Aristotle on the Necessity of Public Education

Aristotle on the Necessity of Public Education

Randall R. Curren

ROWMAN & LITTLEFIELD PUBLISHERS, INC.
Lanham • Boulder • New York • Oxford

ROWMAN & LITTLEFIELD PUBLISHERS, INC.

Published in the United States of America
by Rowman & Littlefield Publishers, Inc.
4720 Boston Way, Lanham, Maryland 20706
http://www.rowmanlittlefield.com

12 Hid's Copse Road
Cumnor Hill, Oxford OX2 9JJ, England

British Library Cataloguing in Publication Information Available

Library of Congress Cataloging-in-Publication Data

Curren, Randall R.
    Aristotle on the necessity of public education / Randall R. Curren
       p.   cm.
    Includes bibliographical references and index.
    ISBN 0-8476-9672-3 (alk. paper) — ISBN 0-8476-9673-1 (pbk. : alk. paper)
    1. Aristotle—Contributions in education.   2. Education, Greek.
  3. Education—Philosophy—History. I. Title.
    LV85.A7 C87   2000
    370′.1—dc21   00-036922

Printed in the United States of America

For

Alan Donagan
Carl Hempel
and
Norton Nelkin

in memoriam

Contents

Preface and Acknowledgments

This book is primarily a reconstruction of Aristotle's neglected account of education and its place in public life, but it also evaluates and explores the significance of his defense of public education for contemporary controversies over educational choice, equality, and the ethical content of public schooling. This dual purpose is motivated by the central place that education holds in Aristotle's political thought, by the conviction that his arguments for public education rest in a more incisive understanding of the relationships between virtue, law, and education than has been recognized, and by my own sense of what is most consistent with the practical aspirations which guide Aristotle's political thought.

What follows is thus first of all an interpretive essay in ancient philosophy, but also an essay in political, legal, and educational philosophy. Insofar as it is the former, it aims to fill a significant void in the literature on Aristotle's practical philosophy, for Aristotle's educational thought has received very little attention. Insofar as it is the latter, its central aim is to reassess the grounds for creating and maintaining a system of education that is public and the same for all, at a time when the merits of public education are increasingly questioned. The issues of public policy at stake in this should be of interest not only to political, moral, legal, and educational philosophers, but to many nonphilosophers as well. With this in mind, I have endeavored to make the chapters that follow as accessible to nonspecialists as possible, without sacrificing interpretive accuracy or analytical rigor. I have relegated many interpretive debates to the endnotes in the interest of readability, but this was not always possible or desirable, and readers will have to judge for themselves whether some sections may be beyond the scope of their interests.

This project grew out of my attempts to reconcile Aristotle's account of responsibility with his remarks on education and the influences on moral character, and some aspects of the substance and presentation of that work, begun in my doctoral dissertation and published as "The Contribution of *Nicomachean*

Ethics iii 5 to Aristotle's Theory of Responsibility," in the *History of Philosophy Quarterly* (Curren 1989), appear in chapter 6 (§6.2) by kind permission of the journal's executive editor.

A summer fellowship in 1991 from the National Endowment for the Humanities, and a Spencer Fellowship which provided a year of academic leave through the 1991–92 academic year, gave me the encouragement and opportunity to develop that work in the direction of a sustained inquiry into the relationships between education and law in Aristotle's political thought. I am grateful to the NEH and the Spencer Foundation for their generous support, to the colleagues and administration at the University of Rochester who kindly accommodated my absence, and to Kurt Baier, John Cooper, Alan Donagan, Tom Green, Deborah Modrak, Israel Scheffler, Robin Smith, and Tyll van Geel for their encouragement and assistance during and since that formative stage of the project. The interim result of that work was a three-part article, "Justice, Instruction, and the Good: The Case For Public Education in Aristotle and Plato's *Laws*," published in *Studies in Philosophy and Education* (Curren 1993–94)*;* "Punishment and Inclusion: The Presuppositions of Corrective Justice in Aristotle and What They Imply," published in *The Canadian Journal of Law and Jurisprudence* (Curren 1995b); and "Justice and the Threshold of Educational Equality," published in Michael Katz, ed., *Philosophy of Education 1994* (Curren 1995a). Material from part 1 of the *Studies in Philosophy and Education* article, "Groundwork for an Interpretation of *Politics* VIII.1," appears with much revision in chapters 1 and 3; part 2, "Why Education is Important Enough to Merit the Legislator's Attention," appears here in extensively revised and expanded form as chapter 4; and material from Part III, "Why Education Should Be Public and the Same for All," appears here in revised and expanded form in chapters 2 and 5. All of this material originally published in *Studies in Philosophy and Education* appears with kind permission from Kluwer Academic Publishers. Material from "Punishment and Inclusion" appears in chapter 6 (§6.1, §6.3, and §6.4) with minor revisions, and material from a review essay on Fred Miller's book, *Nature, Justice, and Rights in Aristotle's Politics*, appears in revised form in the concluding section of chapter 7, by kind permission of the journal's editor. Parts of §7.2 in chapter 7 were presented at the annual meeting of the Philosophy of Education Society in March 1998 under the title "Critical Thinking and the Unity of Virtue," and appeared in *Philosophy of Education 1998* (Curren 1999a), and later with additions as "Cultivating the Intellectual and Moral Virtues" (Curren 1999b).

The Spencer Foundation provided further assistance and encouragement in the form of a grant which provided a summer salary and a research assistant through the 1993–94 academic year. A grant from the National Endowment for the Humanities enabled me to teach a seminar for school teachers on the *Politics* and *Nicomachean Ethics* in the summer of 1998, as I was making revisions to the manuscript. I am grateful for their continued support, and for the extraordinary stimulation provided by an intensive seminar on the themes of this book.

Versions of various parts of this work have been presented as colloquia, at the 1987 Dayton Conference on Aristotle's Ethics and Metaphysics, and at meetings of the American Philosophical Association, the International Association for Philosophy of Law and Social Philosophy, the National Academy of Education, the North American Association for Social and Political Philosophy, the Philosophy of Education Society, and the Communitarian Network. The penultimate draft was the subject of a symposium held at the World Congress of Philosophy in August 1998, sponsored by the Association for Philosophy of Education. I am grateful for the responses of my commentators and audiences on those occasions, and owe special thanks to John Cooper and Fred Miller, who prepared responses to the versions of the opening section of chapter 5 (§5.11–§5.14) and the second section of chapter 4 (§4.2), which I presented at APA meetings in December 1993 and May 1994; to Stephen Salkever and Nancy Sherman, my copanelists at the Communitarian Conference in Geneva, Switzerland, in July 1996; to Amatai Etzioni, whose invitations made the Geneva session possible and enabled me to participate in discussions of character education and government policy in Washington, D.C. in the summers of 1995 and 1996; to Harvey Siegel, for his enduring collegiality and kindness in arranging the World Congress symposium; and to Peter Simpson and Leon Kojen, whose participation in the symposium provided me with valuable and much appreciated reactions to a nearly complete manuscript. I am also grateful to Stephen Macedo and Eamonn Callan for the stimulation provided by a very fruitful exchange on common schooling and the funding of religious schooling, hosted by the former at Syracuse University in December 1998.

It has been my great fortune and pleasure to have studied and practiced philosophy with some extraordinary teachers, and I would like to thank them here, though it would be wrong to think that this book goes very far toward discharging the intellectual and personal debts I have incurred. I must mention particularly Jerry Nosich and the late Norton Nelkin, my mentors at the University of New Orleans; at the University of Pittsburgh, where I was a doctoral student, Annette Baier, Kurt Baier, the late Carl Hempel, Alexander Nehamas, and above all Joe Camp, who was as brilliant and generous as one could wish a teacher and mentor to be; and at the California Institute of Technology, where I began my academic career as an Andrew Mellon Postdoctoral Instructor, my colleague and last teacher, the late Alan Donagan.

My debts to the work of other scholars are great, and will be obvious to readers who are conversant in the literature of ancient philosophy. I would like to acknowledge particularly the work of John Cooper, Richard Kraut, Fred Miller, and David Reeve.

I have been aided in the course of this work by many others who have provided encouragement, advice, invitations, bibliographical assistance, and reactions to versions of various parts of this work. They include Hank Allen, John Bennett, Brian Brent, Harry Brighouse, David Carr, Joseph Dunne, Jan Garrett,

David Ericson, Mary Louise Gill, Robert Holmes, Kenneth Howe, Bruce Kimball, Peter King, Richard Kraut, Sharon Lloyd, Kathleen McGowan, Robert Moffatt, Donald Morrison, Jan Narveson, Ronald Polansky, Jean Roberts, Amelié Rorty, Jim Sterba, Kenneth Strike, Harold Wechsler, my students in three seminars at the University of Rochester, the participants in my NEH sponsored seminar, and an anonymous referee. Finally, I must thank my wife, Tina, and my children, Gabriel, Glenna, and Rosina, who have taught me most of what I know of happiness and how human beings become good. The life of contemplation would be empty without them.

Abbreviations and Notes on Translations

ARISTOTLE

AC	*Athenian Constitution*
A. Post.	*Posterior Analytics*
DA	*de Anima*
EE	*Eudemian Ethics*
MM	*Magna Moralia*
Met.	*Metaphysics*
NE	*Nicomachean Ethics*
PA	*On the Parts of Animals*
Phys.	*Physics*
Pol.	*Politics*
Rh.	*Rhetoric*
Sens.	*Sense and Sensibilia*

Note: Except where indicated, translations are essentially those appearing in Jonathan Barnes, ed., *The Complete Works of Aristotle, The Revised Oxford Translation*, 2 vols. (Princeton: Princeton University Press, 1984). I systematically replace "excellence" with "virtue" as a translation of *aretê*, "noble" with "admirable" as a translation of *kalon*, and "base" with "shameful" for *aischron*.

I have seen no need to document minor stylistic departures from these translations, but in the few instances in which my departures are substantive and no other source is indicated, I insert the transliterated Greek on which I've relied. I follow the same policy with regard to the works listed below.

I have also consulted and relied on the following other translations:

Freese, J. 1926. *Aristotle, The "Art" of Rhetoric*. Cambridge, Mass.: Harvard University Press.
Irwin, T. 1985. *Aristotle, Nicomachean Ethics*. Indianapolis: Hackett Publishing Co.

Kraut, R. 1997. *Aristotle, Politics Books VII and VIII*. Oxford: Clarendon Press.
Lord, C. 1984. *Aristotle, The Politics*. Chicago: University of Chicago Press.
Rackham, H. 1934. *Aristotle, The Nicomachean Ethics*. Cambridge, Mass.: Harvard University Press.
———. 1944. *Aristotle, Politics*. Cambridge, Mass.: Harvard University Press.
———. 1971. *Aristotle, Eudemian Ethics*. Cambridge, Mass.: Harvard University Press.
Reeve, C. D. C. 1998. *Aristotle, Politics*. Indianapolis: Hackett Publishing Co.
Robinson, R. 1995. *Aristotle, Politics Books III and IV*. Oxford: Clarendon Press.
Saunders, T. 1995. *Aristotle, Politics Books I and II*. Oxford: Clarendon Press.
Simpson, P. 1997. *The Politics of Aristotle*. Chapel Hill: University of North Carolina Press.

References to Aristotle's works refer, in accordance with scholarly norms, to the book, chapter, page, column, and line numbers of Immanuel Bekker's 1831 edition of the Greek text of the extant works. Hence, *Pol.* IV.15 1299b24–25 refers to *Politics,* book four, chapter fifteen, page 1299, column b, lines twenty-four through twenty-five. References to other ancient texts refer similarly to the pagination established by editors of those texts. These are page, column, and line numbers that generally appear in the margins of modern editions and translations.

PLATO

Ap.	*Apology*
Cri.	*Crito*
Euth.	*Euthyphro*
Gorg.	*Gorgias*
Hp. Ma.	*Hippias Major*
Phdr.	*Phaedrus*
Prot.	*Protagoras*
Rep.	*Republic*
St.	*Statesman*
Sym.	*Symposium*
Tht.	*Theaetetus*
Tim.	*Timaeus*

Note: Except where indicated, translations are from John Cooper, ed., *Plato, Complete Works* (Indianapolis: Hackett Publishing Co., 1997).

I have also consulted and relied upon these other translations:

Annas, J. and R. Waterfield. 1995. *Plato, Statesman*. Cambridge: Cambridge University Press.
Bury, R. G. 1926. *Plato, The Laws*. Cambridge, Mass.: Harvard University Press.
Fowler, H. 1914. *Plato*, vol. 1. Cambridge, Mass.: Harvard University Press.
Hubbard, B. and E. Karnofsky. 1982. *Plato's Protagoras*. London: Duckworth.

Lamb, W. R. M. 1924. *Plato*, vol. 2. Cambridge, Mass.: Harvard University Press.
Pangle, T. 1980. *The Laws of Plato*. Chicago: University of Chicago Press.
Taylor, C. C. W. 1991. *Plato, Protagoras*. Rev. ed. Oxford: Clarendon Press.

PLUTARCH

Lyc.   *Lycurgus*
Sol.   *Solon*

Note: Translations are those of Bernadotte Perrin, *Plutarch's Lives*, vol. 1 (Cambridge, Mass. Harvard University Press, 1914), with adjustments for contemporary usage.

XENOPHON

Lac. Pol.   *Constitution of the Lacedaimonians*
Oec.   *Oeconomicus*

Note: Translations are those of E. C. Marchant, *Xenophon, Scripta Minora* (Cambridge, Mass.: Harvard University Press, 1925) and *Xenophon, Memorabilia and Oeconomicus* (Cambridge, Mass.: Harvard University Press, 1923), with adjustments for contemporary usage.

Introduction

Considered as a work on the place of education in public life, Aristotle's *Politics* has languished in the shadow cast by Plato's *Republic*, the most conspicuous masterpiece of moral and educational theory in antiquity. This is regrettable, for the causes of the neglect of Aristotle's educational theory have less to do with any shortcomings it may have than with various obstacles which have stood in the way of understanding it. Whatever its limitations, and however much it owes to Plato's educational thought, the *Politics* holds an important place in Aristotle's practical philosophy, it advances beyond Plato's thought in important ways, and it remains instructive and in some respects compelling even now.

One of the more superficial reasons why Aristotle's educational thought has been neglected is that the *Politics* is not a pleasingly polished work in the way that the *Republic* is. While the latter was evidently written to be read, the former is a record of a series of lectures: perhaps Aristotle's own notes, perhaps those of a student who heard them, or perhaps a compilation of two or more sets of notes. These lectures were evidently given repeatedly and evolved over time, without consistency being fully imposed as various amendments were made. Aristotle may have expressed himself more fully than he does in the manuscripts that have come down to us, and he may have made adjustments as he spoke, without correcting the text he was speaking from. Those of us who lecture may recall doing just this sort of thing, and it would explain some of the text's anomalies if what has come down to us was copied in part or in whole directly from Aristotle's own notes. In any case, the reader is faced with a text that is compressed, sometimes cryptic, and occasionally cluttered with apparently inconsistent formulations.

Aristotle's remarks on education in the *Politics* are sketchy and their organization also presents difficulties. Book VIII is devoted entirely to describing the content of public education and defending its necessity, though the discussion breaks off abruptly, a fact only clumsily disguised by an editor's concluding addendum.[1] The arguments for public education which appear in Book VIII are

1

compressed and unimpressive on their face, and the rest of what Aristotle has to say about education is scattered in small pieces through the preceding books. His account of education and defense of the necessity of public education cannot be properly understood without drawing these scattered remarks together, but the difficulties in drawing them all together into a coherent whole are considerable and inseparable from the task of making coherent sense of the work as a whole. Since commentators have only recently come to regard the *Politics* as a coherent treatise, susceptible to a "unitarian" reading,[2] it is not surprising that little progress has been made toward piecing together Aristotle's account of the place of education in politics, or his understanding of the role of educational theory in his "philosophy of human affairs" *(hê peri ta anthrôpeia philosophia)*.

A tradition of "developmental" readings of the *Politics* created until recently a further specific barrier to serious engagement with Aristotle's account of education, quite apart from its role in discouraging unitarian readings generally.[3] Books VII and VIII, where the only sustained discussion of education occurs, were regarded as belonging to an early Platonic phase of Aristotle's philosophical development. The view of Werner Jaeger, which exercised considerable influence until the advent of a more analytical style of close textual work, was that these books are best seen as superseded by the more mature "empirical" middle books (i.e., IV–VI). The account of education in Book VIII was thereby essentially dismissed as uncharacteristic of Aristotle's mature thought. Although this developmental thesis has lost ground in recent years, and for very good reasons, questions about the purposes of the *Politics* as a whole, and the roles in it of Books IV–VI and VII–VIII, have lingered.

Even on a unitarian reading of the *Politics*, it has features which invite the conclusion that the educational program of Books VII and VIII has no significance beyond its role as a component of Aristotle's theory of the best possible polis, which is to say no significance for more ordinary polises nor any for modern societies.[4] Because it is in Books VII and VIII that Aristotle enumerates his arguments for public education and spells out his proposals regarding its substance, it is natural to suppose that he intends those arguments and proposals to pertain only to the extraordinary polis described in those books. If that was his intention, then it seems reasonable to regard his arguments and proposals as inapplicable to any society that is very different from the one he describes there, because it is substantially bigger, for instance, or because it lacks the desire or capacity to endure the unconscionable social stratification which he accepts as part of the best social and political system that is attainable.

As much as the organization of the *Politics* may suggest these inferences, however, it does not justify them. There are anticipations in earlier books of the *Politics* of the arguments for public education that appear at the start of Book VIII, and these arguments are formulated in Book VIII with the obvious intention that they will apply to all governments. This will become more evident when we come to examine the arguments, but it is worth noting more preemptively that the single ground on which one might doubt this is that one of Aristotle's arguments relies on the premise that "the whole city has one end" (VIII.1 1337a21–22). If one takes this to be a claim exclusively about the city described in Book VII, then the argument would of course have a very narrow application; but Aristotle's claim throughout the *Politics* is that it is in the nature of cities in general to aim at the best life for their citizens. Contentious as this is, it is a claim about all cities and the one end they all share. The city which Aristotle describes in Book VII is different not in having this natural end, but in the degree of its success in achieving it. If Aristotle is right about the proper aims of governments or (what is closely related, in his view) the demands of justice, then we can scarcely escape whatever force his arguments have by holding that ordinary polises or modern societies are larger, or more divided, or in some way more principled, or better or less fortunate than the polis he envisioned as the best possible. We may have to conclude instead that the larger size of modern states makes it harder for them to satisfy the demands of justice, and that despite our readiness to condemn Aristotle's complacency about slavery and relegating women and others to noncitizen status, we have a long way to go ourselves to live up to the demands of justice tied up with his arguments for an education that is the same for all. In making these preliminary remarks, I do not mean to offer any definitive conclusions about the merits of Aristotle's educational theory; my concern is rather to identify another feature of the *Politics,* and previous commentary on it, that obscures the importance of education to its larger purposes.

Aristotle's educational thought is by no means confined to the *Politics*, so it is also appropriate to note that attention to the educational dimensions of Aristotle's ethical works has focused almost exclusively on his account of moral development and has not concerned itself much with the politics of education or what the *Politics* has to say about education.[5] This has been encouraged at least in part by the distinctness of the *Nicomachean Ethics* and *Politics*, and what their distinctness may suggest about their intentions to a modern reader, namely that if Aristotle is offering advice to anyone in the *Nicomachean Ethics* it is to private individuals and not to the statesman or political theorist.[6]

The price of failing to read the two texts together is well illustrated by the tenor of critical commentary on Aristotle's account of friendship. Although the topic of political friendship has been debated for some years now (Annas 1977, 1990; Cooper 1977, 1990; Price 1989; Schollmeier 1994; etc.), the relationship of Aristotle's account of friendship to the *Republic*'s prescriptions for unifying a polis through the communal upbringing of children is rarely if ever understood in light of Aristotle's commitment in the *Politics* to the idea that actual cities are *not* sufficiently unified and should be made so through legislative efforts to promote friendship. Many scholars simply do not address the political question of how a city is to be unified by friendship, while others portray Aristotle as believing this will take care of itself. Where Plato proposes the elimination of individual families and of the moral education embedded in family life, Aristotle proposes a less radical course. This moderation and his presumed individualism has apparently invited the implausible conclusion that it is through leaving the naturally occurring familial and social bonds within the polis alone, and not through any form of public intervention, that Aristotle thinks social unity will arise. What has been most noticed, then, has been Aristotle's apparent reinvestment of trust in the spontaneously occurring forms of attachment and learning within the private realm,[7] and not the extent to which he remains committed to the Platonic idea that a central task of statesmanship is to take steps calculated to unify the polis through common schooling and other institutions which educate and bring citizens together in the right way. In this instance and others the political aspects and intentions of the *Nicomachean Ethics* and its connections to the *Politics* tend to be ignored or discounted, when what is essential to an understanding of Aristotle's theory of education is a unified reading of the *Politics* and *Nicomachean Ethics* together.[8]

The style and structure of the *Politics*, its limited, scattered, and apparently "early" account of education, and its distinctness from the ethical works have thus all contributed to the impression that Aristotle has little of importance to say about education, and does not accord education the central place in politics that Plato does. The quantity of scholarly attention devoted to the educational aspects of Aristotle's political thought has been commensurate with this impression, and this is unfortunate, for as I have said a good case can be made for the view that Aristotle's educational thought is not only central to his political theory, but also deeply insightful and challenging. Because it *is* central to his political thought, a good understanding of it is also essential to a full understanding of his accounts of such related topics as friendship, virtue, responsibility, and law.

Aristotle conceives of political science *(hê politikê epistêmê* or simply *hê politikê)* as a field of inquiry, knowledge, and counsel, encompassing both ethics and legislative science *(nomothetikê),* that aims to guide political practice by providing the universal component of political wisdom or *phronêsis.*[9] Ethics provides the statesman with an understanding of happiness *(eudaimonia)* or the highest good for human beings, the importance of virtue for a happy life, and the formation of virtue, so that he may effectively promote the happiness or well-being *(euêmeria)*[10] of all citizens, and perhaps also the noncitizen residents, of his polis. Legislative science aims to guide polises in establishing laws conducive to that end, for law is the essential vehicle of rule through which it may be achieved (*NE* X.9 1180b24–30; *Pol.* I.2 1253a30–35). Law has an *instructional* aspect (*NE* V.1 1129b19–26; V.2 1130b22–27; X.9 1180a6–24)[11] in addition to its *compulsive* and *corrective* aspects, however, and the most important laws are those pertaining to education (*Pol.* V.9 1310a13–20, VIII.1 1337a10–11), to the institutions whose chief function (like law itself) is to enable people to form and to act from good judgments (*Pol.* VIII.5 1340a16–19). Without this education almost no one would become responsive to reason and argument, as opposed to force (*NE* X.9 1180a4–5), and that would not only make a happy life impossible but would foreclose any chance of achieving a legitimate rule of law, which involves rule through voluntary acceptance of law rather than through force (*Pol.* I.13 1259b37–60a2, III.3 1276a8–16, III.4 1277b8–30, III.6 1279b17–22, III.9 1280b30–40 [where Aristotle identifies the aims which people have in voluntarily choosing to live together in a "true" and legitimate, as opposed to a constitutionally corrupt, polis], III.10 1281a22–25, III.13 1283b42–84a3, III.14 1285a27–29, III.15 1286a22–31 [where he endorses popular ratification of laws], IV.9 1294b35–39, IV.10 1295a17–23, IV.11 1295b14–24, IV.12 1296b15–16, V.9 1310a15–17, V.10 1313a5–11, VII.2 1324b23–31, VII.14 1332b16–29; Keyt 1996; Long 1996). Aristotle thus seems to identify law and education as the two fundamental and deeply interdependent tools of political practice.

The use of education by the statesman is consequently a topic of the first importance in Aristotle's practical philosophy, and it is inseparable from his views on the nature of law and its relationships to virtue, happiness, and the requirements of justice. In the twentieth century, the theoretical debate over the nature of law and its relationship to morality has been reduced almost entirely to the narrow question of whether anything can count as law that does not measure up to some standard of natural morality (Hart 1961); but for Aristotle, and before him Plato, the relationships between education and law, and education and virtue, were of no less concern than the relationship between law and the demands of natural justice. What we find in their thought is a concern with the relationships between education, law, and the virtues, the virtue of justice being regarded as both a trait of individuals and a natural measure of the legitimacy of institutions.

From these relationships flow several arguments for public education, advanced in the cause of individual virtue, happiness, freedom, and rationality; political excellence and stability; and the promotion of friendship and social solidarity. The most generally compelling of these arguments rests in the idea that without the right kind of public education, the kind of consent and obedience to law that is essential to the legitimacy of the most necessary forms of state power is not possible. This is an argument diametrically at odds with the classical liberal position that consent to a government and its laws that is grounded in publicly controlled education would be suspect, inasmuch as government schools might be inclined to indoctrinate, inhibit individuality and personal freedom, and cultivate blind obedience to bad laws and bad leadership.[12] Nevertheless, it is as strong and fundamental an argument for public education as we are likely to find, and it has the interesting feature of generating distributive consequences without presupposing any conception of distributive justice or any substantive political ideal beyond a basic opposition to coercion. It generates a mandate for educational equality of a kind that entails much the same content that arguments resting in concepts of deliberative democracy do, and it does so on quite minimal assumptions. It yields the conclusion that justice requires a public system of education which provides all children with adequate moral and political education, instruction in a variety of domains of knowledge and their methods of inquiry, and preparation for work. Several of Aristotle's arguments lend support to this conclusion, but the main line of argument I will develop is built on the ideas that education for self-governance is properly directed toward nurturing virtue in its fullest sense, and that the exercise of virtue in self-governance rests in the possession of knowledge and capacities of critical reason, as much as in habits of moral virtue.

Thus, I will argue that although what Aristotle means by education *(paideia)* is first and foremost *moral education*, his arguments have important implications for public education as we know it at the beginning of the twenty-first century. First, and perhaps most obviously, Aristotle's defense of public education may be usefully brought to bear on the theory and practice of character education, which is currently on the agenda of thousands of school districts in the United States.[13] This is a field which developed very rapidly during the 1990s, and it has developed in part along self-consciously Aristotelian lines, but in the absence of any significant scholarly reconstruction of Aristotle's theory of public education and the place of virtue in it. The potential value of such a reconstruction for this significant arena of educational policy and practice is quite substantial, both with regard to the place of character education in the agenda of public education and to its content.

Second, as the foregoing remarks suggest, Aristotle's arguments provide us with compelling grounds for taking seriously a sort of educational equality that we should care about. Using his case for the legitimacy and desirability of public provisions for moral education as a starting point, one can plausibly develop on Aristotelian premises a mandate for equitable access to a required curriculum of moral and political education, instruction in the academic disciplines, and preparation for work.

Third and finally, Aristotle's defense of public education has a significance for debates about school choice and privatization which is not diminished by his emphasis on virtue. Although we are accustomed to thinking of the purposes of modern schooling as pertaining most of all to the acquisition of knowledge and skills that contribute to economic productivity, the American public school movement was built on rather different concerns. During the early years of the republic, these grew directly out of classical political theory and its idea, which Aristotle develops at length, that the most stable constitutions are "mixed" in the sense of incorporating elements of different forms of constitutions. The American Founding Fathers were well versed in classical political theory, and they concluded from the theory of mixed constitutions that pure democracy would be as unstable in America as the ancient moralists had maintained it was everywhere, unless sound education could be relied upon to reconcile democratic freedoms with the need for good order and excellence in government. They understood the aim of education to be virtue, by which they meant most generally such traits as "discipline, sacrifice, simplicity, and intelligence" (Kaestle 1983, 5), and they argued, in express opposition to John Locke's defense of homeschooling, that the system of public education they envisioned was the best way to promote these and other more distinctly civic virtues. Citing Aristotle's remark in *Politics* VIII.1, that education should be adapted to the form of government under which citizens will live, John Adams argued in his *Defence of the Constitutions* that children "of every rank and class of people, down to the lowest and the poorest" should be "educated and instructed in the principles of freedom" and "in every kind of knowledge that can be of use to them in the practice of their moral duties . . . and of their political and civic duties" (Adams 1778, 168, 197). Noah Webster, Samuel Knox, and Thomas Jefferson all made similar arguments, and all insisted on a public education in the principles of law and government which would enable all citizens to appreciate the virtues of their constitution and laws, and to understand their legal and political obligations (Pangle 1993, 97–99, 106ff.). Jefferson held in addition, and very much as Aristotle did, that universal public education should prepare citizens not only to be ruled, but to rule, with the virtues most conducive to human happiness; he proposed a system which would equip all free citizens to guard their liberties against the incursions of tyranny and share in rule in accordance with their "genius and virtue."[14] Knox and others invoked the Aristotelian argument that public schools which bring children of different social backgrounds together would promote social unity through bonds of personal friendship (Pangle 1993, 92).

By the early nineteenth century a new argument, that prevention of crime through education was better and cheaper than punishment, had emerged (Kaestle 1983, 34–39), and by midcentury the conception of the virtues of citizenship which animated the increasingly successful public school movement had broadened to include other elements that were quintessentially Aristotelian. Specifically, a fear of faction, fueled by the urban poverty and conflict associated with industrialization, inspired the hope that universal schooling might contribute to social equality and social and national unity (91). Between 1750 and 1850, American views of moral education also shifted away from a reliance on punitive methods, and toward character training, moral persuasion, and the internalization of discipline (87–89), so that by midcentury the maintenance of law through moral education that was substantially persuasive rather than coercive was considered to be "part of the republican experiment" (97). In sum, the "unassailable social function of common schooling" as it was understood during the era when the American public school movement was beginning to push its agenda forward was to promote "morality, good order, intelligent citizenship, economic prosperity [most particularly through promoting the virtues of "industry" and "thrift"], fair opportunity, and a common American culture" (95), morality being considered the most important of these goals (96, 100, 137).[15]

Thus, it was largely on the strength of arguments derived directly from classical political theory, and others that were broadly classical and Aristotelian whatever their exact etiology, that the American public school movement was built. Since Aristotle's thought embodies what is arguably the most attractive formulation of the ancient tradition of political and educational theory, a reappraisal of his arguments is a useful approximation to a systematic assessment of the arguments on which our system of free public schools was founded. This would be a useful exercise in any era, if only to remind ourselves of how we have come to the position in which we find ourselves. Today, when the American public school movement has all but collapsed, having been declared dead as early as three decades ago,[16] it has particular importance. School choice and privatization are now widely advocated on principles of market efficiency and respect for individual choice, and generally as a panacea for all that ails the public schools.[17] We must ask, as a question of more than theoretical interest—indeed, as one vitally important to our well-being—whether there are principled and compelling grounds on which to preserve and perhaps reform the system whose fate has become a topic of debate in national politics. I will not attempt to offer an all-things-considered judgment on this question, but as I reconstruct Aristotle's arguments for public education in the chapters that follow, I will examine them with an eye to what they may contribute to this debate.

These arguments are collected together, albeit in highly compressed form, at the start of *Politics* VIII, and their elaboration will be the focal point around which I shall organize my interpretation of Aristotle's educational politics in the chapters that follow. I shall do this through close textual work which places these arguments within the larger context of Aristotle's works and the political, educational, and intellectual world of his time. I will place his educational thought within the broader sweep of Socratic thought, in order to understand both what he contributes to that tradition, and what he takes from it and assumes as premises shared with his audience.

My threefold aim in these chapters will thus be to develop an interpretation and analysis of Aristotle's arguments for public education which places them in the larger context of his practical philosophy, and in the context of Socratic thought generally; to assess the strength of these arguments; and finally to weigh and elaborate their importance for current debates about the nature of and grounds for educational equality, the place of moral education in public schools, and school choice and privatization.

Chapters 1, "Greek *Paideia* and Socratic Principles," and 2, "The Arguments of Plato," set the stage for the main body of the work by reviewing the background of educational practices and theory in which Aristotle's views developed. Given his place in the Socratic tradition and the importance he evidently attached to Plato's arguments for public education, I devote much of these first two chapters to a review of the arguments for public education in the works of Plato, beginning with their origins in Socratic moral and political theory.

Chapter 3, "Groundwork for an Interpretation of *Politics* VIII.1," takes up some important aspects of the setting for Aristotle's own arguments for public education, which are summarized in VIII.1. Here I identify the nature of Aristotle's general enterprise in the *Politics*, the audience he wishes to address, the general outlines of his theory of rule and constitutions, the conclusions he seeks to establish in VIII.1, and what public education that is the same for "everyone" would amount to for him.

Chapter 4, "Why Education is Important," examines the arguments for the first of the two conclusions which Aristotle advances in VIII.1, namely that education is important enough to merit the legislator's attention. I offer multiple reconstructions of both arguments, and argue, through a development of links between *Politics* V and the arguments of VIII.1, that one form of the first of them, Aristotle's *argument from constitutional requirements*, is designed to appeal to the practical politician's desire to remain in power. In the course of developing this interpretation, this chapter advances a unitarian reading of the place of the "empirical" middle books, particularly Book V, in Aristotle's political thought as a whole.

Chapter 5, "Why Education Should be Public and the Same for All," examines the pair of arguments which Aristotle adduces in explicit support of the claim that education should be provided through a public system. The first of these revolves around the promotion of civic unity through the cultivation of the moral and intellectual virtues, and through common schooling that promotes goodwill and friendship. By placing Aristotle's discussion of friendship in its political and educational context, I arrive at a significantly new interpretation of his conception of the role of friendship in unifying a city. I also conclude that Aristotle was concerned about conflict arising from the pursuit of contested goods, and I derive an important lesson from this about the kinds of aims a public system of education can coherently pursue.

The second argument revolves around the idea that the care or education of each citizen is in some sense inseparable from the care or education of the whole citizenry, and I examine several variants of this argument. The most compelling of these focuses on the role of education in securing the foundations of corrective justice. This *argument from the foundations of corrective justice* amounts to an application of Aristotle's concept of a consensual rule of law, which puts education before force, to the problem of when the state may legitimately respond with force to violations of law.

Chapter 6, "Education and the Foundations of Justice," considers some of the difficulties involved in attributing to Aristotle this *argument from the foundations of corrective justice*, and examines the principles on which it might be elaborated and defended. I consider whether Aristotle's concept of corrective justice is applicable in the way this argument requires, and whether his account of responsibility can accommodate the notion that a state's failure to educate would undermine the legitimacy of public censure and punishment. In doing this I develop a new interpretation of Aristotle's remarks about responsibility for character in *NE* III.5 and conclude that he acknowledges there that the statesman's conscientious sponsorship of a public system of education is a necessary condition for a just system of criminal punishment and censure. I conclude that the argument is a strong one, with substantial implications for modern educational and penal practice.

Chapter 7, "Justice and the Substance of Common Care," elaborates the implications of Aristotle's arguments for three topics of perennial educational concern: educational equality, the respective roles of moral education and "critical thinking" in the curriculum, and school choice and common schooling that requires children to be educated together with others unlike themselves. My consideration of the significance of Aristotle's arguments for educational equality begins with an examination of a recent influential account of educational equality developed by Amy Gutmann, and outlines an alternative account which avoids some of the limitations which hers seems to have. In doing this I develop the curricular implications of Aristotle's arguments, and then pursue those implications further by considering his endorsement of the unity of virtue doctrine, and examining the apparent tensions between moral education and intellectual training that nurtures autonomous judgment and reasoning. In the chapter's concluding section, I note the insufficiency of the grounds on which the Aristotelian arguments for public education have been dismissed, and conclude that they provide us with compelling reasons to reaffirm, and do justice to, the fundamental commitments on which the American system of universal public schooling was founded. Turning to the upshot of these arguments for debates over school choice or market approaches to distributing education, versus schools that are "common" or economically, socially, ethnically, and racially mixed, I conclude that there is a strong case to be made for common schooling, and that the prospects for privatizing education in a way that would be acceptable are dim.

1

Greek *Paideia* and Socratic Principles

In those parts of the ancient world known to Aristotle, public education was devoted almost entirely to military training, and was rare even in that form. Having compiled descriptions and histories of some 158 ancient constitutions,[1]
Aristotle remarks in Book VIII of the *Politics* that "the Lacedaimonians are to
be praised, for they pay the greatest attention *(spouden)* to their children, and do
so as a community *(koinê)*" (VIII.1 1337a32–33).[2] In a related passage in the
Nicomachean Ethics, he says that "In the Lacedaimonian state alone, or almost
alone, the legislator seems to have paid attention to questions of upbringing
(trophê) and pursuits *(epitêdeumaton)*; in most states such matters have been
neglected, . . . [yet] it is best that there should be a public and proper care for such
matters" (*NE* X.9 1180a25–30). The Cretan constitution seems to be the only
other one he considers worth mentioning in this regard, since Crete is the only
state besides Sparta that he finds praiseworthy for its efforts to make citizens
"good and law-abiding" (*NE* I.8 1102a8–12).

Aristotle mentions Sparta and Crete together as having education arranged with
war in mind (*Pol.* VII.2 1324b7–10), and having arrangements for citizens to dine
at common meals *(phiditia)* that were educative by design (*Pol.* II.5 1263b37–
64a1).[3] He compares their respective provisions for common meals in *Pol.* II.9
(1271a26–37) and II.10 (1271b20–72b23). We learn in these passages that he
regarded the Cretan constitution as the model on which the more "fully elaborated" Spartan one was based, and superior to the Spartan one in its arrangements
for common meals, if not generally. The Carthaginian system of government is
noted for its similarity to the Cretan and Spartan systems, and Aristotle observes
that it has common meals comparable to those of the Spartans (*Pol.* II.11
1272b24–34). In discussing their "gymnastic" training (*gymnastikê*, which was
preparatory to both athletic and military contests), he also remarks of the Spartans that "there are now some who rival them in education, whereas formerly there
were none" (*Pol.* VIII.4 1338b37–38), so that now "they trail behind others in
both athletic and military contests" (1338b26–27). This claim that the Spartans

11

fell behind others in these ways is consistent with the judgment that they "pay the greatest attention to their children." Aristotle himself attributes this loss of dominance to a mistaken and counterproductive conception of *how* to cultivate courage, not to being outdone in their seriousness about education. By other ac-counts, what made the difference in athletics was the Spartans' loss of interest, and in war the superior numbers of their enemies, the creation of professional armies by other cities which had been without any until the fourth century, and the tactical innovations of the Theban and Athenian generals.[4]

1.1 ATHENIAN AND SPARTAN EDUCATION

Athens itself had gone no farther toward introducing public schooling than in-stituting a system of military training, the *ephêbeia*, which was publicly funded and compulsory for citizens aged eighteen to twenty.[5] This provision would have contributed significantly to the creation of a more professional and tactically proficient military force, but its significance was limited by the nature and dura-tion of the training it called for. The *ephêboi* spent a year in collective physical training and weaponry instruction in the barracks at Piraeus and were then dis-persed to outposts in Attica for a year of service as *peripoloi*, patrolling the fron-tier. Their training prepared them to be hoplites, or heavily armed infantry, but they were not made hoplites, perhaps because the *ephêbeia* was compulsory for all male citizens but only those of considerable wealth could bear the cost of the armaments, which hoplites were normally expected to provide themselves.

Apart from this required military training, what Athenian schooling consisted of in Aristotle's time, for those who desired it and could afford it, were lessons in athletics *(gymnastikê)*; the "arts of the Muses" *(mousikê)*, which included music, poetry, narratives, and above all Homer; and "letters" *(grammata)* and arithmetic.[6] The democratization of Athens had brought with it the introduction of group lessons as a more affordable alternative to traditional one-on-one in-struction, and the introduction of letter-schools, which taught writing, reading, and arithmetic, subjects which had acquired broader commercial utility with the growth of trade. It is impossible to say how many boys attended these various lessons, and there is no clear evidence that any girls did,[7] but there are indica-tions that boys of wealthier families began school at a younger age and may have attended more expensive schools (*Prot.* 326c; Golden 1990, 63). Attending les-sons in all of the available subjects might have entailed walking to three differ-ent places of instruction: to a letter-school conducted by a *grammatistes*; a *palaestra*, or training area equipped for "gymnastics," supervised by a *paidotribes;* and a lyre-school run by a *kitharistes*.[8] Since this entailed children as young as five years old walking from one location in the city to another, the practice of those who could afford it was to assign a household slave to serve as the *paidagôgos*, to lead *(agô)* the boy *(pais, paid-)* or child *(paidion)* from one place to another, providing supervision and security.[9] How many families had to forgo this luxury we can scarcely say, but some of those who lacked a *paidagôgos* might also have done without instruction in *mousikê*, rather than do without schooling altogether, while others would have had no schooling at all.

Education in the sense of formal instruction was thus restricted to Athenians of means, and was discretionary. Its content and quality of supervision varied from child to child, and was more a product of parental assets and choice than of principle. The only provision of Athenian law that induced parents to provide their sons with any form of education before the age of their compulsory military training was a law attributed to Solon that held that parents who had not prepared a son in the skills necessary for a livelihood *(technên didaschesthai)* could not claim support from that son in their old age (Schmitter 1975, 286–89). This provision may or may not have been interpreted to demand attendance at school (287), and it is unlikely that what was taken to be sufficient education was the same for members of every social class. How could it be when Aristotle reports that "the poor, not having any slaves, must employ both their women and children as servants" *(Pol.* VI.8 1323a5–6)?[10]

The "old education" originating in sixth-century Athens was principled in the sense that it was suited to the actual use of leisure *(scholê)* by the knightly warrior class it served. The members of this aristocracy devoted their days to athletic contests and their evenings to the songs and recitations by which they entertained each other at their drinking parties, the *symposia,* which were supplanted in Sparta by *phiditia.* A schooling in *gymnastikê* and *mousikê* was thus well suited to preparing the Athenian warrior class to use their leisure time in a way that was admired and considered good. It was thought to promote manly virtue *(andragathia),* or make men admirable *(kalon)* and good *(agathos,* the adjectival counterpart of the noun, *aretê,* signifying goodness, virtue, or excellence). One might challenge its conception of virtue and what is most truly admirable, but the old education provided plausible means for attaining the goal it set itself, namely a "well-bred" private tutor who established a strong personal relationship with the youth, while providing general moral guidance and most or all of his instruction.

By contrast, the Athenian education of the later fifth and fourth centuries was an indeterminate amalgam of new elements chosen for their commercial usefulness and old elements chosen not quite as the old aristocrats had chosen them, but also because they were coveted symbols of social rank. If education was regarded as a good thing, its content was varied and changing, and the purposes which Athenians had for obtaining it were diverse and in some ways competitive. If the practical arts of literacy and arithmetic were pursued for the economic advantage over fellow Athenians which they might confer, and if cultural attainments were sought by the lower classes, and jealously guarded by the self-styled *agathoi* or *aristoi* (the landed aristocracy, but literally "the good" or "the best"),[11] for the relative social status they conferred, then these were educational goals that

could not have been part of a collectively rational public system of education.
To the extent that *outdoing* each other had become part of the Athenian pattern
of schooling, it was a market-based approach which did not yield any *common*
advantage.[12] And if this was true of Athenian primary education, it was even truer
of higher education among the Greeks generally, insofar as it was a higher education in rhetoric which concerned itself not with truth but with what would appear true, and was sought for its utility in advancing a career of political influence and honor.

Furthermore, to the extent that the earlier ideal of an education in virtue remained, its weight was borne most notably by the *paidagôgos*, who filled the
caretaking and supervisory role as no teacher of group lessons could. This was
evidently the arrangement that Athenians preferred, though our evidence about
this aspect of Greek slave practices is "anecdotal in the extreme" (Finley 1980,
107). From what we know of "pedagogy" it was typical of Greek slavery in the
ambiguous attitude it expressed toward the slave's humanity and moral status (93–
122). The view of the ancient moralists was at least consistent, if also abomi-
nable, in insisting on the moral perversity of entrusting the moral formation of
children to slaves. One could scarcely justify slavery by asserting the slave's incapacity for self-governance, and judge a slave well-equipped to govern a child.

Xenophon, in his *Constitution of the Lacedaimonians,* makes this his first point
of comparison between Spartan education and that of other Greek states:

> In the other Greek states parents who profess to give their sons the best education
> place their boys under the care and control of a *paidagôgos* as soon as they can
> understand what is said to them, and send them to a school to learn letters, *mousikê*,
> and the exercises of the *palaestra*. . . .
>
> Lycurgus, on the contrary, instead of leaving each father to assign a slave to act
> as tutor, assigned the task of supervising the boys to a member of the class from
> which the highest offices are filled. . . . He gave this person authority to gather the
> boys together, to take charge of them and, to punish them severely in the case of
> misconduct *(Lac. Pol.* II.2).[13]

In this task of inculcating obedience, this *paidonomos* was assisted by young
whip-carriers, who accompanied him and punished offenders on his command.
Xenophon goes on to describe, less fully but in much the same terms as Plutarch
does several centuries later *(Lyc.* XVI–XXV), a system in which boys are raised
and trained by the city from the age of seven onward for courage and skill in war,
skill in theft and deception, obedience, the capacity to endure pain and hardship,
and *aidôs*. *Aidôs* is usually translated as "shame," but in many contexts it would
be more fitting to think of it as *a susceptibility to shame*, or—what is very close—
respect for others and for the moral judgments of others.[14] Xenophon's account
emphasizes the importance of obedience and *aidôs*, and their significance for
creating cohesion.

By Plutarch's account:

as soon as [the boys] were seven years old, Lycurgus ordered them all to be taken by the state and enrolled in companies, where they were put under the same discipline and nurture, and so became accustomed to share one another's sports and studies. . . .

Of reading and writing, they learned only what was necessary; all of the rest of their training was calculated to make them obey commands well, endure hardships, and conquer in battle *(Lyc.* XVI.4–6).[15]

They were supervised by the boy captains of their companies, by the "most prudent and warlike of the so-called Eirens" *(Lyc.* XVII.2*)*, who were commanders and military and moral trainers of twenty years of age (XVIII.2–3), and by the elderly men of the city, who watched them "with the idea that they were all in a sense the fathers and *paidagôgoi* and governors of all the boys" (XVII.1).

At the age when a youth would claim the liberties of a free citizen in other cities, Lycurgus is said to have imposed "a ceaseless round of work" to keep Spartan youths out of trouble (Xenophon, *Lac. Pol.* III.1–3). Moreover, they were required to live in barracks from the age of twelve until thirty years old, married or not *(Lyc.* XVI.6–7; Marrou 1956, 20–21). Beyond that, Plutarch records that

The training of the Spartans lasted into the years of full maturity. No man was allowed to live as he pleased, but in their city, as in a military encampment, they always had a prescribed regimen and employment in public service, considering that they belonged entirely to their country and not to themselves, watching over the boys, if no other duty was laid upon them, and either teaching them some useful thing, or learning it themselves from their elders (*Lyc.* XXIV.1–2).

Although Aristotle suggests in some passages that the Spartan system was narrowly concerned with the cultivation of courage, when we consider the whole of his remarks, including his qualified praise for the Spartan *phiditia*, we see that he regarded it, as other ancient moralists did, as a method which was very systematic in inculcating a number of traits which contributed to social cohesion and the attainment of common goods. The Spartans were made by their education both frightening to their enemies and uncommonly devoted to each other and to their city. As distastefully totalitarian as its methods were,[16] this system did eliminate serious points of friction among Spartan citizens and enabled them to secure certain common aims, among them the "leisure" or freedom from the burdens of productive labor, which rested on their ability to control the helot population.

In short, with regard to Athens, Sparta, and the rest of the Greek world, what we learn from both Aristotle and from other ancient sources is that although there were a few cities in Aristotle's world which made some public provision for education, these provisions were concerned almost entirely with training for military service, and even within that narrow scope were rather minimal, except in Sparta.

1.2 WHY WOULD NO ONE DOUBT THAT EDUCATION SHOULD BE THE LEGISLATOR'S FOREMOST CONCERN?

It is rather interesting, then, that Aristotle should open Book VIII of the *Politics* with the remark that "No one will doubt that the legislator *(nomothetê)* should direct his attention <u>above all</u> to the education of the young *(tôn neôn paideian)*" (1337a10–11; emphasis added). It may be that the Spartans regarded education "as the greatest and most praiseworthy *(kalliston)* task of the law-giver" (Plutarch, *Lyc.* XIV.1), but the absence of public education in other cities suggests that this would not have appeared obvious to many other Greeks. So why does Aristotle say that "no one will doubt" that education should be the legislator's foremost concern? How seriously does he mean this, and if he is serious about this why would he think it true?

Aristotle is evidently quite serious in claiming that the desirability of legislative attention to education will be obvious, if not to everyone, at least to his intended audience. This shows itself in his reliance on some closely related claims at the start of the *Nicomachean Ethics*. Aristotle begins by entertaining the possibility that there might be some end which we all choose for its own sake and for nothing beyond itself, "everything else being desired for the sake of this" (I.2 1094a19), and he notes that this would constitute the chief or highest good *(ariston)* for human beings. He suggests that this highest good would naturally be the object of whatever art holds the corresponding top position among arts. This art would be the preeminent master-craft *(architektonikês)*, or the most authoritative art in the sense that the requirements of pursuing its end effectively would establish requirements to be met by the various subsidiary arts (I.2 1094a25–27). Aristotle asserts that there *is* such an art, and that it is called politics *(hê politikê)*.

The first rather remarkable piece of evidence Aristotle offers for this conclusion is that "it is [politics] that ordains which of the sciences should be studied in a *polis*, and which each class of citizens should learn and up to what point they should learn them" (1094a28–b2). This has all the appearance of an empirical claim, but it is clear from what we have already seen that Aristotle knew it was very far from being a true generalization about existing cities. That he offers this more as a normative claim than an empirical one is evident. If this is right, then the sense of the argument is that since politics *should* control and make use of education, it must be the art whose nature it is to aim at the highest good for human beings. A tacit premise on which this evidently relies is the proposition that education is essential to the pursuit of the highest human good. Supposing it is, the art which of all arts is the one that should control and make use of education, or in other words the one to which education is properly subsidiary, would be uniquely equipped to pursue the highest human good. Aristotle will need other arguments if he is to show that politics is *entitled* to take the highest human good as its end, or that it *should* take this as its end, but with this argument he eliminates every other art from contention. On the assumption that education is essential to the enterprise of promoting the highest good for human beings, if it is politics that should control and use education, then no other art could be the one that properly promotes the highest human good. If there is such an art, it would have to be politics.

The argument is thus quite coherent on a normative reading of the premise that it is politics that determines what sciences are to be studied and by whom, and this lends more than circumstantial credence to the suggestion that Aristotle does not intend this premise as an empirical generalization about actual polises. Clearly, he would not offer this argument unless he assumed his audience would readily agree that education should be publicly supervised, and unless he himself believed it should be; and he would not offer it *here*, in the course of laying the foundations of his ethical theory, unless he held this view of education with great confidence. I take it then, that when Aristotle says in Book VIII of the *Politics* that "no one will doubt" that education should be the legislator's first concern, he means it quite seriously. I also take it that he does not say this just on the strength of the arguments he has offered in the course of *Politics* I–VII, since the *Nicomachean Ethics* seems to precede the *Politics* in the sequence of his lectures, the end of the former being obviously intended as a transition to the latter. Whatever significance he attaches to his own arguments for public education, his reliance at the outset of the *Nicomachean Ethics* on the assumption that education is properly subject to political control suggests a prior history of agreement with his audience on this point.

Turning to the question of *why* Aristotle would have supposed that no one would doubt that education should be the foremost concern of legislation, three circumstances are worth noting. First, the Greek world had long been impressed by Spartan military prowess, and Sparta's victory over Athens in the Peloponnesian War, which ended in 404 or roughly seventy years before the composition of the *Politics*, must have contributed greatly to the respect which Athenians and others had for Spartan institutions (Powell 1988, 156–57). Even after the Spartans were outmaneuvered by the Thebans at Leuctra in 371 and Sparta ceased to be a great power (Hammond 1986, 493–97), the educational system that had produced the Spartan hoplite may have remained in the minds of many a model worthy of at least selective emulation.

A second circumstance, quite compatible with the first, is that praise for Spartan institutions was apparently common among the old oligarchs of Athens, and mixed with nostalgia for earlier and less democratic times in Athens. Even if Sparta itself had become more democratic than these Athenians might have preferred, the Spartan system of military and civil discipline might have seemed an obvious way to create an obedient and obliging citizenry. Aristotle was not a champion of oligarchy,[17] but it is conceivable that he assumed the prevalence of such ideas about Spartan education among the leisured and learned who attended his lectures.

Third, it is likely that Aristotle and his audience of students of political science were familiar with arguments about education that had been made by Xenophon, Socrates, and Plato, and possibly others. We have seen something already of Xenophon's sympathetic portrayal of the Spartan system of education, and even though it is doubtful that his arguments or any others would have held the importance in Aristotle's mind that those of Socrates and Plato did, it is useful to observe the grounds on which Xenophon advocated a better domestic education for women in his *Oeconomicus*. The argument is addressed to husbands, though in terms which are suggestive of a theme in Socratic and Platonic educational thought which we shall come to shortly and dwell upon at some length:

> "When a sheep is ailing," said Socrates, "we generally blame the shepherd, and when a horse is vicious, we generally find fault with his rider. In the case of a wife, if she receives instruction in the right way from her husband and yet does badly, perhaps she should bear the blame; but if the husband does not instruct the wife in the right way of doing things, and so finds her ignorant, should he not bear the blame himself?" (*Oec.* III.11).[18]

This is not an argument for *public* education, but Aristotle would not have been blind to the way in which it might be turned into one. The principle which seems to underlie it would suggest that if the city is in a better position than individual citizens to know certain things essential to acting well, and the city may wish in the future to blame those who act badly, then it must first see to it that they are educated in those things.

In any case, Aristotle would have been well aware of the arguments that Plato had made for a public system of education and for the importance of such a system to the legislative art. These arguments play an important role in Plato's work, and Aristotle surely assumed with good reason that his audience was familiar with them. It may be that when Aristotle suggests that "no one" will doubt the importance of education, he has in mind his own audience, which might have consisted of Plato's students and his own, give or take a few.[19] If this is the case, then his confidence in asserting the obvious desirability of a public system of education would reflect a judgment that Plato had given arguments for public education which were strong and recognized as such.

Which arguments of Plato's Aristotle may have found so convincing we can scarcely surmise without examining, first, Plato's arguments, then Aristotle's. In beginning with Plato's arguments, as I soon shall, we may learn something of what Aristotle took for granted in the way of a common understanding with his audience. The background which this provides will prove invaluable when we take up the task of reconstructing Aristotle's own arguments for public education.

The task of the remainder of this chapter and the next will thus be to survey the arguments which Plato offers on behalf of public education, beginning with their roots in Socratic thought. These arguments are by no means confined to the *Republic*, and Aristotle's political works show the obvious influence of not only the *Republic*, but also the *Apology*,[20] *Protagoras*,[21] *Statesman*,[22] and *Laws*. His references to all of these works and their formative influence on his own are clear, as we shall see. Important elements of the educational content of the middle and later Platonic dialogues are already evident in the *Apology* and *Crito*, and by reading these dialogues together we will be able to identify the Socratic principles on which Platonic and Aristotelian political and educational thought are founded.[23] I will take up these dialogues in their apparent order of composition, concentrating on the principles which seem most basic and the arguments which seem most important. In the remainder of this chapter I shall examine the educational ideas of Socrates as we encounter them in the early dialogues, particularly the *Apology* and *Crito,* and in the next I shall examine those of Plato as we encounter them in the transitional, middle, and late dialogues. What I shall provide in this limited space will be little more than a sketch, though one which I hope will suffice to indicate the general contours of the Socratic tradition in which Aristotle labored. Much that would be essential to a full examination of Platonic educational thought must be left to another occasion.

Plato's dialogues may seem an unlikely place to venture in search of palatable and compelling arguments for a public school system. The reaction of students who come upon the *Republic* for the first time is not unlike that of English-speaking scholars writing in the 1930s and '40s who dismissed the *Republic* as the "original philosophical charter of fascism" (Sisson 1940, 143). In an age when Nazi and Communist claims to the legacy of Plato figured significantly in an international struggle for both moral and military supremacy (Morrow 1941, 105–06), this was perhaps not surprising, but with the passage of time it has become easier to see the textual grounds for a more sympathetic reading of Plato's political thought. Morrow (1941) emphasizes Plato's extraordinary commitment to the idea of a just rule of law in the *Laws*, and what emerges from more recent scholarship is a picture of Plato as a champion of government by reasoned persuasion and consent not only in the *Laws*, but through the entire course of his political writings (Kraut 1984; Reeve 1988; Cooper 1999; Bobonich 1991, 1996). A principle which is evident in those writings, and in other Greek sources before Plato, is that it is better to rely on persuasion *(peithô)* than force *(bia)*—that persuasion is to be used instead of force to the extent that it will suffice, and must be given a reasonable chance to succeed before force can be judged necessary.[24] An important feature of the deployment of this principle in the Socratic dialogues is that it is applied to individuals in their dealings with each other and with the city, and to the city in its dealings with individuals, in remarkably similar ways. In the former application it becomes the misunderstood principle that one must either "persuade or obey," but we will be able to see why this is so only when we turn our attention to the *Crito*.

1.3 EDUCATION AND LAW IN THE *APOLOGY* AND *CRITO*

The early Socratic dialogues may seem as unlikely a place to find useful and compelling arguments for public education as the *Republic*, for while the latter is dismissed as repugnantly authoritarian, the former are dominated by a Socrates who challenges all comers to offer any basis of moral knowledge on which they might properly claim to be teachers of virtue. How could Socrates be an advocate of public education, a public education in virtue moreover, if he believes one must have moral knowledge to be a teacher of virtue, and believes no one possesses such knowledge? How could he be an advocate of public education when we find him concluding in the *Meno* and *Protagoras*, two transitional dialogues, that there are no teachers of virtue and virtue simply cannot be taught, on the express grounds that there are no examples of success in teaching it (*Meno* 89d–96d; *Prot.* 319b–20b), and the implied grounds that when he questions those who claim to teach virtue it becomes evident that they lack moral knowledge (cf. *Ap.* 21b–23a)?

The answer to this question must begin in the recognition that Socrates saw good reasons to doubt that complete or true virtue could be taught, but did think it possible and important for cities to ensure that their citizens receive a more elementary form of moral education. The stages of moral education and development which Socrates recognizes are convincingly identified by Richard Kraut in the following terms:

(A) A child receives a conventional moral training, as described by the *Protagoras* and endorsed in the *Crito*. He has many true and many false beliefs, none of them systematically related. He thinks he has knowledge but does not. And he often acts incorrectly.

(B) A person is challenged by Socratic questions and loses his complacency. He sees difficulties in his firmly held beliefs. . . . He cannot defend his beliefs in argument, and he realizes this.

(C) The stage Socrates has reached. He has systematized many of his beliefs and has rid himself of errors. He can defend many of his views in argument, but he is still afflicted by puzzles. . . .

(D) The stage of moral expertise. A person can define the virtues, is free from moral perplexity, and can determine how to act even in difficult situations (Kraut 1984, 230–31).

Socrates seems to place himself at stage *C*, and to place no one else he has met any higher than *B* (*Ap.* 21–23b). Yet he clearly thinks that progress along the path from *A* to *D* is possible through philosophical questioning and inquiry (*Ap.* 30a–b, 38a), and that there is great value in the foundation for virtue laid by *A* (*Cri.* 50d–e; *Prot.* 327b–d; Kraut 1984, 218–24). Since he believes virtue is the greatest good one can possess (*Ap.* 30b, 36c, 38a), this gives him reason to approve of cities whose laws encourage or require conventional moral training while also encouraging or leaving room for the practice of philosophy. Kraut concludes very plausibly that this is the best explanation for why Socrates concedes in the *Crito* that Athens has been "exceedingly pleasing" to him (52b); its provisions for conventional moral training were less systematic than those of the Spartans and Cretans (52e–53a), but that was more than compensated for by its being far more tolerant of the practice of philosophy (Kraut 1984, 228).

Thus, we may reasonably conclude that when Socrates expresses doubts about the teachability of virtue he means virtue that is perfected by the possession of systematic moral knowledge or moral expertise, and not virtue of a more ordinary sort. We have no reason to doubt that Socrates accepts the idea that virtue of this ordinary sort is produced by the conventional upbringing and schooling described in Protagoras's "Great Speech" (*Prot.* 325c–27d).[25] A critic might nevertheless ask in what sense Socrates could be a proponent of public education when he concedes in the *Crito* that he sees no reason to criticize the Athenian law that did no more than "instruct [his] father to educate [him] in the arts and in physical culture" (50d–e)?[26] This seems to be an endorsement of actual Athenian practices, not a call for anything we would be inclined to call public education. This cannot be denied, but what is important about the early dialogues for our purposes is that we meet in them a Socrates not unlike the one we encountered in the *Oeconomicus* of Xenophon.[27] We meet a Socrates who believes that no one does wrong willingly (*Prot.* 352c, 358c–d), and who believes that those who do wrong unwillingly should be instructed and persuaded, rather than punished. More broadly, we meet a Socrates whose insistence on putting reason *(logos)* and persuasion *(peithô)* before force *(bia)* and violence *(biasdoimên)* in the conduct of public life has fundamental implications for the educational burdens which a city must accept and in some way discharge, whether through schools or by some other means.

1.31 Fidelity to Reason in the *Apology*

In pleading his own defense, Socrates argues that it is absurd to suppose that he would have knowingly corrupted his associates, and inappropriate to punish him if he did so unknowingly:

> if I corrupt them unwillingly, the law does not require you to bring people to court for such unwilling wrongdoings, but to get hold of them privately, to instruct them and exhort them; for clearly, if I learn better, I shall cease to do what I am doing unwillingly. You, however, have avoided my company and were unwilling to instruct me, but you bring me here, where the law requires one to bring those who are in need of punishment, not of instruction (*Ap.* 26a).

The setting for this remark is a legal system in which charges for many kinds of offenses were brought by volunteers, rather than by a public prosecutor acting in the name of "the people" (MacDowell 1978, 53–66), so it is Meletus, Socrates' accuser, and not the city itself, who Socrates says should bear a burden to instruct him, rather than seek punishment. This falls short of arguing that the city has an obligation to instruct its citizens in what they need to know to lead just and law-abiding lives, but it does seem to imply that the city can never be in a position to punish unless this educational burden is discharged by *someone*, and this in turn implies that the city cannot establish a general claim to punish whomever may break its laws *unless it makes some general provision for educating everyone*. Whatever burden of instruction the individual prosecuting the case may bear, the jury will presumably be bound by the same principle that instruction is the appropriate response to ignorance, and will be in no position to impose a punishment on one who has not been appropriately instructed.

In this passage Socrates allows that punishment may sometimes be appropriate, and it would seem to follow from this that he assumes that in some instances the burden of instruction will have been adequately borne. It is not entirely clear how he intends to reconcile this qualified approval of the use of punishment with his doctrine that no one does wrong willingly, but it would be natural for him to assume that there will be cases in which the futility of further educative efforts will become evident and the city will have to use other methods to protect itself. Faced with people who do not respond to instruction, what is a city to do? Having put instruction and persuasion first, might it justly defend itself by imposing punishments which purge it of those who have been instructed and discovered to be incurably bad? Could it not hold that those of unjust *character* are unjust *unwillingly*, yet hold that the city may defend itself from *voluntary wrongdoing*—from wrongdoing that springs directly from an unjust character—and that when attempts to defend itself through instruction and persuasion fail, it is entitled to use more forceful means? The doctrine that no one is willingly unjust implies that people cannot simply choose their states of character; to choose the better and the right over the worse and the wrong they must know what is right and best, and often they do not. They require instruction and persuasion, and a city that does not provide these will be in no position to blame and punish them. This creates an educational burden which can, however, be satisfied, and when it has been satisfied the city will be in a position to blame and punish, even though the wrongdoer remains incapable of making himself into a just person. It has placed instruction and persuasion before force, on what is best identified as the principle that *instruction is the appropriate response to ignorance which has not proven impervious to instruction*, and to deny the city the use of force in the face of unyielding ignorance and wrongdoing would be to deny it the means to defend itself and preserve the good order on which the well-being of its citizens depends.

This is admittedly somewhat speculative, but I will try to show now that it reconciles Socrates' statements about punishment and ignorance in a way that conforms to the general pattern of his principle of putting rational persuasion before force. This principle is itself only one aspect of a more general principle of putting reason before force, of putting reason *(logos)* and wisdom *(sophia* and *phronêsis; Ap.* 23a, 29e) first in every way, which I shall call the *principle of fidelity to reason.* In the dialogues of Plato, Socrates does not announce any such principle, but it is embodied in his belief that *the rational soul (psychê) or intellect (nous) is the divine element in human nature, and the one we should cultivate and rely on in ourselves and others, if we are to live well and admirably* (*Ap.* 29d–30b, 30e–31a, 36c; *Cri.* 44d, 47e–48a; *Prot.* 313a–b; etc.). "The god[28] is wise," and "human wisdom is worth little or nothing" by comparison, says Socrates (*Ap.* 23a; cf. *Hp. Ma.* 289b), but wisdom is "the greatest good" (*Cri.* 44d), and those who wrongly believe themselves wise are guilty of "the most blameworthy ignorance" (*Ap.* 21b–e, 29a–b). They are guilty of failing to acknowledge the great gulf that lies between themselves and "the god," and thus fail to love and strive toward a wisdom measured not by man, but by god.[29] Socrates disavows any knowledge of the nature of piety (*Euth.* 15c, 15e–16a; Kraut 1984, 249–52), but he surely believed that piety entails a respect for and striving toward what is divine in ourselves and others.[30] Since Socrates identifies the divine element in us with the rational soul, piety would evidently entail cultivating and relying on rationality and reasoning to the greatest extent that one can. This would mean *cultivating rationality both in oneself and in others* and *relying on reasoning* both in action and in speech, *in moving both oneself and others to act,* and *in judging what to say and what to believe* of the opinions of others. Socrates' respect for reason is on display in all these ways in the *Apology* and *Crito,* and the strategy of his defense at trial is largely to explain that his fidelity to reason, annoying as it may be, is an expression of both piety and goodwill toward the city and its youth.

In its application to cities in their dealings with citizens, the *principle of fidelity to reason* generates corollaries pertaining to the *manner, aim,* and *substance* of rule. Thus in moving citizens to act in some ways and not others, the *manner* in which a city should rule, to the greatest extent possible, is through truthful instruction and rational persuasion, rather than through force; and it should listen to the arguments offered in return by its citizens and endeavor to judge those arguments on their rational merits. The *aim* of the city's laws and rational persuasion should be to produce not fidelity to commands and conventions as such, but fidelity to reason, and through it a grasp and pursuit of what is truly, and not just apparently, good. The city should aim at the highest good of its citizens, in short. In its *substance* the laws, commands, and verdicts by which rule is transacted should strive to embody reason—which is to say divine reason or law (*Ap.* 30d; *Cri.* 54c[31])—wisdom, or what is just and good for the whole city. In sum, the city and its laws should be true to reason in every way.

Similarly, in its application to the conduct of citizens toward the city, the *principle of fidelity to reason* generates corollaries pertaining to the *substance* and *aim* of individual conduct, and to its *manner,* both in *compliance* and *defiance* of law. In the *substance* of their conduct citizens should do what is right, just, or demanded by reason (*Ap.* 32a; *Cri.* 48c, 49a, etc.) and they should *aim* at the good

(*Ap.* 29e–30a; *Cri.* 54b). To the extent that the laws of actual cities are not divinely inspired or grounded in systematic moral knowledge, those laws will sometimes demand the right thing and sometimes demand the wrong thing. When they demand the right thing, fidelity to reason demands that citizens comply in a *voluntary manner*, for in this case what the law demands is what reason demands. To fail in this is to behave not in the manner of a citizen, but of a slave who is unable to govern himself in accordance with reason and must be *forced* to cooperate with it (*Cri.* 52d). On the other hand, when the laws demand the wrong thing, what fidelity to reason demands in the *manner* of their defiance of law is that they make a reasonable effort to persuade the city that what it demands is wrong. Here again, instruction is the appropriate response to ignorance that has not proven impervious to instruction. Socrates reasons that in a good city a citizen's consent to the laws and debt of gratitude for the benefits conferred by those laws creates an obligation to "persuade or obey" (*Cri.* 51b, 51b–c, 51e–52a), and that to fail in this obligation is to do violence to the city (51b–c). One way to avoid doing the city violence is to obey, but when obedience is precluded by the wrongness of what the law demands, the citizen must avoid doing the city violence by making a reasonable effort to persuade it that what it expects is wrong. If the city has already shown itself to be unmoved by reason, an acceptable course may be to simply ignore the law, as Socrates himself seems to have done by defying the unjust orders of the Thirty oligarchs "not in words but in action" (*Ap.* 32c–d). Otherwise, the citizen should attempt to instruct and persuade the city through truthful and rational means, but if he fails to convince it that its law is unjust he must nevertheless do the right thing, even in defiance of its instructions (*Ap.* 29d, 32a–d, 37e–38a).[32] Having put instruction and persuasion first as much as possible, his fidelity to reason does the city no violence.

In the interpretation I am offering here, the demands of justice on citizens in their relations to cities are thus interestingly symmetrical with the demands of justice governing cities in their relations to citizens, and this symmetry is explained by the common origin of these demands in the *principle of fidelity to reason*. Principled defiance of bad law by citizens and punishment of wrongdoing by the city are both acceptable on Socratic principles, but both are subject to the constraints of fidelity to reason and the reliance on instruction and persuasion that entails. The burden of instruction and persuasion which the city and citizen both face is a responsibility to encourage rationality and to provide reasons which a reasonable person would accept as sufficient. For the city's part, it is not a duty to endure injustice when reasonable efforts to instruct and persuade unjust individuals fail, for fidelity to reason entails striving to exemplify rationality ourselves and encourage it in others, and the creation and preservation of good order through good law is essential to doing that. Nor, for the citizen's part, is it a duty to undertake futile and potentially dangerous efforts to reason with rulers who have already demonstrated their disregard for reason, nor ever to persist beyond giving reasons that a reasonable person would be moved by. By ascribing the *principle of fidelity to reason* to Socrates, we can thus make coherent good sense of what might otherwise appear to be unrelated or conflicting Socratic doctrines. I have provided only the barest outline of an interpretation, however, so it is time to return to the text of the *Apology* and examine one further passage before continuing on to the *Crito*.

Several aspects or corollaries of the *principle of fidelity to reason* are evident in the *Apology* in Socrates' explanation to the jury of why he offers a reasoned defense and refrains from the customary appeals to pity (34c) and "pitiful dramatics" (35b):

> Quite apart from the question of reputation, gentlemen, I do not think it right to supplicate the jury and to be acquitted because of this, but to teach and persuade *(didaskein kai peithein)* them. It is not the purpose of a juryman's office to give justice as a favor to whoever seems good to him, but to judge according to law, and this he has sworn to do. We should not accustom you to perjure yourselves, nor should you make a habit of it. . . .
>
> Do not deem it right for me, gentlemen of the jury, that I should act towards you in a way that I do not consider to be good or just or pious, . . . [for] clearly, if I convinced you by my supplication to do violence to your oath of office, I would be teaching you not to believe that there are gods, and my defense would convict me of not believing in them. This is far from being the case . . . (35b–d).

The first thing of great importance that is evident in this passage is that Socrates understands teaching and persuading to be truthful and reasoned, since he contrasts them explicitly and at length with appeals to the emotions, which might induce an unsound judgment. This is important, for without such evidence one might doubt that his expressed preference for teaching and persuading expresses a commitment of fidelity to *reason*. Both here and in his explanation to Crito of how he will judge the arguments for escape, when he awaits death after his conviction (*Cri.* 46b–48a),[33] he displays and praises a reliance on truth and reasoned argument, whatever perils one may face. In the *Apology* he encourages the jury to judge the arguments impartially, and in the *Crito* he holds himself to the same standard. Judging the arguments impartially and heeding those which prove the strongest upon examination seems to be at the core, then, of how citizens and cities should determine what to do, say, and think; compliance with perfect or divine reason is what the good of all human beings rests on, and this seems to be the principal and fundamental means by which Socrates thinks progress toward that end can be made.[34]

A second important feature of this passage is that Socrates advocates teaching and persuasion not only because he does "not think it right" or "good or just or pious" to use more manipulative methods of having his way with the jury, but because using those methods would encourage the jurymen to violate their vow to "judge according to law." Socrates clearly thinks it would be wrong to induce them to violate that vow, and he also clearly thinks that to "judge according to law" entails judging in a way that is reasoned and respectful of truth and evidence. It is reasonable to infer from this that he assumes there is *a natural standard of impartial reason* which should govern the administration of justice, and that he thinks piety and justice demand that citizens encourage the city to embrace that standard. Socrates suggests that to acquit out of pity, in violation of the oath one has taken to "judge according to law," would be to perjure oneself, to make the oath one has sworn false after the fact, or "do violence *(biasdoimên)* to it." Here as elsewhere, violence is contrasted with fidelity to reason, and fidelity to reason is understood to be essential to justice.

Of course, Socrates is not only encouraging the city along the path of reason, but is instructing the city's jury in the very way that he would have the city instruct its citizens. He commends to the jurymen the very virtues of piety and justice which he is accused of lacking, and he does so with the intention of teaching them that these virtues entail a commitment to reason and aim their possessor toward the good of others (*Ap.* 25d; *Rep.* I 335c–d). He thereby endorses these virtues, and the embrace of reason which they entail, as legitimate components of the substance of public instruction. More broadly, he endorses the instruction of citizens through reason and pursuant to virtue and the good when he suggests at *Apology* 36b–37a that it would be appropriate for Athens to subsidize his philosophical examination of his fellow Athenians, and at *Gorgias* 521d–e that his speeches make him a practitioner of the "true political craft."

Third, in this speech to the jury Socrates says that if he convinced the jurymen to do violence to their oath, he would be teaching them "not to believe that there are gods." In saying this he evidently relies on the jurymen's belief that the existence of the gods and their law makes a breach of oath wrong.[35] On these beliefs, and no others we could plausibly impute to them, they could validly infer the denial of theism from the practical equivalent of a denial that a breach of oath is wrong. Thus, it is likely that Socrates said this to the members of the jury on the assumption that they held this view of divine law; and in order for this not to violate the spirit of his condemnation of manipulative arguments, it would seem that he must have believed it himself. This provides us with some basis, beyond Socrates' references to the "laws of god" (*Ap.* 30d) and obeying "the god" (*Ap.* 29d, 38a), for attributing to him the corollary to the *principle of fidelity to reason* pertaining to the substance of law or rule. To make further progress with this attribution, however, we need to turn more directly to the *Crito*.

1.32 Instructing Crito through the Laws

When Crito comes to Socrates in the final days before his execution and urges him to escape and leave Athens, Socrates responds that he "value[s] and respect[s] the same principles as before" (46b–c) and will not measure what is virtuous and true by the opinions of men, even opinions held by all men, but by arguments impartially judged (46c–47c). It is tempting to see between the lines here an implicit rejection of the Protagorean doctrine that "of all things Man is the measure," and this hypothesis is encouraged further by the apparent references to the trial of Socrates that appear in the context of an extended discussion of this Protagorean doctrine in Plato's *Theaetetus*.[36] At *Crito* 46d–47a Socrates insists that we should not value all the opinions of men, but those of wise men, and Plato has him insist on essentially the same point at *Theaetetus* 171d, in express opposition to Protagoras, before launching into a "digression" on "how natural it is that men who have spent a greater part of their lives in philosophical studies make such fools of themselves when they appear as speakers in the law courts" (172c). The philosophical manner of pleading a case is contrasted in the *Theaetetus,* much as it is in the *Apology,* with flattery and currying favor (173a). There are also references to lies, "the policy of repaying one wrong with another" (173a–b), and the natural penalty for injustice (176d–77a), much like those at *Crito* 47c–49e following Socrates' insistence that he will judge the arguments impartially. We also find an express statement there of the idea, which I have attributed to Socrates in the *Apology,* that to escape from evil "means becoming as like God as possible," which a man does "when he becomes just and pure, with understanding" (176b), the measure of justice and understanding being thus obviously divine. The linkages between the two passages are thus strong, and they provide good grounds for thinking that Socrates is implicitly contrasting his own views with those of Protagoras in the opening of his response to Crito.

This reference to Protagoras is significant because it makes it all the more clear that Socrates does not hold in the *Crito* a theory of law and obligation to the laws which would make adherence to human laws unconditionally obligatory, but rather a theory on which human laws are subordinate to a divine standard of justice. Socrates begins his response to Crito by explaining that he is bound to do what is truly just, not what men, even all the men of one's city, hold to be just. On the Protagorean account, all the men of one's city and the laws they establish as a convention or social contract cannot be wrong. The virtues are simply whatever they are taken to be in one's own city, and by this standard Crito's appeal to what the majority of men will say should prevail. But Socrates will have none of it. He denies the assumptions on which the appeal to opinion rests and declines Crito's unjust proposal. Consistency will demand that he also refuse to obey laws which are unjust by the standards of natural or divine law, even if they express the majority view. But what of the judgment of the majority of the jurymen who convicted him, if their verdict was *substantively* unjust, or arrived at in a way that breached their oath of office? This is the question which gives the *Crito* its edge, and I shall return to it after noting some other aspects of the dialogue.

An important role which Crito plays in the dialogue is to speak for legal conventionalism and a conventional ethic of outward success, an ethic which finds virtue in helping one's friends and harming or prevailing over one's enemies. This *agonistic,* or "Homeric," ethic (Adkins 1971) derives its name from *agon,* or "contest," and Crito is depicted as a representative of it when he suggests that

Socrates' trial was a contest which Socrates and his friends should feel shame at having lost (45e), and that they should all be thought lacking in manly virtue if they fail to defeat the enemies of Socrates, who wish to destroy him (45c and 46a). Crito regards law as an arena in which combatants struggle with one another (cf. *Tht.* 172e), and he succumbs at least partially to the view that virtue is measured by success alone when he obtains access to Socrates by bribing the warder (43a) and suggests that Socrates need not feel compelled to stand by what he said in court (45b). Crito has forgotten what is just and virtuous, at least for the time being, and Socrates accepts the obligation to instruct and persuade him (48e), just as he would have the city do, and just as he would have citizens do toward the city. He says, "I think it important to persuade you before I act, and not to act against your wishes" (48e), though clearly he is prepared to act without Crito's approval if persuasion fails.

What happens, then, is that Plato has Socrates respond by allowing the laws of Athens, idealized and deified, to speak to them both. He thereby creates what is on the one hand, in effect, a dialogue between two theories of law and virtue, and on the other hand a model for how cities and citizens ought to go about persuading and acting toward each other.[37] As I have already noted, the laws speak repeatedly of the citizen's obligation to "persuade or obey" their orders (51b, 51b–c, 52a), and I have said enough for our purposes here of the grounds for interpreting this as a requirement to do what is just and attempt to persuade the city that it is wrong if justice requires one to disobey. For the city's part, the laws say "we only propose things, we do not issue savage *(agriôs)* commands to do whatever we order" (52a). They speak repeatedly of persuading Socrates (53a, 54b, 54c), and they present him with philosophical arguments and instruct him to observe *(skopei)* what follows from those arguments (51c). Their mode of persuasion is truthful and philosophically reasoned, and it is they, the laws themselves, who instruct Socrates, and through whom Socrates instructs Crito.

It is unclear, of course, in exactly what way Socrates would have the laws of actual cities persuade and instruct, but it is clear that he is proposing here that they should *in some way* encourage and rely on reason in moving citizens to act. He has the laws say their commands are not *agriôs*, and we must read this in light of Plato's habit of contrasting the godlike *(deiotaton)* with the savage *(agriôs)* and most savage *(agriôtaton)*, the extent to which reason is present and controlling making all the difference between the two.[38] In saying their commands are not savage, the laws thus imply that they are reasonable or rational, and they seem to intend this not simply as a point about their substance and aims, whose merits are invoked at 50d–e, but about their manner. It might be objected that their immediate point about their manner is only that they are open to being persuaded by citizens,[39] but surely this implies that they will also engage in persuasion themselves, if only in answer to questions and objections that are put to them. Socrates is evidently advancing a conception of law as the embodiment of divine or perfect reason, and an instrument by which human beings can be made more godlike, more rationally self-governing, and thereby better and happier. The speech of the laws suggests that they would engage in these educative tasks through reasoning with citizens, though in what venue and by what means they will reason with citizens is, as I have said, unclear. Socrates may think that the very text of the laws should be instructive and contain rationally persuasive arguments, or he may think that there should be laws which direct members of the city to incorporate the law's commands into teaching which provides reasons for respecting and obeying those commands, or he may think that laws should be enacted by assemblies of citizens or more generally through processes of public discussion and deliberation. Perhaps he would regard all three as appropriate.

With regard to the second of these possibilities, it is interesting to note that by instructing Crito through the impartial voice of the laws, Socrates is able to preserve the sympathetic tone without which his attempt to instruct Crito might fail. A less sympathetic tone would tend to inspire a less rational and more spirited and resistant response, and Socrates may recognize this and believe that he owes it to his friend to persuade him in a way that is reasoned but also friendly.[40] He might also think that a city should adopt a sympathetic or friendly tone in attempting to persuade its "offspring," though we cannot assert this with any certainty. We have seen in his speech to the jury in the *Apology* that Socrates condemns the use of emotional appeals which *defeat* reasoned judgment, but his attitude to emotional influences that *encourage* or increase the likelihood of a reasoned judgment is unclear. One might think that fidelity to reason compels one to instruct and persuade in a manner that is reasonably calculated to inspire a rational acceptance of the conclusions one provides reasons for, but one cannot say with much conviction that Socrates consistently makes as much effort to avoid inciting a spirited and resistant response in his interlocutors as respect for truth and reason permit. He may think that reasoned persuasion should not concern itself at all with the emotions and their role in a listener's response to speech, even if some people find the result off-putting. He may think that some forms of emotional encouragement to judge rationally, such as the sympathetic or friendly tone which he adopts toward Crito, are not only permissible but generally advisable or obligatory. He may think that a stance of emotional neutrality can and should be attained through the adoption of an impartial point of view. Or, finally, he may have no determinate view on this matter. The decision to instruct Crito through the laws does at least suggest, however, that he regards the law as an important vehicle of instruction transacted between human beings, and one whose impartiality enables one person to instruct another in a way which is both sympathetic and respectful of reason.

A further point regarding the character of the persuasion which the laws exhibit in the *Crito* is that it relies on the goodness of the laws' substance and aims. The laws suggest that they have aimed at Socrates' well-being by providing for his nurture and education (50d–e), and they urge him at the close of their speech to value goodness above all, warning that

if you depart after shamefully returning wrong for wrong and injury for injury, after breaking your agreement and contract with us, after injuring those you should
injure least—yourself, your friends, your country, and us—we shall be angry with
you while you are still alive, and our brothers, the laws of Hades, will not receive
you kindly . . . (54c).

In Greek theology, Hades is the brother of Zeus and Poseidon, the one ruling the
air and the other the water. For Socrates to speak of the laws of Athens as brothers of the divine laws of another realm is to identify them as themselves divine,
and almost certainly as the laws of Zeus, ruler of the realm inhabited by human
beings.[41] This passage thus provides unequivocal evidence of the divine status
of the laws which speak to Socrates—unequivocal evidence that Socrates holds
that any laws that are entitled to our obedience embody divine reason or systematic moral knowledge, and are good for us. It also illustrates one of the forms of
reasoned persuasion which Socrates believes the goodness of just law makes
possible, namely appeals to the citizen's well-being. The laws have argued at
length (53b–e) that Socrates will be injuring himself if he commits the injustice
advocated by Crito, and their argument complements Socrates' own reasons for
believing that virtue is of all goods most essential to happiness (47e–48a). This
suggests that the city's efforts to persuade citizens along the path of virtue and
justice can and should instruct them in the benefits to themselves of virtue and
voluntary compliance with law.

1.33 The Obligations of Citizenship and the City's Right to Punish

A final aspect of this concluding passage which we must note, before turning to
the *Protagoras*, is the laws' suggestion that if Socrates escapes he will injure the
city and its laws, and will be "breaking [his] agreement and contract with [them]."
I suggested above that a central problem in the *Crito* is how Socrates can accommodate respect for the mistaken judgment of a jury within his natural law alternative to Protagorean relativism, and I will suggest now that he believes gratitude to the city for benefits bestowed by it, and prior consent to its laws and
procedures, both provide reasons to honor its verdicts through obedience or persuasion (51e–52a). At 50c, the laws first refer to Socrates having made an agreement with them when they say that Socrates has agreed "to respect the judgments"
of the city. They then enumerate the benefits of birth, nurture, and education that
they have bestowed upon Socrates (50d–e), insist that he is their "offspring" (50e),
and argue that he therefore must honor them by obeying or persuading them "as
to the nature of justice" (50e–51). The laws then return to and develop their argument from agreement (51d–53a):

by giving every Athenian the opportunity, after he has reached manhood and observed the affairs of the city and us the laws, we proclaim that if we do not please
him, he can take his possessions and go wherever he pleases. Not one of our laws

raises any obstacle or forbids him. . . . We say, however, that whomever of you remains, when he sees how we conduct our trials and manage the city in other ways, has in fact come to an agreement with us to obey our instructions. . . . Yet . . . we give two alternatives, either to persuade us or to do what we say (51d–52a).

Having said this, the laws remind Socrates of a number of facts: that he has been satisfied with Athens and its laws and has chosen to remain there even though he thinks there are other well-governed cities (52b, 52e–53a); that he has made no efforts to publicly persuade the laws that they have wronged him (52c), yet now contemplates "breaking the undertakings and agreements that [he] has made with [them] without compulsion or deceit, and under no pressure of time for deliberation" (52d–e). They point out, in other words, that Socrates will violate the obligation to persuade or obey if he flees, since he has not attempted to persuade the city that any law or the verdict rendered against him is unjust. And they point out that he has acquired this obligation through his own tacit consent (as well as from the benefits he has enjoyed), since he remains there freely and with knowledge of the laws and their administration, and not because he cannot leave, stays for lack of any acceptable alternative, or has been coerced, deceived, or forced to make a hasty decision. Socrates thus takes the idea of free and informed consent very seriously, for by mentioning each of these aspects of a free and informed decision he implicitly acknowledges that if any of these conditions were absent his presence in Athens could not be interpreted as an expression of consent or agreement to its laws and procedures. Indeed, he allows that the absence of some of these conditions may preclude assuming that some other Athenians have entered into an agreement with the city, when he says that "I am among the Athenians who most definitely came to that agreement with them" (52a–b).

The laws offer two arguments then, one appealing to the parent-city analogy and one appealing to the idea of consent or agreement, and both are offered as evidence that Socrates owes the city and its laws the honor of either his obedience or a reasonable effort to persuade them that they are wrong. The first argument places a burden on the laws to *benefit all citizens* if they are to claim the loyalty of all citizens, for the claim to quasi-parental status is grounded in the assertion that the city bestows care and benefits of the kind that good and responsible parents do. There is no suggestion that any parental or quasi-parental right to expect obedience would exist if these normal parental duties of care were not faithfully discharged. The second argument places this same burden on the city, since consent requires satisfaction, but it also places on the city a further responsibility to create the conditions necessary for all citizens to give *free and informed consent* to the laws, if it is to claim the loyalty of all citizens. In sum, the laws must benefit citizens, and citizens must be able to learn about the laws of their own city and other cities and freely examine and discuss the merits and defects of those laws, if the city is to legitimately assert an obligation of obedience.

What this earns the city in return is evidently a reasonable expectation of voluntary compliance with its good laws, which no city can do without and long endure, and a right to explanations from citizens who regard any of its laws as bad. Socrates, for his part, has not attempted to persuade the city that the verdict in his case was unjust, so he must now honor the city with his obedience, and not subvert its laws. Not having put persuasion first, he has no right now to use force, even if the jury's verdict was in fact unjust. By contrast, we have noted that he describes himself in the *Apology* as ignoring without explanation the orders of the Thirty oligarchs to assist them in the prosecution of an innocent man (*Ap.* 32c–d), and we must assume that he regarded his response as acceptable because the orders were unjust and the oligarchy ruled neither by consent nor for the good of the citizens of Athens.

The function of the arguments from the parent-city analogy and from agreement is thus to provide a reason to honor a verdict which reason does not directly commend, and more broadly to honor the laws and judgments of one's city at least to the extent of explaining one's grounds for objecting to them. In doing this, these arguments perform a greater service in the cause of reason than might be apparent, by encouraging public dialogue about justice, and by discouraging unreasonable flaunting of the laws, which can only accomplish their legitimate ends through mainly voluntary compliance. If these arguments create any obligation beyond those generated by the *principle of fidelity to reason*, it is a special obligation to adhere to the corollaries of this principle in relation to *one's own* city. Socrates surely thought that divine justice applies universally to all human beings in their dealings with one another, but he may have thought that it is only in application to a city's dealings with its own citizens that fidelity to reason generates duties of care (i.e., duties to nurture and promote the highest good of others, as opposed to duties of self-restraint, fair dealing, and generosity toward guests), and only in application to a citizen's own city that it generates a corresponding duty of consideration arising from gratitude (*Ap.* 30a). Perhaps he thought these duties of care are voluntarily assumed with the acceptance of positions of leadership or lawmaking (which properly aim at the highest good of all citizens), much as the obligation to obey or persuade is incurred by one who makes a free and informed choice to remain in the city as a citizen. On this account, cities are naturally bound to treat aliens and other cities in a just manner, but not to bestow upon them the care that is due to a citizen, and citizens must similarly act justly, but can ignore the bad laws of other cities without explanation. In the absence of any history of living together as one community, or any agreement to do so, neither is under any obligation to make such efforts.

Having addressed this matter of the citizen's obligation to obey, and what a city must do to properly claim it, we must now ask what if anything these arguments imply about a city's right to impose punishment. Can we infer that the laws must benefit all citizens and create the conditions for them to give free and informed consent—perhaps even refrain from punishing infractions by those who openly withhold consent to the specific laws they break—if a city is to punish justly? Does the agreement of citizens *create* the city's right to administer the most burdensome kinds of punishments that cities rely on, as Kraut (1984, 190) suggests?

I think we must be careful to resist the idea that these arguments by which the laws seek to establish that citizens have obligations to the city have any direct implications for the foundations of the city's right to punish. Nowhere does Socrates suggest that he is offering a theory of punishment, as opposed to a theory of citizens' obligations and how they should respond to unjust laws and verdicts. On the other hand, on the Socratic natural law theory I have outlined here, it is clear that only just laws can be enforced, and in order to be just a law must benefit all citizens, must embody divine reason or justice, and must be administered in a manner that promotes rational acceptance of, and voluntary compliance with, good law. Thus, for the law to honor the *principle of fidelity to reason*, all the conditions for free and informed consent to law and for the city to claim quasi-parental status must be present, for otherwise the law will fail in its proper aim of encouraging rationality and virtue. Only under the conditions for free and informed consent to law will compliance with good law exhibit the qualities of motivation and intention present in virtue. Moreover, we have seen that Socrates holds that punishment cannot be justified unless instruction and persuasion have run their course, and clearly they could not have run their course if any of the conditions for free and informed consent were absent. So it may well be that Socrates develops the arguments from the parent-city analogy and from agreement with the understanding that they reflect the conditions for a city's claiming both a right to the voluntary obedience of citizens and a right to punish violations of law. He could do this, however, while holding any number of views of what justifies punishment: the tacit agreement of citizens, the city's right to defend itself, or the city's duty to create and maintain a social order that is good and conducive to the highest good of as many citizens as possible. Thus we can justifiably conclude that Socrates believes the city must bear certain educational burdens if punishment is to be justified, while withholding judgment about whether one might attribute to him an *authorization* or *contractarian* view of the city's right to punish.

1.34 Conclusion

Drawing together the lessons of this examination of the Socratic dialogues, we can sum up the arguments for public education generated by Socratic principles in the following list:

1. The natural *aim* of a city is the highest good of its citizens, which consists of being wise, or having and exercising systematic moral knowledge. As it happens, cities are without this knowledge and thus lack the capacity to make citizens truly virtuous and wise, but they should pursue this aim to

the extent that they can by encouraging conventional moral education followed by rational moral self-examination.

2. In their *substance*, human laws should embody and communicate perfect
   or divine reason. (Absent moral knowledge, only divine inspiration would
   allow them to succeed in this.) Law is thus properly an instrument of public instruction, and it should be incorporated in some way into a program
   of instruction which involves engaging citizens in reasoned persuasion.

3. Justice demands that cities govern citizens in a *manner* that puts truthful
   instruction and persuasion that is reasoned and impartial before force. Cities cannot justly demand the loyalty or voluntary obedience of citizens without creating the conditions for free and informed consent to their laws, nor
   can they establish a general right to punish lawbreakers without providing
   for the education of all citizens.

These features of the city's aim, the substance of its laws, and the manner of
its rule all derive from what I have called the *principle of fidelity to reason*, which
may be summarized together with its corollaries as follows:

Intellect is the divine element in human nature, and the one we should cultivate and
rely on in ourselves and others, if we are to live well and admirably.

In thought: In deciding what to believe, rely on reason and evidence and let the
stronger argument prevail.

In speech: Speak the truth, and rely on reason and evidence in persuading others
of the truth. Respect the reasons and evidence that others give and encourage them
to speak the truth and render and rely on well-reasoned judgments.

In action: Act in conformity with the dictates of reason. In moving others to act,
rely to the greatest extent possible on rational persuasion and instruction instead of
force and violence.

2

The Arguments of Plato

We have seen that Plato's early dialogues present Socrates as an advocate and human exemplar of fidelity to reason, and that the *principle of fidelity to reason* suggests that a good and just state will encourage and rely on reason in the manner, aim, and substance of its legislation and dealings with citizens generally. We have also seen that fidelity to reason creates educational burdens associated with each of these aspects of rule, though Socrates does not say that these burdens necessitate the creation of public schools. His view, as we have seen, is that since human beings lack moral knowledge, the best course for a city is to promote the goodness and thereby good of its citizens by promoting conventional moral education, which will inevitably inculcate some true moral beliefs and some false ones, and leave philosophers free—if not also pay them—to engage in and induce others to engage in moral self-examination through elenctic questioning.[1] This much we may confidently attribute to Socrates, but between him and Aristotle stands Plato, whose efforts to perfect Socratic thought we must now consider.

Plato develops his own accounts of education most conspicuously in the *Republic* and the *Laws*, the major political works of his middle and late dialogues, but we must also consider the *Meno* and *Protagoras*, which deserve our attention as transitional works in which Plato confronts and begins to move beyond the limitations of Socratic thought.[2] What we will find in these dialogues is a continuing commitment to the *principle of fidelity to reason*, together with efforts to develop and modify Socratic thought in ways intended to resolve its problems, underwrite its unguarded commitments, and elaborate its implications. Our dominant concern, of course, will be to see how Plato's attempts to perfect Socratic thought generate his arguments for public control and sponsorship of education. What will become evident is that these arguments originate in part in the *principle of fidelity to reason* itself, in part in Plato's repudiation of the elenchus as a mode of instruction suitable to the role in moral education which

Socrates assigns it, and in part in Plato's rejection of the Socratic assumption that virtue is akin to a craft, the possession of either being no more than the possession of a form of expert knowledge. Plato's repudiation of the widespread use of philosophical questioning to lead people toward higher levels of moral development is important to his arguments for state control of conventional moral education, and his rejection of the craft analogy provides the foundation for a broadening of the aims and content of that education to include both instruction to overcome ignorance and training of the passions to develop the capacity to comply with reason.

Plato's criticisms of the place of the elenchus in Socratic moral education serve to discredit its widespread use in promoting moral development, and restrict the dialectical examination of moral beliefs to those few who will employ it with the right end in view, which is to acquire truth and wisdom. Those who would employ the elenchus in this way are those of a "philosophical nature," from whom the rulers of the city of the *Republic* are to be drawn, or in the *Laws*, those of advanced age and secure virtue. In the former work, this denial of any prospect for a citizenry at large to be morally improved by dialectical examination leads Plato to shift the entire burden of establishing true moral beliefs to conventional moral education, and eliminates any substantial hope of more than a few people rising beyond the possession of consistently true moral beliefs to any higher form of moral understanding. By contrast, the latter work introduces non-elenctic forms of reasoning suitable to providing all citizens with justifications for the moral beliefs that are inculcated, enabling them to reach a higher level of moral and rational development than the citizens of the *Republic*. Plato also appears to regard these forms of reasoning as having a *limited* capacity to change the minds of those who have fallen into error,[3] but he does not consider reliance on them any substitute for doing everything possible to establish true moral beliefs from the outset. To this end he describes in these works two different foundations on which a city might take control of moral education to ensure that it inculcates nothing but true moral beliefs.

In the city of the *Republic* these true moral beliefs will be identified by one or more philosopher-kings who have come to possess moral knowledge through a course of higher learning preparatory to grasping the Form of the Good. The Kallipolis, or best city, of the *Republic* is in this sense a city of *moral knowledge* in which virtue can be more systematically cultivated than Socrates may have thought possible, since he thought no human being possessed moral knowledge. It is the ideal that should be kept in view as people endeavor to create a humanly feasible city "that most nearly resembles it," Plato says in the *Laws* (V 739d–e).

By contrast, the second-best city of the *Laws* seems to be one in which education and the laws rest not in moral knowledge, but in *divinely inspired true moral belief*, assisted by limited rational insight into the nature of virtue.[4] The dialogue opens with the word "god" *(Theos),* uttered by the Athenian Stranger in eliciting and respectfully acknowledging the customary view that the laws of Crete and Sparta were conferred upon those cities by Zeus and Apollo. Later, in Book VII, having identified the aims and principles of law and public education, and the general features of the constitution of the city of Magnesia, the Athenian says that in "this discussion of ours, which has lasted from dawn up to this very moment . . . I think I sense the inspiration of heaven" (811c). At the dialogue's close in Book XII, the Athenian refers to law as a "god-given" institution (957c), to "our divine foundation" for the city (965c–d), and to "God himself" as "guiding us" in the elaboration of the city's laws (968b), and suggests that it is God who will give the city whatever name it acquires (969a). These remarks are too numerous to be lightly dismissed, especially in view of the many other indications in this work, including the lengthy proof of the existence of god(s) in the prelude to the law of impiety in Book X, that Plato considers lawgiving to be "a religious task" (Stalley 1983, 166). One can speculate that Plato assumes the Athenian, who is evidently his fictional counterpart, has overcome all the errors of his own conventional moral education through some form of philosophical inquiry, elaborates the laws of Magnesia through the powers of his own reason alone, and suggests divine inspiration as a rhetorical ruse. However, what he suggests with these invocations of divine inspiration is that much as an ideally just city would require the moral knowledge of a "god among men," a second-best city whose law and education rest in systematically true moral beliefs would require a divinely inspired lawgiver. By contrast with the philosopher-king(s) of the *Republic*, the elders of the "Nocturnal Council" of the *Laws* are introduced in order to secure the "complete and perpetual security" of the legislation or "preservation of the laws" provided by "God himself" through a human founder or lawgiver (XII 960b–d), and to that end require not a godlike knowledge of the Forms (which are not mentioned in the *Laws* and Plato's other late works), but a more easily attainable understanding of the nature and unity of the virtues sufficient to provide a criminal with "a full explanation and description of the effects of virtue and vice" (XII 964c).[5] As Plato describes this "enlightenment and instruction," it is designed not to correct errors induced by conventional moral education (as Socrates had thought the elenchus might), but as a supplement to it which repeats the instructional component of the training and instruction which Plato hopes will be effective in inducing justified true moral beliefs in most citizens. It is a form of instruction which involves reasoning that is not elenctic, and one which Plato evidently believes may promote a more complete form of virtue than one which stops at habit and true belief, but there is no indication that he thinks it will lift any of the citizens of Magnesia to a state of moral knowledge equal to the gods'.

Plato also abandons the craft analogy and takes seriously the phenomenon of "weakness of will," of failures to act well not owing to a lack of instruction and understanding but owing to weakness in the face of danger or the enticements of pleasure. In doing so he does not abandon the idea that the truest or most complete

form of virtue *involves* the possession of knowledge, or the idea that wrongdoing always *involves* ignorance, but he does amend the Socratic conception of
virtue by attaching far more importance to the capacity and disposition to act in
the right way, and by holding that rationality, including the capacity to act as one
has reason to, is something that *develops* and this development must be systematically promoted by education. These changes broaden the educational burden
to be borne in making citizens good, to include not only *encouragement* to rely
on reason and *instruction* that will overcome ignorance, but also *training* that will
strengthen the capacities of rational action.

Plato's concerns about the adequacy of elenctic questioning, the craft analogy,
and Socrates' model of moral education are evident in the transitional dialogues,
Meno and *Protagoras*, and Book I of the *Republic*, and it will be instructive to
review these before proceeding to the proposals and direct arguments for public
education which appear in the middle and late dialogues. I will begin by reviewing Plato's criticisms of the elenchus in *Republic* I and the *Meno*, then take up
the nature of virtue and the burdens of moral education in the *Protagoras*, and
proceed from there to *Republic* II–X and the *Laws*.

2.1 IGNORING THE GADFLY

Without ever directly declaring his intentions, Plato brings four charges against
the elenchus and Socrates' conception of himself as a "gadfly" (*Ap.* 30e) who
deploys the elenchus to moral educative ends:[6] (1) the elenchus can be ignored
or blunted by resistance to its ground rules; (2) it is not clear how it would morally improve a person who already firmly holds true moral beliefs; (3) it is more
likely to corrupt than improve a person whose moral convictions are not firm;
(4) it presupposes a respondent whose moral beliefs are already largely correct.
There are connections between these complaints and Plato's abandonment of the
elenchus as his method of inquiry, a method which is displayed in all its weakness in *Republic* I but is conspicuously absent in the remainder of that dialogue
and later ones, as well as his abandonment of Socrates' conception of virtue as
craft knowledge which enables those who possess it to make the right choices.

(1) The first limitation of the Socratic reliance on elenctic questioning to dislodge false moral beliefs is that it would leave the city's efforts to promote virtue hostage to the willingness of individual citizens to listen and respond appropriately to whatever philosopher may accost them. The Socratic two-stage
conception of moral education would require enough willing philosophers to
examine every citizen in need of moral examination, but even a city that met this
requirement would face the problem that any number of citizens *may not be willing to listen*. Indeed, one would suppose that the farther citizens are from having systematically true moral beliefs the less receptive to listening they will be.
The philosopher's views and mode of life will seem all the more strange, mistaken, and annoying.

This theme is evident in the *Republic* from its opening lines, which describe Socrates and Glaucon being approached by Polemarchus, Adeimantus, and several others:

> Polemarchus said: It looks to me, Socrates, as if you two are starting off for Athens.
> It looks the way it is, then, I said.
> Do you see how many we are? he said.
> I do.
> Well, you must either prove stronger than we are, or you will have to stay here.
> Isn't there another alternative, namely, that we persuade you to let us go?
> But could you persuade us, if we won't listen?
> Certainly not, Glaucon said.
> Well, we won't listen; you'd better make up your mind to that (I 327c).

This is stage-setting, but the allusion to the Socratic principle of putting persuasion before force and the futility of trying to persuade those who will not listen is no accident. Before anyone in this dialogue submits to Socrates' questioning, he is confronted with the telling observation that no one need do so. Plato would seem to point out with this exchange that while it may be true that a gadfly does not require the voluntary cooperation of its host, a questioner does require the voluntary cooperation of a respondent, and may not receive it. Beyond that, he foreshadows a central theme of the *Republic* and the *Laws*, and the *Nicomachean Ethics* and *Politics*, which is the importance of an education which prepares people to be receptive and responsive to reason.

The cooperation that is required by the elenchus goes far beyond a simple willingness to listen. In addition to simply ignoring the philosopher's conversational overtures, an interlocutor can blunt the effectiveness of an examination by ignoring its ground rules. These ground rules require the respondent to offer a thesis, answer each question that follows with only a "yes" or a "no" that expresses his own opinion, and admit defeat when led by the questioner to a contradiction. In his exchange with Socrates in *Republic* I, Thrasymachus challenges these ground rules at several points (336c, 349a, 350d–e), and although Socrates repeatedly insists that Thrasymachus answer with his own opinion (346a, 349a, 350e), the latter gives no assurances that he does and remains unconvinced (351d, 352b, 353e, 354a). Thrasymachus insists that it is his *account* that Socrates should be refuting (349a), and thereby identifies another important aspect of the elenchus, that it does not refute an account so much as a person's attempt to defend it. Although Socrates insists it "makes no difference," this bears tellingly on the effectiveness of the elenchus, since a respondent may have more faith in the account or thesis which is examined than in his own ability to adequately defend it. In effect, the elenchus requires that the respondent place no more confidence in the thesis than in his dialectical ability and other beliefs elicited by the examiner, and this is a requirement that many will resist when faced with a dialectician of Socrates' strength. As Adeimantus suggests later in Book VI, your [Socrates'] hearers . . . think that, because they're inexperienced in asking and answering questions, they're led astray a little bit by the argument at every question. . . . Yet the truth isn't affected by this outcome (487a–b).

An elenctic refutation may rely on errors of fact or inference quite independent of the thesis at issue, and a respondent with more confidence in the thesis than in his own dialectical ability may assume with some justification that the error lies in something else that was said. So an elenchus which culminates in a contradiction does not compel a respondent to give up his thesis. The respondent not only can ignore the gadfly altogether, but he can refuse to answer in the way required, or do so yet refuse to admit defeat on what may be subjectively reasonable grounds.

(2) The exchange with Cephalus which follows the opening lines of the *Republic* establishes the point that the elenchus lacks the capacity to morally improve one who already has substantially true moral beliefs and holds them firmly, as a person of good upbringing, experience, and simple piety might. Cephalus holds many of Socrates' own most cherished beliefs and in much the same terms in which Plato will present them later in the dialogue,[7] yet when Socrates presses him to say "unconditionally" whether justice "is speaking the truth and paying whatever debts one has incurred" (331c), he yields to the opening set of objections and withdraws to attend to a sacrifice (331d). He is a person of considerable virtue and firmly held true moral beliefs, much as Socrates is, but unlike Socrates he is very far from having an examined life or being equipped to meet the demands of one. His early departure from the dialogue may be intended to suggest not only that nothing could be gained by continuing to examine him, but also that unexamined, firmly held, true moral belief may be sufficient for the purposes of most people. This suspicion is reinforced by the fact that Plato has Socrates argue in the *Meno*, contrary to what we have every reason to think was his own view, that true moral belief is sufficient for virtue (97a–99b), and by Plato's portrayals of Socrates himself in the early dialogues as possessing the virtues he is unable to define.[8] These are indications of a retreat from the identification of virtue with expert moral knowledge, at least to the extent of allowing that virtue may be present by degrees without moral knowledge.

(3) A third problem Plato identifies with Socrates' suggested use of the elenchus is that it is more likely to corrupt than improve those who have had a conventional moral education but lack mature conviction. The danger is illustrated by the exchange between Socrates and Polemarchus in *Republic* I, which generates a refutation of the youth's conventional understanding of justice but produces nothing to replace it (331d–336a). This danger is later described in Book VIII in terms which unequivocally condemn the practice of the historical Socrates:

. . . We hold from childhood certain convictions about just and admirable things; we're brought up with them as with our parents, we obey and honor them. . . .

And then a questioner comes along and asks someone of this sort, "What is the admirable?" And, when he answers what he has heard from the traditional lawgiver, the argument refutes him, and by refuting him often and in many places shakes him of his convictions, and makes him believe that the admirable is no more admirable than shameful, and the same with the just, the good, and the things he honored most. . . .

And so, I suppose, from being law-abiding he becomes lawless. . . .

. . . isn't it only to be expected that this is what happens to those who take up arguments in this way? . . .

And isn't it one lasting precaution not to let them taste arguments while they're young? (538c–39a)[9]

This argument would seem to preclude the use of the elenchus not just with the young, but more generally with those whose convictions are so fluid that they might be induced to give up their true moral beliefs.[10] And since Plato shows no sign of thinking that people hold their true beliefs with greater conviction than their false ones, it would thereby seem to preclude using the elenchus on anyone whose *false* moral beliefs might be dislodged. It is thus an argument for not using the elenchus to shape people's moral beliefs at all, and it will not be until the *Laws* that we shall see Plato prescribe a more suitable form of argument for inducing people to discard some moral beliefs and adopt others.[11]

(4) A fourth problem, which becomes evident in Socrates' interrogation of Thrasymachus in *Republic* I, is that elenctic questioning cannot be expected to dislodge the moral errors of one who is consistently or dominantly vicious. Faced with how *consistently* corrupt Thrasymachus's views are, Socrates remarks that his consistency in praising injustice makes it "harder" and not "easy . . . to know what to say" in response (348e). The aim of the elenchus is to demonstrate the inconsistency of an interlocutor's beliefs by deriving an open contradiction from them, but this can only be achieved through valid inferences if those beliefs are inconsistent, and Thrasymachus's are uncomfortably close to avoiding inconsistency.

The content of his account of justice contributes to this challenge by suggesting the possibility that whole cities of people might share consistently or dominantly false moral beliefs. According to this account, it is the stronger in each city who rule,

> and each makes laws to its own advantage. . . . And they declare what they have made—what is to their own advantage—to be just for their subjects, and they punish anyone who goes against this as lawless and unjust. This, then, is what I say justice is, the same in all cities, the advantage of the established rule (338d–39a).

With this account, Thrasymachus holds that the strong rule in order to secure pleasures without end for themselves—to "outdo others and get more and more *(pleonexian)*," as Glaucon says in Book II (359c)—and that the "craft" of rule (334b–c) is an art of exploitation which promotes this pleonectic satisfaction of the rulers through establishing standards of conduct favorable to the rulers but not the ruled (Reeve 1988, 15). Since this is grounded in an account of human desire as *universally* pleonectic, it suggests the possibility that law and all the forms of instruction associated with it might be used in *every* city to indoctrinate citizens in corrupt systems of belief which they could not be led out of by elenctic questioning.

Even if the effect of this indoctrination were merely to induce dominantly and not consistently false moral beliefs, one could not expect elenctic examinations to purge the false and preserve the true. For if one's beliefs are mostly mistaken, and one seeks to preserve as many of one's beliefs as possible, then the beliefs one will be prompted to abandon under questioning are more likely to be true than false. One's beliefs will converge toward consistent error, rather than consistent truth.

Even when it is used and submitted to in accordance with its ground rules, then, Socratic questioning cannot be expected to promote progress toward more systematically true moral beliefs, if there is any reason to doubt that those who submit to examination begin with mostly true moral beliefs. Plato seems to provide such a reason in Thrasymachus's account of justice, and he seems to have been concerned with this limitation of the elenchus as early as when he wrote the *Meno*. His introduction of the theory that learning is recollection in that work (81b–d), in response to Meno's "paradox of inquiry," is probably intended to underwrite the assumption that there is a bias toward truth in human belief (Fine 1992, 213–15).[12] It suggests that what comes to mind in contemplating questions will be shaped not simply by the limited wisdom or deceptions accumulated in this life, but by the soul's having "seen all things here and in the underworld" in previous lives (81c). What rises to consciousness from the depths of a soul which has learned everything will presumably be biased strongly toward the truth. This would provide a reason to believe that the elenchus can be effective in dislodging the false moral beliefs acquired in the course of an imperfect or even systematically deceptive conventional moral education, but it is not clear how serious a suggestion this is in the Meno,[13] and there is no sign of Plato taking it seriously in the *Republic*. The suggestion of both *Republic* I and the *Meno* is that the success of the elenchus depends upon truth already having a strong foothold, and the lesson Plato seems to have drawn in the *Republic* is that virtue depends upon entrusting the burden of ensuring a strong foothold for truth to the city itself.

All told, then, Plato argues that the elenchus cannot be used in moral education in the way that Socrates advocates because it would be insufficient on several grounds, unnecessary as far as the general public is concerned if sound and firm moral convictions can be induced by conventional moral education, and more likely to corrupt than improve those whose convictions might be influenced by it. It is evidently at least largely on these grounds that he concludes that conventional moral education should be more carefully controlled to ensure sound content, for without the elenchus or a replacement for it which can be used to later purge false moral beliefs and induce true ones it is unclear how the deficiencies of a conventional moral education might be corrected.

Having displayed the inappropriateness and futility of conducting elenctic examinations of interlocutors such as Cephalus, Polemarchus, and Thrasymachus, Plato allows the dialogue to proceed through Books II–X of the *Republic* with interlocutors who already possess true moral beliefs and philosophical natures.[14] Socrates punctuates his accounts of justice and the Kallipolis with invitations to agreement, but his manner of argument is not elenctic and his aim is not the moral improvement of his interlocutors. His manner of argument owes much to Protagoras's, in fact, and it is to the *Protagoras* that we must now turn.

2.2 BLAMING WHAT IS LEARNED: IGNORANCE AND INCAPACITY IN THE *PROTAGORAS*

The Socratic dialogues introduce the idea that fidelity to reason commends efforts to encourage others to be rational, but they do not portray the rational powers or capacities as developing and needing assistance to develop and prevail over the passions.[15] By contrast, one encounters in the *Protagoras*, in Protagoras's "Great Speech" (320c–328d), an account of early education as lifting human beings up from a savage state by disciplining the passions and harmonizing the soul. Plato stages in the *Protagoras* a fictional dialogue between Socrates and Protagoras, and although Socrates prevails in his characteristic way, it would be wrong to think that he is presented in a better light than Protagoras or that his conception of virtue stands unchallenged at the dialogue's close. Whatever the views of the historical Protagoras, Plato has chosen in this dialogue to present through him some of the ideas he will use to correct and supplement Socratic thought in the *Republic* and other works (Stalley, 1995). The accounts in Protagoras's Great Speech of conventional moral education, and of the educative nature of punishment, are unlike anything in the Socratic dialogues and much like the accounts in the *Republic* and the *Laws*.

Protagoras begins his speech with a creation myth and the story of Zeus making it possible for human beings to live together in cities. Zeus sends Hermes "to bring justice *(dikên)* and a sense of shame *(aidô)* to humans, so that there would be order *(poleôn kosmoi)* and bonds of friendship *(despoi philias)* to unite them" (322c). With this start, Protagoras then holds that "the virtue of a man" *(andros aretên)*, "justice, temperance, and piety" *(dikaiosunê kai sôphrosunê kai to hosion* (324e–325a)), must be universally possessed, and thus "taught and carefully developed" (323c), if cities are to exist and not be torn apart by mutual wrongdoing (322b, 323a, 324e, 327a). In a passage later echoed in *NE* III.5 (1114a22–31), he argues that this view that virtue is a product of teaching and training is shared by the Athenians and others:

> In the case of evils that men universally regard as afflictions due to nature *(phusei)* or bad luck *(tuchê)*, no one ever gets angry with anyone so afflicted or reproves, admonishes, punishes, or tries to correct them. We simply pity them, . . . someone who is ugly, for example, or scrawny or weak. . . . But in the case of the good things which accrue to men through careful attention *(epimeleias)* and training *(askêseôs)* and teaching *(didachês)*, if someone does not possess these goods but rather their corresponding evils, he finds himself the object of anger, punishment, and reproof. Among these evils are injustice, impiety, and in general everything that is opposed to civic virtue. . . . The key, Socrates, to the true significance of punishment lies in the fact that human beings consider virtue to be something acquired through training (323d–24a).

Having thus distinguished what is owing to nature or chance from what is acquired by careful attention and teaching *(epimeleias kai matheseôs)*, and having insisted that it is universally acknowledged that only the latter is subject to blame and punishment, Protagoras then goes on to argue that reasonable punishment is and should be regarded as educative, and that the burdens of punishment nevertheless oblige parents to attend carefully to the formation of virtue through conventional moral education (325b–c).

"Reasonable punishment is not vengeance for a past wrong . . . but is undertaken to prevent *(apotropês)*" future crime, and is thus imposed with the understanding that "virtue is learned," Protagoras says (324b–c). In the context of the dialogue this statement is intended to provide more evidence for the claim that virtue is, and is widely believed to be, something that is taught and learned; but it also expresses the view that punishment is itself educative or imposed with educative intent.[16] The idea that it is educative is expressed in the language of correction or setting straight *(euthuna, euthunousin)*, in the account of moral instruction that follows:

> As soon as a child understands what is said to him, the nurse, mother, *paidagôgos*, and the father himself fight for him to be as good as he possibly can, seizing on every action and word to teach him and show him that this is just, that is unjust, this is admirable, that is shameful. . . . If he obeys willingly, fine; if not, they straighten *(euthunousin)* him out with threats and blows as if he were a twisted, bent piece of wood (325c–d).

Later, at school, the teachers pay similar attention to these things, give the children literary models worthy of imitation, make them gentler and more restrained through musical training that harmonizes their souls and improves their speech and movements, and train their bodies so they "will not be forced to cowardice in war or other activities through physical deficiencies" (325e–26d). "And when they quit school," he says,

> the city in turn compels them to learn the laws and to model their lives on them. . . . An analogy might be drawn from the practice of writing teachers, who sketch the letters faintly with a pen in workbooks for their beginning students and

have them write the letters over the patterns they have drawn. In the same way the city has drawn up laws invented by the great lawgivers in the past and compels them to govern and be governed by them. She punishes anyone who goes beyond these laws, and the term for this punishment in your city [Athens] and others is, because it is a corrective *(euthunousês)* legal action, "correction" *(euthunai)* (326d–e).

In a passage echoed in later dialogues and in Aristotle's *Politics* I.2 (1253a30–39), Protagoras adds that even the most unjust person "reared in a human society under law" is a paragon of justice compared with savages *(agrioi),* who lack "education and law courts and the pervasive pressure to cultivate virtue" (327c–d).

This contrast with savages, who are ungoverned by reason presumably, and the images of instruction and correction at home, and musical training which civilizes *(hêmerôteroi)* children by causing their souls to make desirable rhythms and scales their own *(kai tous rythmous te kai tas harmonias anagkasdousin oikeiousthai tais psychais tôn paidôn* [326b]), all suggest a conception of education as embracing both instruction and training, which enables children's reason to prevail over their passions. The description of how writing is taught also suggests roles for both instruction and practice overseen by someone who can detect and correct deficiencies of performance. Such a notion of practice is very far from instruction which aims simply to overcome ignorance, and suggests that the *capacity* to do what one understands one should (in the case of letters, to form the right shapes reliably) is not a gift of nature or chance, but a product of instruction, attention, and training. Considered in its analogical application to law, this notion yields the propositions that the laws instruct citizens in how they are to conduct themselves and that punishment plays a role in this instruction when necessary by "compelling" the citizens to listen to the laws, to "learn the laws and model their lives on them." The laws try to persuade and instruct, it would seem, and the punishments try to ensure that they are able to—that no one refuses to listen and everyone uses the laws as models of action long enough to acquire the disposition to do so voluntarily.

Instruction is thereby put before force, but force is also enlisted in the service of instruction as necessary, and has an educative nature of its own. This does not diminish the Socratic burden to place instruction and persuasion as much as possible before force and violence, but it does reflect Plato's recognition that instruction and persuasion are sometimes resisted. Similarly, one might assume that a weakening of the mandate to place instruction before forceful punishment would follow from the thesis that all reasonable punishment has an educative and thus beneficial character, but there is no indication of this in the *Protagoras.* Having argued that virtue is widely regarded as teachable, Protagoras argues that the burdens of punishment would compel a parent to provide all the attention and moral instruction possible:

Since it [virtue] is something that can be taught and nurtured, is it possible that they [good men *(agathoi andres)*] have their sons taught everything in which there is no

death penalty for not understanding it, but when their children are faced with the
death penalty or exile if they fail to learn virtue and be nurtured in it—and not only
death but confiscation of property and, practically speaking, complete familial catastrophe—do you think they do not have them taught this or give them all the attention possible? (325b–c)

Protagoras thus defeats the supposition that the educative capacity of punishment
entails that it is without serious costs to the person who is "set straight." He does
not say in so many words that parents or cities are *obligated* to provide prior
adequate education as a foundation for compliance with law and the imposition
of corrective justice, but he holds that *good* parents *do* provide such education
in light of the burdens of punishment, which is tantamount to holding that *all*
parents *should*, and he holds that such education makes all the difference between
lacking and having the capacity to live just and self-restrained lives. The Socratic
obligation to put teaching before punishment would thus seem to be preserved,
and the scope of that teaching expanded to overcome not only ignorance but also
any incapacity that might stand in the way of compliance with the demands of
reason and law.

Soon after Protagoras has concluded his Great Speech, Socrates poses the
question of whether "you necessarily have all the parts [of virtue] if you have
any one of them" (329e), and Protagoras's denial of this "unity of virtue" thesis
leads into a series of arguments which eventually force him to retract that denial
"on the basis of what we have agreed upon" (360e) and concede that justice, temperance, and courage are all knowledge or wisdom and thus all identical. Along
the way, however, Protagoras interrupts his examination (334a–348c) and after
some discussion puts to Socrates a question of poetical interpretation (339), eliciting from the latter a parody of exegesis and a merciless denunciation (347c–e)
of the former's suggestion "that the greatest part of a man's education is to be in
command of poetry" (339a). This parody generates a number of claims which
Socrates seems to endorse, including the dictum that no one does wrong willingly (345e). Among these are some claims about incapacity which seem to be
relied on later in the *Laws* (I 644b–47d)[17] and by Aristotle in the *Nicomachean
Ethics* (III.5):

incapacitating misfortune would overthrow only someone who is capable
(*eumêchanon*), not the chronically incapable (*amêchanon*). . . . For the good is susceptible to becoming bad, . . . But the bad is not susceptible to becoming; it must
always be. . . .
  . . . a good man may eventually become bad with the passage of time, or through
hardship, disease, or some other circumstance that involves the only real kind of
faring ill, which is the loss of knowledge (344d–45b).

Given the importance in this dialogue of the theme of having and lacking the
capacity to conform oneself to the dictates of reason and law, it is hard to imag-

ine that Plato would put these words in the mouth of Socrates just to mock those who take literary exegesis to be a serious form of inquiry. The passage presents some difficulties, but several aspects of it suggest the theme of possessing and losing the capacity of rational control, on the one hand in the face of external forces which exceed one's capacity, as in the case of the ship's pilot caught in a hurricane (344c–d), but more importantly by the corruption or degradation of the capacity itself by trauma, disease, or other conditions which involve the "loss of knowledge." Protagoras has developed in his Great Speech the idea that human beings must be civilized by education if they are to be responsive to reason, which is to say both able and disposed to be moved by reason, and now comes Socrates himself suggesting that this capacity and disposition can be "overthrown" and "thrown down" by "incapacitating misfortune," which would be understood by the tragedians and other Greeks to mean hardship or misfortune which leads one to act from destructive emotions and lose sight of what one knew.[18] Knowledge retains a salient role in this drama, but not a determinative one, as it does in the analysis of courage and cowardice which closes the dialogue. Having called Socrates into service for an assault on the claims of poetry, Plato gives every appearance here of enlisting him in an oblique challenge to his own doctrine.

Socrates' closing arguments for the unity of virtue depict failures of courage as lapses of perception, in order to sustain the idea that cowardly wrongdoing is not just accompanied, but caused, by ignorance owing to misperception. "Most people . . . are going to say that most people are unwilling to do what is best, even though they know what it is and are able to do it, . . . because they are overcome by pleasure or pain," Socrates says (352d–e). Yet the truth is that people perceive the more distant pains associated with pleasures close at hand to be smaller than they are, just as *all* things at a distance appear smaller than they are (356c). Their failing is thus not in seeking what is pleasant and avoiding what is painful, but in judging from appearances rather than knowledge or the "art of measurement" (356d–e). He holds, on the strength of these claims, that it is owing to a lack of knowledge that people "make mistakes with regard to the choice of pleasure and pain, . . . good and bad" (357d). If there is any acknowledgment here of a role for education in remedying the limitations of people's capacities to hear and comply with reason, it is in Socrates' suggestion that the "art of measure-ment . . . would make the appearances lose their power" over us (356d–e), but this will appear and be rightly judged inadequate by anyone, including Plato, who is familiar with reversals of perception in the face of danger, and doubtful of the capacity of most people to acquire moral knowledge. Socrates holds out the idea that knowledge would stand firm where mere belief succumbs to such reversals, but his own views on the topic of moral knowledge preclude him from offering this as a practical approach to cultivating courage. If Protagoras has been undone by his attempt to illicitly assimilate his own teaching of "political art" or exper-tise to the dispositional virtues required of all citizens, that was a conflation in-vited by Socrates' offer of the expression "the art of citizenship" *(politikê technê)* at 319a (Adkins, 1973), and Socrates has been implicitly undone himself by a similar failure to acknowledge the distinction between expertise and virtuous dispositions. The failings of the craft analogy are pointed up as much by Protagoras's failure to survive Socrates' questions as by the cogency of his account of conventional moral education, Plato's acceptance of Socrates' argument that knowledge or wisdom is essential for true or complete virtue notwithstanding.

Plato will endorse the Socratic paradox to the end, in the sense that he will accept the idea that wrongdoing always involves ignorance, but he will assert that ignorance cannot be overcome and the truth kept in sight without training that shapes the desires toward the good and allows thought and reason to prevail when pain threatens and pleasure beckons. With this modification of the Socratic view, Plato sets *incapacity* beside *ignorance* as a cause of wrongdoing which can and must be overcome, at least by degrees, by education. In this view, no one does wrong without ignorance or incapacity and the corruption of perception which attends it. One may have the capacities of endurance that are integral to courage and moderation but have deficient moral beliefs, and thus make the wrong choice in some situations, but one may also have true moral beliefs, yet lack the capacity and disposition to handle pleasures well (lacking moderation) or pains well (lacking courage), and consequently do the wrong thing, seduced into believing, as one would not in a moment of repose, that what one does is right. This is already a considerably more complex account of virtue than Socrates', and it will be associated in Plato's middle and late works with more complicated accounts of education which incorporate important elements of the account offered in Protagoras's Great Speech.

2.3 "FOSTERING THEIR BEST PART WITH OUR OWN": EDUCATION AND LAW IN THE *REPUBLIC*

The moral educative scheme of the *Republic* is in some ways just what one would expect Plato to construct on the foundations laid in the transitional dialogues and its own Book I: the Kallipolis will not expose the young to elenctic examinations (VII 537d–e, 538c–39d), but will attempt on the strength of the rulers' higher studies leading to moral knowledge (V–VII 473b–541b)[19] to lay a foundation of wholly true moral beliefs and train the passions in such a way as to strengthen rationality (II–III 376c–412b), so that when reason comes to a young person it will *confirm* the true beliefs which have already been absorbed (III 402a; cf. *Laws* II 653b) and be heeded. It will cultivate a responsiveness to reason and a disposition to rely on it, for Plato is committed no less than Socrates to the *principle of fidelity to reason* (II 383b–c, IX 586e, 598d 590c–d, *Phdr.* 247d–48c; *Tim.* 90c; *Tht.* 176b–c; *Laws* IV 715e–16d, etc.), its corollary that justice requires citizens and city alike to put instruction and persuasion before force (III 411d–e, VII 519e, VIII 547b, 548c, 552d–e), and the related thesis that law is "useless and accomplishes nothing" without education (IV 427a).

These starting points, and the premise that a city grounded in a human being's moral knowledge is at least possible, form the basis of Plato's elaboration of a set of educational provisions suitable to a city that is said to be ideally just. Justice aims at the good of all citizens (I 335c–d, IV 420b–c, VII 519e), a life "divine and supremely happy" (*Tht.* 176c–e; cf. *Tim.* 90a–d) to the greatest extent possible, and the Kallipolis is accordingly a city which promotes all its citizens' wisdom or fidelity to reason as much as possible:

> . . . it is better for everyone to be ruled by divine reason, preferably within himself and his own, otherwise imposed from without, so that as far as possible, all will be alike and friends, governed by the same thing. . . .
>
> This is clearly the aim of law, which is the ally of everyone. But it's also our aim in ruling our children; we don't allow them to be free until we establish a constitution in them, . . . and—by fostering their best part with our own *(to beltiston therapeusantes tô par)*—equip them with a guardian and ruler similar to our own to take our place (IX 590d–91a).

The core commitments of fidelity to reason and their applications to education and law are evident in this passage. The city and parents alike are to nurture the development of reason and autonomous virtue, and do so guided by reason, "fostering their best part with our own."

These commitments warrant some comment, especially in connection with the law, the use of force, and the scope of the city's educational provisions. I will address each of these topics very briefly, noting along the way the arguments for public control of education which Plato offers, and close with a few words about the character of the education proposed.

The topic of law and its relationship to education is treated briefly in Book IV. The law is spoken of there as educative (430a, 433c, etc.), much as it was in the *Protagoras*, but the thesis that receives more development is that law cannot achieve its ends without education. Education is described, to begin with, as "the one great thing" or rather "sufficient" to achieve the city's ends, for "if by being well educated they [the guardians] become reasonable men, they will easily see" how the city should be managed and what laws should be enacted (423d–e). This is to say that the one important or sufficient aspect of defining the constitution of the Kallipolis is defining its system of education. A second and related claim which is then developed is that the "musical" arts *(mousikê)*, physical training *(gymnastikê)*, and games must be supervised by the guardians to ensure that they are consistent with good order, since these formative aspects of education and culture (*paideia*, in its broad sense[20]) cannot be changed without the existing laws, both written and unwritten, being undermined (424c):

> . . . Our children's games must from the very beginning be more law-abiding, for if their games become lawless, and the children follow suit, isn't it impossible *(adunaton)* for them to grow up into morally serious *(spoudaious)* and law-abiding men?

But when children play the right games from the beginning and absorb lawful-
ness from *mousikê*, it follows them in everything and fosters their growth . . . (424e–
25a).

To say that it is *impossible* for children to mature into morally serious and law-
abiding adults is to say that they lack the power or capacity *(dunamis)* to listen
to the claims of reason and law and comply. This is as much as to say that law is
impotent without education, and that a primary aim of the supervision of
children's activities must be to develop this capacity, and beyond it a disposition
to listen and respond to reason. We thus have here a pair of linked arguments for
the necessity of public provisions for education, which come together in an image of the correct way to legislate: not in the normal way by simply enumerating and amending laws to prevent cheating on contracts and other wrongdoing,
which is "useless and accomplishes nothing" since it is "really just cutting off a
Hydra's head," but by putting instruction and persuasion first,[21] so that legislation will rest in good judgment and citizens will receive that legislation already
willing to do the right thing, rather than be eager to exploit its "loopholes" (426e–
27a).

The references to contracts and laws pertaining to the marketplace (425c–d,
426e) make it clear that this discussion of putting education before law pertains
to the producers as much as to the soldiers and rulers (i.e., the guardians), or in
other words to all three social classes in the Kallipolis. This is what the *principle of fidelity to reason* demands, and it is confirmed by the passage from Book
IX discussed above, by remarks which are made in passing, and by other indications that Plato envisions the Kallipolis as a city ruled not by force, but by persuasion and agreement. Taking up the matter of force first, Plato attributes the
virtue of moderation to the Kallipolis, and holds that moderation exists when the
three parts of a soul or city enjoy "friendly and harmonious relations, . . . when
the ruler and ruled believe in common that the rational part should rule" (IV 442c).
He speaks similarly of the citizens agreeing about who should rule and exhibiting unanimity on this matter (IV 431e, 432a), and any such agreement would
presumably have to rest on upbringing and instruction that would enable them
to achieve at least a limited understanding of what is agreed to and why, and to
acquire capacities of self-restraint or moderation which enable them to comply
voluntarily with what is agreed to, in the manner of a free citizen, and not only
in response to force, in the manner of a slave. Plato's remarks about inferior constitutions in Books V and VIII make it clear that the members of the Kallipolis's
producing class are *not* slaves but free citizens, who rightly regard the city as
promoting their happiness as much as anyone else's, and willingly accept the rule
they are subject to on account of that (V 463a–b, VIII 547b, 548c).[22]

The basis for Plato's claim that the Kallipolis aims at the happiness of every
class of citizens is evidently that in this city each is able to enjoy most fully the
kind of pleasure it most values: the rulers the pleasures of the intellect, the sol-

diers or auxiliaries the pleasures of honor, and the producers or money-lovers the pleasures that money can buy. What he says in Book IX with reference to the soul is meant to apply with as much force to the city:

> . . . those desires of even the money-loving parts that follow knowledge and argument and pursue with their help those pleasures that reason approves will attain the truest pleasures possible for them, because they follow truth. . . .
>
> Therefore, when the entire soul follows the philosophic part, and there is no civil war in it, each part of it does its own work exclusively and is just, and in particular it enjoys its own pleasures, the best and truest pleasures possible for it (586d–87a).

One of the claims that Plato makes here is that these three kinds of pleasures are not equally real, and that people are not equally able to enjoy them all (580c ff.). Only a few people will progress beyond the enjoyment of bodily pleasures to the pleasures of honor, and only a few of those few will ever acquire a taste for the truest pleasures, those of the intellect. No one will make the ascent without education that "turns the soul"—its desires—toward higher and better things (VII 518d). This is the very point of education, Plato says, and he implies in the passage above that in following the rule of philosopher-kings the citizens of the Kallipolis will all receive training and instruction which will nurture the ascent of their desires as much as possible, enabling them "to attain the [best and] truest pleasures possible for them."[23]

The attainment of these pleasures also depends upon each class doing its own work, in each case the form of work by which its most preferred pleasures are earned, and leaving to others what they most prefer. It depends upon justice, as Plato conceives it: "the having and doing of one's own" (IV 433e–34a). This requires not only that all citizens be directed toward the work they are best suited to (IV 423d), but that everyone gets the elements of conventional moral education, with its contents controlled for suitability, and grows up imitating suitable things. Although the education described in Books II and III is introduced as appropriate for the guardians, Plato refers near the end of Book III to "the upbringing and the education we gave" not only the guardians (soldiers and rulers) but also "the rest of the city" (414d), and he refers in Book V to the training in craftsmanship which the children of craftsmen receive (467a). This suggests that although some specific elements of the education prescribed for future guardians, such as the attention to courage, would not be part of the education of a future producer, the efforts to ensure that children's exposure to stories, music, athletics, and games promotes receptivity to reason, virtue, and lawful conduct would apply to both. Neither should be allowed to hear the wrong kinds of stories and music, or play games which reward vice, but while the future guardians would be raised communally and receive schooling in *mousikê* and *gymnastikê* from the city itself, the future producers would receive only the *mousikê* that is incidental to family and civic life and instruction and practice in a craft, apparently through private means.[24]

Plato's basic argument for political control of the content of education first appears in Book II, at the start of his discussion of the education of future guardians. A human being is "most malleable" in its youth, he says, "and takes on any pattern one wishes to impress on it" (377a). The beliefs acquired thereby "are hard to erase and apt to become unalterable" (378d), so we should not carelessly allow children to hear stories from which they might acquire beliefs that are false and morally ruinous (377b). Since we should not, he says, it is necessary to select the stories that are admirable and "persuade nurses and mothers to tell their children" only those (377c). First of all, "a god is really good . . . and must be described as such" (379b) to encourage piety and friendliness (III 385e–86a); fear of death should not be encouraged, lest courage be undermined (III 386a ff.); truthfulness and endurance should be presented in a favorable light (III 389b); and the belief that virtue is essential to happiness should be encouraged (392a–b).

Turning from the content of stories to their style of narration, Plato introduces the idea that the patterns one habitually imitates "from youth become part of [one's] nature and settle into habits of gesture, voice, and thought" (III 395d). Thus, all children (IV 423a) should be guided to imitate in youth only those who exhibit the virtues they themselves should possess (395c–96a), and only those occupations which it will be suitable for them to practice in adulthood (395b–c, 396a–b).

Plato's basic argument regarding stories and music is then extended to painting, architecture, and all other aspects of the city which might influence the formation of character, judgment, and the perception of good and evil. We must not allow our guardians to "be brought up on images of evil, as if in a meadow of bad grass," he says, but

> seek out craftsmen who are by nature able to pursue what is fine and graceful in their work, so that our young people will live in a healthy place and be benefitted on all sides, and so that something of those fine works will strike their eyes and ears like a breeze that brings health from a good place, leading them unwittingly, from childhood on, to a resemblance, friendship, and harmony with the beauty of reason (401c–d).

This education, he says, will induce an admiration for what is admirable and hatred for what is shameful, and by means of this harmony with reason, a receptivity to reason which will mature into a capacity to grasp why some things are to be admired and others condemned (401e–2a). The emergence of sound judgment is thus understood by Plato to require exposure to good character and images of good character, and protection from exposure to their opposites, while a person is young. This much of Plato's educational scheme may be understood as resting in the notion that one grows comfortable with and imitates what is familiar and presented in a favorable light. A second concept of learning seems to underlie his further prescription that *gymnastikê* and *mousikê* be used in such a way as to strengthen and harmonize the reasoning and spirited parts of the soul, so that the reasoning part can assume its properly dominant role (410b–12a). Here the concept is one of exercise, development of strength and influence through exercise, and atrophy in its absence, as much in the sphere of desire as in ability. Without *mousikê*, Plato says, the "love of learning" becomes "enfeebled, deaf, and blind" and a person "no longer makes use of persuasion but bulls his way through every situation by force and savagery like a wild animal" (411d).

Plato's case for public provision for education is thus, in short, that it is necessary to a just city because it is essential to good order, consensual rule, and human virtue, happiness, and rationality, which is to say the fulfillment of the divine aspect of human nature. To frame things just in this way, however, would be to ignore the evidence that Plato is not only concerned to promote these Socratic ideals, but to overcome the evils of war, civil war, and poverty. His embrace of Socratic ideals does not fully explain the prominence of the virtue of moderation in the *Republic*, and a fuller account would have to address in connection with this his account of the origins of war in pleonectic desire (II 373d–e). Nor does his promotion of Socratic ideals fully explain his embrace of social unity as a paramount civic virtue and his related defense of the common "possession" of women and children (V 457c ff.) as a bastion against civil war (465b). Nor does it explain his insistence that "the greatest of all evils" is for a city to allow people to become "totally impoverished," unable to support themselves, and reduced to begging or stealing while others become "excessively rich" (VIII 552a–e). These features of the *Republic* suggest that the best city would attend to education and upbringing in order to secure the greatest well-being of its citizens, but lacking this aspiration the avoidance of disaster and misery at home and abroad would be reason enough.

2.4 JUSTICE AND COMMON CARE IN THE *LAWS*

The *Laws* is Plato's work on legislation, and so just the place where one would expect to find his most detailed development of the implications of the *principle of fidelity to reason* for the substance, aim, and manner of rule. In this respect it is a work that does not disappoint, for the *Laws* is an extraordinary elaboration of the idea of a rule of law which benefits everyone and no one stands above, a rule of law which embodies divine reason, is transacted through informed consent, and aims at the common good.[25] Its point of departure is the merits and shortcomings of the laws and educational arrangements of Sparta and Crete, which were conceived with a view to developing courage, and not the whole of virtue, with a view to war, and not peace and good will (I 628d). A good legislator will have the highest or whole of virtue in view (I 630), the "divine" goods of the soul: good judgment *(phronêsis)*, moderation, justice, and courage, all of which "look toward reason, which is supreme" (I 631d–e). With this invocation of the divinity of reason, and insistence that the cultivation of rationality is the statesman's most fundamental concern and the means to enable "the citizens to live supremely happy lives" (V 743c), Plato signals his continued commitment to the *principle of fidelity to reason*, and its corollary pertaining to the *aim* of legislation. I noted, at the opening of this chapter, the suggestion that the laws of Magnesia embody divine reason in their *substance*, and we shall see in what follows that those laws are to be imposed in the *manner* demanded by fidelity to reason as well.

Plato says that the entire system of legislation will promote various lesser goods, such as health, strength, and wealth, with a view to the ethical virtues, and will promote the ethical virtues with the cultivation or perfect exercise of reason as its highest aim (I 631c). This not only makes the cultivation of reason the highest aim of legislation to which everything else is subsidiary—so that other goods, including the ethical virtues, are to be pursued in whatever way, and to whatever extent, is most conducive to the flourishing of the divine aspect of human nature—it recognizes the ethical virtues of *phronêsis*, moderation, courage, and justice as essential *means* to the flourishing of reason. This relationship between the virtues and reason was evident in the *Protagoras* and *Republic*, in the proposition that reason needs assistance if it is to prevail over the passions, and the related proposition that the training of desire which inculcates the ethical virtues provides such assistance. The *Laws* will continue the development of this line of thought, most notably by arguing that the development of moderation calls for training analogous to what is used to develop courage in soldiers. Beyond this training and other more conventional measures to promote virtue, the city of the *Laws* will establish a more complete form of virtue than most of the citizens of the Kallipolis would possess, and something closer to the knowledge that is identical with divine reason,[26] by providing its citizens with rational justifications for their moral beliefs.

By contrast with the *Republic*, the *Laws* seems to abandon the tripartite division of character types suited to three distinct social classes (Stalley 1983, 108–11) and with it the notion that the philosopher-kings alone will have the moral insight, understanding, or rational justification requisite to advancing beyond mere habitual virtue and firmly held true moral belief. It envisions, instead, a city of citizens who all share in landowning, military service, and rule, who rely on the labor of slaves and metics (resident alien workers), but for their own part are all, males and females alike, to be educated in public day schools and provided with substantial rational understanding of virtue. The intent behind providing them with this rational understanding is evidently to nurture the autonomous reason which Plato referred to in the *Republic* as what is most preferable (IX 590d), not just because it is essential to complete or true virtue, but because the highest end of legislation should be to enable all citizens to exercise as perfectly as possible the divine element in their own souls. The training and instruction which this requires is to be provided through public day schools, regulation of culture, work, and other aspects of daily life, and by making law itself as instructive as possible by prefacing the laws with truthful and reasoned "preludes." These preludes are essential to Plato's conception of how the law will pursue its highest aim: they will provide as much as possible of the moral understanding essential to full virtue and the perfect exercise of reason. They are also essential to his conception of how the legislator will put persuasion and instruction before force as much as possible.[27]

Several arguments for public education appear in the *Laws*, and they coincide for the most part with those we encountered in the *Protagoras* and *Republic*.[28] What is distinctive in its case for the necessity of public education is best seen, however, through its view of the foundations of legitimate authority.

2.41 Legitimate Rule

The grounds on which authority is claimed are several, Plato says, but the most widespread is the claim of the stronger to rule the weaker, and the most in accordance with nature is the "natural rule of law, without force, over willing subjects" (III 690b; Bury 1926), administered by men and women (*Laws* VII 804e–805a) of practical wisdom. These competing views of the grounds for authority are introduced by Plato in Book III (at 690a–c) in the course of an argument running from 683b, where the question of what it is that *preserves* a regime is first posed, to 693d. That argument is then repeated in a somewhat different form at 693d–702a, and the two versions of it together provide a defense of his view that the authority to rule rests on aiming at the common good with the informed consent of the citizens whose good is to be pursued.

The first version of this argument purports to examine the causes of Sparta's having outlasted Argos and Messene, and concludes (at 689d) that in general what is necessary to preserving a city is "the greatest wisdom" and fidelity to reason. The second version regards the Persian monarchy and the Athenian democracy as representative of coercive rule by the one and the many respectively, and argues again from what is conducive to stability to a conclusion which is compatible with that of the first argument, in holding that rule by force, rule that is in the interest of those who rule rather than in the common interest (implied at 697d), and rule that does not promote friendship and community (697d, 701d) are inconsistent with the preservation of a city. Assuming as we must that self-sufficiency or the capacity for self-preservation is serving here as an implicit test of what is natural,[29] it is reasonably evident that both versions of the argument are designed to refute the claim that the rule of the stronger is natural or legitimate. Rule of this sort does not exhibit the fidelity to reason which the first version of the argument concludes is essential to preserving a city, and the suggestion seems to be that it suffers from all three of the defects identified in the second version as well. By contrast, the one form of rule which could claim legitimacy, if these arguments are accepted, is a rule of law by consent, aiming at the common interest and at friendship and unity.[30]

A few pages later, in Book IV, Plato has the Athenian Stranger ask whether it is not the case that, when the stronger rule by superior force, they punish those who fail to do the things they have named as just (714d), and the Athenian announces in summary fashion a few lines later that those who rule in this way and stipulate laws "which are not established for the good of the whole state" (715b) produce ordinances that are just in name only.[31] The clear implication is that these so-called laws have no legitimate claim to be obeyed or enforced. What follows then, by way of spelling out what is involved in legitimate rule, must be understood in part as an elaboration of the necessary conditions for just enforcement of law, even though Plato's view of punishment is that it is most often (though not always) intended as a therapy for the soul and to provide compensation and restore friendship (IX 862b–63a).[32] As he says at IV 718b, the laws themselves will show one how to order one's life through persuasion, and "when they have to deal with characters that defy persuasion" they will resort to "compulsion and chastisement."

2.42 An Education in Virtue

Plato's account of the place of public instruction in a just system of law seems to divide into two parts, one of which he describes as instruction and persuasion which, "provided it is not made to utterly savage souls *(pantapasin ômais psuchais [labomena])*, will help to make people more amenable and better disposed to listen to what the lawgiver recommends" (IV 718d). This instruction is intended to make people "easier to teach" and will be spelled out in prefaces to the laws themselves and taught in schools. It is itself a form of rational persuasion, however, and presupposes prior nurture, training of the passions, and education to ensure that the citizens are not "utterly savage," but instead "supremely easy to persuade along the paths of virtue" (IV 718c).

Plato provides an account of this basic education in virtue in Book I, where he argues that "those who are able to rule themselves are good *(agathôn men ontôn tôn dunamenôn archein autôn),* those who cannot are bad" (644b). Given what we have encountered in the *Protagoras* and the *Republic*, there should be no surprise that he does not say here that those who are not *ignorant* of the good and the right are good. He does not say or imply that having the ability or power *(dunamis)* to control or rule *(archô)* oneself requires nothing more than having knowledge or true opinion. Indeed, there is a discussion of the importance of training and practice in withstanding the "natural attraction of pleasures," no less than the natural impulse to flee in the face of dangers (I 635c—d ff.), which gives us an account of becoming good that is predicated on the view that no attempt to overcome ignorance can succeed in enabling us to do the right thing unless we are also trained in a way that develops our self-control in the face of dangers and pleasures.[33] The point is that self-control does not come naturally, but only through guided practice, and that in the absence of this practice it is useless to try to inform people of what it is they should do (cf. II 653a–b). It is useless, he says, for the Spartan law to forbid drinking parties, for "if they [Spartan men] are not trained to stand firm when they encounter" the seductions of alcohol, those who later succumb will "only in a limited sense . . . deserve to be called courageous and free" (I 635c–d).

On the other hand, Plato does not say that the capacity to rule oneself is simply a kind of self-control or disposition to act as one thinks best. Rather, he describes it as a disposition to guide oneself in accordance with reason, and he identifies self-rule by reason with self-rule in accordance with the divine reason encoded in the common law. The "golden and holy lead-string of calculation *(tou logismou agôgên chrusên kai ieran)* is called the common law of the city *(tês poleôs koinon nomon),*" he says, and he cautions that

> we must assist *(sullambanein)* that most admirable *(tê kallistêi)* lead-string *(agôgêi)* of law; for since calculation is admirable *(kalou),* but gentle rather than violent *(praou de kai ou biaiou),* its efforts need assistants, so that the gold in us may prevail over the other substances (I 645a).

The work of education, as Plato defines it at the outset of this discussion, is precisely to provide such assistance. It is to be an "education from childhood in *virtue,* a training which produces a keen desire to become a perfect citizen who knows how to rule and be ruled as justice demands" (I 643e–44a). Without proper education it is *unlikely* that conformity with reason and law will be very widespread, for the capacities of reason and harmony of reason and desire must be developed by proper instruction and exercise if a person is to acquire self-control and succeed in conducting him- or herself in accordance with just law (II 659d).[34] We are like "divine puppets," Plato says, in which the fear of pain, the anticipation of pleasure, and the faculty of calculating what is better and worse

> work within us like tendons or cords, drawing us and pulling against one another in opposite directions toward opposite deeds, struggling in the region where virtue and vice lie separated from one another (644e; Pangle 1980).

The cord we should always follow is calculation or reason, he says; but his view, as we have seen, is that the work of education is essential to the success of those who do succeed in following it. He rejects here any notion of a will that is *simply* free or can be counted on to attain full powers of reason just with the passage of time.

2.43 Preludes and Overtures

The other claim, that laws should be presented and prefaced in a way that will "make the one who listens . . . more agreeable and a better learner," is pursued in Book IV through the elaboration of two models of medicine and legislating, and the notion that the laws should be preceded by "preludes." The two models of medicine correspond to the two titles to authority already invoked, and serve to sharpen the contrast and make it more vivid. The kind of doctor who does not follow nature, he says, does not "give or receive any account of the illness afflicting" the patient, but instead

> he gives him orders on the basis of the opinions he has derived from experience. Claiming to know with precision, he gives his commands just like a headstrong tyrant and hurries off . . . (720c; Pangle 1980).

This is typical of doctors who deal with slave-patients, while the other kind of doctor, who treats the illnesses of free men, he says,

> investigates [the illnesses of free men] from their beginning and according to nature, communing with the patient himself and his friends, and he both learns something himself from the invalids and, as much as he can, teaches *(didaskei)* the one who is sick. He does not give orders until he has in some sense persuaded; when he has on each occasion made the sick person gentle *(hêmeroumenon)* by means of persuasion, he attempts to lead him back to health (720d–e; Bobonich 1991, 370).

This superior "double method" of the doctor who acts from knowledge and with the informed consent of the patient is then illustrated in the domain of legislation by contrasting (at 721a–d) a law set down as a simple command and threat of punishment, the threat being the only reason of any kind given for obeying, with a law preceded by a "prelude" which explains the rationale for it, "to make the person to whom he promulgated his law accept his orders—the law—in a more cooperative frame of mind and with a correspondingly greater readiness to learn" (723a–b). The immediate example given is the law requiring marriage between the ages of thirty and thirty-five, which includes a prelude that explains at some length the important role in human life of having children. Other preludes, offered elsewhere in the *Laws*, display a similar intention to explain why conformity with the laws is in the interest of those expected to obey them, and to put encouragement before threats.[35]

The general preamble to the legal code does even more than this, however, for it begins by explaining the first principle of the Socratic moral tradition in a way that is grounded in an account of the soul, just as the good doctor's explanation of a patient's illness will take as its natural starting point an account of bodily health:

> Of all things a man can call his own, the holiest (though the gods are holier still) is his soul. . . . There are two elements that make up the whole of every man. One is stronger and superior, and acts as master; the other, which is weaker and inferior, is a slave; and so a man must always respect the master in him in preference to the slave. Thus when I say that next after the gods—our masters—and their attendant spirits, a man must honor his soul, my recommendation is correct (V 726e–27a).

The prelude continues by enumerating the various forms of dishonor to the soul, emphasizing the importance of making "as perfect as possible what is deficient" in this superior part of oneself (V 728c), and provides accounts of the relative values of various goods (V 728d–29a), of the varieties of duties, vices, virtue, and happiness (V 729a–34e), concluding that

> The courageous man does better than the coward, the wise man than the fool; so that, life for life, the former kind—the restrained, the courageous, the wise and the healthy—is more pleasant . . . and infinitely happier (V 734d—e).

This prelude to the laws as a whole thus provides a general understanding of Plato's theory of the good, the way specific moral directives and beliefs are justified by it, and the advantages of virtue. This is consistent with the Athenian Stranger's observations that the good doctor uses "arguments that come close to philosophizing, grasping the disease from its source and going back up to the whole nature of bodies" (IX 857c–d; Pangle, 1980), and that the legislator is concerned with educating *(paideuei)* the citizens, not imposing laws on them (IX 857e), and will "explain the nature" of virtue and goodness and justice "and how they should be reflected in our conduct, if we aim to be happy" (IX 858d). All of this is reinforced later with more philosophically elaborate arguments, in the preface to the law of impiety in Book X, which are intended to "demonstrate by means of argument" *(apodeixaimen metriôs tois logois)* the priority of the soul and the existence of the gods (887a ff.).[36]

These preludes must precede not only the laws as a whole, but each of them individually, Plato insists (IV 723b), and the inference we must draw is that it is largely through this means, and the education of the capacities of reason already mentioned, that the legislator will endeavor to obtain the citizens' cooperation and consent to the laws. Plato regards the laws enumerated by the Athenian Stranger as eminently worthy of consent, and the aim of the preludes is to state the considerations that may be adduced on their behalf in a cogent and rhetorically effective way. The preludes "are persuasion at the high level of rational insight suffused with emotion" (Morrow 1960b, 558), which is what they should be if they are to nourish not only the desire but the understanding essential to virtue and the fulfillment of the citizens' rational potential.[37]

The laws and their preludes will not be merely announced and written down, moreover, for Plato holds that the instructional aspects of legislating should be assigned first and foremost to public schools. He describes the institutional framework of a system of public education in Book VII:

> it has already been said that buildings for gymnastics and for common instruction should be located at three places in the center of the city, and that outside, at three places again around the city, there should be gymnasia and open spaces arranged for horses as well as for archery and the other long-range weapons, where the young can learn and practice. . . . In all these buildings there should dwell teachers of each

subject, strangers persuaded by pay to teach those who attend all the things they should learn. . . . And it will not be left up to the father's wish to decide who shall attend and whose education shall be neglected, but rather, as the saying goes, "every man and child insofar as he is able" must of necessity become educated, on the grounds that they belong more to the city than to those who generated them (804c–d; Pangle 1980).

These teachers will evidently inherit much of the burden of the good legislator to "commun[e] with [each youth] himself and his friends, . . . learn[ing] something himself from [them], and . . . making [each] gentle by means of persuasion," in order to induce a commitment of fidelity to reason, a sympathetic acceptance of law, and cooperation in the arduous enterprise of acquiring the capacities and dispositions of virtue. The teacher's job, in a sense, is to make the case for a youth's becoming a member or citizen of his or her community, bound by the norms of that community, and to do this by "communing"—by creating the personal bonds of friendship and trust that must inevitably precede an acceptance of those norms. If the laws must "appear in the light of a loving and prudent father and mother" (IX 859a), then they must do so at least in part through these public school teachers.

Education is to be "a process of attraction, of leading children to accept right principles as enunciated by the laws," which begins by presenting the child with models worthy of emulation (II 659d–60a) and ends with the preludes to the laws. Plato suggests in a truly remarkable passage that his own preludes or speeches in praise of the laws, indeed the *entire text of the* Laws *itself*, would be an appropriate model for the literary content of school lessons:

> when I look back over this discussion of ours, which has lasted from dawn up to this very moment . . . it's come to look, to my eyes, just like a literary composition. Perhaps not surprisingly, I was overcome by a feeling of immense satisfaction at the sight of my "collected works," so to speak, because . . . it's *these* that have impressed me as being the most eminently acceptable and the most entirely appropriate for the ears of the younger generation. So I could hardly commend a better model than this to the Guardian of the Laws in charge of education (VII 811c–d).

It is thus abundantly clear that Plato regards the law as educative, and that its instructional (as opposed to its corrective) aspect is to be transacted at least primarily through the "system" of public education which he describes at VII 804c–d, and is to provide philosophical arguments sufficient to nurture a significant level of moral understanding—arguments no less truthful and rational than those which the Athenian Stranger offers his interlocutors.

2.44 Consent and Corrective Justice

These elements of Plato's view of proper legislation alone suggest a remarkable meditation on the truth that a rule of law does not create itself. Construed as a kind of consent theory, these elements imply that a just and consensual rule of law, accepted on the strength of persuasion rather than imposed by force, has not been created if people have not been provided with the means to acquire the capacities of reason and rational self-control, and have not been at least moderately well-informed about the reasons for laws being as they are, by people who have earned their trust. As a foundation for arguing that justice demands public measures to ensure that all children are properly educated, this theory provides a basis for regarding appropriate education as a necessary element in any attempt to create an *enforceable* legal order in a society, and for regarding a fair share in that education as a condition for justly punishing any individual for a breach of it. If the authority of law rests on *consent* that is both informed and rational, then education which informs and strengthens reason is presupposed. But if this is so, then it is essential that education be publicly supervised to assure equality and proper content, for otherwise the unification of a society under a common rule of law might be precluded by the deficient or deviant educational practices of a family, clan, or class which was unwilling or unable to comply with voluntary educational standards. The legislative enactment of common law might prove largely unenforceable, not only as a matter of fact, but as a matter of justice.

It should be noted in this connection that Plato reiterates in a number of places the necessity of putting persuasion before threats and punishment (IV 718b, V 727c, VI 783d, IX 880a, X 907d, XII 964b–c) and indicates most explicitly in his prelude to the law of capital offenses in Book IX, and the remarks following it, that punishment presupposes reasonable efforts on the legislator's part to provide suitable education. Regarding the law of capital offenses, he says that

> The very composition of all these laws we are on the point of framing is, in a way, a disgrace: after all, we're assuming we have a state which will be run along excellent lines and achieve every condition favorable to the practice of virtue. . . .
>
> But if any citizen is ever shown to be responsible for such a crime . . . the judge should regard him as already beyond cure, considering the kind of education and upbringing he has enjoyed since infancy, and how after all this he has still not refrained from acts of the greatest evil (853b, 854e).[38]

The reference here to vice as a diseased state of the soul, which may be regarded as incurable when it persists through systematic efforts to inculcate virtue, suggests in connection with Plato's remarks that the "lead-string of law" or calculation must be assisted by education if it is to prevail in us (I 645a), a version of this *argument from the foundations of corrective justice* which hinges, in the manner of Socrates' argument at *Apology* 26a, on the idea that the legitimacy of punishment presupposes prior efforts to nurture the *ability* to comply with the requirements of law.[39]

Although Plato never *offers* either version of this argument in so many words, his views on punishment, education, moral development, and the authority of law do seem together to imply in both of these ways that public administration of education is necessary if there is to be properly enforceable law, and that the justice of regarding all citizens as equally punishable for the offenses they commit requires that education be in some respects the same for all. The dominant argument of the *Laws* is, of course, as it was in the *Republic*, that the supervision of education in all its aspects is essential to assure the fulfillment of the divine aspect of human nature. What this *argument from the foundations of corrective justice* gives us, however, is elaborations of the concept of *consensual* rule traceable to the *Crito*, and of the *ability to comply* with law traceable to the *Apology*, which suggests in two ways that public education is a requirement not only of an ideal state, but of any that can claim legitimacy.

Let us return now to Aristotle, taking in hand this sketch of the moral and educational architecture of the Socratic tradition he was to carry forward.

3

Groundwork for an Interpretation of *Politics* VIII.1

The arguments for public education which open Book VIII of Aristotle's *Politics* have been neglected to such an extent that we cannot even take it for granted that the *conclusions*, or *number*, or intended *audience* of these arguments have been properly identified. Considered in isolation they do not seem particularly compelling, and this has undoubtedly discouraged many commentators from investing the effort required to parse and analyze them. A number of preliminary tasks are thus in order before we can properly address the substance and significance of these arguments. First, we must note the essentials of the theory of rule and constitutions that runs through the *Politics*, since it is the most important and most formative constituent of the setting in which the arguments of VIII.1 are embedded. Second, we must identify Aristotle's audience and his purposes, for this will also put us in a better position to understand the purposes and strategies of these arguments. Third, we must resolve some preliminary questions concerning the arguments of VIII.1 themselves, including particularly what they are arguments for. Some of them are arguments for education that is "public and the same for all," and we will want to know what falls within the scope of public education for Aristotle, and who is included in the "all" who are to receive it. These are the tasks of the present chapter, and I shall undertake them in the order I have enumerated here.

3.1 THE THEORY OF RULE AND CONSTITUTIONS, IN OUTLINE

Book I of the *Politics* seems to have been inspired above all by Plato's identification of the king with the statesman in his dialogue the *Statesman*, for he says in its opening chapter that, "Some people think that the qualifications of a statesman, king, householder, and master are all the same, and that they differ, not in kind, but only in the number of their subjects" (I.1 1252a7–10).[1] Plato's purpose in the *Statesman* was evidently to argue that kings should rule in the manner of statesmen, aiming at the common good and ruling by persuasion and consent to the greatest extent possible, a purpose broadly compatible with that of the *Laws*.[2] In both works, entitlement to rule rests in the possession of wisdom, and correctness in the aim and manner of rule is a matter of aiming at the common good, which requires aiming above all at virtue and the cultivation of reason, and putting persuasion before force. Both works carry forward the contrast between rule over free citizens and rule over slaves first referred to in the *Crito*. In opening the *Politics* in the way he does, Aristotle gives notice that he will take issue with some aspects of Platonic political thought. What we will find, in fact, is that he agrees almost entirely with these fundamental aspects of Platonic political theory, but openly disagrees with Plato on two points: he modifies Plato's conception of the qualifications for sharing in rule in a way that leads to wider participation in rule, and he argues that slaves should be ruled through instruction and persuasion, with a view to promoting virtue, much as free citizens are. In these and other ways, Aristotle's theory of rule displays not only a thorough commitment to what I have been calling the *principle of fidelity to reason*, but a willingness to push its application even farther than Plato did.

Politics I is organized as an argument for the claim that there are several legitimate forms of rule, and the significance of this for political rule is the incorporation of Plato's conception of rule over willing subjects into a conception of citizens ruling and being ruled by turns. Aristotle argues in opposition to Plato that although it is the possession of wisdom alone that creates an entitlement to rule, the possession of wisdom must be considered *in relation to* the rational powers and wisdom of those who are ruled. Different distributions of wisdom yield different forms of rule, as evidenced by the different natural forms of rule in households. "There is one rule exercised over subjects who are by nature free, another over subjects who are by nature slaves" (I.7 1255b18–19), he says, while the father and husband's rule over the free members of his household is royal or kingly in relation to his children, whose deliberative faculty is "immature," but constitutional in relation to his wife, whose nature and deliberative capacities are the same as his but "without authority" *(akuron)* (I.12 1259a39–b17, I.13 1260a8–14).[3] The master's title to rule his slaves rests in his possession of an ordinary share of deliberative capacity and the slave's lack of any capacity to deliberate, but the father's title to rule his children and the husband's title to rule his wife are different, because his children and wife have the power to deliberate in some degree.

In cities, wisdom may also be distributed in different ways, yielding different legitimate forms of rule which are all alike in according citizens shares in rule proportional to their capacity to contribute to wise political decisions. Aristotle holds that the most basic question for a city is whether or not it can call upon the wisdom of someone fit to rule as a king. Entitlement to rule as a king would require not just having wisdom, but having *incommensurably* more wisdom than everyone else in a city, so that even the collective wisdom of all of them together would add nothing (*Pol.* III.13 1284a4–11). In the absence of such a "god among men," a city of citizens who share a common rational nature, and differ merely in their degree of practical wisdom, will be a city which is properly constitutional, in the sense that all citizens should share in rule, ruling by turns and succeeding each other in accordance with law or constitutional principles. In general, the view that emerges is that *the possession of normal deliberative capacities and a share of virtue or practical wisdom entitles one to rule oneself and gives one a prima facie right to participate in ruling one's polis*. The possession of a prima facie entitlement to share in political rule is a function of how virtuous, and thus how practically wise, one is, and it is generally best for a city, for all its citizens who have a share of practical wisdom, to contribute to the management of the city in ways that combine their individual partial shares of wisdom into judgments grounded in a more complete and well-rounded understanding of things.[4] Because practical wisdom is for Aristotle largely a matter of grasping the particulars of situations in their fullness and proper significance, he regards it as largely (though not entirely) a function of experience, whether additively across a population or cumulatively over a lifetime.[5] He does, as I have said, note the bare possibility— not unlike the one contemplated by Plato in the *Republic*—of someone being so incomparably or divinely wise that the contributions of others would add nothing, making it natural and desirable for the other citizens to grant that person the power to rule alone (VII.3 1325b10–14). Aristotle's *ideal* of rule is thus bifurcated according to whether a city happens to be blessed with a leader who can act from complete or god-like wisdom, though in the end he will hold that no city is or can expect to be blessed in this way.

3.11 The City's Aim and the Correct Manner of Ruling

Book I begins with an account of the origins and growth of cities, and Aristotle's well-known claim that human beings are "political animals," that is to say city-dwellers, by nature *(phusei politikon zôon)*. Aristotle's language reveals three aspects of the naturalness of cities and of city life: (1) the possession of speech gives human beings alone the capacity to discuss and collectively pursue the good, making it possible for them alone to live together in pursuit of the best kind of life (I.2 1252a8–18); (2) social sentiments incline human beings to live together (I.2 1252a26–31, 1253a30); (3) a city, and no social unit smaller than a city, is self-sufficient for the purposes of providing what is essential to the best kind of life for human beings (I.2 1252b28–32). In sum, city life is natural for human beings in the threefold sense that they are *capable of* living together in cities in pursuit of the best life, they are *inclined to* do so by sentiments of mutual attraction, and they *need to* if they are to live the best kind of life (Miller 1995, 30–45). Through this discussion of the growth and origin of a polis, Aristotle describes each stage of aggregation or association as consensual and mutually beneficial, including the husband-wife and master-slave relationships within households.

The natural and proper aim of the household, village, and city is the best life, and not merely life itself, nor the worse kinds of life, says Aristotle (I.1 1252a4–6, I.2 1252b28–31, VII.2 1324a24–25; *NE* I.2 1094a18–28, I.9 1099b29–32). What kind of life *is* the best kind we are not told in the *Politics* until Book VII, though Aristotle may have assumed that his audience had already heard his lengthier treatment of this topic in the *Nicomachean Ethics*.[6] In *Pol.* VII.1 he says, much as Plato implies at *Laws* I 631c, that "it is for the sake of the soul that external goods and goods of the body are desirable at all," since a person's happiness is proportional to the measure of his or her moral virtue and wisdom, just as "the gods are . . . happy and blessed . . . by reason of their own nature" (1323b15–24). The gods are invoked again in VII.3 as a standard of perfection by which human beings and the quality of their lives are properly judged: the life devoted to contemplation as its highest end (i.e., the end to which everything else is made subsidiary) is the best and preferable to the life devoted to statesmanship as its highest end because "thoughts and contemplations are independent [of external goods] and complete in themselves" just as the gods "have no external actions over and above their own energies" (1325b29–30).

Happiness, Aristotle says in *NE* I.2, is held to be "the highest of all goods achievable by action" (1095a16–19), and a highest good, he says in I.7, is complete in itself: "always desirable in itself and never for the sake of something else" (1097a34–35). By this measure, a life devoted to the most perfect exercise of the rational soul or intellect, "the most divine element in us" (*NE* I.8 1098b11–17; X.7 1177a16, 1177b30), is the natural highest good for human beings, the happiest life, because it alone is not only desirable for itself (being marvelously pleasant [1177a25]), but aims at nothing beyond itself (X.7 1177b19–20). The action of the statesman, by contrast, aims at something beyond itself, whether power, honors, or the happiness of some or all of the city, "a happiness different from political action, and evidently sought as something different" (X.7 1177b14–15). The life of contemplation is thus the only one that can meet this test of what can constitute a highest end, i.e., the only one that is a complete good in the sense of being desirable in itself and not desired for anything beyond itself. The life of statesmanship may be a happy one and desirable in itself, Aristotle concedes, but only "in a secondary degree" (X.8 1178a9). The contemplative life is also the most divine, in the sense of being the most like the life Aristotle imagines the gods to lead (X.8 1178b8–23), as well as in the sense of being the most self-sufficient (X.7 1177a27, 1177b21), and the one which is "in accordance with the highest virtue" or the virtue of "the best thing in us" (X.7 1177a12–14), namely *sophia* or contemplative wisdom, which is "knowledge of the highest [most divine] objects which has received as it were its proper completion" (*NE* VI.7 1141a18–19, 1141b2–7).[7]

If these arguments for the superiority of the life of contemplation were not enough to make Aristotle's endorsement of the *principle of fidelity to reason* obvious, he adds that "intellect *(nous)* is something divine *(theion)*" and we

> must, so far as we can, make ourselves immortal, and strain every nerve to live in accordance with the best thing in us; for . . . it is the authoritative and better part. . . . And . . . that which is proper to each thing is by nature best and most pleasant for each thing; for man, therefore, the life according to intellect is best and pleasantest, since intellect more than anything else is man. This life therefore is also the happiest (X.7 1177b30–78a8; cf. X.8 1179a23–27).

With this passage and what we have just reviewed, we have all the elements of the *principle of fidelity to reason,* just as we first encountered it in Socrates: intellect is the divine element in human nature, and the one we should cultivate and rely on in ourselves and others, if we are to live well and admirably. To live most happily, Aristotle says, one must make the life of the intellect, of the pursuit of contemplative wisdom, one's highest end, and it is the natural and proper business of households, villages, and polises to enable its members to do so, and to be partners in doing so. A community of this sort requires that its members not only cultivate and rely on their own intellectual capacities, but share a common commitment to the fulfillment of reason and intellect. It also evidently requires that fellow citizens, members of households, and friends use "the power of speech" to discuss "the just and the unjust" (*Pol.* I.2 1253a14–16), with the regard for truth that piety requires (*NE* I.6 1096a16), but there is no indication that Aristotle believes this must be political speech or that participation in politics is necessary for happiness or a natural aim of the city.[8]

Aristotle's view is thus that what is most in accordance with nature, or right, is that cities form partnerships "in which every man, whoever he is, can act best and live happily" (Pol. VII.2 1324a24–25), which is to say as much as possible a life devoted to intellectual contemplation as its highest end. This being so, what are we to say of those whom Aristotle does not regard as capable of contemplation, such as slaves, free metics and farmers, and perhaps many women? If cities are formed of people who are drawn together by bonds of mutual attraction and choose to live together for mutual advantage, where will the mutual advantage lie for these kinds of people? The best answer the text seems to permit is that Aristotle sees the city as properly promoting their well-being too, by promoting their virtue. This will advance them along the proper and desirable path of human development (toward the autonomous exercise of practical and contemplative reason), which is good for them, even if they can never reach its terminus. They will not be *full* partners in the city, which all the citizens ideally will be, but they will be partners in a secondary degree. They will not be full partners because they will not be capable of living the best kind of life or contributing to conversations about the good and the right, but they will derive advantage from living in the city, and will contribute in turn to its capacity to provide the necessary things on which the advantages of city life for all the city's inhabitants depend. Just as Plato says in the *Republic* that "it is better for everyone to be ruled by divine reason, preferably within himself and his own, otherwise imposed from without" (IX 590d–91a), Aristotle suggests here that even those who lack the potential for rational self-governance can and should be made better and happier by training, instruction, and arrangements which make them more responsive to reason and allow them to live more in compliance with it.[9]

As I have said, Aristotle breaks with Plato in regarding even slaves as properly participating to some degree in the city's common advantage, and thus as deserving instruction and persuasion within the household, to the extent this can make them more virtuous. Although it is hard to know how to reconcile all of the images of the relationship between master and slave which Aristotle invokes, there are strong indications that he regards all master-slave relationships as unnatural and unjust unless they are mutually advantageous and do not *merely* rely on force. His characterizations of a "natural slave" are in fact generally at odds with his uses of the term "slavish" to suggest unresponsiveness to anything but force or the prospect of bodily pleasures (*NE* I.5 1095b19–20, III.10 1118a23–25, etc.). Aristotle says that "he who participates in reason enough to apprehend, but not to have, is a slave by nature" (*Pol.* I.5 1254b22–23), and it may be that he means by this that the natural slave possesses capacities of both understanding *(sunesis)* and judgement *(gnômê),* but no capacity to deliberate and generate appropriate plans of action of his own (i.e., no share of practical wisdom or *phronêsis*). In any case, it suggests that slaves will need to understand what is entailed by instructions, and act, whether from a habit of obedience, out of loyalty, in the expectation of rewards, or in some other way. There is no suggestion in this definition of natural slavery that force will be required, though neither is the selective use of force precluded, any more than it is precluded in dealing with children or free citizens.[10] Indeed, at the end of the sixth chapter of Book I, Aristotle holds that, "where the relation of master and slave between them is natural they are friends and have a common interest, but where it rests merely on convention and force the reverse is true" (*Pol.* I.6 1255b12–15).

The most important part of the discussion of the idea of natural slavery occurs in *Pol.* I.13, for it is there that Aristotle takes up and attempts to resolve a basic puzzle in this idea:

> A question may indeed be raised, whether there is any virtue at all in a slave beyond those of an instrument and of a servant—whether he can have the excellences of temperance, courage, justice, and the like; or whether slaves possess only bodily services. And whichever way we answer the question, a difficulty arises; for, if they have virtue, in what will they differ from freemen? On the other hand, since they are men and share in rational principle it seems absurd to say that they have no virtue. A similar question may be raised about women and children . . . (1259b21–31).

Aristotle's answer to this dilemma begins from the idea that those who rule and are ruled must both have "a share of virtue" (1260a3), the one having "virtue of the rational, and the other of the irrational part" of the soul (1260a7–8). As we have seen, Aristotle suggests that the parts of the soul are present in different degrees in freemen, women, children, and natural slaves, and that "the slave has no deliberative faculty at all; the woman has, but it is without authority, and the child has, but it is immature" (1260a12–14). What this allows Aristotle to say, then, is that although human virtue, per se, is determined by human nature and is not relative to one's particular city or civic role (III.4 1276b33–36), there are virtues proper to the various classes of people for whom human virtue itself is unattainable (1260a28–33). The natural slave does possess virtue, but a virtue belonging to the irrational or desiring part of the soul, and manifesting itself in *obeying well* the commands of reason imposed by the master.

A natural slave is to that extent not a *wild* animal, who can only be moved by force, for to obey well surely means to obey from desires which lead one to do willingly what the voice of reason commands (in this case the voice of a master who possesses reason and exercises it in accordance with virtue). He is, as I have suggested, more like a *tame* animal (I.5 1254b10–12) whose social instincts make him responsive to social rewards and thus potentially responsive to commands that embody reason. For Aristotle says of the irrational soul that

> in a sense it shares in [reason], in so far as it listens to and obeys it; this is the sense in which we speak of paying heed to one's father or one's friends. That the irrational element is in some sense persuaded by reason is indicated also by the giving of advice and by all reproof and exhortation (*NE* I.13 1102b30–3a1).

To obey in a manner expressing the virtue proper to the irrational part of the soul, then, is to obey in response to the reasons and advice that are given, normally out of love and respect, as a child does his or her father (*Pol.* I.12 1259b10–13).

Aristotle's depiction of the natural slave's psyche thus suggests that a slave can be induced to act more in conformity with reason by persuasion, instruction, and praise. He closes with the revealing remark that

> the master ought to be the source of virtue in the slave, and not a mere possessor of the art of mastership which trains the slave in his functions. That is why they are mistaken who forbid us to converse with slaves, and say that we should employ command only, for slaves stand even more in need of admonition than children (I.12 1260b3–8).

The reference here may be to *Laws* VI 777e,[11] as Saunders (1995, 101) says, but the contrast between the slave and free doctor in *Laws* IV 720 constitutes a far more prominent statement of the legitimacy of ruling slaves through bare commands. Plato there describes the slave doctor as treating slaves, and as merely ordering or telling them what to do. It is hard to imagine that Aristotle would refer to 777e without also having 720 in mind, so it is reasonable to surmise that he is insisting here that Plato has fallen short of the demands of reason in the lessons he draws from the analogy of the two doctors. Plato uses the analogy to illustrate the proper method of ruling free citizens through instruction and persuasion, and Aristotle reveals here his disapproval of treating slaves any differently. The art of managing slaves, like any art of managing human beings, properly aims at developing virtue and responsiveness to reason to the extent they can be developed, and that requires moving them to action through methods of instruction, training, and persuasion as much as possible. His general commitment to rule by consent and without force is, as I have said, clear.[12] Aristotle thereby pushes the *principle of fidelity to reason* a step beyond the high plateau to which Plato carries it, and we shall see him do so in another politically significant way in his account of constitutional rule.[13]

3.12 The Theory of Constitutions: Obligation, Legitimacy, and Consent

The arguments of Book I of the *Politics* aim to show that there are several different forms of rule in general, but it is only in Book III that Aristotle elaborates his account of constitutions and the proper forms of rule in polises. He distinguishes the true, just, or legitimate forms of constitution from those that are corrupt, unjust, or illegitimate, and we get an indication early in Book III that he understands the citizen's obligation to obey to depend upon a government's legitimacy. He raises in III.3 the question of what distinguishes an act of the state which demands respect from an act which is not an obligation-creating act of state. In answer, he reports what people say, namely that what is "established by force, and not for the sake of the common good" (1276a13–14) is no act of state, but a private act without authority. He corrects this only to point out, to the friends of democracy who say this, that it applies as much to democracies as to tyrannies, and he would presumably add, if there were any need to, that it applies to oligarchies as well. This simply makes explicit what is mostly assumed through the discussion that follows, namely that the laws of corrupt regimes are laws in name only and are without authority, as Plato says in the *Laws*.

In III.6 Aristotle returns to the central themes of Book I and holds that

> The conclusion is evident: that governments which have a regard to the common interest are constituted in accordance with strict principles of justice, and are therefore true forms; but those which regard only the interest of the rulers are all defective and perverted forms, for they are despotic, whereas a polis is a community of freemen (1279a17–22).

Here as elsewhere Aristotle conjoins rule over freemen, or rule that is consensual, with rule which aims at the common good or advantage. It is natural for him to assume that the two are strongly linked, for it is natural to assume that it is mutual advantage that would induce people to give their consent, and that in the absence of mutual advantage it would not be possible to govern them except by force or despotically. In general, Aristotle repeatedly endorses rule by consent as essential to the legitimate forms of constitution, including at III.14

1285a27–28, where he says that "kings rule according to law over voluntary subjects."[14]

The typology of constitutions which Aristotle then develops is a refinement of Plato's in the *Statesman*, as he later notes himself in Book IV (IV.2 1289b6–11). There are true and corrupt forms of rule by one, by a few, and by the many, he says, monarchy, aristocracy, and "polity" or constitutional government being the true forms, which aim at the common interest as all cities properly should, and tyranny, oligarchy, and democracy being the corrupt forms, which aim at the "private" interest of the rulers themselves. Since the natural aim of the city is the best life for all its citizens, and *just law is law that conforms to that natural end*, and thus promotes virtue (III.6 1279a17–22, III.9 1280b5–12, *NE* V.1 1129b17–26), Aristotle regards these corrupt forms of government as lawless or unconstitutional. Our contemporary conception of a democracy, a constitutional democracy which effectively protects common interests against the potential infringements of majoritarian power, is closer to what Aristotle means by a polity or constitutional government than to what he means by democracy. He understands democracy to be rule by the *dêmos*, the class of poor citizens who were most numerous in Greek cities, a rule aiming at the "private" interest of this class, unchecked by effective legal protection of the interests of members of other classes.

In III.9, which we will have occasion to examine at greater length in a later chapter, Aristotle settles the question of who is entitled to share in rule by first settling the question of what the proper aim of the city is. What he says here follows from the importance of virtue to the best life: that virtue is a city's proper concern, and so entitlement to rule is a function of one's share of virtue.[15]

Aristotle then turns in III.10 and 11 to the related but distinct question of who or what is properly sovereign. It is here that he departs profoundly from Plato in holding that

> the many, of whom each individual is not a good man, when they meet together may be better than the few good, if regarded not individually but collectively. . . . For each individual among the many has a share of virtue and practical wisdom, and when they meet together . . . some understand one part, and some another, and among them they understand the whole (III.11 1281a42–b9).

In response to objections to popular government grounded in the Platonic idea that good political judgment requires special and rare knowledge, Aristotle adds that

> there are some arts whose products are not judged of solely, or best, by the artists themselves. . . . the master of the house will actually be a better judge [of it] than the builder, just as . . . the guest will judge better of a feast than the cook (1282a18–23).

These arguments point toward the possibility of a city less paternalistic and static than those envisioned by Plato. Both rest in the premise that practical wisdom *(phronêsis)* "is concerned not only with universals but with particulars, which become familiar from experience" (*NE* VI.8 1142a13–15), and might be justified also in some measure by the related premise that the universals belonging to practical wisdom can be widely known.[16] Aristotle holds as Plato did that knowledge takes as its objects things that are necessary, universal, and eternal (*NE* V.3 and 6), but by contrast with Plato's middle period identification of separable or transcendental Forms as the objects of knowledge, and belief in the extreme difficulty of grasping those Forms, Aristotle identifies the forms or species of human character types and political constitutions as objects of knowledge known to himself and accessible to people of ordinary good upbringing and schooling through the instruction in political science embodied in his lectures on ethics and politics.[17] He thus regards the knowledge of universals belonging to *phronêsis* as in principle widely accessible, and in holding that practical wisdom is concerned with what shall be done, with a *particular*, an "object not of knowledge but of perception" (*NE* VI.8 1142a23–30), he also insists that even without a knowledge of these universals citizens will be able to contribute incrementally or additively to the well-rounded perception of a situation in need of an action. Parmenides held that if anything is knowable it is the same through and through eternally, somewhat like a child's ball which looks the same on all sides, and Aristotle responds in effect that what we require then in the domain of action is *knowledge* of the timeless natures of the species of things we must act upon and *perceptions* which take in all sides of the "particular circumstances of the action and the objects with which it is concerned" (*NE* III.1 1110b33–11a1).[18]

The political effect of this is highly progressive in comparison with Plato's static theocracy, for it regards human communities as possessing the capacity to improve upon the limited wisdom of any one merely human person through collective exercises of judgment. This is a capacity which must be exercised as a matter of justice, according to Aristotle, for he holds, as I have said, that citizens are entitled to share in rule in proportion to their virtue or share of practical wisdom.

This argument for the collective wisdom of the many does not in itself resolve the issue of who or what should be sovereign in a polis, however. For as I have said, Aristotle does hold that a kingship would be desirable if there were "a God among men" available to rule (III.13 1284a11). The question of whether the law or some number of men should be sovereign must also be resolved. As it happens, Aristotle's view is that law will be essential to rule in any of its legitimate forms, and he holds that "the rule of law . . . is preferable to that of any individual" (III.16 1287a19–20), for

> he who bids the law rule may be deemed to bid God and Reason alone rule, but he who bids man rule adds an element of the beast; for desire is a wild beast, and pas-

sion perverts the minds of rulers, even when they are the best of men. The law is reason unaffected by desire (1287a29–33).[19]

Law, then, shall be sovereign, and the sovereignty of law amounts to the sovereignty of divine or perfect reason, just as it did for Socrates and Plato. Aristotle's view seems to be that the most direct way to make such reason sovereign is to consent to the rule of a divinely wise king, but failing that to rely on the collective wisdom of all citizens who have any share of virtue and wisdom. The *manner* of rule in the latter case would obviously involve public persuasion, deliberation, and consent through the action of a citizens' assembly, but in what manner is a king's rule over "voluntary subjects" exercised? One would suppose on general grounds what is suggested by the proposals of the *Statesman* and the *Laws* taken together, that new citizens at the stage of their *dokimasia*, or enrollment as independent citizens (MacDowell 1978, 68–70), need to give consent informed by knowledge of the *existing* laws and their purposes, and *new* laws require general consent on the occasion of their enactment. Both are necessary if all laws are to be imposed by consent or agreement, as Aristotle surely realized, so there is some reason to assume that he takes both forms of consent for granted when he speaks of rule over voluntary, willing, or consenting subjects. What we have seen already of his endorsement of the *principle of fidelity to reason* suggests he would also hold that this consent must be informed, free, and neither deceived nor hurried. If a city is properly a partnership in pursuit of the best and most divine life, a life of activity in accordance with the highest virtue, then all of these requirements are just as essential to Aristotle's conception of political life as they are to those of Socrates and Plato.

In what way, then, will laws be enacted? What Aristotle says of the passing of laws in a kingship is this:

> The best man, then, must legislate, and laws must be passed, but these laws will have no authority when they miss the mark, though in all other cases retaining their authority (III.15 1286a22–24).

Aristotle speaks here of the best man, the king, as legislating, but possibly of others as passing the laws, a function he ascribes to the "deliberative element" of a government at *Pol.* IV.14 1298a5. This is consistent with the Athenian conception of a legislator as one who drafts and proposes legislation which must be enacted by an assembly (see §3.2 below), with references in other Greek sources to kings placing their legislative agendas before assemblies (Gagarin and Woodruff 1995, xv), and with what I have attributed to Plato in the *Statesman*. We can say on strong inferential grounds that Aristotle must have assumed that, even in the case of a kingship, legitimate rule will proceed through public consultation and approval of law, to the greatest extent possible, and this passage may well be an acknowledgement of this. A second important aspect of this passage is its insistence that laws which "miss the mark," which presumably fail to accord with natural justice or divine reason, have no authority even if they are consented to. We seem to have here an endorsement of the Socratic principle, displayed most prominently in the *Apology*, that what properly commands the assent and obedience of citizens is not the laws that have been enacted, but the laws that are natural, divine, or consistent with reason. This amounts, then, to an endorsement of the *principle of fidelity to reason* in its application to the substance of rule as well as its manner.

Before concluding this preliminary review of Aristotle's theories of rule and constitutions, we must take brief note of his account in Book IV of the constitutional form of government, or polity. Book IV begins with a general pronouncement regarding the scope of political science. The political scientist should know not only what is the best that may be achieved in human affairs in the best of circumstances, but also what is the best that most cities will be able to attain; what is best for any particular city that might be encountered, and how to attain the best for each that is possible in the circumstances; and how in various specific conditions cities may be established and preserved. Aristotle then says that

> Of kingly rule and aristocracy we have already spoken, for the inquiry into the perfect state is the same thing as the discussion of the two forms just named, since both imply a principle of virtue provided with external means (IV.2 1289a30–33; cf. IV.18 1288a33–b2, V.10 1310b32–33).[20]

Having spoken of these two forms of rule in Book III, he will undertake a fuller elaboration of the most perfect *attainable* state in Books VII and VIII, regarding it there as an ideal aristocracy in which rule is shared and alternates, a god-like king being "unattainable" (VII.14 1332b16–27; cf. V.10 1313a5–11). He spells out in those books the external means the perfect attainable state will require and the attention it will have to devote to marriage, childbirth, nurture, and education in order to achieve its natural and proper aim of providing all its citizens with a life of contemplation. It is here, of course, that he describes the system of public education that he envisions. His purpose through the intervening books, however, will be to provide instruction in the other aspects of political science just enumerated, beginning with an account of the "second best" city, the polity or constitutional form of government, which is the best that most cities can hope to attain. Aristotle has some revealing things to say about the importance of education in achieving even this second best, and the lessons are in some ways more important than his advice on how to create the most perfect attainable state, since they pertain more to the avoidance of what is intolerable than to the achievement of what is ideal.

A polity is a second best city for Aristotle because it does not succeed in allowing all its citizens to lead the best kind of life, but nevertheless avoids the evils of tyranny, oligarchy, and democracy. These corrupt forms all involve one individual or social class dominating and exploiting the others, and managing to do so by force and by appeal to some title to rule other than virtue. Having described oligarchy and democracy at some length, Aristotle comes to polity at the end of IV.8, identifying it as a form of government which bases entitlement to rule on some combination of wealth, which oligarchs appeal to, and freedom, which democrats appeal to. It is thus a form of government in which rich and poor both participate, so that neither is able to promote its interests to the exclusion of the other, and neither is lacking in reasons to prefer the survival of the constitution and voluntarily accept its laws.[21] In one sense it is a "mixed" constitution, and in another it is a "middle" constitution. The word *politeia* (constitution) signifies both the institutional aspects or arrangement of offices of government (III.6 1278b9), and the social order of a polis (III.1 1274a39). In its institutional aspect, the constitution of a polity is mixed, combining elements typical of both oligarchy and democracy, which is to say institutional roles or offices for both rich and poor. In its social aspect, a polity is a "middle" constitution in the sense that the social classes are not polarized or inclined to factional conflict, but are more equal (IV.9 1294b24), which they cannot be without converging toward what is economically and socially the middle (IV.11 1295b25–29). It is not a city in the truest sense, a partnership in pursuit of what is really good, for its citizens will probably pursue a *variety* of merely *apparent* goods, and they may not be particularly virtuous. Neither will it assign shares in rule on the correct principle. Yet it does meet the conditions Aristotle lays down for constitutional legitimacy, and it avoids some of the worst problems. We will speak much more of this in due course.

3.2 THE PRACTICAL INTENT OF ARISTOTLE'S POLITICAL THOUGHT

By the time Aristotle wrote the *Nicomachean Ethics*, he had come to regard political science *(hê politikê)* as encompassing both moral and political inquiry,[22] and he understood the principal aim of this science to be to guide political practice toward its natural and proper ends (*Pol.* IV.1 1288b21–89a7, III.8 1279b12–25; *NE* VII.11 1152b1–2), and its secondary aim to be to guide households toward theirs (*NE* X.9 1180a25 ff.). It was thus an emphatically practical enterprise in its intent, and Aristotle's recurrent use of medical metaphors for statesmanship suggests that he thought political science would achieve its practical purposes—that political science could guide political (and household) practice—in a manner analogous to the way in which medical science aims to guide the practice of medicine.[23] Aristotelian political science is thus addressed to legislators, whether directly or indirectly, no less than medical science is addressed to doctors, and it is an art of the possible, aimed at producing what good may be produced in each individual case that may present itself.[24] If medicine must take its patients as it finds them, then political science must similarly take cities as it finds them, and we may note that in acknowledging the political importance of social and material conditions, not just in the context of founding a state, but in reforming the variously constituted states which already exist, Aristotle has in this respect accepted more fully than Plato the implications of the guiding metaphor which the latter bequeathed to him.[25] It is no less true, however, that the political scientist or philosopher who wishes to bring about reform must take his audience of actual and aspiring legislators as he finds them, and must find a way to make reform attractive to even those who are drawn to politics for the wrong reasons. Plato seems to have grappled repeatedly with this problem of how philosophy can make a difference to politics,[26] and we must infer from the practicality of Aristotle's intentions that it must have concerned him greatly as well.

It is sometimes held, on the strength of Ingemar Düring's reconstruction of the *Protrepticus* (Düring 1961), an early work of Aristotle's addressed to Themison, the king of Cyprus, that Aristotle had at one time held (as Plato had) that philosophy should make a difference to politics through kings becoming philosophers, or philosophers becoming kings, but that (as Plato did) he later abandoned this view and came to hold instead that "a good king should listen to the true philosophers and be agreeable to their advice" (von Fritz and Kapp 1977, 114). And even if one discounts this disputed developmental thesis, it cannot be doubted that Aristotle was aware of Plato's having undergone such a development himself, and that he would have attached importance to the question which this line of development inevitably suggests, namely *why* a king should pay attention to what a philosopher says. Indeed, given its importance to the prospects of political science coming to guide political practice in the way that Aristotle wanted it to, one could reasonably expect this to be a topic of central importance in the *Politics.*

Aristotle may seem to foreclose any satisfactory answer to this question with his remark in *NE* III.3 that "We deliberate not about ends, but about what contributes to ends. For a doctor does not deliberate whether he shall heal, nor an orator *(rhêtôr)* whether he shall persuade *(peisei),* nor a statesman *(politikos)* whether he shall produce good order *(eunomian),* nor does anyone else deliberate about his end" (1112b12–15). One thing this signifies is that Aristotle regards the creation of good order or the conditions conducive to the best kind of life for the citizens of a polis as the natural end of statesmanship as of a city, and that he would not consider anyone who does not pursue this end to be a true statesman. But placing the identity of our ends beyond the reach of deliberation—perhaps beyond the reach of rational scrutiny of any kind—creates something of a puzzle about how philosophy could ever succeed in shaping the ends of rulers and political leaders through instruction and argument.

This puzzle seems at first only to be deepened by the fact that Aristotle limits his audience at the outset of the *Nicomachean Ethics*, and again in its closing transition to the *Politics,* to those who are already morally serious (*NE* I.2 1094b28–95a12, 1095b1–8; X.9 1179b4–10). He suggests that only those who have been brought up and educated correctly, and thereby possess true moral beliefs or the moral "facts," can benefit from the study of political science. This suggests that he believes political science will rest its arguments in appeals to what is good and admirable, and is incapable of persuading those who are not already moved by such considerations. How then will it encourage corrupt rulers toward reform, when they are neither suitable students of political science nor moved by appeals to what is good and admirable?

Aristotle's ideas about moral development reinforce and explain this restriction of his audience in a way which, again, only seems to make things worse. What shapes our desires and what we perceive and believe to be good, according to Aristotle, is what we are habituated to, which is to say both what we grow accustomed to and what we practice or do habitually. These are the "starting points" or "first principles" (*archas*), which "the man who has been well brought up has or can easily get" (NE I.2 1095b6–8) and which he must build upon when learning political science.[27] Aristotle's view of desire and moral belief is thus not unlike Plato's in holding that upbringing and training or habituation are at least the principal source of true moral beliefs and admirable desires, and that the ascent to moral knowledge must rely on those as its foundation. Some people, whom Aristotle describes as "bestial,"[28] never rise above being moved by the pleasures that entice and the pains that threaten. Others acquire the capacity to act expediently, which is to say in a way that is calculated and thus rational in the limited sense of being suitable to the agent's ends, whether to secure pleasure, honor, or some other end. Presumably, a corrupt leader will have developed morally no farther than this (or will have regressed to this) and so could not be considered a suitable student of political science. Aristotle suggests that such a leader would not share the starting points of the arguments deployed in that science and could not be expected to employ it effectively or toward suitable ends.[29]

Since Aristotle's desire was nevertheless to encourage such leaders toward reform, we must conclude two things. First, we must infer that although Aristotle would not have regarded corrupt leaders as suitably equipped students of political science, his hope was to influence those leaders in a way that did not require their mastery of political science. To do this he would presumably have to call upon arguments which do not appeal to what is good and admirable, and so it is likely that somewhere in the *Politics* there are such arguments. Second, although it is possible that he hoped these arguments might have a direct and beneficial effect on the practices of any actual or aspiring leaders of bad character who might hear his lectures for themselves, he would have expected their inability to master political science to prevent them from engaging in an effective program of reform. Since effective political reform would require the advice and guidance of someone who *had* mastered political science, the means by which Aristotle could have hoped to bring about the reform of corrupt regimes would be by training political scientists of good character to advise and encourage the leaders of those regimes toward reform. Evidently those political scientists, then, would be equipped with arguments which do not appeal to what is good and admirable, but rather to "starting points" or motives widely shared by corrupt leaders.[30]

I will argue in §4.3 that the empirical study of constitutions on which the middle books (IV–VI) of the *Politics* are most obviously based provides Aristotle with a powerful, if ultimately problematic, way of making the kind of argument required. Beyond this we might speculate that by inducing different habits of statesmanship, political science or scientists might bring about an evolution of those corrupt leaders' desires and perceptions, not by argument that changes their minds about what is good, but by a kind of retraining of their desires.

If the *Politics* is thus addressed to legislators, if only in many cases indirectly, before continuing on we must still say a few words about who these legislators are. Aristotle is concerned with the formation and reform of constitutions or political societies (*politeiai*), and so most obviously with legislation on a scale that can be described as a program of reform, or something more ambitious still. Legislation on such a scale would have been an infrequent occurrence in a polis as stable as Athens, being confined largely to the framing of constitutions, as by Solon, e.g., and major episodes of recodification carried out by lesser "law-givers," such as Draco. Legislation of a more piecemeal nature and many nonlegislative aspects of rule may also make an important difference to the constitution or character of a society (*politeia*), however, and one can scarcely doubt Aristotle's interest in guiding such reform as might be possible through these means as well. The first among the distinctions of terminology which must be noted, then, is Aristotle's distinction, at II.11 1273b4–5 and elsewhere, between a legislator or law-giver (*nomothetês*), such as Solon or Draco, and one who rules or holds office (*archein*). Rule, in this sense, is what is exercised by the ruling or governing class or body (*Pol.* II.2 1261b4, III.6 1278b31–32, III.7 1279a29–31, III.8 1279b16–20). However, in enumerating the three elements of a constitution which a good law-giver in this first sense must attend to, Aristotle identifies narrower forms of both ruling and lawmaking. "There is one element which deliberates about public affairs," he says, a second "concerned with the magistracies" or elective offices, and "thirdly that which has judicial power" (IV.14 1297b41–98a3). The deliberative element "passes laws" among other things (IV.14 1298a5), and so rule does involve legislating, though of a more incremental sort than "law-giving" would seem to involve. Aristotle also identifies the holders of public offices (occupants of *archas*) as rulers or magistrates (*archontas*) at V.8 1308b32–37 and elsewhere, but a "ruler" in this sense may or may not be a legislator. In Athens, for instance, before the democratic reforms of Ephialtes, six of the nine annually elected archons were law-setters (*thesmothetai*), but later, in fourth-century Athens, there were some four hundred public offices with very diverse but usually routine responsibilities.[31]

The audience which Aristotle ultimately hoped to influence probably included both law-givers and rulers in the larger senses of these terms, and thus lawmaking on both a grand and a small scale. Some of what he is concerned with may seem to fall beyond the effective range of lawmaking, such as the affairs of the oligarch's household (at V.9 1310a12–26, e.g.), but law-making is in any case the *primary* instrument of statesmanship, in his view. In addition, it is likely that he hoped to shape the beliefs and practice of the actual or aspiring "politician" (*rhêtôr*) whose influence in democratic Athens would have depended largely on a reputation for sound advice and judgment, and less, if at all, on the powers of any office.[32] No formal role for political leadership existed in the Athenian system, but the sovereign *ecclêsia* (Assembly) did rely upon the advice and proposals of "leaders," such as Pericles, Cleon, and Demosthenes, and it is not much of a distortion to regard these leading politicians as legislators of a sort, inasmuch as it was they who formulated and put forward many of the proposals the Assembly voted on. It was perhaps the "demagogues" among them, who made their way by cultivating the *dêmos*, whom Aristotle was most eager to influence, since it was from their ranks that he thought a tyrant most likely to emerge (*Pol.* V.10 1310b11–17).

One might accommodate the breadth of the audience which Aristotle hoped to influence by understanding the term "legislator" to include not only law-givers and members of the state's ruling deliberative body (though probably not every adult male citizen of Athens, even though the Assembly was open to them all under the democracy[33]), but also in Athens those who relied not on *sovereign* authority, but on the authority of expertise and rhetorical skill in arguing their proposals before the Assembly. Alternatively, one might use the term "statesman" to denote these rulers, "leaders," and legislators, whom Aristotle wished to influence. I will use in the following both "statesman" and "legislator" in these inclusive senses, and "ruler" in its larger sense, where appropriate, in each case meaning one who has control or influence over the design or composition (the "constitution," properly understood) of the state.

I am inclined to say then, that although we can infer from Aristotle's remarks about the qualifications of a student of political science and the limitations of lecture or instruction by reasoned discourse that his primary audience was aspiring political experts and leaders (*Pol.* IV.1 1288b21–89a7) who were well-bred and already morally serious, he did also intend to provide the political experts-in-training in his audience with knowledge and arguments which could be used to persuade the leaders and rulers of all forms of regimes to engage in reform (IV.1 1289a1–3). Even if Aristotle believed that only the morally serious could actually master political science, it is clear that the audience he hopes to ultimately influence with his arguments is much wider. I will return later, as I have said, to the important question of how Aristotle can expect his arguments to be successful with that wider audience of leaders who do not share his fundamental ethical commitments.

3.3 THE TWO CONCLUSIONS OF *POLITICS* VIII.1

Apart from Aristotle's closing praise for the educational conscientiousness of the Spartans, the opening chapter of Book VIII of the *Politics* consists entirely of what

appears to be a series of four distinct arguments, which I here separate and label
for convenience of reference:

The Argument from Constitutional Requirements

The neglect of education in polises harms their constitutions (*politeias*). The
young should be educated toward (*pros*) each constitution, for the character (*êthos*)
proper to each both safeguards it (*phulattein*) and establishes it to begin with, for
instance a democratic character a democracy, and an oligarchic character an oligarchy. And in all cases better character produces (*aition*) a better constitution
(*politeias*) (1337a10–18).

The Argument from the Origins of Virtue

Again (*eti de*), for the exercise of any faculty or art a prior education and habituation (*propaideuesthai kai proethisdesthai*) are required; clearly therefore [these are
required] for the practice of virtue (1337a18–21).

The Argument from a Common End

And since (*epei d en*) the whole city has one end, it is manifest that education
should be one and the same for all, and its care (*epimeleian*) public (*koinên*) and
not private (*idian*)—not as at present, when everyone looks after his own children
privately, and gives them private instruction (*mathêsin idian*) of the sort which he
thinks best. The training (*askêsin*) in things which are of common interest should
be made common (*dei . . . koinên poieisthai*) (1337a21—27).

The Argument from Inseparability

At the same time (*hama*), one should not suppose that any of the citizens belongs
to himself, but rather that each belongs to the polis, since (*gar*) each of them is a
part of the polis (hekastos tês poleôs), and it is natural for (*pephuken*) the care of
each part to look to (*blepein pros*) the care of the whole (1337a27–31).

There are important connections between these several arguments which must
not be ignored, and there are also a number of ways in which each may be elaborated, given the rich resources of Aristotle's thought. This initial partitioning does
follow the divisions suggested by linguistic markers (viz., the various forms of
conjunction) in the passage itself, however, and it is compatible with the division of the topics indicated at the close of the preceding chapter (i.e., in VII.17).
Aristotle says there that he will first

investigate whether some arrangement (*taxin*) should be made (*poiêteon*) regarding children; next, whether it is advantageous for the care (*epimeleian*) of them to
be done in common or on a private basis, which is what happens even now in most
cities; and third, what quality this should have (1337a3–7; Lord 1984).

Newman seems to be on track in suggesting that the first of these questions is
addressed by the first two arguments (occupying 1337a10–21), the second by the

third and fourth arguments (1337a21–31), and the third by VIII.2–7 (Newman 1902, vol. 3, 499–501). There seems, in fact, to be little alternative to this reading, given the evidence that Book VIII does indeed follow the plan laid down at the end of Book VII.[34] The content of these questions is not immediately clear, however, despite Aristotle's announcement of his intentions.

To begin with, the word "*taxin*," which I have here followed Lord and Simpson in translating as "arrangement," is sometimes rendered more speculatively as "regulation," as in Jowett and Barnes's version of 1337a3–4, "Let us first inquire if any regulations are to be laid down about children. . . ."[35] Less common, but equally misleading, is the reference to regulation which Jowett and Barnes impute to the opening sentence of VIII.2, immediately following the arguments of VIII.1 and its praise for the Spartans. Aristotle's conclusory statement there is that there should be *nomothetêteon peri paideias* (legislation about education), but this does not entail, as they would have it, that "education should be regulated by law" (1337a33). *Taxin* is the nominal form of the verb *tassein*, to order or impose order on, and there are ways of imposing order which do not amount to imposing regulation in the sense in which we would speak of "government regulation."[36] One way of legislating about education would be to *provide* education for those who are unable to pay for it, but without controlling in any way the alternatives available. This would be an educational reform not unlike Aristotle's proposal that the costs of participation in religious observances be subsidized (*Pol.* VII.10 1330a9–10). In the Athenian context it would have imposed some order on education, insofar as it would have made school attendance more uniform. Another way of legislating about education would be to enact penalties for failure to educate one's children, but without laying down any laws about the content of that education. This would be an educational measure similar in form to the Solonian law referred to in chapter 1 (§1.1) and laws assigning penalties for failure to serve on juries or attend the Assembly (*Pol.* IV.5 1293a5–7, IV.13 1297a14–b1), and it is obviously one that might also contribute to making school attendance more uniform. Neither of these measures would amount to what we would call regulation of education, but they would both be ways of legislating about it and imposing order on it. These measures would also be ways of attending to, or taking pains about, children, and so would also satisfy the terms of Aristotle's first ground for praising the Spartans, namely that they "pay the greatest attention (*spoudên*) to their children" (1337a32). Since his second ground of praise is that they make these efforts "as a community (*koinê*)" (1337a33; Reeve 1998), we have an apparent match to the two questions addressed by the arguments in VIII.1, and so a second backward reference that we may consult, together with the forward one at the end of VII.17, in attempting to identify the intended conclusions of those arguments.

None of these forward or backward references gives us any reason to think that the question addressed by the first pair of arguments in VIII.1 is concerned specifically with the *regulation* of education by the state, for regulation is but one means through which the legislator might make some arrangement regarding education. This first question anticipates further questions about the form and substance of the arrangements which the legislator should make, but it is itself concerned with no more than the preliminary issue of whether education is important enough to merit the legislator's attention and efforts. The character of the arguments themselves confirms this, moreover, for they provide the legislator with several reasons for regarding education as important, but offer no advice as to the *kind* of measures he should take.[37]

The second question has been the subject of some controversy, in large part because Aristotle's remarks about education in *NE* X.9 seem to note two advantages of individual home instruction. He says there that the father's instructions will have "even more force" than public laws, because the child will tend to obey out of "natural affection and disposition to obey" (1180b6–7), and that like others, such as boxing coaches, who teach through individual and not group lessons, he can tailor the instruction to fit the individual child's case (7–13). This has led at least one commentator, Maurice Defourney, to suggest that in both works Aristotle is only concerned to argue for state *supervision* or *regulation* of education (Defourney 1932, 194–95), but this ignores a great deal of evidence, including that of *NE* X.9 itself. The whole point of X.9 is that the proper culmination of the ethical inquiry undertaken in the *Nicomachean Ethics* lies in legislation. Cities should aim to promote virtue through good laws, much as the Spartans have (1179b32–80a30), and they will thus require knowledge of legislative science. "But if [these matters] are neglected by the community it would seem right for each man to help his children and friends toward virtue," Aristotle goes on to say (30–31), adding that heads of households will thus require knowledge of legislative science too. What follows, then, is a series of highly compressed arguments for why there is a point to them acquiring this knowledge: they need not write down the laws for it to help (1180b1); they need not be educating a group, even though that is what the city does (2–4); they need not have compulsive force in the way the city does, for a head of household can rely upon natural affection (4–7); and they can even use legislative science to better effect than the city can, since they can tailor their prescriptions individually (7–28). Without a knowledge of legislative science, however, the possibility of giving *individualized* instructions will not enable them to formulate *good and beneficial* ones, so in the absence of public education in political science itself there is no reason to expect that parents will have the capacity to instruct their children well.

We cannot ignore the Socratic background to this, which is to say Socrates' observation in the *Meno* (92e–94e) and *Protagoras* (319d–20b) that even the most virtuous parents who lack systematic moral knowledge seem unable to make their children good. Aristotle shows every sign of agreeing with this when he closes his remarks about parents in X.9 by saying that surely he who wants to make men, whether many or few, better by his care must try to become capable of legislating, if it is through laws that we can become good. For to get anyone whatever—anyone who is put before us—into the right condition is not for the first chance comer; if anyone can do it, it is the man who knows, just as in medicine and all other matters which give scope for care and practical wisdom (1180b24–28).

A parent need not be able to make "anyone whatever" good, of course, but the children within even one family can be remarkably different and difficult to understand and instruct, and parents left to their own devices will not only be "unscientific," but will fail to "stud[y] accurately in the light of experience what happens in each case" (17–18). They will not even know "what is just and what is unjust," which involves knowing "how actions must be done," since that "is a greater achievement than knowing what is good for the health . . . [which in turn] is no less an achievement than that of being a physician" (*NE* V.9 1137a9–17).

The general sense of this, then, is not at all that it would be better to leave education to private households. Aristotle is simply embedding, within a general point about the need for systematic public attention to virtue, some reasons to think that parents who are versed in legislative science will be able to make good use of it. It seems clear, then, that *NE* X.9 does nothing to undermine the conclusion that Aristotle means to be arguing for education that is public in the sense of publicly provided, and not just publicly regulated. Moreover, there is further evidence for this conclusion in Aristotle's reference at *Pol.* VII.17 1336a1 to children being educated at home "until they are seven years old," which implies they will not be educated at home thereafter, and his consistent references to public education as education in which children are educated *together* (e.g., at *Pol.* IV.9 1294b19–24).

A question that remains, however, is whether Aristotle has in mind public day school, which would leave children in the care of their parents much of the time, or a public system more like the Spartan one. One might look again to *NE* X.9, and suppose that it provides evidence that Aristotle would think a system of day schools best, but this too is problematic. It is quite inaccurate to suggest, as Nancy Sherman does, that *NE* X.9 provides evidence that Aristotle is "eager to offset" the "less personalized aspects of public education" by preserving a place in each child's education for parental love and individual attention (Sherman 1989, 150). Aristotle surely thought parental love and attention were good things, but the point about parents he is seeking to establish in X.9 is that their close attention to their children will not enable them to make their children virtuous if parents lack systematic knowledge of virtue and how to make human beings better. There would be as much justice in construing his praise for affection and individual attention as evidence for his views on the manner in which public instruction should be conducted, as evidence for eagerness to preserve a role for parental moral education.

A more promising piece of evidence is Aristotle's critique of Plato's *Republic* in *Pol.* II.3 and 4, which suggests the view that attachments of affection within families provide an essential foundation for the ties of friendship that create civic unity. This suggests a system of public education less all-encompassing than the Spartans', as do some of his criticisms of the harshness of the Spartan system and the narrowness of its goals. As we have seen, the virtues of military prowess, unity, and absolute obedience composed the core of what the Spartan system aimed at, and those aims might be well served by boarding boys in barracks and subjecting them to continuous military discipline, but these are not Aristotle's goals.

One detects a similar shift in Plato's position on this point, between the *Republic* and the *Laws*, and it is quite possible that when Aristotle makes his case for public education he has in mind a scheme of public day schools not unlike what we have seen Plato describe at *Laws* 804c–d.[38] That Aristotle had an intimate knowledge of these and many other parts of the *Laws* is now well beyond dispute,[39] and Newman would seem to be right in suggesting that Aristotle had this and related passages from the *Laws* in front of him in composing *Pol.* VIII.1 (Newman 1902, vol. 3, 501–2). Given Aristotle's usual eagerness to note any differences between his own views and those of his former teacher, it is likely that if he were defending a significantly different conception of the institutional structure of public education from what Plato had advocated, then he would have said so. His discussion of the character of public education that begins in VIII.2 treats both the ends and means of education as controversial—i.e., both the relative priority of moral virtues, intellectual virtues, and things that are useful (1337a39–43); and which subjects should be taught (1337b1–16)—but *not* its organizational framework. One can scarcely treat such evidence as conclusive, but it gives us some reason to conclude that when Aristotle says that education should be common or public (*koinên*) he means substantially what we would mean in saying that education should be public. He means that the city should establish and operate day schools, choose and appoint the teachers who will teach there, and determine what is to be taught and to whom, and who must attend and for how long, while nevertheless leaving children in the care of their parents when lessons are not taking place.

3.4 CULTURE, SCHOOLING, AND LAW

If it is true that in arguing for public education Aristotle means in large measure what we would mean in saying that education should be public, it is however also likely that his conception of public education includes more than public schooling, and it is possible that he intends his arguments to apply to aspects of educational practice and educational activities of the state which would not fall within the arrangements described by Plato at *Laws* 804c–d. These might well include common meals, the educational practices of households (including their use of slave pedagogues), and the educational dimensions of culture and law.

We saw at the outset of chapter 1 that Aristotle regarded the Spartan and Cretan "common meals" (*phiditia*) as educationally important, and that this was a view he shared with other ancient moralists.[40] The "best possible" city, which he describes in *Politics* VII and VIII, would accordingly make provisions to "defray the cost of common meals" so they will be "open to all the citizens" (VII.10 1330a3–13, 17 1336b9–10). The use of slave pedagogues by Greek families, described in §1.1, was also apparently a matter of some concern to Aristotle, for he says in VII.17 that the directors of education (*paidonomois*) should keep an eye on children's upbringing, "taking special care that they are in the company of slaves as little as possible," since contact with them would be morally detrimental (1336a39–b5; Kraut 1997). Whether he envisioned providing children with some other form of supervision on the way to and from school is not clear. More generally, Aristotle endorses controlling children's exposure to indecent or shameful speech (1336b4–8), and to inappropriate explanations, stories, pictures (1336a29–31 and b13–15), games (1336a28–29), and theatrical performances (1336b19–24). He reiterates and goes beyond this in *NE* X.9, in holding that "upbringing (*trophên*) and occupations (*epitêdeumata*) should be fixed by law" not only for the young but, in the case of pursuits, for "the whole of life" (1179b35–80a4), in order to ensure the growth and preservation of virtue.[41] This rather sweeping suggestion that everyone's pursuits should be regulated is indicative of the strongly interventionist character of Aristotle's political views as a whole (Barnes 1990), and there are strong indications that he intends this to embrace cultural pursuits as well as others, to the extent that they have some connection with character. Passages such as 1342a2–5 and 25–27 in *Pol.* VIII.7 suggest that performers are to be granted latitude in some aspects of their work but not in others, and that the license that is granted pertains to the aspects of the work that have no potential to corrupt character. Those who have reached maturity and are well educated may be less subject to corruption than others (VII.17 1336b19–24), but Aristotle may nevertheless understand public education to include the sponsorship of theatrical "contests and exhibitions" that provide forms of adult recreation that are beneficial in preventing the erosion of good judgment, as Carnes Lord has argued (*Pol.* VIII.7 1324a16–21; Lord 1982).

These aspects of Aristotle's political thought raise the question of where, if at all, he would draw the line between those things which promote virtue and constitute education and those which promote virtue but are not forms or aspects of education. In general, he demonstrates little concern to clarify this point, and he invites a virtual identification of education with the means through which one becomes virtuous, with such remarks as that "all else [beyond what nature provides] is the work of education; we learn some things by habit and some by instruction" (*Pol.* VII.13 1332b10–11).

If this remark can be taken literally, then the law itself qualifies as educative, insofar as it communicates the substance of divine reason (*Pol.* I.16 1287a29–

33), instructing the inhabitants of a polis in what they are to do and not do, and promoting and maintaining desirable habits through both this instruction and the threat of sanctions. In a passage which brings to mind the analogy between a city's laws and the practice of the writing teacher in Protagoras's Great Speech (*Prot.* 326d–e), Aristotle says that

> the law bids us do both the acts of a brave man . . . and those of a temperate man . . . and those of a good-tempered man . . . and similarly with regard to the other virtues and vices, commanding some acts and forbidding others; and the rightly-framed law does this rightly, and the hastily conceived one less well (*NE* V.1 1129b19–26).

The laws thus provide a kind of instruction in the varieties of acts performed by virtuous and vicious people. Later, in *NE* X.9, Aristotle adds that the importance of good law to the development of virtue is the reason why some think that "legislators should urge people toward virtue and exhort them to aim at what is admirable, on the assumption that anyone whose good habits have prepared him decently will listen to them" (1180a6–8; Irwin 1985). The lines that follow this make it clear that the reference is to Plato's proposal that all laws be prefaced by persuasive preludes that encourage citizens to comply and instruct them in the reasons underlying the laws.[42] Although Aristotle does not commit himself in this passage to the idea that legislation will instruct through preludes, his commitment to rule that is by consent and not by force, and is directed at the development of virtue and the flourishing of reason, carries with it a commitment to instruction of some kind that would do the job for which Plato's preludes are intended. What is not clear is whether he regards this instruction as properly part of the laws themselves, or as independent but preparatory to a citizen's grasping and cooperating with the divine reason which the laws do embody. In either case, however, good laws would be on Aristotle's account both instructive and supervisory in ways that nurture and preserve virtue and fidelity to reason, and are thus educative.[43] His view seems to be that a legislator who aims at the well-being of the citizens and knows how to attain it will enact laws which cover as much as possible the full range of actions pertaining to justice and injustice, or the whole of virtue.

This being granted, we may enumerate the possible objects of Aristotle's advocacy of public education in *Pol.* VIII as follows. He may be arguing that

   (i)   the state should *mandate* specific courses of instruction, study, and exercise for the young;

  (ii) the state should *sponsor* mandatory courses of instruction, study, and exercise for the young;

 (iii) the state should *sponsor* public offerings of appropriate theater, music, and poetry;

(iv) the state should *control* what is available in the way of theater, music, poetry, games, etc., and should prohibit the use of slave pedagogues;

(v) the state should exercise broad control over what people do and how they do it, through the dictates of law and the compulsive and corrective dimensions of its enforcement;

(vi) the state should create and fund a system of common meals.

We have already dispensed with (i) as less adequate to the text than (ii), and so the question we have come to now is which, if any, of (iii), (iv), (v), and (vi) might also fall within the intended scope of the arguments in *Pol.* VIII.1. Given that those arguments pertain explicitly to the "education of the young (*tôn neôn paideian*)" (1337a10–11), we may note first that to the extent that (iii), (iv), (v), and (vi) concern adults, they are to that extent not the concern of VIII.1. This consideration eliminates (iii) altogether, because the evidence bearing on sponsorship of theatrical events suggests a concern with adults rather than children, and because Aristotle's position in VIII.6 is that the musical education of the young consists of acquiring and practicing skills of musical *performance*. He seems to regard this early education in performance as providing the basis for correct judgment of character as it is portrayed in music, and perhaps also thereby a basis for a higher or continuing adult education through *listening* to music.[44] Whether this consideration also eliminates (vi) altogether is not clear, since it is not clear whether he envisions any role for youths in the common meals. Youths will not dine at the public tables (*Pol.* VII.171336b9–10, 20–23), but that does not preclude them from serving those who will.[45]

Turning to (iv) and (v), it appears that Aristotle did have both of these in mind in addition to (ii), when he argued in *Pol.* VIII.1 for public education. The remarks in VII.17 that we have reviewed suggest a fairly comprehensive scheme of legal provisions which would not only control several aspects of the content of "paternal command," but supplement its insufficient compulsive power, which a child may resent more than the impartial dictates of law (*NE* X.9 1180a19–20). It would limit parental educational discretion in many ways, including their use of pedagogues.

Again, if the compulsive power of law is required as a component of education in general, then it is presumably required in the context of public schooling as well, so we must understand public schooling itself to involve not only *preparation* for a life in conformity with law, but also ongoing *practice* in conformity to law. But then, if law is the servant of instruction as much as instruction is the servant of law, there is some reason to regard the practices of law in the polis at large as essential to the success of schooling. If, for instance, it is important to the mission of the schools that indulgence in luxuries be avoided, then it would seem to be important that such indulgence be prevented outside of school as well, since the young will spend time both in and out of it. We must say, then, that Aristotle probably conceived of public *schooling* as encompassing not only (ii) but also an element of (v), and that he may have been arguing for (v) in its own right, as well as public schooling, in arguing for public *education*. The evidence for his having this in mind in *Pol.* VIII.1 is indirect, but not insubstantial.

The conclusions at which the four arguments of *Pol.* VIII.1 aim, then, are most certainly these: that children should be educated, and that this should take place through common instruction by state-appointed teachers in publicly provided places, though not to the exclusion of the education which would occur as a matter of course within the home. In addition, we may now add, first, that this may well in its content include an element of instruction in, and practice in conformity to, the laws of the state; second, that quite apart from this public schooling, Aristotle is arguing for a comprehensive code of juvenile law, aimed at the development of virtue; third, that a component of this juvenile law would specify what is and is not acceptable by way of cultural diversions and adult supervision; and fourth, that this juvenile law might possibly include a role for youths in the common meals in which their fathers participate.

Having thus clarified to the extent that we reasonably can here the institutional character of the education which Aristotle proposes in *Pol.* VIII.1, I will, in the examination of these arguments in the chapters that follow, confine my remarks to an assessment of the case that they make for public *schooling* alone. Thus, I shall make little further reference to any but the first of the four conclusions of secondary importance just enumerated.[46] Two further preliminaries remain, however, and I shall take up the first of them, namely the content of the education that is to be public and the same for all, in the next section.

3.5 THE CONTENT OF PUBLIC EDUCATION

The content of the public schooling which Aristotle envisions is inescapably related to the substance of his arguments for public education, so it is best if we begin from at least a cursory acquaintance with that content. His account of the substance of education in general is shaped by his view of the natural order of human generation:

> reason (*logos*) and intelligence (*nous*) are the end of our nature. Therefore it is by reference to them that one must concern oneself with birth and the development of habits. Second, just as soul and body are two, so too we see that there are two parts of the soul, one that is without reason and another that has reason. . . . Now, just as the body comes into being before the soul, so too the part that is without reason comes into being before the part that has reason. . . . That is why attention must be paid first to the body, before the soul; and then to desire. But attention paid to desire must be for the sake of intelligence, and that paid to the body must be for the sake of the soul (*Pol.* VII.15 1334b14–27; Kraut 1997).

We see here, to begin with, another expression of Aristotle's view—an endorsement of the Socratic view—that the rational soul is the highest element in human nature, and the one whose flourishing is tantamount to the fulfillment of our nature and most essential to our happiness. Not surprisingly, it is this principle that he sets down as properly determining the aims and order of the best possible polis's public education and laws regarding marriage and the care of children. The natural order of human development dictates giving attention first to the body, which is the topic of *Pol.* VII.16, and attending next to the desiring part of the soul, which is the topic of VII.17 and much of VIII. Aristotle makes it clear here that the training of desire requires that the right habits of conduct be established, and that this training is foundational for, and should aim toward, the development and exercise of intellectual virtue. He believes, as Plato did before him, that one does not become *responsive* to reason or *capable* of accurately perceiving what is good and evil without moral virtue, the virtue of the desiring part of the soul. As he says in *NE* X.9, it takes the cooperation of nature, habituation, and teaching for people to become good, for without them they are unresponsive to reasoned arguments and lack any conception of what is admirable (*NE* X.9 1179b4–31).[47]

Turning to Aristotle's account of public schooling in Book VIII, we encounter three announced goals: what is necessary in the way of practical arts, such as reading, writing, and drawing (*Pol.* VIII.3 1337b25–26); virtue; and the capacity to engage in intellectual activity (VIII.2 1337a40–b10). With regard to the practical arts, Aristotle's main concern is to warn that they are not to be pursued beyond what is really necessary, by which he might mean necessary to keeping body and soul together, necessary to virtue, or necessary to intellectual flourishing. All would be consistent with the structure of aims we have just described. More concretely, this might mean what is necessary to a landowner who will be prohibited from farming himself (VII.9 1328b39–40), but will need to manage the affairs of his farm, keep his own accounts, and maintain a moderate amount of wealth. It might mean the practical arts that are necessary to participating in the political life of a polis whose offices may require literacy and the keeping of accounts. Finally, it might mean the practical arts that are necessary to intellectual pursuits, which might include reading, writing, drawing, arithmetic, and geometry. Considered either individually or collectively, these possibilities suggest that Aristotle's list of necessary arts would be dominated by reading, writing, and elementary mathematics.[48] More abstractly, these would include whatever practical arts are necessary to maintain a moderate amount of wealth, since that is a circumstantial prerequisite for sharing in rule and engaging in intellectual pursuits.

To the extent that the practical arts are pursued beyond necessity, an education becomes *banausic* and not liberal or fit for a freeman, as it should be. A *banausic* education is one "that makes the body or soul or mind of the freeman less fit for the practice or exercise of virtue" (VIII.2 1337b9–10), whereas a liberal education is one which keeps the proper dominant end of education in view. That dominant end is preparing citizens for the most worthy use of their leisure, namely contemplation:

It is clear, then, that there are branches of learning and education which we must study merely with a view to leisure spent in intellectual activity, and these are to be valued for their own sake; whereas those kinds of knowledge which are useful in business are to be deemed necessary, and exist for the sake of other things (VIII.3 1338a9–13).

As we have seen, the burden of preparing citizens to engage in intellectual activity falls first of all on education for moral virtue. It also surely requires instruction in the intellectual pursuits themselves, though we learn remarkably little of these in what we have of Book VIII.

What occupies most of Aristotle's attention is music. He notes that "gymnastics is taught because it contributes to courage" (VIII.3 1337b26–27; Kraut 1997), and he endorses the teaching of it (VIII.4 1338b39–40), presumably for that very reason. His main concern in discussing athletic training, however, is to make the point that the Spartans are wrong to regard courage as the principal end of education, and that they are unproductively brutal in their methods (1338b9–18). By contrast, Aristotle places the greatest emphasis on music and its capacity to help people take pleasure in the right things, thereby shaping their character and capacity to form good judgments:

> Rhythm and melody supply imitations of anger and gentleness, and also of courage and temperance, and of all the qualities contrary to these, and of the other qualities of character, which hardly fall short of the actual affections, as we know from our own experience, for in listening to such strains our souls undergo a change. The habit of feeling pleasure or pain at mere representations is not far removed from the same feeling about realities . . . (VIII.5 1340a19–25).

Aristotle borrows a page from Platonic learning theory here, in suggesting that we acquire dispositions of character at least partially through imitation.[49] The account of character acquisition in *NE* II provides a necessary supplement to this, in holding that "every virtue is both produced and destroyed" by our own conduct (II.1 1103a7–8). If we must consistently act in the right ways to become virtuous, there are however different ways in which we might be led to do so: in response to compelling supervision, by our native desires if we are lucky enough to be good-natured by birth, out of affection or respect for an elder, or from desires or emotions engendered by music, as we see here.

Beyond this, it is important to bear in mind that Aristotle's description of the laws and education of the best possible polis in *Politics* VII and VIII emphasizes the highest aspirations of cities and how they can achieve those aspirations in the best of circumstances. We will see, as we proceed, that in his discussions of cities that are less admirable and less fortunate, Aristotle devotes more attention to other aspects of public education, such as the equalizing effects of schooling all of the citizen children of a city together.

This brings us, however, to one final preliminary, which is the matter of who is understood to fall within the scope of "all" when Aristotle says that this is to be education that is "one and the same for all" (*Pol.* VIII.1 1337a23).

3.6 EDUCATION THAT IS THE SAME FOR "EVERYONE"

As we have just seen, Aristotle describes the public education of the best political system as a "liberal" education suitable for freemen, so although we have also seen that he advocates instructing and guiding slaves toward virtue, we can safely conclude that the education of slaves will be a domestic affair and not the task of the city itself. We can speculate that Aristotle might deem it appropriate to prescribe domestic education for slaves as a matter of law, for in Book I of the *Politics* he seems to depict a true city as mutually advantageous for all its inhabitants. He clearly thinks that natural justice demands mutual advantage and the avoidance of force whenever possible, so to the extent that the well-being of slaves requires moral instruction, and the avoidance of force requires relying on persuasion, natural justice would seem to warrant regulation of the treatment of slaves to encourage moral instruction.

On the other hand, Aristotle says in Book III that "a polis is a community of freemen" (6 1279a21–22), and that "the members of a polis, if they are truly citizens, ought to participate in its advantages" (1279a32–33). Both of these formulations are troubling, for unless the many noncitizens of a polis who are quite necessary to it (VII.8 1328a23–40, 9 1329a25–26) share in the city's advantages, it is not clear how a fundamental reliance on force can be avoided. And Aristotle insists even concerning war with other cities that only defensive wars and those which "obtain empire for the good of the governed" (VII.14 1333b42) are just. That is, even in its conduct toward other cities, just rule requires mutual advantage. The one way to resolve this interpretive difficulty that suggests itself is to regard all inhabitants of a city as entitled to share in some of its benefits that will promote their well-being, but regard only citizens as partners in *eudaimonia,* or the best life, to which the city is properly devoted.

Thus, although Aristotle speaks in Book VIII of the "liberal" education suitable for freemen, his assumption seems to be that even the most just city possible is only obligated to educate its freemen who are citizens.[50] Presumably he would prefer on his principles to make the proportion of citizens in a city as large as possible, but he apparently saw no possibility of a city being composed entirely of citizens, and he believed it sometimes necessary to manipulate the criteria for citizenship in order to preserve political stability (IV.13 1297b1–8, VI.4 1319b6–19). On this interpretation, a city should strive to make citizens of as many of its inhabitants as possible, and to provide a public "liberal" education to all those who are citizens. Aristotle apparently could not conceive of an economy that could forego the services of slaves and free resident aliens (metics), however, and their children would evidently receive only domestic or privately acquired education.

Another question that arises is whether the public education which Aristotle describes might only be provided to full or male citizens, since he does not seem any more inclined to regard women as full citizens than Athens did. When he speaks of educating women or girls he speaks of them as free persons, but not as citizens:

> women and children must be trained by education with an eye to the constitution, if the virtues of either of them are supposed to make any difference in the virtues of the state. And they must make a difference: for the children grow up to be citizens, and half the free persons in a state are women (I.13 1260a15–21; cf. *Rh.* I.5 1361a8–12).

This makes it quite clear that public education is to be provided for girls as well as boys, but in speaking of women as free persons and not citizens, and as a class of persons having different characteristic virtues from those of men (I.13 1260a20–31), Aristotle gives us some reason to doubt that he has in mind the same education for boys and girls. This passage in I.13 echoes *Laws* VI 781a–b, where Plato says after similar remarks about the neglect of women's virtue that "all our arrangements should apply to men and women alike," but it is not clear that Aristotle is willing to follow Plato quite that far. He says neither that they will receive the very same education, nor what the education of girls will be if it is different.

It is thus with regard to male citizens that Aristotle says without qualification that all will receive the same liberal education, which provides what is necessary of the practical arts, cultivates virtue, and aims above all to nurture the capacities of reason and intellect. As regards rich and poor, Aristotle's view seems to be that in ordinary cities they should be educated together in the same curriculum, to help equalize and unify them. In the ideal aristocracy of Books VII and VIII, it may be improper to speak of rich and poor, given how successfully they have been equalized. Let us accept, then, as a tentative conclusion requiring further development, that it is with regard to rich and poor that we encounter what was most significant for Aristotle in his suggestion that "all" children be educated publicly, and thus at public expense.

4

Why Education Is Important

I have said that the first two arguments of *Politics* VIII, the *argument from constitutional requirements (CR)* and the *argument from the origins of virtue (OV)*, are more readily interpretable as arguments for the claim that education is a desirable thing, and so worthy of the legislator's attention, than as arguments for the claim that education should be regulated:

The Argument from Constitutional Requirements
   The neglect of education in polises harms their constitutions *(politeias)*. The young should be educated toward *(pros)* each constitution, for the character *(êthos)* proper to each both safeguards it *(phulattein)* and establishes it to begin with, for instance a democratic character a democracy, and an oligarchic character an oligarchy. And in all cases better character produces *(aition)* a better constitution (1337a10–18).

The Argument from the Origins of Virtue
   Again *(eti de)*, for the exercise of any faculty or art a prior education and habituation *(propaideuesthai kai proethisdesthai)* are required; clearly therefore [these are required] for the practice of virtue (1337a18–21).

Neither of these arguments makes any reference to the nature of the educational arrangements that might be called for. *CR* says that citizens should be educated so as to have the virtues that will promote the form of political life they will collectively lead, but nothing is said about the nature of the legislator's role in this. *OV* says that virtue cannot arise without education, but again says nothing about the kind of efforts the legislator should make. What is at stake, then, is something more preliminary than the character of the commitment to education that a legislator or polis should make. What is at issue is why any public arrangements concerning education should be made at all.
   The task before us now is first of all to reconstruct or flesh out the details of these arguments on the foundations laid in the preceding chapter, and in light of

the various remarks about education scattered throughout the *Politics* and other works of Aristotle's. In the compressed form in which these arguments are presented in VIII.1, they give an appearance of simplicity which is quite deceptive. There are more than two arguments here, and some of them make use of *OV* as a premise of *CR*. More specifically, I will argue that there are at least three distinguishable versions of *OV* taken as an argument in its own right, a version of it which involves *CR* as a premise, and at least six versions of *CR*, all of which require *OV* as a premise. I will distinguish five versions of *CR* which appeal in different ways to the health or quality of a constitution, and one which appeals to a leader's interest in perpetuating his rule. Since I stated at the outset that these arguments are not mere historical curiosities, I shall also offer some assessments of the extent to which they provide ancient polises, modern states, and their leaders with compelling grounds for devoting attention and effort to education.

4.1 ARISTOTLE'S TWO ARGUMENTS FOR THE IMPORTANCE OF EDUCATION

I have said that this initial division of VIII.1 into four distinct arguments, of which *CR* and *OV* are the first two, is on the one hand quite reasonable, but on the other hand a potential source of error if we ignore the important connections between the four arguments. On the face of it *CR* and *OV* do provide in sequence two quite distinct reasons for thinking that education is important, as Newman says,[1] and those reasons seem to rest in appeals to distinct goods. *CR* seems to link education to the good of the constitution or polis as a whole, and *OV* may be intended to link education to the good of its individual parts, i.e., its citizens, inasmuch as virtue is essential to a person's well-being (*Pol.* VII.1 1323a27–35, 1323b21–26, VII.8 1328a37–38, VII.9 1328b35–37, 1329a22–23, VII.13 1332a9–10, etc.).[2]

On this reading, *OV* is undoubtedly an argument of preeminent importance which builds directly on Aristotle's conception of the natural and proper end of a polis:

The Argument from a City's Natural End

P1: The natural aim of a polis and of political science is the highest good for human beings (*Pol.* I.1 1252a1–6, I.2 1252b28–31, VII.1 1323a14–22, VII.2 1324a23–25; *NE* I.2 1094a18–28, 1095a15–16, I.9 1099b29–32).

P2: The highest good or best life for human beings "is the life of virtue [i.e., activity "in accordance with the highest virtue" or "best and most complete" virtue, namely *sophia* (*NE* I.7 1098a16–18, VI.7 1141a18–19, 1141b2–7, X.7 1177a12–14), when excellence has external goods enough for the performance of good actions" (*Pol.* VII.1 1323b39–24a1).

P3: The practice of virtue requires prior education and habituation *(OV)*.

C1: The fulfillment of the natural aim of polises and political science requires education *(P1–3)*.

P4: Legislators should regard as important anything which the fulfillment of the natural aim of polises and political science requires (a role-obligation deriving from natural justice; assumed).

C2: Thus, legislators should regard education and habituation as important *(C1, P4)*.

On this reading, we have a valid argument resting squarely in central tenets *(P1, P2)* of Aristotle's moral and political theory, which he has been at pains to reiterate and apply to more preliminary matters, such as marriage and early child care, in the chapters of Book VII leading up to the statement of *OV* at the start of Book VIII. It is thus as obvious a reconstruction as we are likely to find, though it is not the only reconstruction of *OV* we could justifiably attribute to Aristotle.

Since this *argument from a city's natural end* is rooted ultimately in a conception of piety, of the moral necessity of respecting what is divine, namely the intellect and reason (the capacities and deliverances of reason) in ourselves and others, we may also with good reason recast it in terms that will sound Kantian, but should be regarded as nonetheless Socratic. Respect for the reason in others entails not only duties of noninterference (i.e., duties to use persuasion and not force, to be truthful, to respect free, informed, and unhurried agreements, and so on), but duties to encourage and aid others in the fulfillment of their rational potential, which, as *OV* says, requires education:

The Appeal to Respect for Reason

P1: Human beings are subject to a natural duty to respect the reason in themselves and others.

P2: That duty of respect entails a duty to encourage and cultivate one's own and others' rationality.

P3: The cultivation of a human being's potential rationality entails the cultivation of virtue and requires education *(OV)*.

C1: Human beings have a duty to contribute to the education of others *(P1–3)*.

C2: Legislators have a duty to contribute to the education of others *(C1)*.

This may be regarded in Kantian terms as an appeal to an "imperfect" duty of beneficence, or in Socratic terms as a direct appeal to the *principle of fidelity to reason*. Either way, it rests in the assertion of a natural duty to respect the reason in others, which is as fundamental to the western moral tradition as any proposition one will encounter. Since it is not my purpose here to find deeper or more purely secular grounds on which to assert this duty, I would simply observe that if one grants its existence—as I believe one should—then one has strong grounds for regarding education which promotes the fulfillment of human rationality as important, if not also a collective obligation of any society.[3] The grounds are strong because the premise *(P3)*, that rationality and virtue do not emerge to maturity spontaneously and in just any conditions, but require education, is not only a central tenet of Platonic and Aristotelian moral psychology, but sustainable on the evidence.[4] No form of untutored goodness, moral innocence, or cleverness can be imagined to equip one to handle a very wide range of circumstances consistently well, and no one who cannot do this would count as virtuous or wise. The capacity to endure what must sometimes be endured, to resist what must at times be resisted, to see what does and does not matter in a situation, and judge well, will not often, if indeed ever, be acquired without guided practice and instruction.[5]

Stepping back from this direct appeal to first principles, it is clear that another equally legitimate reconstruction of *OV* is possible. Aristotle seems to believe, just as Plato did, that even short of exercising the highest form of virtue, lives are happier and more pleasant the more they are lived in accordance with reason or virtue. We do not find in Aristotle's works any counterpart to Plato's brilliant depiction of the descent of the best city and person toward tyranny, viciousness, and misery in *Republic* VIII and IX, but there can be little doubt that Aristotle is convinced that lives are generally more pleasant as they are more virtuous and thus more in accord with reason, since virtue is both essential to the internal goods of the psyche and instrumental to securing various external goods.[6] One aspect of these broad associations between happiness, pleasure, and virtue pertains to friendship. As we shall see in chapter 5, Aristotle holds that friendship is the external good most essential to happiness (*NE* VIII.1 1155a3–5), and he holds that the best and most gratifying kind of friendship can arise only between those who are virtuous (VIII.4 1157a17–25). Only the virtuous can let themselves be known to each other, trust each other, and be liked for themselves, and it is thus in an important sense only the virtuous who are not alone in the world. In light of this, we might set down as a third, and wider-scoped, reconstruction of *OV*:

The Argument from the Promotion of Happiness

P1: Legislators should promote the happiness of all citizens as much as possible, and regard anything essential to the fulfillment of that end as important.

P2: Promoting the virtue of citizens is essential to promoting their happiness.

P3: The practice of virtue requires education and habituation *(OV)*.

C: Legislators should regard education as important.

What is important about this version of *OV* is that it has application even with regard to those who, for whatever reasons, will not be able to lead a life of contemplation, and that it has application even in cities in which such a life is impossible. From a modern viewpoint, its assumptions are also more modest than those of the *argument from a city's natural end*. The promotion of happiness is a sensible goal for political activity, all else being equal, and since no contentious position on the substance of a happy life is taken in this version of the argument, the main burden of supporting argument and evidence would pertain to its second premise *(P2)*, that virtue is essential to happiness, and its third premise *(P3)*, which my discussion of the preceding version of *OV* bears on. With regard to *P2*, we shall see in §4.3 that Aristotle regards virtue as essential to happiness through its various contributions to the quality of life in a city, and that he is on solid ground in doing so. This is important, for although one can imagine an individual ignoring Aristotle's arguments that true friendship and the internal goods of the psyche require virtue, and trying to free-ride on the quality of life created by the virtue of others, free-riding is at best an individually rational strategy for securing happiness, not a collectively rational one. If virtue in relation to others is a general requirement of a social order capable of sustaining happy lives, as it surely is, and education is essential to establishing virtue, then education is a general requirement of a social order capable of sustaining happy lives and a proper object of political concern.

Turning to *CR, the argument from constitutional requirements*, it is not immediately obvious how one might place *CR*'s appeal to the good of the constitution within the framework of Aristotle's theory of rule and constitutions. On general grounds, one might suppose that the character or ethos corresponding to a form of constitution would consist of patterns of beliefs, perceptions, and habits conducive to a full realization of the form of rule, and full compliance with the laws, characteristic of that form of constitution. We get some hint of this in Aristotle's remark that "there are two parts of good government; one is the actual obedience of citizens to the laws, the other part is the goodness of the laws which they obey" (*Pol.* IV.8 1294a4–6). This suggests that with greater compliance a constitution would, in a sense, be more fully realized and more successful. The passages that bear on patterns of participation in rule tell a more complicated story, but our success in reconstructing *OV* and these possible starting points for reconstructing *CR* lend at least prima facie plausibility to the idea that *CR* and *OV* are no more or less than two independent arguments which appeal to two distinct goods.

Yet, this simple parsing of the arguments has serious problems which show that as much as Aristotle may have had in mind the versions of *OV* which I have elaborated, more is at work here than meets the eye. The first of these problems is that *CR* is incomplete without *OV*, since the former only establishes a link between the quality of a constitution and the character of the citizens, and it is in the latter that the link between character and education is made. That is, the good of the state depends upon education because it depends upon the character of its citizens, *and* the character of its citizens depends in turn upon education. To concede this, however, is to grant that *OV* must be regarded as the continuation of, or in other words a part of, *CR*, even if it may also be regarded as an independent argument in its own right.

As paradoxical as it may sound, there is also a reading of these arguments which regards *CR* as part of *OV*. While there can be no doubt that Aristotle thinks that education is essential to the development of virtue, and that *OV* can stand on its own as an argument, it is also clear that he regards good law and city life as essential to the development and exercise of virtue, and thus to happiness. We noted in the preceding chapter Aristotle's view that no social unit smaller than a polis is self-sufficient for the purposes of living the best life (§3.11) and that "it is through laws that we can become good" (§3.3, §3.4; *NE* X.9 1180b25–26), and we will see more evidence of this in what follows. Against this background, the reference in *OV* to "prior habituation" invites the thought that Aristotle, having argued elliptically in *CR* that education is beneficial to a polis's constitution, notes in *OV* the importance of living in a good city to receiving the "prior habituation" required "for the practice of virtue." On this reading, there is an argument to the effect that education is not only of direct importance to the acquisition of virtue, but also indirectly important, inasmuch as education contributes to establishing and preserving the aspects of city life, including a rule of law, that provide the habituation that is essential to virtue. This may be regarded as a reading on which *CR* becomes part of *OV*, in the sense that it is premised on the common good of the citizens, the importance of virtue to that good, and the multiple roles of education in promoting virtue.

The third and most serious problem with regarding *CR* and *OV* as independent arguments which appeal to two distinct goods, the good of the polis or constitution itself, and the good of the citizens, is that this seems to entail a violation of Aristotle's conception of natural justice. What is naturally just, according to Aristotle, is what contributes to the common good of a polis's citizens, or in other words what enables as many of them as possible to live the best kind of life. This requires promoting in all of them the virtues proper to a human being *per se*, those that enable reason and intellect to flourish, and it is only under the best constitutions that the virtue of a citizen will coincide with this naturally desirable "human virtue" (*Pol.* III.4–5, esp. 1278b1–3). Since *CR* seems to call for molding citizens to fit whatever form of constitution a polis happens to have, it seems to license efforts to inculcate the virtues and habits of participation in rule and compliance with law characteristic of citizens in tyrannies, oligarchies, and unconstitutional democracies. Since these virtues would diverge significantly from those of a good human being as such, and since the efforts to inculcate them would tend to make at least some citizens less virtuous as human beings than they would otherwise be, it is very hard to see how Aristotle could intend this argument in the way we have supposed. Since there would be no good reasons for many of these laws, a training in conformity would presumably have to involve deceit and discourage the development of critical intelligence, which he could scarcely commend. Since shares in rule are distributed in oligarchies, democracies, and tyrannies in ways that violate natural justice, education which promotes acceptance of those distributions would arguably also be unjust. Rather than attribute to Aristotle an argument so clearly in violation of his own conception of natural justice, we would do well to survey what he has to say elsewhere about the place of education in establishing, preserving, and improving constitutions— above all, his advice to corrupt regimes about how to preserve themselves. In doing that, we will learn that the ethos which preserves a constitution and makes it better is *not* one which allows the fullest realization of the principles of a deviant form of constitution—which makes a democracy more democratic, or an oligarchy more oligarchic—but rather one which makes it less deviant or more like a polity.[7]

A fourth problem with interpreting these arguments as independent and resting in the good of the constitution and of the citizens respectively is that it seems to leave Aristotle with no argument that could be expected to have much sway with the corrupt leaders whom he evidently wished to persuade toward reform (§3.2). Leaders who cared about the good of their subjects could have been induced through *OV* to care about education, and perhaps through other arguments to care about other aspects of their cities essential to the citizens' well-being. A leader who cared about the citizens' well-being, and also regarded the health of the city's constitution as important to that well-being, might also find in *CR* other reasons to care about education. Although Aristotle's view seems to be that the value of cities derives from their contributions to their inhabitants' quality of life, the "common good" of a city being nothing other than the good life which as many of them as possible participate in (*Pol.* II.5 1264b15–24, VII.13 1332a32–38; Miller 1995, 45–56, 194–224),[8] it is conceivable that *CR* might also persuade leaders who are motivated by a conception of the good or goodness of a polis's constitution as something distinct from the good of the citizens. However, Aristotle's contrast between legitimate and corrupt constitutions presents us with a simple dichotomy between those who rule with the common interest in view, i.e., the individual good of citizens of every social class, and those who rule with only their own interest in view, i.e., the individual good of the one tyrant, few oligarchs, or many poor who rule in a democracy (*Pol.* III.7 1279a29–32). Nowhere in the elaboration of his typology of constitutions is there any suggestion of leaders who would rule with any other end in view besides these two. Thus, if Aristotle is to persuade corrupt rulers, whom he seems in Books IV–VI of the *Politics* to regard as far more prevalent than good ones, then he will do so by his own account, through arguments which appeal to their self-interest, not to the good of their subjects or some distinguishable good of the constitution.

Together, these third and fourth difficulties suggest that there is a linkage in *CR* between the references to safeguarding or preserving a constitution and to better character making a better constitution. I will argue that there are several arguments embedded in *CR* and *OV* in addition to the versions of *OV* already identified, that none of these arguments gives encouragement to corrupt regimes to use education simply to preserve their constitutions as they are, and that one argument offers corrupt leaders the promise of greater longevity in power as an inducement for ruling more wisely and instituting constitutional reforms, including the introduction of education favorable to the citizens' well-being. Thus, I will argue that we can read *CR* and *OV* together as appealing not only to the good of the polis as something compatible with the good of its citizens, but to the self-

interest of the legislator himself.[9] I suggested in chapter 3 that there can be little
doubt that Aristotle was concerned with the question of how philosophy can make
a difference to politics, and in particular with the question of how it can move a
legislator to engage in reform, and here I will argue that there is a clear echo in
VIII.1 of the strategy for encouraging reform which is evident in his discussion
in Book V of the causes and prevention of political conflict *(stasis)* and change.
The essence of that strategy is to appeal to the interest that most rulers and politicians will naturally have in perpetuating their own rule or ascendancy, and to
appeal to facts about the causes of revolution which point up the importance to
constitutional longevity of taking measures which will, as it happens, make a
regime more just and conducive to the well-being of the citizens. The same kind
of connection between education and the prevention of instability seems to be
made in V.9 and in VIII.1, so it may well be that the intent of the two is the same,
and that the argument of VIII.1 amounts to a summary recapitulation of the one
in V.9.

It will be useful to examine the textual basis for this *appeal to a desire for
stable rule (SR)* first, before continuing with the larger work of reconstructing
the *appeal to constitutional requirements (CR),* for this will enable us to bring
to the latter enterprise a better understanding of the relationship between the references in *CR* to establishing and safeguarding constitutions and making them
better.

4.2 THE APPEAL TO A DESIRE FOR STABLE RULE

Aristotle's *appeal to a desire for stable rule (SR)* is an argument intended to move
the legislator toward the good of the citizens, and thus the city as a collective
whole, through an appeal to his self-interest. The argument moves from a concern with stability or the avoidance of revolution to what will best prevent it,
namely above all else—since perceived injustice is the most important general
cause of serious political conflict (V.1 1301a36–b4)—a certain moderation and
avoidance of injustice and divisive policies, a course that will reduce inequality,
unhappiness, and perceived injustice. Education appears in this argument, not as
a substitute for making cities more just, but as the culmination of doing so.

With regard to oligarchies and democracies, Aristotle says in *Pol.* V.9 that

> of all the ways that are mentioned to make a constitution last, the most important
> one, which everyone now despises, is for citizens to be educated in a way that suits
> their constitutions. For the most beneficial laws, even when ratified by all who are
> engaged in politics, are of no use if the people are not habituated and educated in
> accord with the constitution—democratically if the laws are democratic and
> oligarchically if they are oligarchic. . . . But being educated in a way that suits the
> constitution does not mean doing whatever pleases the oligarchs or those who want
> a democracy. Rather, it means doing the things that will enable the former to gov-

ern oligarchically and the latter to have a democratic constitution. In present-day oligarchies, however, the sons of the rulers live in luxury, whereas the sons of the poor are hardened by exercise and toil, so that the poor are more inclined to stir up change and are better able to do so (1310a12–25; Reeve 1998).

In this passage, which is remarkably similar to the argument of VIII.1 *(CR),* it is clear that education which suits an unjust constitution and tends to preserve it will not allow those who hold power to rule and enjoy the fruits of their illicit dominance in the ways they are inclined to. The implication is that the education which is suitable to a constitution characterized by inequality and the disenfranchisement of one class or the other is education which makes the members of those classes, rich and poor, more alike. The classes being more alike, the constitution would be less threatened by envy and factional conflict, which is to say more unified. Democratic education and oligarchical education would be *no different* in this respect, which is surprising given the suggestion in VIII.1 that democracy is preserved by a democratic ethos and oligarchy by an oligarchic ethos, but not surprising given the importance of unity as a measure of constitutional health in the tradition of political thought Aristotle is carrying forward.

Aristotle says more generally of democracies and oligarchies that they are destroyed by disproportion, by the inclination of those in power to deny members of other classes shares in rule proportional to the virtue they possess (V.9 1309b18–24). "Neither the one nor the other [form of constitution] can exist or continue to exist unless both rich and poor are included in it," or allowed to share in rule (1310b38–40).[10] This means that no oligarchy or democracy can continue to exist unless it becomes a mixed regime, and thus something closer to a polity. The trajectory of efforts to preserve constitutions of these kinds is thus necessarily toward greater justice, by Aristotle's lights, a theme further exemplified by his insistence that neither form of constitution should attempt to divide the city by quarrels, or to treat either rich or poor unjustly (1310a5–13). Education suitable to constitutions which must preserve themselves in these ways would presumably not only aim to make all citizens more like each other, as we have just surmised, but would also aim to encourage friendly feelings across class lines and inculcate the virtues of justice and self-restraint.

Turning now to tyranny, the measures to be used in preserving tyranny which Aristotle suggests in *Pol.* V.11 are almost invariably introduced as things that must be done to give the *appearance* of caring about the common good, but which would in fact have the effect of actually promoting the common good. To begin with, the tyrant "should *pretend* concern for the public revenues" but in order to do so "he should give an account of what he receives and of what he spends" (1314a40–b14; emphasis added), which would at least make it more difficult for him to ignore the common good. Again "he should *appear,* not harsh, but dignified. . . . Yet it is hard for him to be respected if he inspires no respect, and [thus] . . . His conduct should be the very reverse of nearly everything which has been said before about tyrants" (1314b18–38; emphasis added). A final and very important example of this rhetorical pattern is that Aristotle advises tyrants that they should encourage both the rich and poor "to *imagine* that they are preserved and prevented from harming one another by his rule, and whichever of the two is stronger he should attach to his government" (1315a34–36; emphasis added). For both classes to imagine their interests are protected, those interests must surely receive some actual protection, and to attach one of these classes to his government is to give it a share in rule, which is more in accordance with justice than retaining it in whole himself. The pattern, then, is to argue from what is required to preserve the regime, but the measures to be taken amount to a path of reform *(epanorthoun),* toward a more just or correct *(orthê)* form of government. "The salvation of tyranny is to make it more like the rule of a king," Aristotle says (1314a35–36), and "the more restricted the functions of kings, the longer their power will last unimpaired" (1313a20–21). The education suitable to preserving a tyranny would thus be one suitable to a kingship, which is to say one that aims at the highest good of all the citizens: virtue and mutual trust, rather than the mistrust, impotence, and humiliation tyrants normally prefer (1314a13–29).

The pattern of Aristotle's Book V advice to corrupt regimes thus seems to consistently move from the premise that the preservation of such regimes requires reforms that would make them less corrupt, the "most important" of which is to arrange for education that promotes virtue and constitutional unity. This lends credence to the suggestion that Aristotle's insistence that education is important to preserving constitutions can be legitimately construed as both an appeal to constitutional health as an end compatible with the good of individual citizens, and as a direct appeal to political leaders' predictable desire to stay in power. To make a more thorough case for these claims, however, we must sort through some of the debates that have surrounded Book V and Aristotle's advice to tyrants.

Book V belongs to the so-called "empirical" books (i.e., IV–VI) of the *Politics,* and the relationship of those books to the rest of the work has been a matter of some controversy. Jaeger's developmental view of their relationship, that the "empirical" books belong to a later and more objectively scientific phase of Aristotle's political thought and supersede the "Utopian" books (Jaeger 1948, 169–70), is now widely rejected, and the once common editorial practice of placing IV–VI after VII–VIII has fallen into disfavor.[11] Books IV–VI do rely more overtly on Aristotle's comparative study of actual constitutions than do I–III and VII–VIII, but they are clearly prescriptive and intended to encourage reform; and neither can it be argued that the project of VII–VIII is in any way incompatible with an empirical study of constitutions. The description of the scope of political science which opens Book IV (1288b21–89a7) gives us every reason to believe that there is a place in Aristotle's mature vision of political science for all of Books I–VIII as they have come down to us, so whatever the correct explanation may be of the textual anomalies which have so puzzled commentators, those anomalies can scarcely be thought to show that Aristotle intended his approach in IV–VI to *replace* that of the other books of the *Politics.* Some puzzles regarding the place of Books IV–VI in the *Politics* as a whole do remain, however.

The debates concerning Books IV–VI that are of significance for the present inquiry bear on the following questions: What does the empirical study of constitutions, which is much more closely linked to the content of IV–VI than to the rest of the *Politics*, contribute to the work as a whole? Why does the topic of stability receive the extended treatment that it does? Is it true that the role of the good is less apparent in IV–VI than in the rest of the *Politics*, and if so why? How can Aristotle think that it is morally proper to offer all forms of regimes, even tyrannies, advice on how to preserve themselves? There again, why does he *say* (e.g., in IV.1) that he will offer advice on how to preserve each kind of regime, but offer advice which would actually change the form of some of them? Why is the mode of exposition so straightforward, with "less dialectical discussion of problems or of his predecessor's views" than in the rest of the *Politics* (Mulgan 1977, 116)?

A view of Aristotle's mature vision of political science which is now widely shared is that it encompasses a great deal that his early and essentially Platonic view did not, while (contrary to Jaeger's view) still retaining a place for the study of ideal constitutions. An early view along these lines, which still retains some of the flavor of the Jaegerian view, is G. H. Sabine's:

> It is not to be supposed that Aristotle consciously abandoned [the Platonic, ethical] point of view, since the treatise on the ideal state was left standing as an important part of the *Politics*. At some date not far removed from the opening of the Lyceum, however, he conceived a science or art of politics on a much larger scale. This new science was to be general: that is, it should deal with actual as well as ideal forms of government and it should teach the art of governing and organizing states of any sort in any desired manner. This new general science of politics, therefore, was not only empirical and descriptive, but even in some respects independent of any ethical purpose. . . . The whole science of politics, according to the new idea, included the knowledge both of the political good, relative as well as absolute, and also of political mechanics employed perhaps for an inferior or even a bad end (Sabine 1973, 91).

Christopher Rowe, Richard Mulgan, Richard Bodéüs, and others have correctly pointed out, however, that the program announced in IV.2, and executed in IV–VI as a whole, is concerned for the most part with the *reform* of existing states, with reference to an attainable ideal (V.9 1309b18ff.). That ideal is defined as a mean between oligarchy, understood as the domination of the poor by the rich, and democracy, understood as the domination of the rich by the poor (III.7 1279b7–10). The attainment of this "middle" and "mixed" "constitutional" form of government or "polity" would eliminate a good deal of injustice and yield a state in which both rich and poor would have the political means to protect their own interests and their access to the means for pursuing a good life. In including a sufficient number within the political life of the state this form of government would also yield a more stable state, since neither the rich nor the poor would have to resort to extraconstitutional means to protect their interests.

It is not accurate to suggest, then, as Sabine does, that Aristotle is indifferent to the "manner" of governance and organization of a state, and that he offers here a science of "political mechanics" that may be employed even for a "bad end." Yet "the general standpoint of the three books as a whole is that injustice is to be avoided because it leads to *stasis*," i.e., to political conflict which may be expressed through extraconstitutional means, and which would not infrequently lead to constitutional change *(metabolê),* notes Rowe (1991, 68). Rowe adds, again quite accurately, that the avoidance of injustice is presented as "a means to an end, rather than being an end in itself" (68), and that the role of the good receives little attention, even though the implementation of Aristotle's advice would yield better and more just states. Rowe takes this mode of presentation to be a reason for concluding that Aristotle's political science has two distinct practical aims, and he offers as a second reason the odd assertion that although a state cannot secure the good for its citizens without attaining stability, "it patently does not follow from this that a stable constitution will in itself be better in terms of the other standard [the *eudaimonistic* one] than an unstable one" (69). The two independent aims which Rowe imputes to Aristotle's political science on the strength of these considerations are the attainment of the best life for all citizens and, quite apart from that, the promotion of order and stability. On this interpretation of Rowe's, then, Aristotle's political science is not the science of "political mechanics" which Sabine describes, but neither is it guided unequivocally by moral aims.

Four responses to this are in order. First, the argument that stability *per se* need not make a state better with respect to the promotion of human thriving is beside the point. Aristotle asserts repeatedly (as he notes himself at V.9 1309b16–18) that stability depends above all on at least a majority of citizens deriving enough good from the constitution to desire its continuation.[12] Moreover, as we have seen, the methods for promoting stability Aristotle *advocates,* and insists are more effective than other more oppressive and divisive means (a direct comparison of the two is made at V.11, 1314a13–15b10), *would* have the effect of making states better from a *eudaimonistic* standpoint, even if it is true that a mere balance of power between the rich and the poor is less ideal from this standpoint than the ideal aristocracy or community of the virtuous envisioned in *Pol.* VII–VIII. The polity's "mixed" and "middle" constitution will still allow more opportunity, and provide more citizens with at least some of what is required, to pursue the good privately, if not as a collectivity.

Second, this view of Rowe's is in conflict, as he notes, with the fact that Aristotle "talks as if the enterprise of IV–VI were a simple and straightforward extension of that of VII–VIII" (69). The introductory remarks of IV.1 do suggest a unity of purpose which Rowe's interpretation does not capture, and it is plain enough what it is. Aristotle has described the best form of constitution in Book III (namely aristocracy or kingship, except that the latter is unattainable), and he continues in Book IV by describing in more detail the second best or more generally attainable constitution, a "polity" or "constitutional" government. Much of what follows in V and VI is shaped by the idea that this second best constitution is what worse forms of constitution should aim at if they are to be better cities, i.e., more in conformity with the requirements of natural justice, and also more stable cities.

Third, Rowe offers no explanation for why Aristotle would have devoted so much of his effort in the domain of political science to a second and distinct goal. Given the overarching moral aims which Aristotle evidently does have, one must explain what purpose the empirical elements serve in a way that places them within his larger moral enterprise.

Finally, to the extent that Rowe's hypothesis of two distinct goals is prompted by the observation that the good plays little explicit role in IV–VI, I would suggest first, that Aristotle does in fact offer some very direct moral judgments of tyranny, and second, that there is a better explanation of the empirical emphasis of his discussion of tyranny and other corrupt constitutions in Book V. With regard to the first of these points, Aristotle does say quite plainly in introducing the topic of tyranny that it is "made up of two evil *(kakôn)* forms of government" and has "the perversions and errors of both" (V.10 1310b4–7), and he says similarly a page later that "tyranny has all the vices *(kaka)* of both democracy and oligarchy" (1311a9). The second point, that there is a better explanation of Aristotle's empirical emphasis, is best prefaced by noting the difficulties that attend two other recent and largely sound readings of Books IV–VI.

Richard Mulgan's view is compatible with Rowe's in most matters of importance to us here, but he takes political instability to be important to Aristotle for the twin reasons that it "threaten[s] the pursuit of Aristotle's good life" and because "most rulers are anxious to avoid" it (Mulgan 1977, 119). This is right on target, as far as it goes, but Mulgan does not explore the possible relationships between these two considerations. Much as Rowe does, he asserts the dominance of an "attitude of strict ethical neutrality" (130) and observes that the thrust of IV–VI is nevertheless a strongly reformist one (130–38), but he sees significance that Rowe does not in the fact that Aristotle's advice would often lead not to the preservation of a constitution, but to the replacement of it with one that is both more stable and closer to Aristotle's *eudaimonistic* ideal. This generates a complaint which we may reasonably regard as a symptom of a defect in Mulgan's interpretation:

> The task that Aristotle has set himself is in fact impossible. Believing that extreme constitutions are inherently unstable, he is unwilling to support means of making them stable which do not involve making them less extreme and so altering their character. One wishes that he had recognized this inconsistency and had consciously abandoned the attempt to preserve every type of constitution whatsoever. . . . He certainly has advice to give extreme oligarchs, democrats, and tyrants but he should have admitted more openly that he considers their position untenable and that they must change the nature of their rule or be overthrown (136).

What Mulgan identifies here as a tension in Aristotle's thought is arguably a tension in his own interpretation. It is likely that he has been misled by the inconspicuousness of moral judgment in this book, and errs in thinking that Aristotle really does aim "to preserve every type of constitution whatsoever."

Rather than impute to Aristotle an ambition which is rather obviously "impossible," as Mulgan charges, it is more charitable to suggest that his ambition was not in fact to preserve all regimes, in the sense of preserving both continuity of rule *and* the form of rule in place, but rather to reform those in need of reform, even though that might sometimes require an alteration of their form. One could then attribute his manner of presentation to a conviction that the prospects for persuading those who hold power to engage in reform would be better if his moral aspirations remained in the background. His view, on this interpretation, would be that the political expert should aim at the good, but formulate his proposals in a way which would engage the ruler's practical concern with preserving his own rule, in order to persuade and retain the confidence of rulers who could not be counted on to act from good intentions, and whose trust might be lost if the theme of the good were sounded too openly. Because Aristotle believed that unjust regimes, such as oligarchies and tyrannies, are the shortest-lived (*Pol.* V.12 1315b11–12), his advocacy of this strategy for encouraging reform does not amount to an advocacy of deception. The arguments which the political expert would present a corrupt ruler with would be sound, but they would engage the ruler's motives rather than the expert's. The wisdom in this seems rather clear, and so, from a practical standpoint, Mulgan would appear to be quite mistaken in the assertion that Aristotle "should have admitted more openly that he considers [the] position [of extreme oligarchs, democrats, and tyrants] untenable." The political expert cannot hide the fact that his proposals call for making changes in untenable regimes, but neither morality nor practicality demands that he engage in open moral condemnation of the rulers he advises, nor that he announce *ex ante* that the course of reforms he may eventually secure agreement to will change the form of rule which they exercise.

Mulgan, in a related passage, holds that Aristotle's "inconsistency" regarding whether corrupt regimes will have to alter their form in order to be stable makes his advice to such regimes "unreal and unconvincing," since those who engage in extreme forms of rule would surely realize that moderation would change the form of rule they practiced (134). This is scarcely a cogent objection, however, for to be fully open at the start about the necessity of a fundamental change in the form of the regime would only make that necessity obvious from the start, rather than at some time after the political scientist has been able to establish a relationship of trust and influence with the leadership of a regime. Over the course of time, a tyrant's experience of engagement in better constitutional practices might also have some potential to retrain his perceptions and dispositions, making him "virtuous, or at least half virtuous," as Aristotle says (V.11 1315b3–4), and more receptive to further moderation of his regime.

Aristotle explains in his introductory remarks in IV.1 that

> one ought to introduce an arrangement *(taxin)* such that easily out of existing cir-
> cumstances *(paidiôs ek tôn huparchontôn)* they [the leaders of existing regimes] *will
> be persuaded (peisthêsontai)* and will be able to participate in it *(dunêsontai
> koinônein)*, since to reform a constitution is no less a task than to institute one from
> the beginning. . . (1289a1–4; emphasis added).[13]

These opening remarks are addressed to students of political science, and they draw the student's attention to the practical importance of proposing arrangements which will be not only feasible, but which can also be made attractive to those in power. Viewed in light of these opening remarks, the analysis of the causes and means of prevention of *stasis* in Book V may with good reason be regarded as intended to equip the student to meet the challenges of both feasibility and persuasion. We may see Aristotle as providing the student with a model of the kind of argument that is most likely to succeed with those who hold power: an argument which appeals to the leader's predictable interest in preserving power and is moved along always by vivid appeals to the lessons of history, and not by recourse to ethical premises or dialectical reliance on what philosophers and other intellectuals have been able to agree on. It is an argument which seems in all respects suited to winning the confidence of an ambitious man of action, and moving him to modify his rule in ways he would otherwise not wish to.

How many rulers of the more extreme varieties might actually be led more than a little way down this path of reform would depend on many things, including how consistently expedient and mistrustful they were, and what kind of relationships they came to have with their political scientist advisers. Reasonable grounds for skepticism are not hard to find, but for all that it is a powerful argument that Aristotle develops. Mulgan's grounds for judging it "unreal and unconvincing" are confused, I have argued, and no better is Ronald Polansky's alternative suggestion that it is not to the tyrants and extreme democrats and oligarchs that Aristotle offers his advice, but rather only to the morally serious aspiring statesman (Polansky 1991). This alternative would spare Aristotle the alleged embarrassment of trying to address real legislators without any argument that could be expected to move them, but it ignores the evidence of 1289a1–7 which we have just considered, and it would relegate Aristotle's political science to a less thoroughly practical status than he envisions for it. Moreover, Polansky is put in the position of having to explain why Aristotle might have "some good use" for tyranny, since on his reading, Aristotle is advising the statesman on how to actually preserve tyranny, rather than how to transform it. As resourceful as Polansky's arguments are on this point (342–43), they are ultimately unconvincing.

Aristotle offers advice on preserving the rule of tyrants, but this is not a sign that he would be pleased to see either a true statesman *attempt* to preserve tyranny, or a tyrant *succeed* in preserving tyrannical rule. His advice on preserving the rule of tyrants may indeed contribute to the "edification of the statesman," as Polansky says (342), but the audience it is ultimately intended for is probably at least equally the tyrants themselves and especially the extreme democrats of Athens. In an extreme democracy the *demôs* constitute a monarch whose rule may be no more lawful and enlightened than that of a tyrant, he says at *Pol.* IV.4 (1292a10–38), and most tyrannies arise out of such democracies, he says in V.10 (1310b11–17). Like his warning in V.9 (1309b18–10a2) that a democratic state may be destroyed by pushing democracy to an extreme, it is likely that his remarks on tyranny are addressed as much to the political class of the post-Periclean Athenian democracy as anyone—to the Cleons and Hyperboluses, whose methods and policies had evidently alienated a significant portion of the upper class—and were intended to warn them of the potential for degeneracy and the need to moderate democracy, above all through the observance of law and the inclusion of "both rich and poor" in the government (1309b39–40), if it is to be preserved.[14]

In sum, then, there are difficulties in the existing interpretations of *Politics* V which can be avoided if we accept the notion that there is a continuity of ethical purpose that runs through the whole work, and see Aristotle as attempting to provide the student of political science with an argument for reforms, including the institution of some arrangements regarding education, which will enlist the motives of leaders who can only be counted on to promote their own interests. Aristotle clearly is concerned with the reform of "perverted" forms of rule in Book V and speaks directly of the importance of finding a way to easily, in the face of "existing circumstances," persuade the leaders of such regimes, so there are reasonable grounds for supposing that he takes himself to have developed an argument which will engage the existing motives of those leaders. The obvious candidate, as we have seen, is an appeal to their interest in staying in power.[15]

There are also grounds for concluding that the importance which the empirical study of constitutions came to have in Aristotle's political thought was due, at least in part, to his desire to develop an argument of this kind to its full potential. He was undoubtedly familiar with the argument of *Laws* III (683b–702a; discussed in §2.41) that Sparta outlasted Argos and Messene because rule by force is inconsistent with the preservation of a city, and he would have seen the value in developing a more robust empirical basis for an argument of this kind. A massive comparative study of constitutions focused on the factors that "preserve and destroy states [in general], and what sorts [of factors] preserve and destroy the particular kinds of constitution" (*NE* X.9 1181b16–19), would be most useful in this regard. The view of von Fritz and Kapp is that it was only after Aristotle became preoccupied with "the question of what means can or may be used to bring a state, even if it were only by a little, nearer" to the best that is possible for it to be, that the historical study of constitutions acquired particular significance for him (von Fritz and Kapp 1977, 128). If this is right, then the empirical turn in Aristotle's political thought was a natural outgrowth of his enduring ethical concerns, motivated by the desire to identify for each form of constitution a set of ethically progressive reforms which would be both feasible and attractive to the regime in power. If necessity is the mother of invention, then Aristotelian political science was born of the weightiest barriers to political reform: the absence of not only knowledge, but desire.

The upshot of all of this for our understanding of *Pol.* VIII.1 should be clear, given our previous formulations of Aristotle's *appeal to a desire for stable rule*, as I have called it. Education "relative to the regime" is called for in order to promote constitutional stability, but in the context of Aristotle's reformist program, the education which will be appropriate to a regime is that which, together with the other stabilizing reforms which will precede it, will produce in a state the best constitution attainable in the circumstances. In the language of *Pol.* VIII.1, this education will produce "better character" not merely relative to the constitution which precedes these reforms, but absolutely; and that better character will in turn produce a constitution that is "better" not merely relative to its kind, but absolutely. Construed as an appeal to a leader's desire for stable rule, it appeals to a leader's perceived self-interest, but it may also be construed as an appeal to stability as a virtue of constitutions which may be desirable on other grounds, as we shall see in the section that follows.

While this would be a very complicated argument to fully and properly assess, it is important to observe that it is grounded in the assertion of a close relationship between justice and political stability, which Aristotle apparently had systematic and weighty empirical evidence for. The prospects for retaining power through repression are undoubtedly greater in the modern era than they were in Aristotle's time, and to that extent the empirical basis of the argument will have been undermined. Nevertheless, as regards those modern societies in which recourse to such repression is not contemplated or possible, it is likely that education which promotes justice and broader participation in political life would be a stabilizing force in those societies in which extraconstitutional conflict was already being redressed through the kinds of equalizing, or nearly equalizing, reforms that Aristotle calls for.

4.3 ARGUMENTS FROM CONSTITUTIONAL QUALITY

We need to return now to Aristotle's *argument from constitutional requirements (CR)* and attempt to identify the various aspects of constitutional quality that he may consider education important to. As we saw in the preceding section, education that is suitable to a constitution and tends to preserve its stability is not education that will enable it to exhibit most fully its characteristic form, but education which *improves* it by contributing to its absolute quality or conformity with natural justice. Given this and the principles underlying Aristotle's ranking of constitutions, there is every reason to conclude that when he says "in all cases better character produces a better constitution," he means "better" absolutely, not relative to constitutions as they are. The education which establishes, preserves, and improves the quality of a constitution is thus education which promotes the well-being of city and citizens alike by promoting human virtue itself, and not merely the citizen virtues demanded by a constitution as it stands. This is as it should be, given what we observed in §3.5 of the aims of the education described in the pages following the arguments of VIII.1, namely, what is necessary in the way of practical arts, virtue, and the capacity to engage in intellectual activity, which is to say the highest virtue possible. The education that is called for by *CR* is thus highly progressive, and I will try to show in what follows that it is intended to be progressive with respect to both the social and institutional aspects of a constitution.

The results of our discussion up to this point suggest that the education suitable to a constitution will improve it institutionally in two ways: by improving the stability of the city's political system or government, and by making its rule more just, wise, and equitably distributed among the citizens. Similarly, Aristotle's remarks about the causes and prevention of *stasis* and revolution in democracies, oligarchies, and tyrannies suggested that the education suitable to a constitution will promote equality and social unity. In what follows, we shall see that equality is to be promoted especially with regard to virtue and wealth. The former is essential to a city's fulfilling its natural end, and succeeding in this as a community or partnership, but so too is the latter, since it pertains to the "external goods enough for the performance of good actions" (*Pol.* VII.1 1323b40–24a1), which are essential to lives of virtue. To promote equality or relative equality in wealth is to promote a "middle" constitution, one dominated by a middle class, which is the social counterpart of an institutionally "mixed" constitution, which provides roles in governance for citizens of each class. Aristotle's goal for political reform is to make a city as much as possible a polity, a city whose constitution is both "mixed" and "middle," so it is safe to infer that the moderation of wealth is an important aspect of education suitable to improving a constitution. Unity is also an important measure or aspect of constitutional health for Aristotle, just as for Plato, so in what follows I will regard moderation in wealth and social unity as the two goals of education intended to improve the social aspect of a constitution.[16]

To the extent that all education in deviant regimes is properly directed toward these four aspects of constitutional quality necessary to becoming as much as possible a polity, the education suitable to all deviant regimes is the same, and escapes any suspicion of violating the requirements of natural justice. If oligarchic and democratic education are similarly progressive and alike in these four respects, however, they are not alike in all respects. Aristotle would not speak in VIII.1 of a democratic ethos and an oligarchic ethos unless they were in some respects different, and the obvious reason why they would be, despite his reformist agenda, is that he regards the capacity of cities to transform themselves into polities or aristocracies as *limited*. Cities can only improve themselves by degrees, and only by so much even in the long run, given the nature of their populations and circumstances. Although it would be better for the citizens of such imperfect cities to live in better cities and possess a correspondingly higher form of virtue, it is nevertheless better for them to live in stable, imperfect cities, and possess the less perfect virtue which that enables them to possess, than in a state of war or no city at all. There is thus some justice in preserving such cities, and because Aristotle regards education, not law, as the fundamental means by which any constitution exists at all, this means that education cannot be *wholly* progressive, but must also maintain the currently feasible best ethos that a city has achieved, and establish in citizens from their youth onward the citizen virtue consonant with it, if also reaching beyond it.

The upshot of this is that our list of four progressive ways in which suitable education improves the quality of a constitution is incomplete. We must add that education must be suitable to a constitution in the sense of promoting voluntary acceptance and habitual compliance with its laws and customs, a task distinguishable from promoting virtue *per se* to the extent that the laws fail to embody divine reason, but contributing to it to the extent that they do. The constitutional good that is thereby promoted is good order *(eunomia),* or order that is at least better than the chaos which exists beyond the reach of any law at all.

As I have just said, order is not a product of law itself, according to Aristotle, but a product of training and instruction, as one can see in his remark in *Pol.* V.9 that "the most beneficial laws, even when ratified by all who are engaged in politics, are of no use if the people are not habituated and educated in accord with the constitution" (1310a15–17). The issue in this passage, which is part of the longer one we examined at the start of §4.2, is apparently compliance with laws in general or the acquisition of virtue, and the implication is that although the possession of reasons for ratifying laws may carry weight with those who are involved in ratifying them, that will not suffice to insure universal compliance or the acquisition of virtue in most cities. The democracies and oligarchies which are referred to immediately following this passage will have citizens who are politically disenfranchised, citizens who do not grasp the reasons for the laws being as they are, and citizens who may grasp the reasons but lack virtue and the capacity to heed those reasons. All cities will have laws ratified in the past, before those who are currently adults reached maturity and could participate in ratifying laws. Thus all cities, to some degree or another, must rely on education beyond what is intrinsic to participation in lawmaking itself, in order to secure voluntary and habitual compliance with the laws, and all must provide education preparatory to that participation in order for the reasoning involved in ratification to produce a rational response.

In this sense, to be educated in the spirit of a constitution is to be prepared through training and education to live in voluntary compliance with both the letter and spirit of its laws; in modern terms, this means not just the laws belonging to what we would call "constitutional law," but the laws generally, both written and unwritten, to the extent that a well-ordered city depends upon cooperation with not only written laws but also customs and codes of civility in small matters. Aristotle implies that *none* of the laws are of any use without education in the spirit of the constitution, and we can understand this in light of his remark at *Pol.* III.1 1274b39 that a *politeia*, a constitution, is an arrangement *(taxis)* of the inhabitants of a polis, or a "way of life" *(bios)* (IV.2 1295a40–b1, VII.8 1328b1– 2). A government, or *aition politeia*, is the source *(aitia)* of that arrangement, according to Aristotle, and is itself based on the guiding or controlling principle *(aitia)* from which that arrangement arises. Thus, we may speak of a constitutional *ethos* in the sense of habits *(ethê)* of lawful and civic-minded conduct that are essential to the full realization of the social order or "arrangement" that constitutes the *politeia*.[17] In modern English it is most natural to refer to this "arrangement" as the "order" created in society by its various laws, customs, and standards, since we restrict the signification of "constitution" to the controlling principles or even, in the American tradition though not in the English, to the document in which those principles are declared. Aristotle says in *Pol.* IV.4 that "where the laws have no authority there is no constitution" (1292a32–33), and he evidently means by this that where there is no compliance with law there is no social order or coherent way of life.

All told, then, Aristotle would seem to hold that education is important to securing a number of constitutional goods which contribute in turn to a city's capacity to promote the best life for its citizens: good order; stability; moderation or relative equality in wealth; just, wise, and equitably distributed governance; and unity or social harmony. Let us examine these in this order in the subsections that follow.

4.31 *Nomos, Eunomia,* and *Eudaimonia*

Aristotle's conception of what is good about a society being well ordered rests with his view that man is the "most savage of animals" without the order created by law. "A social instinct is implanted in all men by nature," he says:

> and yet he who first founded the state was the greatest of benefactors. For man, when perfected, is the best of animals, but, when separated from law and justice, he is the worst of all; . . . without virtue, he is the most unholy and the most savage of animals, and the most full of lust and gluttony. But justice is the bond of men in states; for the administration of justice, which is the determination of what is just, is the principle of order in political society (*Pol.* I.2 1253a30–39).

Aristotle insists here, as he does in the passage from *NE* X.9 discussed in §3.4, that people will not become virtuous unless they live under law and justice, and without virtue are "unholy" and, by implication, very far from being happy. He suggests here, and elsewhere, that law (i.e., true law that embodies reason) prescribes virtue and does so with an educational intent. In *NE* V.2, for instance, he says that "the things that tend to produce virtue taken as a whole are those of the acts prescribed by the law which have been prescribed with a view to education for the common good" (1130b25–27).

Speaking to the relationship of virtue to happiness first, we may note that virtue is essential to *eudaimonia* internally, but also externally through the importance to *eudaimonia* of leisure and external goods, including friendship, which can only arise through forms of social organization which depend in turn upon virtue. As we have seen, Aristotle regards virtue as an internal requirement for *eudaimonia* in the sense that happy lives *consist* of virtuous activity, but also in at least two other senses. First, a happy life is one arranged with the exercise of *sophia* or political *phronêsis* as its highest end, and the arranging which this involves requires the exercise of good judgment or *phronêsis*. Other ends must be examined for their compatibility with the highest end, and pursued in a way that facilitates and does not undermine its pursuit. Good judgment is thus *instrumentally* essential to any efficient or effective pursuit of *sophia* or political *phronêsis* as one's highest end, and the possession and exercise of *phronêsis* is itself impossible without virtue, given the unity of virtue thesis we have already noted.[18]

Second, Aristotle seems to hold something like the Platonic view that *eudaimonia* (literally, having a good, *eu*, god, *daimon*, within) involves a kind of psychic peace resting in virtue or a share of divinity, for he remarks in *Pol.* VII.1 that

> no one would maintain that he is happy who has not in him a particle of courage or temperance or justice or practical wisdom, who is afraid of every insect which flutters past him, and will commit any crime, however great, in order to gratify his lust for meat or drink (1323a27–31).

No explanation is given here, but the images in this passage together suggest that without virtue a person is subject to psychic disturbances of various kinds arising from the dominance of unbounded fears and bodily desires.

Virtue is also related to the best or happiest life through the external goods which depend upon the moral virtues. Friendship is one of these goods, as we have already said, and there are others which depend equally but less directly upon virtue, insofar as they arise from a city's good and productive order, which can only exist if its citizens are virtuous. The virtues exercised in relation to others are traits which are essential to maintaining a self-sufficient system of roles and occupations through which anyone can have a reasonable expectation of having a good life, for, as we have seen, there is nothing smaller than a polis that is sufficient for the purposes of living a good life, according to Aristotle, and a polis cannot exist without its inhabitants fulfilling their various roles well. The external goods required for a happy life and supplied by a good city include most notably the leisure necessary to cultivating and exercising virtue (*Pol.* II.9 1269a34–36, II.11 1273a32–35, VII.9 1328b39–29a2).

As for the relationship between law and the virtue necessary to these various goods, the view that is evident in this and other passages, such as *NE* II.1 1103b3–

6 and X.9 1179b31–80a5 (which we noted in §3.4), is that people do not become virtuous *spontaneously*, but only through habituation and training, which can only be uniformly effective within a framework of good law. Aristotle's view, as we have seen, is that people do not acquire true moral beliefs either spontaneously or simply by being spoken or lectured to, since their beliefs will follow and conform to what they are pleased and pained by, and what they are pleased and pained by is usually not very advantageous to virtue and must be shaped in the right direction through habituation and training. This training, even though it will rely fundamentally on instruction, exhortation, and musical training to nonviolently shape the desires in a favorable direction, will require a background or element of compulsion if it is to succeed in overcoming the stronger recalcitrant passions and tastes which some may have, and direct those who still require training toward respect for reason and the development of better habits and tastes. And it is only law or the authority of the state itself that has such compulsive power to a sufficient degree, and only law in its impartiality that is not resented when it opposes people's impulses (*NE* X.9 1180a19–24). It is also only the law, true law, that can produce consistent and systematic virtue, inasmuch as "law is reason unaffected by desire," while the rule of even the best man is corrupted by desire (*Pol.* III.16 1287a30–33). Rule that does not uniformly communicate the substance of divine reason would fail to uniformly and fully promote virtue, though as we have noted it would still be better to live under such law than live in the absence of law.

Living under good law *(eunomos)* is a condition for human flourishing or happiness, then, since it is essential to the development of virtue, and virtue is essential to happiness. The order arising from good law *(eunomia)* is consequently a good or excellence of a state without which a state cannot perform its natural function of promoting human flourishing, but it is also a good that can only come about through education. So if one cares about what is good for human beings, or cares about good order as an aspect of constitutional quality on which that good depends, then this argument provides one with reason to also care about education and regard it as important.

This is a quite compelling argument, for we can scarcely doubt the importance or necessity of education to prepare children for a life in conformity with the civilizing norms of public life, even if we may doubt the justice of many of the norms of actual societies. It is, in fact, not unlike the Hobbesian appeal to a state of nature, to the extent that both suggest the awfulness of life without good order. For while Aristotle does argue from a conception of the best life, he also argues from the claim that we are "the worst of animals" without good law, much as Hobbes argues that in a "state of nature" (i.e., beyond the rule of law) life is unacceptably awful.

4.32 Stability and the Authority of Law

Turning now to what I shall call the *argument from constitutional stability (CS)*, it is clear that stability is an important aspect of constitutional health, according to Aristotle no less than according to Plato.[19] To see why it is also an aspect of constitutional health or a quality that is important to human well-being, we need only note Aristotle's remarks in *Pol.* II.8 regarding the nature of the law's power to command obedience. "The habit of lightly changing the laws is an evil," he says,

> and, when the advantage is small, some errors both of lawgivers and rulers had better be left; the citizen will not gain so much by making the change as he will lose by the habit of disobedience. . . . For the law has no power to command obedience except that of habit, which can only be given by time, so that a readiness to change from old to new laws enfeebles the power of the law (1269a14–23).

As we have seen, Aristotle regards stability as an important aspect of constitutional health, and argues that progress toward a more just constitution is essential to the longevity or stability of deficient regimes, but he adds here the important qualification that stability in the sense of the laws not changing too massively or rapidly is essential to securing the benefits of good law. It is essential, he says, because the development of habits of compliance takes time; the work of training and instruction necessary to creating the good order which instantiates a code of law takes time. His thinking here is obviously that if the code changes too quickly, there simply will not be enough time for the educative processes to keep up, and the ability of the law to command respect will be undermined. Thus, neither the disruption involved in revolution nor that involved in rapid changes in the laws under the aegis and direction of a continuing and progressive regime is desirable, for in either case an important constitutional good and the advantages of good order for the city's population are compromised or destroyed.

There is an air of paradox about all of this, however. We have just seen that Aristotle holds that education in virtue requires the compulsive force of the law, yet we are now told that the law *has no* compulsive power apart from the force of custom or habits established over time through training and practice. What compelling power could the law have then over a youth whose education has not advanced very far yet? The answer, I would suggest, is that the law does have its special forms of compulsion which can effectively supplement the authority of parents and teachers, and the natural bonds of affection alluded to in *NE* X.9, but these forms of compulsion are themselves dependent upon a high level of habitual, uncoerced conformity, if the whole system is to escape collapse. Such collapse may occur not only through the overwhelming numbers of cases which the mechanisms of surveillance and "correction" might face if noncoerced compliance breaks down, but also in part through those mechanisms falling into disarray, as they are apt to do when the public at large weakens in its resolve to preserve the norms of public life through those sanctions that are available to it. We could take Aristotle's first point, then, to be that compliance cannot on the whole be coerced, but instead can only be ensured through instruction and habituation over time, and his second point to be that, although we can succeed with the aid of law in initiating the young into the operative norms of a common life, we would lack any adequate response to the collapse of those norms that would result if the habitual respect for the laws under which the inhabitants of the polis were prepared to live should fail to transfer to a new set of laws.

In a world which was generally without police forces and (apart from Sparta) standing armies which could be used for domestic control,[20] this was probably a reasonably accurate assessment of the law's power to command obedience, except that it takes no explicit notice of the role of a collective sense that the political system and its laws are on the whole and in the long run collectively advantageous. In the absence of such a conviction it is unlikely that a habit of obedience would be sufficient, but neither would this conviction alone suffice, since it does not in itself provide any disincentive to free-riding. As we have seen, Aristotle does acknowledge repeatedly this second constitutive aspect of the law's authority, and because he does there can be no grounds for suggesting, as some may be tempted to, that he is advocating the use of education as an instrument of repressive social control. In his account of constitutional legitimacy, he provides in principle for the foundations of a *rational* conviction in the collective advantage of life in a polis, and in his account of the causes of factional conflict, sedition, and revolution he identifies the sense of injustice arising from the domination of one class by another as the most important general cause of conflict and constitutional instability.[21]

This principled commitment to policies of mutual advantage and pursuit of the common good was limited, however, by Aristotle's proscription of wars of conquest (at *Pol.* VII.14 1333b29–34a2), for in resisting expansionism the statesman would have faced his task without the one tool that we know was effective in the ancient world in securing stability through the prospect of collective advantage. Few polises of the classical period managed to escape a "bloody oscillation between oligarchy and democracy, or between one oligarchic faction and another," writes Moses Finley:

> The main variable was the extent of stabilization; that is what requires explanation, and I find it in the fact that the successful conquest-states, Sparta, Athens, Rome, were also the stable ones . . . (Finley 1983, 106).

In a world that was "always on the edge of disaster in the countryside and of food shortages in the cities" (197), the focus of political conflict involving the poor was debt bondage and "land hunger," and this conflict seems to have been mitigated only rarely and through conquest. "In Athens during the imperial period perhaps ten thousand citizens—8 or 10 percent of the whole citizen body—were settled in cleruchies or were assigned arbitrary and substantial 'rents' from estates retained and worked by the conquered population," writes Finley (1983, 111).

That the Athenian aristocracy resisted redistributive solutions to this conflict is not surprising, but conquest had a price of its own, which might help to explain the opposition to *it* expressed by aristocratic moralists. Athenian expansionism was built on a large naval force drawn predominantly from the *dêmos*, and this "increased their contribution to the well-being of Athens" in such a way, writes Adkins, that

> the *agathos* must have felt that the claims of his *aretê* were being infringed—it was he, not the *dêmos*, who should perform such services for the city, since doing so was in the last resort the justification for his being termed *agathos* (Adkins 1967, 315).

Adkins links this to Plato's unkind words for seaborne soldiers in the *Laws* (IV 707a4 ff.), and to his sharp distinction between the craftsman and warrior classes, and related praise for moderation *(sôphrosunê)* and minding one's own business *(apragmosune* and *ta hautou prattein),* in the *Republic* (II 374b ff.):

> *Polupragmosune,* or "busybodiness" is manifested in a *polis* by transgressing the bounds of the traditional system based on *moira*—the system which gave to each his share in society and politics, a larger share to the *agathos*, a smaller share to the *kakos*—and upsetting the status quo (Adkins 1967, 325).

It is hard to resist the conclusion, then, that the class interests of the *agathoi* did play a role in the opposition which Plato expressed toward expansionist foreign policies. We may suspect Aristotle of this too, given his remark in *Pol.* VII.6 that "there is no necessity that the sailors should be citizens" (1327b8–9), but motivations notwithstanding it is hard to fault an opposition to military expansionism on moral grounds. Plato and Aristotle did both call for the enactment of laws which would eliminate or sharply reduce the inequality in landholdings among citizens *(Pol.* II.6 and 7, II.9 1270a15–b7, VII.5 1326b26–37), though Aristotle adds that in order to prevent poverty it is "even more necessary to limit population" (II.6 1265b5–7). He also insists that since "men always want more and more without end" (II.7 1267b2–3), "it is not the possessions but the desires of mankind which require to be equalized, and this is impossible, unless a sufficient education is provided by the laws" (II.7 1266b30–32). What is necessary, in his view, is not that strict equality be established, but rather that all citizens "should have so much property as will enable [them] to live not only temperately but liberally" (II.6 1265a32–34), and that they should choose for themselves a better kind of life than one devoted to endlessly accumulating the sorts of goods that cannot be possessed without denying them to someone else.[22] Whatever shortcomings this view may have, it cannot be accused of ignoring the importance of a well-founded collective belief in the utility of the political system and its laws to a willingness to obey the laws. And while Aristotle does not regard these considerations as making it important for everyone to be educated, he does take them to provide grounds for teaching those who may be active in public life to avoid a life devoted to the competitive, and therefore potentially destabilizing, pursuit of *not only property but honor,* the danger in the latter instance arising not from the envy or anger of the poor, but from instability within the political class itself (II.7 1266b37–67a2, 1267b4–8, V.1 1302a10–11).

The danger of lawlessness arising from massive or overly frequent changes in the laws may be exaggerated, of course, but this is no easy matter to assess, and it is perhaps not unreasonable to close off this phase of the argument by suggesting that Aristotle makes here a reasonable, if not completely convincing, case for the importance to the quality of a constitution and to human well-being of education which will promote a stable orderliness in society. As we saw early in §4.2, the education which Aristotle believes can do this will aim to inculcate not only the spirit of the laws, but also the virtues of justice and self-restraint, and will promote equality, mutual trust, and friendly feelings among the citizens.

4.33 Moderation in Wealth

Moderation in wealth, which is to say a social order in which all the citizens or as many as possible possess wealth in moderation and are content with that, was a constitutional good of great importance to Aristotle. First, as we have just seen, it was related to stability in the size of a polis, another measure of constitutional— no less than biological—health, through the fact that military expansionism was the primary means to economic expansion in a world in which land was the salient unit of production. If constitutional health is incompatible with growing endlessly, and unlimited desires can only be satisfied by annexing land without limit, then the training and limiting of desire by education is essential to constitutional health. Moreover, it is also essential to international justice, to the extent that expansion can only be achieved through force. Beyond this, moderation in wealth is important to the city being a partnership in pursuit of the best life because it is: (1) required for mutual advantage and the exercise of virtue; (2) a condition for alternately ruling and being ruled in the manner of citizens; and (3) a condition for relative equality, and thus for friendship. Our concern in this subsection will be with the first of these points, with the bearing education has for moderation in wealth on a constitution's capacity to promote mutual advantage and the virtue that is inseparable from it. The second and third points, bearing on governance and friendship, will be addressed more briefly in what follows.

The acquisition of wealth is first addressed in Book I of the *Politics* in connection with the art of household management. There is a natural limit to the accumulation of wealth, says Aristotle, and pursuing more than what is necessary is not a proper pursuit of households (I.9 1257b31–33). In making this point, he adopts the Platonic distinction between necessary desires and unnecessary desires for wealth and pleasures, and follows Plato in holding that it is better and more conducive to the best kind of life to avoid pursuing the unnecessary ones. He also relies on the idea that some purposes for wealth are more in accordance with nature than others, and that there are associated natural or proper limits on the acquisition of wealth.

This theme is developed further in II.7, where it becomes clear that Aristotle regards too much wealth as just as much a problem as too little. He considers at length Plato's proposals in the *Republic* regarding the holding of property in common, but there are also important passages in *Pol.* II.6 and II.7 where he reviews proposals for egalitarian private holding of property. The thrust of his critique of these proposals is that while justice does not require *full* equalization of property holdings, it does require legislative action to ensure that everyone has property in moderation:

> . . . where there is equality of property, the amount may be either too large or too small, and the possessor may be living either in luxury *(truphan)* or penury. Clearly, then, the legislator ought not only to aim at the equalization of properties, but at moderation in their amount. Further, . . . it is not the possessions but the desires of mankind which require to be equalized, and this is impossible unless a sufficient education is provided by the laws (1266b24–32).

Aristotle goes on to say that it is not even enough for this education to be equal, for "there is no use in having one and the same for all, if it is of a sort that predisposes men to avarice, or ambition, or both" (35–37). The references to avarice and living luxuriously signify a range of problems arising from excessive desire for bodily pleasures. Luxuriousness *(trumphêros)* is a quality closely associated with softness or lack of endurance, effeminacy, and voluptuousness, in the work of both Plato and Aristotle. It is thus quite opposed to the manly virtues, most obviously to courage *(andreia)* and *sôphrosunê* (moderation or self-restraint), and a debilitating distraction from more admirable and fulfilling pursuits. Avarice or the desire for a larger share of wealth is associated with the lack of discipline this implies, and is regarded by Plato and Aristotle alike as tending to engender desires that are not just unnecessary but unlawful *(paranomoi)*.[23] This is evident in the discussion of the causes of crime which follows in 1267a, where Aristotle says that "the greatest crimes are caused by excess and not by necessity" (1267a13–14), by desires "going beyond the necessities of life, which [prey] upon" their possessors (1267a7), and not by need.

The matter of property holdings is taken up again in Book VII, where Aristotle describes how property is to be partitioned in the best city. He says there that the land is to be divided into public and private parts, "while of the private land, part should be near the border, and the other near the city, so that each citizen having two lots, they may all of them have land in two places; there is justice and fairness in such a division . . ." (1330a14–16). Fred Miller cites this passage (Miller 1995, 326) as evidence of the claim that Aristotle has a conception of distributive justice applicable to distributions of property, and that seems right. What is just according to Aristotle is what makes people better and enables them to live the best life, and the point here is to ensure that everyone has property holdings conducive to virtue, neither too much nor too little. In a city designed from the ground up this can be arranged from the beginning, but in existing cities in which there are rich and poor, the one having more than necessary and the other less, Aristotle counsels constitutional reforms which would tend to equalize wealth. He is clearly opposed to the unconstitutional seizure and redistribution of property which takes place or is threatened in democracies (VI.5 1320a4–6), but this does not preclude laws which will discourage or prevent further concentration of wealth (I.10 1258b1–8, II.9 1270a15–29), nor the use of public revenues to offset poverty which threatens the character of the constitution.

Speaking of democracies, Aristotle says that

> measures . . . should be taken which will give them [the people] lasting prosperity; and as this is in the interest of all classes, the proceeds of the public revenues should be accumulated and distributed among its poor, if possible, in such quantities as may enable them to purchase a little farm, or, at any rate, make a beginning in trade or farming. And if this benevolence cannot be extended to all, money should be distributed in turn according to tribes or other divisions, and in the meantime the rich should pay the fee for the attendance of the poor at the necessary assemblies (VI.5 1320a35–b3).

The fee referred to is one which would compensate the poor for lost work time to enable them to participate fully in the political life of the polis, and in addition to this Aristotle suggests that "a generous and sensible nobility" would "divide the poor amongst them, and give them the means of going to work," perhaps by "sharing the use of their own property" (1320b7–11). He holds more strongly in Book VII that although a common holding of property introduces problems of its own and should be avoided, property should be used in common "by friendly consent" so that "no citizen should be in want of subsistence" (10 1330a1–3), and in Book II that it is "the special business of the legislator . . . to create in men [the] benevolent disposition" this common use requires (5 1263a38–39).

Aristotle's conception of education for moderation in wealth thus includes not only training to moderate the desire for wealth and the pleasures it can buy, but also the nurturing of benevolence. He regards moderation in property holdings and moderation in the desire for property as making for a better constitution, a constitution dominated by a middle class or citizens of moderate wealth, and he regards the latter type of moderation, and even to some extent the former, as a product of education. The education in question would consist above all of a training of the desires, an eradication as nearly as possible of pleonectic desire for material wealth, and an effort to cultivate the most truly satisfying and satisfiable desire, that for the pleasures of contemplation (II.7 1267a11–13). Insofar as this argument is predicated on the assumption that a healthy city and its economy do not grow, it will seem peculiarly wrongheaded or irrelevant from the vantage point of a modern economy predicated on growth and material consumption without end. Insofar as it rests in a moral psychology which regards the fulfillment of material desires beyond necessity as antagonistic to the cultivation of desires for higher things it is overstated. But to the extent that it rests in the premise that human well-being and the exercise of virtue are promoted by the possession of moderate wealth and contentment in that possession, it is not a bad argument. Let us see now how it is strengthened by Aristotle's accounts of the contributions of a middle constitution to political life and civic unity.

4.34 Education for Good Government

Aristotle says in VII.13 that "a city can be excellent only when the citizens who have a share in the government are excellent, and in our state all the citizens share in the government" (1332a33–35; cf. 1294a1–2). He says of this best possible city but also the second best, or best generally attainable, city—a polity, whose constitution is institutionally "mixed"—that "all the citizens alike should take their turn of governing and being governed" (VII.14 1332b25–27) and that this requires not only a capacity and inclination to rule well, but the capacity and inclination to accept being ruled in the manner of a citizen and not a slave (IV.11 1295b14–23). These passages evidently refer to virtue as it is exercised in the conduct of political affairs, or excellence in legislation, the conduct of trials, and other aspects of public administration. This would presumably include above all the good judgment needed to perform well in various administrative offices, on juries, and in the legislative assembly, but also possibly the ability to keep accounts, the ability to speak publicly, and other lesser virtues. The education described in Book VIII is designed to promote good judgment and what is necessary in the way of practical arts,[24] and to the extent that some offices and positions of leadership require a higher learning and skill in public speaking, Aristotle's own *Politics*, *Nicomachean Ethics*, and *Rhetoric* are intended, as we have seen, as a fitting alternative to the offerings of the Sophists, and perhaps even more the school of Isocrates.

If the participation of all citizens in the political affairs of the state through either a mixed or aristocratic system is a constitutional good, as Aristotle contends, and is better for the city to the extent that their participation contributes to just and wise administration of the common good, then the education necessary to these qualities of participation is a matter of great importance, unless there is no reason to think that education can contribute to them. Moreover, since affairs of government, including the conduct of its courts, are also a "school of citizenship" of sorts (*Ap.* 34–35; *Prot.* 326d–e; *Tht.* 172c–73b; *Pol.* I.2 1253a36–40; Miller (1995, 56–59), in which youths who have come of age are instructed and habituated in the ways of public life and the meaning of justice, the education which contributes to the quality of public administration also contributes indirectly to the habituation of political virtue.[25]

These are the obvious ways in which Aristotle thinks that education can contribute to the quality of governance, but there is a passage in *Politics* IV.11, concerning distributions of property, that may be regarded as a more oblique point about the significance of education for the quality of political life. Aristotle's concern there is that a city should arrange for its citizens "to possess the gifts of fortune in moderation," since "in that condition of life men are most ready to follow rational principle" (1295b1–6). What follows bears quoting at length:

> those who have too much of the goods of fortune, strength, wealth, friends, and the like, are neither willing nor able to submit to authority. The evil begins at home; for when they are boys, by reason of the luxury in which they are brought up, they never learn, even at school, the habit of obedience. On the other hand, the very poor, who are in the opposite extreme, are too degraded. So that the one class cannot obey, and can only rule despotically; the other knows not how to command and must be ruled like slaves. Thus arises a city, not of freemen, but of masters and slaves, the one despising, the other envying; and nothing can be more fatal to friendship and good fellowship in cities than this . . . (1295b14–24).

We have already seen that Aristotle regards moderation in wealth as a constitutional good which contributes to political stability and to a polis's natural aim of promoting the best life and the virtue that requires, and here we see him add that great inequalities of wealth not only generate envy and throw up obstacles to virtue, but make it impossible for citizens to rule and be ruled as justice demands. The rich are incapable of obeying because they lack self-restraint, and the poor are so degraded by poverty that they can neither command nor obey in accordance with reason, which is to say voluntarily when there is reason to. Aristotle may assume here that the great gulf of economic power and social class that lies between them will also make it seem inevitable that the rich alone will rule, but whether or not this is the case, he implies that these differences will be insuperable obstacles to a mixed regime of shared rule, which requires mutual trust and a perception of shared interests. To the extent that both classes do have a share in power, how will they be able to regard themselves as acting pursuant to a common good, and if they cannot how will they act from a conception of shared justice and the impartiality of law?

These remarks make it clear that Aristotle does not expect a schooling in virtue to be efficacious in making people reasonable when they rule, nor reasonable in their obedience and resistance to rule, unless other important conditions, such as moderation in wealth, are present. Of course, he does believe that an equalizing effect on a population can result from the right kind of schooling, namely a schooling not just in political virtue, but in moderation with respect to wealth, and perhaps even more importantly a schooling *together*. To the extent that Aristotle understands public education to be a common education, in the sense of an education which all will receive together, and understands it to be equalizing, we can infer from the position he takes in this passage that he would expect public education to promote a capacity to both rule and accept rule with greater justice. It is a powerful argument that is hinted at here, for it is not at all implausible to think that in order for adults to exercise their collective wisdom in a way that effectively promotes the common good, they require a foundation of previous experience in mutual trust, common action, and common benefit arising from that action.

To conclude, then, Aristotle does not offer specific grounds for believing, of each of the political virtues arising under each form of constitution, that it can only arise, or that it can be better cultivated, through education rather than through spontaneous practice. Nevertheless, it is probably true of most forms of government that it would be profitable to promote at least some political virtues through education. The thrust of this piece of Aristotle's advice to the legislator, then, is that some effort should be made to identify these and provide education that is appropriate to them.

I will conclude this examination of Aristotle's arguments for the importance of education by taking brief notice of one last sense in which he suggests education may improve the quality of a constitution.

4.35 The Argument from Constitutional Unity

Aristotle says in *Politics* II.5 that the state "is a plurality, which should be united and made into a community by education" (1263b37–38), and although no such remark appears explicitly in VIII.1, the idea is an important one in the *Politics* as a whole and closely related to the avoidance of faction and factional conflict or *stasis* (*NE* VIII.1 1155a21–26). In III.9 the idea is developed at some length in the context of arguing that the oligarchic and democratic conceptions of justice or entitlement to share in rule are deficient because they rest on conceptions of equality or entitlement to rule which have no claim to authority beyond the preference of those who hold power. His argument there for an authoritative principle of entitlement to rule begins with the claim that the polis exists by nature and has a natural aim, and it culminates in the view that it is in proportion to citizens' contributions to the common end of living happily and admirably (i.e., in proportion to their possession and exercise of virtue) that they should share in rule:

> a polis exists for the sake of a good life, and not for the sake of life only: ... [hence[26]] virtue must be the care of a polis which is truly so called, and not merely enjoys the name: for without this end the community becomes a mere alliance which differs only in place from alliances of which the members live apart; and law is only a convention, "a surety to one another of justice," as the sophist Lycophron says, and has no real power to make the citizens good and just. . . .
>
> . . . It is clear then that a polis is not a mere society, having a common place, established for the prevention of mutual crime and for the sake of exchange. These are conditions without which a polis cannot exist; but all of them together do not constitute a polis, which is a partnership of households and of [extended] families [or clans] *(koinônia kai tais oikiais kai tois genesi)* in well-being, for the sake of a perfect and self-sufficing life. . . . But these are created by friendship *(philia)*, for to choose to live together is friendship. . . .

... Hence they who contribute most to such a society have a greater share in it.
.. (III.9 1280a32–81a5).

This passage, one of the richest and most striking in all of the *Politics*, encapsulates the theory of the nature of a polis elaborated in Book I, and situates within that framework the account of (prima facie) entitlement to share in rule deployed in Book III. It is the pursuit of virtue or the best life as a common end that makes a political association a true polis, and not a mere artifact of convention, we are told. From this natural end there arises a conception of justice which can claim the authority of nature in opposition to those espoused by democrats and oligarchs. What is just is what promotes the common good (*Pol.* III.6 1279a17–19, III.12 1282b16–18, III.13 1283b35–42, etc.) or cultivates and encourages the citizens' exercise of intellect and reason; and what promotes the common good and respects the reason in others in the matter of determining entitlement to rule is the assignment of shares in rule in proportion to the virtue or practical wisdom which each citizen will bring to the business of governing the polis. This is true both as a direct application of the *principle of fidelity to reason*, which demands that one respect the reasons and evidence that others may offer and rely on reason in moving them to agreement and action, and instrumentally, insofar as a polis can be more efficient in its pursuit of the common good to the extent that its structures of governance are designed to secure wise choices.

This implies an association which operates through cooperative acts of collective wisdom, exercised toward a common end, and so as Aristotle suggests here, it is also in the nature of a polis to be a community or partnership *(koinônia)* "of equals, aiming at the best life possible" (VII.8 1328a35–36; also I.1 1252a1–7, III.3 1276b1–2, etc.).

The polis is a form of association, then, in which persons are properly united in pursuit of a common purpose and by bonds of friendship (II.4 12627–10; *NE* VIII.1 1155a23–28). Aristotle regards friendship as "the greatest good of states *and* what best preserves them against revolutions" (II.4 1262b7–8; emphasis added; cf. *NE* 1169b9–10, *Pol.* V.11 1313a41–b6, 1314a12–29). The polis remains a plurality, inasmuch as a self-sufficient community requires the contributions of "different kinds of men" (II.2 1261a24), but it is held together by common purpose, friendship *(philia),* and the reciprocal goodwill *(to philein)* and consequent trust which friendship involves and engenders (*Rh.* II.4 1380b36–81a2; *NE* VIII.2 1155b31–34, VIII.1 1155a23–28, VIII.4 1157a21–25).

All of this rests on justice, for "a constitution is a partnership, and partnership rests on justice" or sharing in a system of law or an agreement (*EE* VII.9 1241b13–15; *NE* VIII.11 1161b5–8). Sharing in a system of law or legal justice makes political friendship possible, Aristotle seems to say, but in another sense the friendship present in a constitution is a function or product of the *degree* to which it is just:

Each of the constitutions may be seen to involve friendship just in so far as it involves justice. . . .

. . . Therefore while in tyrannies friendship and justice hardly exist, in democracies they exist more fully; for where the citizens are equal they have much in common (*NE* VIII.11 1161a10–b10).

What these and related passages suggest is that justice underlies friendship in two distinguishable ways, one apparently related to the idea that human beings are savage without law (*NE* VIII.11 1161b5–8) and one related to Aristotle's more expansive conception of justice as what is conducive to partnership in pursuit of the best kind of life. Justice in the former and narrower sense establishes ground rules of social conduct which demand certain minimal forms of mutual respect. To the extent that it succeeds in engendering such respect, it generates a rudimentary form of *philia* or friendship—the translation of *philia* as friendship is in this instance rather strained—which can exist even under deviant constitutions (*EE* VII.1 1234b24–31), but does not give rise to the friendship or unanimity required to unify a city in those circumstances. Justice in the broader sense, which entails rule aiming at the common good and distributed in accordance with virtue, and such things as common schools which educate the rich and poor together, is present in widely varying degrees in different cities and creates the conditions for politically unifying forms of friendship to the extent that it equalizes people, gives them things in common, and unites them in a common enterprise (*NE* VIII.11 1161a31–b10).

I will attempt to show that it is reasonable to conclude from these and related remarks about friendship and education that Aristotle holds that constitutional unity is a good associated with unanimity and the absence of faction, and that constitutional unity can and should be promoted through education by cultivating friendship and commitment to the common purpose of living happy lives. The *manner* in which he thinks this may be achieved is not yet clear, so the argument must be regarded as somewhat speculative until the suggested relationships between education, friendship, and the sharing of a common end are clarified. To clarify these relationships would, however, take us most of the way toward an analysis of Aristotle's first argument for education being public, his *argument from a common end* as I have called it, and so I will (somewhat arbitrarily) consign all further consideration of these matters to the section devoted to that argument, which follows in chapter 5.

5

Why Education Should Be Public and the Same for All

After laying the groundwork for an interpretation of *Pol.* VIII.1 in chapter 3, we examined in chapter 4 the first of two pairs of arguments which Aristotle presents there. Those arguments aim to establish that education is important enough to merit the legislator's attention, a conclusion which I described as a preliminary to the further conclusion that education should be provided through a public system. The second of Aristotle's two pairs of arguments in VIII.1 is devoted to establishing this latter conclusion, and it is these arguments that we shall turn our attention to now. I set them out in chapter 3 as follows:

The Argument from a Common End (CE)
   And since *(epei d en)* the whole city has one end, it is manifest that education should be one and the same for all, and its care *(epimeleian)* public *(koinên)* and not private *(idian)*—not as at present, when everyone looks after his own children privately, and gives them private instruction *(mathêsin idian)* of the sort which he thinks best. The training *(askêsin)* in things which are of common interest should be made common *(dei . . . koinên poieisthai)* (1337a21–27).

The Argument from Inseparability
   At the same time *(hama)*, one should not suppose that any of the citizens belongs to himself, but rather that each belongs to the polis, since *(gar)* each of them is a part of the polis *(hekastos tês poleôs)*, and it is natural for *(pephuken)* the care of each part to look to *(blepein pros)* the care of the whole (1337a27–31).

I shall examine the *argument from a common end (CE)* first, and shall consider it in relation to the *argument from constitutional unity (CU)*, which we left off with at the end of chapter 4, the argument that education is important because it is essential to unifying the state and making it into a community (*Pol.* II.5 1263b37–38).

5.1 THE ARGUMENT FROM A COMMON END

Aristotle's arguments for the importance of education are intimately connected with his arguments for its public sponsorship, and nowhere are these connections more obvious than in the case of his arguments from constitutional unity *(CU)* and a common end *(CE)*. The former may be considered the culminating argument for his first conclusion, and the latter his first argument for the second conclusion, but they are linked to each other by the fact that Aristotle takes constitutional unity to consist largely of the sharing of a common end. The most efficient way ahead now, in light of this, is to analyze these two arguments together by examining the cluster of ideas through which they are linked.

We began in the final section of chapter 4 with Aristotle's suggestion that education is the means, or primary means, through which the polis "should be united and made into a community," and we identified friendship, and the reciprocal goodwill and trust associated with it, as a fundamental basis of unity *(Pol. II.4 1262b5–10, III.9 1280b32–81a2; NE VIII.1 1155a23–28)*, alongside a shared commitment to the city's natural end, or *telos,* of living the best or happiest life *(Pol. III.3 1276b1–2, III.9 1280b7–10, VII.8 1328a35–36)*. Aristotle is not very explicit about the ways in which friendship and commitment to this common purpose may be promoted by education, unfortunately, and his commentators have done little to clarify what he does say, even though it goes to the heart of his concept of statesmanship,[1] but we concluded that it is evidently through promoting these two things that Aristotle believes education may promote unity. To continue with this now, it makes sense to begin with the one clear aspect of his conception of the means for promoting friendship and a commitment to the city's natural end, namely the central role which he assigns to the cultivation of virtue, both moral and intellectual.

5.11 Virtue, Unanimity, and Goodwill

Education in the virtue which is essential to leading a happy life would promote *participation* in the city's natural end, which is one distinguishable aspect of sharing in that end. Since the virtues whose exercise is essential to a citizen's *eudaimonia* are also necessarily socially beneficial,[2] an education in such virtue would also promote in each citizen a wish and disposition to promote the good of the city and all its citizens. That is a second distinguishable, though for Aristotle inseparable, aspect of sharing in that common end. Taken together, then, the ability and inclination of each citizen to not only participate in the best life himself, but also assist his fellow citizens in doing so, would seem to be just what is meant by the citizens of the city sharing or being partners in the common end of living the best life. "Unanimity seems . . . to be political friendship," says Aristotle, and

> such unanimity is found among good men; for they are unanimous both in themselves and with one another, . . . and they wish for what is just and what is

advantageous, and these are the objects of their common endeavor as well. Bad men cannot be unanimous except to a small extent, any more than they can be friends, since they aim at getting more than their share of advantages, while in labor and public service they fall short of their share; and each man wishing for advantage to himself criticizes his neighbor and stands in his way . . . [and soon] they are in a state of faction (*NE* IX.6 1167b2–14).

By promoting unanimity in the pursuit of a way of life which each citizen can enjoy without loss to any other (1167a28–30), an education in virtue promotes a form of civic harmony, or reciprocal goodwill and partnership, which Aristotle regards as a kind of *philia* or friendship.

We may observe, further, that unity depends upon a certain measure of trust (*Pol.* V.11 1313b16–18, 1314a17–18, 1314b36ff.; *NE* VIII.4 1157a21–24) and equality (*Pol.* VII.8 1328a35–36; *NE* VIII.5 1158a1, VIII.7 1159a4–5, VIII.8 1159b2–4; *EE* VII.10 1242b22), equality *in virtue* being both the most authoritative (*Pol.* III.9 1281a2–8) and the most important (*Pol.* II.7 1266b26–32). In the absence of virtue one may reasonably expect injustice to occur, and anticipate that its occurrence would undermine trust and civic unity. Aristotle's view is therefore not surprisingly that the only *stable* foundation on which trust may be established is a mutual *recognition* of virtue (*NE* VIII.4 1157a21–25). This same relationship between trust and virtue which he asserts in his discussion of friendship in the *Nicomachean Ethics* is evident in his observation in the *Politics* that tyrants fear the bonds of loyalty *by which the good are united* (*Pol.* V.11 1314a19–21) and seek to create mistrust and quarrels among their subjects in the misguided belief that power can be preserved by dividing the citizenry against itself (V.11 1313b16–18, 1314a17–18 and 27–28, 1314b36ff.).

Successful education for virtue would not only serve to establish a common end, therefore, but would also provide a foundation for common trust and promote equality of the kind that is most essential to creating a partnership "of equals, aiming at the best life possible" (VII.8 1328a35–36). Thus, it would promote unity in the polis in at least three distinguishable ways.

The common beliefs which Aristotle reports in *Rh.* II.4 would have led his audience to conclude that education for virtue could accomplish even more than this, however. Virtue plays a remarkably dominant role in his enumeration there of the kinds of people we are thought to like or feel friendly toward, and so wish the good for, for their own sake. Although Aristotle does not subject these common beliefs to a methodical philosophical examination, he may well have shared many of them himself, and thus may have regarded education for virtue as tending to create civic unity by nurturing traits of character which inspire friendly feelings in others. "We feel friendly to those who have treated us well, . . . provided it was for our own sake. And also to those who we think *wish* to treat us well," he reports (*Rh.* 1381a12–15). He also observes that we feel friendly toward the just (22), the temperate (25), those who are good tempered (31), those whose attitudes toward their neighbors are befitting a good person (1381b7–9), those whose goodwill toward us is unwavering (24–26), those who show themselves to be good friends (26–29), and those who are honest with us (29). Given his definition of liking or feeling friendly toward *(to philein)* as "wanting for someone what one thinks good, for his sake and not for one's own, and being inclined, so far as one can, to do such things for him" *(Rh.* II.4 1380b36–81a1; Cooper 1977, 621), this means that education for virtue will promote goodwill not only by cultivating a disposition to feel and act from it, but also by enabling people to inspire it in others.

This much of Aristotle's view is fairly obvious, as I have said, but it leaves a number of questions that are fundamental to the analysis of *CU* and *CE* unanswered: Is the partnership in pursuit of the common end of living well a partnership of citizens, of larger social entities, or both? Is the bond that unites them friendly feeling, friendship, some combination of these, or these and something else as well? How will education establish that bond and why need education be public in order to establish a common end?

5.12 Partnership and the City's Parts

In order to begin answering these questions, we must return to the passage in *Pol.* III.9 we had begun to consider at the close of chapter 4, and we must examine a part of it which we have so far ignored:

> a city . . . is a partnership of households and of [extended] families [or clans]
> *(koinônia kai tais oikiais kai tois genesi)* in well-being, for the sake of a perfect and
> self-sufficing life. Such a community can only be established among those who live
> in the same place and intermarry. Hence there arise in cities family connections,
> brotherhoods, common sacrifices, amusements which draw men together. But these
> are created by friendship, for to choose to live together is friendship. The end of
> the city is the good life, and these are the means towards it. And the city is the union
> of [extended] families [or clans] and villages *(genôn kai kômôn)* in a perfect and
> self-sufficing life . . . (1280b32–81a2).

The opening and close of this passage taken together call to mind Aristotle's remarks on the growth and origin of cities in *Pol.* I.2, with its sequence of levels of social aggregation, each more nearly sufficient than the preceding for sustaining the best kind of life, and each in that sense natural.[3] The city, being a culmination of such aggregation arising from bonds of mutual attraction and made possible by the capacity of speech, is said in the passage at hand to result from the unification of villages and extended families or clans, those being aggregates themselves of individual households. Thus, in all three of these senses in which a polis is natural *(kata phusin)*—i.e., with regard to self-sufficiency or the capacity to sustain the best kind of lives, with regard to the inclination to aggregate arising from bonds of attraction, and with regard to the use of speech in pursuit of a good life—households, villages, and clans would all seem to be natural. Thus,

Aristotle's intent in the passage at hand may be to define a city as a partnership among the natural social aggregates coexisting within it.

Aggregates of any of these three types can function as political entities which might or might not pursue the common interest of the polis as a whole, and this may be the reason why Aristotle regarded a true polis as a partnership among entities of *all* of these types. Most obviously, he undoubtedly recognized the existence of competition between individual households as well as between extended families or clans, and regarded the most natural form of a village as one populated by a single extended family (*Pol.* I.2 1252b18). Cooperation between households within a clan or village is quite compatible with competition between those larger units and between the households of a polis generally. It is also conceivable that a household which acts through its citizen-head in partnership with all other households, in all matters in which they might be able to do so, might nevertheless through its village stand opposed in some ways to other villages. Similarly, a cooperative agreement between villages might produce unanimity at that level, but coexist with tensions between individual households and families. Cooperation at or within one level of aggregation may not entail cooperation at all levels, then, and Aristotle may recognize this in describing the (truly unified) city as a partnership between the aggregates of each natural kind that occurs in it. He may understand by this a partnership at each politically significant level of aggregation.

If this is correct, however, it creates something of a puzzle, since Aristotle fails to mention the aggregates whose political influence he was evidently most concerned with, namely the rich and the poor. If genuine unity is the more ambitious goal which is continuous with but transcends the mere elimination of *stasis*, then one would suppose that he is particularly interested in unifying the city at a level of aggregation that stands between the extended family and the city as a whole, namely the socioeconomic class, for *stasis* is a form of conflict between socioeconomic classes. So why does Aristotle not say, then, that the city is a partnership between not only households, families, and villages, but also the rich and the poor? He does not, I would suggest, even though he is most concerned to create unity across class divisions, because his view is that cities capable of fulfilling their natural function will not exhibit, and will take care to prevent the emergence of, such class divisions. Households, families, and villages may all be natural and necessary to a city, but socioeconomic classes are not, and we have noted already in our discussion of moderation in wealth in the previous chapter Aristotle's reasons and proposals for eliminating them. In the ideal city described in *Pol.* VII and VIII, or any city true to its nature and capable of fulfilling its natural function, the rich and poor would converge toward moderation in wealth and would thus cease to exist, and so it cannot be in the nature of a city to be a partnership between these two classes. Nevertheless, it is clear that Aristotle's interest in avoiding faction and *stasis* is strongly associated with his interest in constitutional unity (*NE* VIII.1 1155a21–26, IX.6 1167b5–15), a concern that the units of the city that hold political power be of one mind in the pursuit of the common interest or best life for everyone (i.e., exhibit unanimity or political friendship), and that no divisions within the city remain which would exclude, or draw away, any citizens from the partnership of the whole.

5.13 Political Friendship

Turning now to the nature of the bond that is to unite these various partners in the common interest, the passage from *Pol.* III.9 set out above identifies as the vehicles of civic unification such things as intermarriage, brotherhoods, and common religious rites and amusements, and it identifies friendship as the bond through which these operate. The suggestion seems to be that these forms of association bring members of different households, clans, and villages together, and build friendships between them. Those households, clans, and villages are then linked to each other through the friendships between a few of their members, but how that linkage is supposed to result in partnership, and what this partnership of households, clans, and villages would entail in the way of direct bonds between one citizen and another, is not immediately obvious.

Does Aristotle suppose that citizens will all be bound to each other individually by bonds of *civic* or *political friendship*, as John Cooper (1977, 1990) and others following him[4] have suggested, and is it through such friendship that he thinks a city may be unified? The view I shall defend here is that Aristotle does have a concept of civic or political friendship, as Cooper has argued, and that the extent and quality of such friendship is inseparable from the extent to which a city or polis is unified in pursuit of its natural and proper end, but that this tells us next to nothing about the *means* and interpersonal *bonds* by which cities may be unified. Aristotle acknowledges that there are forms of friendship corresponding to every form of community, including political communities (*NE* VIII.9 1159b27–31, 1160a9–30; *EE* VII.10 1242a1–13), but his remarks suggest that the form of friendship which all or most of the citizens of a good city have toward each other can be, in one respect, no more than a foundation on which the more substantial bonds which unify a city rest, while in another respect this form of friendship can be their product. What the statesman must do, I will argue, is promote the possession and exercise of the moral and intellectual virtues and use common schooling and other measures to bring citizens together in settings which nurture friendly contact, common desires and character traits, and the formation of networks of substantial friendships spanning the city's disparate social and economic sectors.

The term "*philia*" is commonly recognized as having a wider signification for Aristotle than the corresponding term "friendship" does for us, a friend being by his lights, as he says in *Eudemian Ethics* VII.10, "a partner either in [one's] family or in one's scheme of life" (*EE* 1242a21–22). Fellow citizens who are partners in each other's lives only in the sense that each desires and pursues in cooperation with others (i.e., through a just system of rule) the same thing, namely a happy life, may then qualify as political friends to each other. As we have seen, other passages suggest that the participants of every community of any kind are bound together by friendship to "the extent to which justice exists between them" (*NE* VIII.9 1159b25–31; cf. *EE* VII.10 1242a19–22). I interpreted this at the end of the preceding chapter to mean in the case of a polis not just that they exist under a common system of law and governance, but that they are induced by it to exhibit toward each other the forms of respect and acceptance of each other's good demanded by justice, just as Aristotle says in *NE* VIII.9, in illustrating the claim that "in every community there is thought to be some form of justice, and friendship too," that "men *address* as friends their fellow-voyagers and fellow-soldiers" (1159b27–28; emphasis added). This suggests a very low threshold of intimacy, common history, and shared activities and sentiments, but also some mutual recognition of mutual goodwill. Other passages suggest that a form of friendship exists whenever there is unanimity in any kind of joint undertaking, such as the unanimity that exists at the moment when a commercial agreement or contract is struck. In *EE* VII.10, Aristotle says that civic friendship rests on equality and is "based on utility," that citizens "no longer know" one another "when they are no longer useful to one another, and the friendship is merely a temporary one for a particular exchange of goods" (1242b22–27). This again suggests a very low threshold for what can count as *philia*, but again some requirement of direct recognition of the other's acceptance of the mutually beneficial terms on which the common endeavor is transacted; knowing each other and being civic friends are regarded here as contemporaneous and extinguished when the commercial exchange is terminated.

As we have seen, Aristotle describes political friendship as a kind of unanimity, but also as present in polises to the extent that they are just. These propositions converge in the notion that all forms of justice involve mutual benefit and unanimity, but their natural culmination lies in Aristotle's conception of justice as what is conducive to the common good or a polis's natural aim of securing the best life for all its citizens. To the extent that a polis is just, its citizens will exhibit unanimity in common and cooperative pursuit of the best life, and to be united in that common pursuit is to be political friends in the truest or most complete sense, and in the way that is required for a polis to be unified in the manner that its natural end calls for. We must conclude, then, that there are different kinds of political friendship, some transitory and falling far short of what is present when a city is unified, such as that which arises from commercial agreements; some more durable but also too rudimentary to constitute a partnership in pursuit of the best life, such as that which arises from the elementary forms of mutual respect or self-restraint demanded by legal justice; and some grounded in the civilizing effects of common law, but rising by other means to a partnership in pursuit of the best life.

Although Aristotle describes civic friendship as motivated by utility, and as mere "friendship of association," since it rests "on a sort of compact" (*NE* VIII.12

1161b14–15), there is some reason to think that he means that this is generally true, not that it is true of this third and rarest, but also most unifying, category of civic friendship. First, he says that friendships of utility are "full of complaints; for as they use each other for their own interests they always want to get the better of the bargain" (NE VIII.13 1162b17–18). The kind of civic friendship which is present when a city is truly unified and free of faction must be something better than this, even if it is motivated in part by utility. Second, Aristotle says that virtue is the concern of a true city which is *not* a mere alliance resting in a compact or convention (*Pol.* III.9 1280b5–12), and this suggests that in such a city the remark that civic friendship is mere friendship of association resting in a compact is void, and that citizens will care about their fellow citizens being virtuous. If they care in the sense of being distressed when their fellow citizens *lack* virtue, they must surely also be pleased when they possess it, and must be drawn to them and be happy to associate with them on that account. To that extent, their friendship, just insofar as they are fellow citizens, is based in virtue and not merely utility. Third, Aristotle regards cities and marriages alike as natural in the three-fold sense noted previously, and he notes that "if the parties are good" it is possible for marriages to be based not only on pleasure (which corresponds to the mutual attraction which makes marriages and cities natural) and utility (which corresponds to the gain in self-sufficiency for a good life that makes marriages and cities natural), but also on virtue or goodness of character (which corresponds to the capacity to engage in conversation about the good which makes marriages and cities natural) (*NE* VIII.12 1162a25–26). The best kind of marriage is thus a character friendship, and not merely a friendship of utility and pleasure. Friendship based in character is a more complete fulfillment of the potential of marriage associated with its threefold naturalness, and because a city's potential is similarly defined by the same threefold naturalness, there is some reason to infer that the best kind of civic or political friendship would also be based on character, as well as pleasure and utility. Although political friendship could not be as complete or intimate a form of character friendship as other character friendships, it would be exhibited in "sharing in discussion and thought" much as they are (*NE* IX.9 1170b11–12), though on a large public stage, rather than a small private one.

The evidence on this point is admittedly mixed, and on the positive side merely inferential. Aristotle says that one cannot have friendships based in character with very many people,[5] and nowhere does he directly say that in an ideal city the citizens will be friends to each other on the basis of not only utility, but also their appreciation of each other's virtue. Yet it is hard to see how friendship based merely in utility could suffice to unify a city in the way Aristotle envisions. By his own account, it does not provide stable security against faction. Nothing that I say here hangs on resolving this, however, and it may be that this is an aspect of his account which he never fully resolved.

Julia Annas has argued in response to Cooper that Aristotle can scarcely hold that there is a special form of civic friendship which can bind every citizen to each of his fellow citizens, since friendship as Aristotle understands it is not a relationship which a person could have to more than a few fellow citizens (Annas 1990). She notes in evidence Aristotle's remark at *NE* VIII.2 1156a2–5 that friendship involves mutual recognition of liking or goodwill, and the five marks said to characterize friendship which he lists at *NE* IX.4 1166a2–10,[6] and which point, she says, to the necessity of both intimacy and shared activities (243). The objection is overstated, since intimacy is not a clear requirement of friendship in Aristotle's account (see, e.g., *Rh.* II.4 1381b33 and *NE* IX.10 1171a14–21), and since he is apparently willing to countenance the transaction on the large stage of public life of such features of friendship as sharing each other's joys and sorrows or making the same choices. Aristotle indicates that unanimity may be displayed by a citizenry in making and supporting political choices about such things as alliances, who shall rule, and the like (*NE* IX.6 1167a31–33), presumably with their votes in a legislative assembly, and through their subsequent show of support for the choices arrived at.

Mutual recognition of mutual goodwill is a less easily disputed requirement for *philia*, however, and Cooper's defense of his position is built in large measure upon taking it to be not only necessary but sufficient for *philia* (Cooper 1990, n. 18), an interpretation authorized by Aristotle's statement in *NE* VIII.2 that "goodwill when it is reciprocal" and recognized is friendship (1155b33–35).[7] Yet in a city too large to allow all citizens to be acquainted with every other citizen, it seems implausible to suggest that such a bond could exist between *all* individual citizens, and there are no passages in which Aristotle unambiguously says that it does occur even in an ideal city. The expression and recognition of mutual goodwill seems to require that every citizen communicate directly with every other citizen, and the textual evidence we have considered suggests that Aristotle thinks justice gives rise to friendship only when people actually address each other in a friendly way (*NE* VIII.9 1159b27–28; *EE* VII.10 1242b22–27). Generally speaking, one cannot impute *specific* attitudes toward each fellow citizen on the strength of a *general* attitude of goodwill toward all citizens, even though the general attitude may entail or be linked to a disposition to exhibit goodwill toward each fellow citizen with whom contact is made.[8]

Annas may be correct, then, in asserting that not *all* of the citizens of a polis can be political friends toward each other if a polis is too big for all of them to have contact or communications with each other, but a polis is a face-to-face political enterprise in which most citizens do at least see each other in legislative assemblies, and to the extent that a polis is politically just, Aristotle nevertheless seems to think that its citizens are united by a kind of political friendship, at least insofar as they interact and exercise influence over each other's well-being. Annas may also be right in holding that the civic friendship of each citizen to another is not the *means* by which Aristotle envisions cities being unified, but her interpretation sheds little light on what is. "Nothing in the passage [*Pol.* III.9 1280b29–40] demands that we find in a well-run polis citizens who have not only a general civic concern for all other citizens, and friendships with some of them, but also in addition to these a special kind of friendship with all other citizens," she says (Annas 1990, 243). Yet her own view of Aristotle's claim that it is friendship that unites the state is scarcely adequate either, her most specific suggestion being that "concern for the common good is fostered by the particular kinds of friendships produced by smaller, personal kinds of interaction," since "(at the least) without these the citizens could be mutually hostile or indifferent and wary" (243). This does not take us very far toward understanding the way in which friendships within the forms of association that Aristotle mentions will generate, or may be used by the statesman as the means to generate, a concern with the common good or a partnership in pursuit of it. Nor does it say as much as one would wish about the relationships of one citizen to another and of one social aggregate to another in the partnership Aristotle envisions.

A. W. Price provides a somewhat more suggestive image of Aristotle's intentions, in speaking of "the unification of expanding circles of loyalty" grounded in associations beyond the family (Price 1989, 200), but his interpretation comes up short in the same respects that Annas's does. What is entailed by the idea of a "circle of loyalty," and how will the legislator ensure that the circles expand outward to embrace every citizen and group in the city, and not stop at the chasms dividing different kinds of people from one another? Not by simply allowing the commonly occurring forms of association in cities to *exist*, for in that case one would expect any city left to its own devices to be adequately unified, whereas Aristotle regards such unity as a rare achievement at best. As we have seen, he holds that there is little friendship in deviant constitutions, just as there is little justice, and that most actual cities have deviant constitutions.

What seems necessary to unity, as far as the substance of the bond is concerned, is not that every citizen be a friend to every other citizen, nor even that they all like each other, but rather, first, that every citizen and political aggregate standing between the household and the city itself display a commitment to the common good in the policies they advocate and adopt. That is, the political actors of the city must support and choose the common interest or best life for everyone over the exclusive pursuit of their own interests when collective and corporate choices are contemplated and made. Secondly, when contact (whether direct or indirect) occurs between individual citizens it should be colored and guided by friendly feeling or goodwill. A city could hardly be a partnership in pursuit of the common interest or best life for all its citizens unless both of these conditions were met, and it seems likely that Aristotle took this much for granted.

These two conditions do entail more than citizens having "general civic concern for all other citizens" (Annas 1990, 243), since a *general* concern of this sort entails neither goodwill toward *specific* individuals who are not friends, as noted already, nor anything about the policies or choices of aggregate entities. At the same time these are weaker conditions than the requirement of *universal* civic friendship, since they require neither actual friendship, nor even mutual friendly feeling, between individual citizens who are unaware of each other's existence. With respect to the bond of one individual citizen to another, these conditions require only that friendly feeling be *generated* and endure when contact *occurs*. That feeling must, of course, be mutual, and must also before long be recognized mutually if it is to endure, and this does meet the minimum requirements for political *philia* which Aristotle suggests and Cooper advocates. Collectively, it also constitutes unanimity of the highest and most politically significant order, which Aristotle equates with political friendship and contrasts with faction. Beyond people treating each other in a friendly way, what is required is simply that enough general goodwill exist to ensure a cooperative, collective pursuit of the common good or best life. Together these forms of goodwill seem not only sufficient for Aristotle's purposes, but also possible by his lights, given his remarks about the ways in which friendly feeling is generated.

5.14 Common Schooling, Religion, and Meals

We have noted already the importance of virtue itself to the spread of friendly feeling, but there is something quite independently significant about Aristotle's observations at *Rh*. II.4 1381a15–16, that we feel friendly to "our friends' friends, and to those who like, or are liked by, those whom we like ourselves," and at 1381b15 and 17–18, that we like "those who are like ourselves in character and occupation" and "those who desire the same things as we desire." These tendencies would together permit the spread of goodwill within the memberships of associations based on common character, occupations, or desires, and also through the pools of participants in shared activities which arise from and nurture common traits. More basic than these tendencies, of course, are the bonds of affection within families, which provide the strongest and most fundamental link of one individual to another and one household to another.

These tendencies to friendly feeling would also permit the spread of friendly feeling *between* the members and participants in these different associations and common activities, but the extent of this would depend on both the extent of the differences and commonalities between those memberships and participant pools, and on the extent to which those memberships and participant pools overlap.

The commonalities between these various groups might be enhanced by common religious observances (*Pol*. III.9 1280b37, VII.8 1328b11–12, VII.10 1330a9–10), common meals (*Pol*. II.5 1263b37–64a1, II.9 1271a27–35, VII.10 1330a3–23, etc.), and especially common education, in which all citizens would share, and so the institution of these would be an important means through which the legislator could promote unity. Aristotle refers to common meals in saying in *Pol*. II.5 that a polis "should be united and made into a community by education" (1263b36–37), and he suggests in other passages that arrangements should be made to ensure that the poor can participate in these meals and in common religious observances (*Pol*. II.9 1271a27–35, VII.10 1330a3–23). As we saw at the outset of chapter 1, his assumption is that these institutions will not spontaneously exist in forms which will include all citizens, and that the statesman should take measures to remedy this. Not all leaders will, and in his description of the kind of tyrannical rule which involves dividing citizens against each other, Aristotle suggests the unifying capacity of such measures with his remark that "common meals, clubs, education and the like" are avoided by tyrants (*Pol.* V.11 1313b1–2). A "common upbringing," which makes people more alike, "contributes greatly to friendship" (*NE* VIII.12 1161b34–35), he says, so even without making all citizens virtuous the institution of a common education could be expected to promote goodwill and social unity by enhancing the kinds of similarities of character and aspiration which tend to generate friendly feeling.

Common schooling which brings all children together, in the sense of mixing children of all kinds together in each school, might also be expected to facilitate the adoption of a common end by broadening each citizen's sphere of sympathetic acquaintance and friendship, since it would make it possible for people from different parts of the city, who would otherwise never come to know each other, to become both acquaintances and friends. Aristotle notes at *Rh.* II.4 1381b33–34 that we feel friendly toward "those with whom we do not feel frightened or uncomfortable," and it is reasonable to suppose that he would regard familiarity as increasing comfort and reducing fear and mutual suspicion. Since fear and discomfort are surely obstacles to feeling and exhibiting goodwill, the familiarity promoted by being schooled together would tend to widen the range of fellow citizens whose good each child will be willing to promote.

To the extent that the memberships of various groups do overlap, it will be possible for friendly feeling to spread from one group to another through those who belong to more than one. Given the ways in which Aristotle says friendly feelings are understood to propagate, anyone associated with one's friend through a club to which one does not belong will tend to inspire one's goodwill, all else being equal. Similarly, through participating in a common festival with some members of other villages, one might tend to feel goodwill toward the other members of those villages, on the assumption that they too like those from their village whom one has come to know. Again, most basically, "the same person is called by one man his own son whom another calls his own brother or cousin or kinsman—[by] blood relation or connection by marriage . . . and yet another his clansman or tribesman," as Aristotle says in *Pol.* II.3, the point being, contra Plato, that unity in the state depends not on the elimination of familial bonds as we know them, but on the propagation of a social network through those very bonds and others like them (1262a9–14). It is in such ways, then, that Aristotle may suppose that goodwill can be transmitted through the city widely enough to guide all the actual dealings of one citizen with another and all the collective decisions made.

The transmission of goodwill through personal connections of these sorts, and an education in the virtue and general goodwill proper to a citizen, are thus both important to Aristotle's view, and there are reasons to think he would regard them as quite interdependent. The transmission of goodwill through personal connections will not proceed very far among people who are not likeable or are generally indifferent to the good of others, so providing a common upbringing and common practices which make people more alike and familiar with one another will scarcely have the desired unifying effect without an education in virtue. Nor will such common experiences generate the desired common end unless the possession and exercise of intellectual virtue is made the paramount goal of education. Given Aristotle's view that virtue is acquired by practicing the kinds of action in which it will find expression (*NE* II.1 1103a16–17 and b21–23, II.3 1105a13–17),[9] it is also hard to see how a training in moral virtue could proceed very far without actual friendships and friendly contact being attempted and established. One cannot acquire or preserve the moral virtues without practicing them in relation to others, and one cannot practice them in relation to others without establishing friendly relationships with others who are prepared to reciprocate. The range of those others should be as wide as the city itself, moreover, for the general possession of the moral virtues is no security against error if one has not acquired a well-rounded understanding of those with whom one must act. The creation of a just community, unified in the pursuit of the best life as its common end, and the preparation of individuals for their role in it is in these ways inseparable.

One would expect the overlap of memberships which I have described here to arise spontaneously to some extent, in the case of extended families through intermarriage, for instance, and in the case of clubs and brotherhoods through people having a plurality of interests and attachments. Yet there is no reason to expect that the memberships of the various associations and groups in a city would spontaneously overlap in such a way as to include every citizen in a network through which friendly feeling might be transmitted and arise mutually between any two citizens who have contact with one another. Distinctions of class, among others, might divide the entire city, so that little if any friendly association takes place between those so divided, and no form of association brings them together. In that event, a natural course for legislative intervention would be to regulate the *membership policies* or conditions of participation in clubs, brotherhoods, religious festivals, and the like, in order to prevent any segregation of citizens into classes or groups which would not intermingle in a friendly way through these associations. Aristotle's remarks in *Pol.* VII.10 regarding the need to secure the public wealth required to make common meals and religious worship open to all citizens suggests that he would accept a great deal of public control of these matters, and there is at least one passage in which he advocates direct political control over the membership of various social groups. In his remarks on how to establish and improve democracy, Aristotle says that,

> Fresh tribes and brotherhoods should be established; the private rites of families should be restricted and converted into public ones; in short, every contrivance

should be adopted which will mingle the citizens with one another and get rid of old connections (VI.4.1319b23–27).

Whatever importance Aristotle may attach to families and other private associations providing venues for the private cultivation of virtue, he makes it abundantly clear in this passage that he does not assume they will do this in the most desirable way if left to their own devices. He recognizes here that they may be prone to policies of exclusivity and competition which can contribute to destructive social divisions and factional conflict.

All told, then, we may conclude that Aristotle probably envisioned three means through which civic unity and the sharing of a common end could be promoted by the legislator: first, through education which promotes the possession and exercise of the moral and intellectual virtues, and thereby trust, goodwill, equality, and common participation in the way of life which constitutes a city's natural aim (namely, a life devoted to the exercise of *sophia* or contemplative wisdom as its highest end); second, through common schooling and other measures which bring all citizens together in settings which permit and encourage friendly contact, and nurture common desires and character traits; and third, and most speculatively, through regulating the membership policies of clubs, brotherhoods, and the like. The first two of these fall within the domain of education as we are concerned with it here,[10] so the means by which Aristotle would have the state unified in pursuit of a common end are for the most part, and most clearly, educational. At least some of these educational means are also *essential* to securing unity, since it is only through instruction and habituation that the trait of generalized goodwill and exercise of intellectual virtue necessary to unity can be established. As we saw in chapter 4, Aristotle's view is, quite plausibly, that such traits cannot come into existence in any other way.[11]

5.15 The Arguments from Constitutional Unity and a Common End

This allows us to now conclude this reconstruction of the argument *CU* by representing it as concluding that education is important enough to warrant the legislator's attention, on the grounds that unity in the state is desirable and unattainable without education, and that it may be effectively promoted by education of the sort we have identified. The twin interrelated proximate goals of this education are the universal adoption of the city's natural end as a common end and the promotion of friendly ties between citizens and the various social entities or aggregates they belong to. Having come to a reasoned if modest understanding of how Aristotle may envision securing the first of these goals, we are also finally in a position to offer a credible statement of the argument *CE*. Education should first of all be *the same for all*, since the city's attaining its natural end requires that every citizen be prepared to both live the best life himself and cooperate in his fellow citizens' doing so. Secondly, it should be *public* both to *ensure* that it will be the same for all, which it will not be if "everyone looks after his own children separately, and gives them separate instruction of the sort which he thinks best" (1337a24–26), and to ensure that the children of the city are educated together, if not all in one place because there are too many of them, then in schools which are common in the sense that each of them mixes together children of each relevant kind (above all, children of all socioeconomic classes), since this is more conducive to mutual goodwill and the sharing of a common end than education which does not facilitate children coming to know each other. In the background of this argument is the assumption that without public control of education the divisions within a city will tend to preclude friendly contact among those divided from each other, and that such education as occurs will be oriented not to the common interest but to private factional interests.

In assessing these arguments, one must consider both the worthiness of the aims to be secured and the usefulness and appropriateness of using public schooling as a means to attaining those ends. With regard to aims, the ideal of a state aiming at the happiest life, or contemplative life, for its citizens might be contested on the grounds that there is no adequate basis on which to assert the existence of a single happiest life for human beings as such. A more modest position would be that states should aim at the happiness of all their citizens, recognizing the variety of lives which may qualify as happy. The acceptance of such variety, of a kind of *pluralism* of the good, would make for a less unified society than Aristotle envisions. Citizens would share fewer traits in common, and would probably lack the common religion which he takes for granted, but it is conceivable that in a society that is sufficiently just and unified by intergroup friendships a more abstract sense of unity in pursuit of happiness could exist and would serve as a sufficient counterweight to the centrifugal forces exerted by the presence of competing conceptions of the good.

With this adjustment to accommodate pluralism, the argument for common schooling becomes more problematic, insofar as the capacity of common schools to make children more like one another may illegitimately undermine the capacity of families to pursue the distinct visions of the good they wish to pursue. That is, even if common schools do not impose any unjustified conception of the good life, they may nevertheless make children more alike and thereby less distinct from one another in ways their families legitimately desire them to be. On the other hand, the acceptance of plurality can be regarded as creating greater obstacles to mutual goodwill and a society's capacity to govern itself with justice and constancy of commitment to the common good, and this would seem to create an even greater need for common schooling than a more homogeneous society would have. Another complication introduced by pluralism is that, although the nurturing of intergroup friendships in common schools would remain a sensible strategy, the identity of the common curriculum which children should receive is thrown into doubt. What is necessary in the way of practical arts will ramify in any case in an economy based not in land capital, but in evolving and disparate forms of human capital, but it will do so perhaps even more with the abandonment of the view that the cultivation of the intellectual virtues provides the singular foundation for human happiness by making a life of contemplation possible. Without a common highest end, there will be no uniform line between what is preparatory to productive labor and what is preparatory to the most admirable and pleasant use of leisure, and what remains of a common curriculum must be predicated on assertions of the universal utility of whatever arts and virtues are cultivated.

The evaluation of these arguments must also recognize that they are animated by a concern with the requirements of political stability and the closely affiliated requirements of justice as mutual advantage, which may be regarded as more compelling than the achievement of partnership in pursuit of the singularly most happy life, both from the legislator's point of view and from that of the citizens, for whom it is a basic requirement of a tolerable existence.[12] If justice demands impartiality in the promotion of mutual advantage, and the achievement of happy lives requires education, as Aristotle holds, then justice surely requires equitable educational investments in children, whether through providing the very same education or through providing education that is equally suitable to promoting different forms of happy lives for different children. Thus, even on their more minimal, pluralistic interpretation, these arguments *CE* and *CU* can be understood as resting squarely in the idea that a just state exists to promote mutual advantage. Indeed, *CE* becomes almost indistinguishable from the *argument from the promotion of happiness* identified in chapter 4, §4.1.[13] Moreover, if mutual advantage is associated with political health and stability in the way that Aristotle asserts, then at stake here is not only social justice, but the matter of how dysfunctional and degenerate a society may become without some sense of unity in pursuit of mutual advantage or happy lives. This raises difficult and perhaps intractable questions about our ability in the present era to promote a sense of unity in pursuit of a common end in a large, multicultural society, the costs of doing so, and the price of failing to. Suffice it to say that Aristotle's arguments are anchored in part in the results of his empirical study of constitutions, and that a proper assessment of their significance for contemporary societies would require a comparably serious attempt to get straight the facts about civic unity and commitment to shared ends.[14]

With regard to justice, these arguments point up a feature of public systems of education as objects of collective choice which I alluded to near the start of this work,[15] namely that it is only collectively rational to support such systems if they are designed to confer benefits which can be simultaneously possessed or enjoyed in common. Aristotle is acutely concerned about the destructive aspects of competition arising from *pleonectic* desires, and prescribes education preparatory to a pursuit of contemplation not only because he regards the contemplative life as the happiest, but because he regards the desire for the pleasure of contemplation as unlike others in being satisfiable without cost to other citizens. The pleasure of contemplation is not an essentially contested good—one which a person can possess only to the extent that others lack it—like honor or social status, or the enjoyment of luxuries. The lesson in this to be carefully observed is that although we may reject this conception of the contemplative life as the singularly most happy one, we cannot erect a collectively choice-worthy public system of education by designing one with the purpose of preparing children for happy lives devoted to the endless pursuit of essentially contested goods.

This is a telling point, since the pursuit of education is now often regarded as worthwhile because it confers competitive advantage in the pursuit of desirable employment, which is to say employment that confers a higher social status and greater access to luxuries than one could otherwise obtain. If the willingness of individuals to create and maintain a public system of education rested in this alone, it could not be collectively rational for them to do so, since it is evident that competitive *advantage* rests in obtaining an educational credential which others lack, and it is all but inevitable that those with antecedent advantages will generally prevail in obtaining those credentials.[16] It is possible, of course, that there can be genuinely common goods arising from economic and social competition, since these are the primary motor of technological innovation and economic expansion, but the existence of such goods is far from obvious in our present circumstances, since a primary effect of such innovation and expansion is to make an ordinary standard of living more expensive and replace free public goods (i.e., economic "externalities" such as clean air and pleasant open spaces) with costly commodities (i.e., objects of economic consumption such as cancer therapies and properties with big yards in gated residential communities). It seems to follow, then, that the arguments *CU* and *CE* not only give us reasons to have a public system of education, but bring to light the incoherence or injustice of establishing a system with the end in view which most Americans seem to have— incoherence if construed as a ground of collective rational choice, but injustice if construed as the ground on which one class promotes its own competitive advantage at the expense of another.

Descending from what is politically ideal, just, and prudent to the most mundane requirements of a satisfactory existence, we come to a further level on which these arguments may be understood and assessed. With regard to even the most basic of day-to-day dealings of one citizen with another, the trust and goodwill entailed by unanimous acceptance of mutual advantage as a fundamental principle of public life are highly desirable, and to some extent essential, social assets. How much goodwill and how much trust—how much *civility* or respect for fellow citizens—is essential for a society to function at all? Not much, perhaps, but it is clear that life is better with more, and worse with less, and if civility is in decline in America, as many insist (Carter 1998), there is all the more reason to take these Aristotelian arguments seriously.

Still, if these are goals which should command universal assent, and which are not too costly to pursue in some measure, important empirical questions remain about whether public education is necessary, and can contribute substantially, to securing them. Aristotle provides us with *plausible* answers to these questions about the roles which education might play in cultivating goodwill and unifying the state in a common pursuit of the good life, but a final assessment of the quality and scope of the grounds which these answers provide for full public control of education must again rest with a knowledge of these matters that is securely grounded in empirical research. Without such knowledge, one can scarcely conclude that the consequences of foregoing common schooling are intolerable in any one society, let alone *every* society.

Such research is available in the form of studies of the American experience of desegregation in the years since *Brown v. Board of Education*, the landmark Supreme Court decision of 1954,[17] and it does lend support to Aristotle's conception of how one might promote unity through common or integrated schooling. While the strategies through which school desegregation has been halfheartedly pursued in the United States have generated resistance and "white flight," including a proliferation of private "racist academies" (Arons 1986, 165–69), there is evidence that where integration has occurred it has increased the incidence of friendships and successful workplace relationships which cross racial lines. Several studies through the early 1980s bear this out (Braddock, Crain, and McPartland 1984),[18] and although no fully effective strategies for integrating the schools of an entire metropolitan area have been developed, the available research suggests that, even in the unfavorable political climate which has prevailed, considerable good can be done through voluntary desegregation plans (Rossell 1990), especially when classrooms are organized on cooperative learning models (Slavin 1979, 1983, 1995).

The studies of this period support the quite plausible and Aristotelian-like hypothesis that the gains in social unity which can be attained through integrated schooling require contact in which status is equal, interaction is cooperative, and goals are shared.[19] Since most racially mixed public schools in the United States segregate students into distinct "tracks," and assignment to different tracks is influenced not only by prior performance but also very substantially by race and other socioeconomic factors (Ballantine 1983; Oakes 1985), such schools not only do not create the conditions of status equality required to promote socially unifying friendships, but may be worse in this respect than privately operated schools without "tracks." Not only does assignment to lower tracks or to the inferior schools typical of American inner cities confer and communicate lower status in and of itself, the differences in curriculum, pedagogy, moral climate, and probable life outcomes associated with these tracks directly undermine any sense of shared aims or common trajectory toward happy lives.[20] Aristotle's appeals to unity and a common end provide us with substantial reasons to create a less invidious status system and a more credible commitment to providing the basis for happy lives in our schools.

On the other hand, without some further premises these arguments do not suffice to show that the common schools we should aspire to can only be publicly operated, as opposed to publicly funded and regulated, and the same is true of the other arguments we will consider in this chapter. As we shall see, they all show at most that a *public system* of some kind is required, not that it must be a system in which schools are directly operated by the state. I shall revisit this topic in chapter 7, in considering the significance of Aristotle's arguments for the debate over school choice.

5.2 THE ARGUMENTS FROM INSEPARABILITY

Turning now to Aristotle's second and final argument for education that is public and the same for all, we find in lines 1337a27–31 of *Pol.* VIII.1 what appear to be two subarguments sharing the common premise that citizens are parts of the state. The first of them proceeds from this initial premise to the claims that citizens *belong* to the state, and thus do not belong to themselves. From this we are evidently expected to conclude that citizens have no claim based in possession of themselves (or their children) to educate themselves (or their children). The second subargument joins the premise that citizens are parts of the state with the further premise that it is natural for the care of the parts to "look to" or be guided by the care of the whole, yielding the unstated but obvious conclusion that the education of citizens should be guided by the good of the whole city. Together these two component arguments may be considered to provide the statesman with a reason to undertake the education of the citizens of the city himself, and to deny those citizens a basis for claiming it as their own prerogative. In sum, they provide grounds for education being public.

As regards their provenance, there is clear precedent for these arguments in Plato's writings, and most particularly in *Laws* 804a, 903c, and 923a. We encountered the first of these passages in chapter 2 (§2.43) in Plato's description of the institutional framework of the system of education he envisions:

> Children will not be allowed to attend or not attend school at the whim of the father; as far as possible education must be compulsory for "one and all" (as the saying goes), because they belong to the city first and their parents second (804d).

Newman (1902, vol. 3, 501) mentions this passage from the *Laws* in connection with the argument *CE* immediately preceding these arguments from inseparability, and clearly there is an order of thought in this passage from Plato that is mirrored in the sequence from *CE* into what follows it: the reference to the practice of separate instruction, followed by the idea that children belong more to the state than to their parents. This coincidence in the order of ideas is suggestive of influence, but comparison of the two passages sheds less light on the character of Aristotle's argument than one might hope.

One of the two remaining links to the *Laws* is illuminating, however. Newman asserts that in holding that the individual belongs to the state, "what Aristotle has especially before him is the language of Plato in *Laws* 923a," and in holding that each is a part of the state he has before him *Laws* 903b (Newman 1902, vol. 3, 502). The latter of these links to Plato is particularly suggestive, as one might reasonably expect from the fact that Aristotle considers possession by the state to rest on the citizen's being part of the state, and 903bff provides some explanation of this notion that citizens are parts of the state. At 903c, Plato invokes a craft analogy, according to which the physician or skilled craftsman's natural concern is the quality of the whole, and his handling of his materials and parts will naturally reflect that. The implications of this for a legislative point of view are that the good of the whole city is the proper aim of legislation—that since the city is composed of citizens, and its good depends upon theirs, that they should be regarded as its parts and the statesman should be at liberty to form them in whatever way is conducive to the good of the whole.

Read in light of this, Aristotle's argument at 1337a27–31 does not seem terribly attractive in either its logic or its implications. Logically, the craft analogy does not provide any real defense for the inference from citizens being *parts* of the state to their *belonging* to the state—to the statesman, in effect—any more than it would the idea that the patient's organs *belong* to the physician. The best that could be said on its behalf is perhaps that there could be no such thing as a *right* of self-education in Aristotle's scheme of thought, because what is *just* is what is conducive to the good of the whole city, namely legislative control of education, and what is right, or in accordance with a right, is not distinguished from what is just. This is a less disastrous position to hold than it may at first appear, since it can in fact accommodate many of the concerns that are expressed in the modern era through the language of rights. One illustration of this is Aristotle's conception of corrective justice and the associated idea of an actionable wrong (i.e., a wrong against an individual for which a legal remedy exists), and another is Plato's proposal that various wrongs against individuals committed by public officials be actionable (*NE* V.4; *Laws* 761e, 846b).[21] Yet there is a simple flaw in this Aristotelian-like argument, which is that it should, but does not, give us a reason to believe that legislative control of education is more conducive to the common good than the alternatives. It assumes the very thing to be demonstrated.[22]

If this most textually plausible reading of the *argument from inseparability* must be judged a failure, as I think it must, it may nevertheless be profitable to pursue the question of whether there are other more palatable reconstructions of it to which the larger body of the *Politics* lends support.

5.21 Inseparability and the Good

The next question worth asking, then, is on what grounds Aristotle might regard the good of individuals as dependent upon the good of the whole polis, when he says that it is natural for the care of each to be guided by the care of the whole. For if there is such a linkage of goods, that would provide a different and more compelling basis for regarding public control of education as natural and desirable. If the good of individuals depends upon the good of others or the whole polis, and the latter is best pursued, or can only be pursued, collectively, then there is reason to pursue the education of those individuals collectively. So on what grounds can Aristotle hold that the good of individuals or the pursuit of their good is inseparable from the good, or the pursuit of the good, of the whole? At least three such grounds suggest themselves, each yielding a distinct argument for public education. As a class they constitute a distinct form of the inseparability argument, and I will refer to them here as *arguments from the unity of care*.

The first of these is suggested by the notion of functional interdependence implicit in Aristotle's idea that human beings are "political animals." As I noted in chapter 3, §3.11, his view is that we are city-dwellers by nature, in part because only a polis can provide the conditions necessary for a good life. He envisions cities doing this by bringing together the incomplete but complementary capacities of different individuals in ways that yield the various forms of goods required for such a life—most of all leisure for contemplation—and this requires that those capacities and the associated dispositions to use them be properly developed and exercised. Thus, the good of each individual depends upon the good or proper functioning of the whole, and that requires in turn that each individual be properly educated in the capacities and dispositions required by his or her (*Pol.* I.12 1259b29–60a24, 1260b9–21) role in the whole. Since each has a stake in how others perform their various roles, it is rational for each to support public measures to ensure adequate preparation for those roles. Some coordination of education by the state would seem rational, then.

But what form of public coordination of education does this provide a justification for? Does this show that it is desirable or essential for education to be public, i.e., for the schooling of children to be *undertaken* by the state? It does not seem to. Unless there is some further way to develop this line of argument, it would appear to support nothing more than state certification of the readiness of individuals to assume those roles in society vital to its well-being, or certification together with measures to ensure a sufficient "supply" of people prepared well enough to secure certification in the roles needed, and measures to ensure a sufficient preponderance of those virtues which are demanded by every role. Those measures might include regulating and mandating private education, as well as ensuring access to it (which may require public subsidies or full funding), but it is not at all clear that they need include a state monopoly on the schooling of children. In contemporary terms, it remains an open question whether a regulated market system in which private schooling could be paid for in full with government vouchers might be equally or more satisfactory.

Moreover, if my conclusions in §3.5 and §3.6 were correct, then Aristotle's own view would seem to be that only citizens, who share in rule and military service but little if any in productive labor, and their wives, whose function is restricted to the domestic sphere, are to be schooled at all. The laboring or productive classes in society are apparently expected to acquire their productive skills and moral training through private instruction and practice at the work, and precursors of the work, they will engage in, as well as experience of the city at large and its laws. Since they are without leisure *(scholê)*, they have no time for school and no need of a "liberal" education to prepare them for the best use of leisure *(Pol.* VIII.2). So although this notion of functional interdependence is important to Aristotle's conception of the self-sufficiency of the polis, it is relevant to education, as Aristotle understands it, only to the extent that the roles of citizens and their wives are different, demanding different virtues, and the role of the citizen has several dimensions, each demanding specific virtues. He does not suppose that the relationships of interdependence between the different classes in the city offer any argument for providing or requiring public education for those who spend their time in productive labor.

Neither does this notion of functional interdependence capture the manner in which *all* of the goods belonging to a good life are generated. It pertains most directly to the goods of commerce and perhaps governance, and to that extent also to leisure *(Pol.* VII.5 1326b30–33, VII.9 1329a1–2), but not in any obvious way to either friendship or personal security. These latter goods both involve interdependence, and so at least some broadening of an individual's good to include that of others, but the interdependence does not seem to involve any *differentiation of function*. Rather, these are goods that require the sharing of a *common* set of virtues, and the interdependence involved is among the citizens themselves, rather than between the citizens and others.

The same is true of rule in a system in which all citizens share in it, inasmuch as their individual well-being depends upon the quality of rule, and the quality of rule depends upon the extent to which citizens all share common moral and intellectual virtues. We considered the dependence of good governance on education in §4.34, as an argument for the importance of education. So it is perhaps sufficient in the present context to simply note that the dependence of the good of each on the good of all through common participation in governance constitutes another reason in support of a public system of education, to the extent that the adoption of a public system improves the prospects of a large number of citizens acquiring the moral and intellectual virtues that are necessary to contribute constructively to the conduct of government, and to the extent that *common schooling* provides "a foundation of previous experience in mutual trust, common action, and common benefit arising from that action."[23]

Taking up friendship and its place in a good life first, it is obvious that fellow citizens are not mere fellow workers in the productive and administrative life of the city. They are, at least some of them, companions without whom one could be neither happy nor virtuous. Aristotle does not regard a solitary life as a happy one, and neither does he regard virtue as an attainment that is possible without the help of virtuous companions. As noted in §5.14, virtues cannot be practiced, or consequently acquired, without the participation of companions, and this is just one of the ways in which the acquisition of the virtue necessary for a happy life is dependent upon having access to virtuous companions. The young especially need good role models and become better by imitating and being coached by models of virtue for whom they feel affection, most notably, but by no means only, their fathers (*NE* X.9 1180b4–7). Young and old alike need good companions with whom to share activities and projects expressive of virtue, and good people generally become better through friendship with each other, by molding each other "in what they approve of" (*NE* IX.12 1172a11–14). Just as importantly, we need virtuous friends if our perceptions of what is morally significant in our lives and the situations we face are to develop and become well rounded. "Through collaboration on projects and through listening to and identifying with the viewpoints of others, an agent's vision becomes expanded and enlarged (cf. [*NE*] 1112b11, 1112b27, 1143a12–16)," writes Sherman (1989, 30). The pursuit and exercise of virtue thus "requires (external) dialogue and audience" (27), as well as models, partners, and beneficiaries of virtue. In all these ways, then, the virtue and happiness of any individual are influenced by the probability of encountering virtuous rather than vicious people, and are thereby dependent upon the goodness of the city as a whole.

All told, this interdependence in the acquisition and exercise of virtue may be counted a distinct and important aspect of our *need* to live in a city if we are to fulfill our human potential and live the best life. It suggests not only that the education of each child should have a public dimension designed in part "to bring [the child] into contact with the exemplary characters of his culture and tradition" (Sherman 1989, 156), but also that each citizen has a stake in the goodness of others, and so has reason to accept and desire that all shall be similarly educated. Still, there is no clear argument here for a state monopoly on schooling, so our conclusions regarding the previous argument apply to this variant as well. The grounds for some public arrangements regarding education are strong, but the case for publicly operated schools is not.

5.22 Justice and Inseparability

One further aspect of the notion that human beings are "political animals" or city-dwellers by nature, in the sense that they require a city to live well, can be detected in Aristotle's remark, in the opening pages of the *Politics*, that "man, when perfected, is the best of animals, but, when separated from law and justice, he is the worst of all" (*Pol.* I.2 1153a31–33). We have considered this passage already, in §3.4 and §4.31, in connection with the contributions of law to the internal goods of character, but it might also be interpreted as concerned in part with security, another aspect of good order. Security is an external good fundamental to individual well-being, and one which depends upon the contributions of all citizens— upon their capacity and inclination to accept rule and the requirements of law in the manner appropriate to citizens (Pol. IV.11 1295b14–23).

The argument from the unity of care which this suggests may be at least approximated, then, by saying that the care of each necessarily involves and must be guided by the care of the whole *because* the care of each requires law, and law is an essentially common institution which aims not at the good of any one individual, but at the common good. While law may be described as a public institution and a medium of education, however, it does not constitute public education in the sense that concerns us here, for we are concerned rather narrowly with public schooling. Still, we noted that Aristotle regards lawmaking without schooling in the spirit of the laws as *futile*. "The best laws, though agreed upon by every citizen of the state, will be of no avail unless the young are trained by habit and education in the spirit of the constitution," he says (*Pol.* V.9 1310a15–17). Given this, we may amend this argument so that it holds that it is natural for the education of each to be guided by the care of the whole, since the care of the whole requires law and the effectiveness of law requires that each be educated for compliance with that law. This modification establishes the relevance of the argument to public schooling and secures this argument's position among the more appealing reconstructions of Aristotle's inseparability argument.

Even in this form, however, this argument that law is a medium of common care requiring public schooling is plagued by the very limitations shared by the preceding arguments from the unity of care. It may show that it is desirable, from both the legislator's and the individual citizen's point of view, to ensure in *some* way that education conducive to compliance with law takes place, but it does not in itself show that public sponsorship of education is the only approach that would suffice.

Furthermore, the grounds for asserting even the former of these conclusions may be contested. The risk that spontaneously occurring forms of education might fail to be adequately conducive to compliance with law might be quite small in some societies, and might be insignificant compared to the risks of giving the state jurisdiction over educational matters. Similarly, the risks in the absence of regulation might be substantial, but the likelihood that state regulation of education would reduce those risks might be small. Putting this somewhat differently, it might seem obvious that in the absence of any supervision of education by the state there will be some people who are not adequately educated for compliance with the law, yet one may wonder why that should lead us to favor such supervision if the number of such people is small and there are drawbacks of any kind to state supervision. In short, the argument hinges on the *risk* involved in legislative *in*action, and fails to acknowledge the risks which legislative *action* may involve. The magnitude of those risks may be quite different in different societies, so it is reasonable to conclude that the considerations raised by this argument are not uniformly compelling across all social orders.

Moreover, *the same is true of the preceding arguments from the unity of care,* since they rest no less than this final one does on the thought that the adequacy of education should not be left to chance. All of these arguments provide substantial grounds for public intervention to ensure the adequacy of education, but ones which may not be compelling in all societies.

The question we are left with, then, is whether these explorations of Aristotle's arguments have exhausted the considerations which he might adduce in support of public education, or whether there remains some more powerful argument which he could offer. We may take it as evident that any remaining argument will be more implicit in his works than explicit, and so all the more difficult to attribute to him with confidence and adequate justification. Only the prospects of an argument of considerable merit could warrant continuing the search in these circumstances. Yet we do have such warrant in the evidence for Aristotle's general commitment to the *principle of fidelity to reason*, and its requirement that instruction and persuasion be put before force and violence as a matter of fundamental respect, piety, or justice. I will argue that Aristotle's commitment to putting instruction before force, not just for its utility in securing compliance but as a requirement of justice, provides the foundation for a decisive argument in favor of a public system of education.

The argument from the uselessness of law without education is vulnerable to the objection that the risks arising from a small number of uneducated residents may be less significant in the aggregate than the risks or costs involved in state control of education. The most obvious way to remedy this weakness would be to argue that education for compliance with law is a matter of individual justice and not just one of reducing aggregate risk. I noted in the section just concluded that although Aristotle lacks a well-developed conception of justice as respect for individual rights, he does have a concept of *corrective justice*, and the suggestion I shall now pursue is that he follows the Socratic principles laid out in chapter 1 in assuming that the justice of criminal sanctions rests, not only generally but in individual cases, on the education that is required to create a rule of law imposed not by force but by consent, and to prepare each citizen for compliance with the law. The argument which this will yield is that the authority to impose criminal sanctions on individual citizens can only be secured through a public system which requires suitable education and guarantees access to it, and that it is therefore a fundamental requirement of justice that some form of *public system of education* be maintained, since no state can exist without law and the enforcement of law, nor claim to be just if its laws and enforcement of them are not. I called this in chapter 2, §2.44, the *argument from the foundations of corrective justice (FCJ)*, and I will devote the final section of this chapter and all of the next to its elaboration and the questions that arise in attributing it to Aristotle.

5.3 THE ARGUMENT FROM THE FOUNDATIONS OF CORRECTIVE JUSTICE

We saw in the opening chapter of this book that Socratic political thought rests in what I have called the *principle of fidelity to reason*, and we saw how that principle yields a duty of natural justice to govern in a way that puts reasoned persuasion and instruction before force. One application of this to the legitimacy of punishment, which we saw most clearly in the *Crito* and the *Laws*, is that punishment cannot be properly used to secure compliance with the laws in the absence of conditions favorable to free and informed consent to the laws, including truthful and reasoned instruction for the young in the reasons for existing laws being as they are, and venues for public discussion and approval of new laws. For convenience, I will call this the *consent version* of *FCJ*.

A second application, which was most evident in *Apology* 26a and Xenophon's depiction of Socratic doctrine in *Oeconomicus* III.11 (§1.2), begins in the propositions that without instruction people will often be ignorant of what is right and required by the law, that when they are ignorant in this way they do wrong unwillingly, and that one who does wrong unwillingly does not need or deserve punishment but rather instruction. Without the middle term "unwillingly," this would collapse into a direct application of the injunction to put persuasion and instruction before force and violence. This is what we seem to have in Xenophon's account, in fact, but the presence of this term in *Apology* 26a provides a point of entry for the Socratic paradox that no one does wrong unwillingly, and the assertion of this paradox seems to strengthen the application of the prohibition on punishment without prior instruction, by establishing wrongdoing as *evidence* in itself of educational failure, and by precluding the possibility that a person's education and upbringing were adequate and he or she simply chose to do the wrong thing.

What we saw in the *Protagoras,* the *Republic*, and the *Laws* is that in rejecting Socratic intellectualism, Plato broadens the educational burden preparatory to virtue and compliance with law to include not only instruction but training which shapes the desires toward the good and enables thought and reason to prevail over the passions, especially in the presence of dangers and pleasures that may cause one to lose sight of moral truths, as if intoxicated. The Socratic suggestion that ignorance is the sole determining cause of wrongdoing is replaced with the claim that ignorance cannot be overcome and the truth kept in sight without training the desires, that without such training it is impossible to become a "morally serious *(spoudaious)* and law-abiding" person with the capacity *(dunamis)* to listen to the claims of reason and law and comply (*Rep.* IV 424e–25e). On this Platonic account of moral development, to properly put instruction and persuasion before force and violence requires a comprehensive education providing not only instruction in what is right and what wrong, as even the "slave doctor" of the *Laws* may be said to do, but systematic exposure to good models portrayed in a favorable light, a proper balance of "musical" and physical training, training in moderation and courage, and instruction which traces the reasons for the laws being as they are back to the nature of the soul. This is the Platonic version of the argument that it is the one in a position to educate and punish—the state, or polis in its legislative capacities—that is to blame, and not the wrongdoer, if the former did not provide suitable education. I will call this the *complicity version* of *FCJ*.

Aristotle's foundational commitment to the *principle of fidelity to reason* and its injunction to put instruction and persuasion before force and violence is clear, his adoption of the Platonic view that virtue and compliance with just law rests on not only instruction but also training and habituation is also clear (*NE* I.1 1103a14–20, 1103b17–25, II.4 1105b2–4, X.9 1179b4–19), and his own regard for punishment as a last resort is evident in his remark that "just punishments and chastisements . . . are good only because we cannot do without them—it would be better that neither individuals nor states should need anything of the sort" (*Pol.* VII.13 1332a12–16). These commitments entail both versions of *FCJ*, whether or not Aristotle saw any need to expressly formulate either. Let us consider these points in more detail.

We have seen that Aristotle's political thought rests in the *principle of fidelity to reason* and its corollaries pertaining to the *aim, manner,* and *substance* of rule (§3.11). It shares Socrates' conceptions of intellect as the divine element in human nature (§3.11; *NE* I.8 1098b11–17, X.7 1177a16, etc.); the cultivation and exercise of the capacities of reason or intellect as constitutive of the best and happiest life (§3.11; *NE* X.7 1177b30–78a8); law and rule as properly aiming at the best life for all (§3.12; *Pol.* I.1 1252a4–6, III.6 1279a17–22, VII.2 1324a24–25, etc.) and embodying divine or perfect reason in their substance (§3.12, §3.4; *Pol.* III.16 1287a29–33); and the moral necessity of putting persuasion before force and ruling in a manner consistent with consent (§3.11, §3.12; *Pol.* I.13 1259b37–60a2, III.4 1277b8–30, III.6 1279b17–22, III.10 1281a22–25, III.13 1283b42–84a3, III.14 1285a27–29, III.15 1286a22–31, IV.9 1294b35–39, IV.10 1295a17–23, IV.11 1295b14–24, IV.12 1296b15–16, V.9 1310a15–17, V.10 1313a5–11, VII.2 1324b23–31, VII.14 1332b16–29). Aristotle regards regimes as illegitimate and corrupt to the extent that they rule by force and without consent, and acknowledges that what is established by force and without consent lacks authority and creates no obligation to obey (*Pol.* III.3 1276a8–16; cf. *Laws* IV 715b).

The *consent version* of *FCJ* follows so directly from the injunction against rule by force, and the associated proposition that what is established by force creates no obligation to obey, that one could regard Aristotle's endorsements of these as tantamount to an endorsement of the argument itself. What the argument assumes beyond the injunction itself, or the proposition that without an obligation to obey there can be no breach of obligation or crime, is simply that (1) meaningful consent requires an understanding of the laws and the reasons for them; (2) a public system of education is required to ensure a common grasp of the laws and their rationales; and (3) rule that is maintained through punishment in the absence of consent would obviously violate this injunction. It is reasonable to think that Aristotle took all three of these assumptions for granted, and that he grasped the requirement of rule by consent as an argument in itself for a public system of education. We reviewed in §3.11 some evidence of his acceptance of the first of these assumptions, and the third is self-evident. With regard to the second,

Aristotle's views on faction and stasis, the lingering influence of a Homeric *agonistic* ethic in Greek culture, and the knowledge of political science required to effectively promote virtue make it clear that he would not have supposed that the upbringing and home instruction within the different classes and clans in a city would have spontaneously converged on the common law.

The evidence bearing on Aristotle's endorsement of the additional (moral developmental) premise on which the *complicity version* of *FCJ* rests, and on his endorsement of that version of the argument itself, is more complicated. We have seen, but must take further note of the fact, that Aristotle does not believe that human beings can know what is good or have the capacity to do the right thing all on their own without the proper training and habituation. Although he regards individual effort as essential to the development of virtue, he also regards virtue as an achievement which depends upon far more than the efforts of the individual. "Now some think that we are made good by nature, others by habituation, others by reasoned speech or teaching," Aristotle says (*NE* X.9 1179b20–21). These are the opinions which are held with most authority, and they are all in part correct, he indicates, but also partly wrong, since the contributions of all three of these must be favorable if one is to become virtuous. Each is necessary, but not in itself sufficient, to produce virtue. "Perhaps we must be content," he says (*NE* X.9 1179b18–19), "if, when all the influences by which we are thought to become good are present, we get some tincture of virtue."

Aristotle rejects the idea that teaching or reasoned speech alone is the origin of virtue on the grounds that

> he who lives as passion directs *will not hear argument that dissuades him, nor understand it if he does*; and how can we persuade one in such a state to change his ways? . . . The character, then, must somehow be there already with a kinship to virtue, loving what is admirable and hating what is shameful (*NE* X.9 1179b26–30; emphasis added).

The character "must *somehow* be there already," he says, but the lesson in this for the statesman is that he must ensure the presence of such character through habituation and training that will lay the groundwork for instruction through reasoned speech. This prior education must be devoted to the development of appropriate tastes and dispositions, to cultivating a receptivity to reason, and to developing habits of correct action far enough to enable a person to be pleased rather than pained by doing the right thing, and not undermined in doing the right thing by the presence of seductive but less worthy competing pleasures or the specter of pain. This training and habituation need not come to an end with the start of teaching through reasoned speech, and some forms of training will surely involve such teaching, but it provides a civilizing foundation without which teaching cannot gain a foothold.

"It is on account of pleasure that we do bad things, and on account of pain that we abstain from admirable ones," Aristotle holds,

Hence we ought to have been brought up in a particular way from our very youth, as Plato says, so as to both delight in and to be pained by the things that we ought; for this is the right education (*NE* II.3 1104b10–13).

It is in this way, he says, that we become temperate and brave: through practice in abstaining from pleasures we become able to abstain from them, and through practice in standing our ground in the face of perils we become able to stand our ground in the face of them (II.2 1104a27–b3). Thus, "as a condition of the possession of the virtues, knowledge has little or no weight, while the other conditions count not for a little but for everything, i.e., the very conditions which result from often doing just and temperate acts" (II.4 1105b2–4; cf. *MM* 1182a15–23).

As we have seen, Aristotle regards training and practice as determining the ends one is moved to pursue, which is to say one's desires, but also the major premises of one's deliberations, which is to say one's moral beliefs and conception of what is good and worthy of pursuit (*NE* I.5 1095b5–8, VI.5 1140b6–19, VI.12 1144a31–35).[24] States of moral character are formed by practice, and "each state of character has its own ideas of the admirable and pleasant," he says,

and perhaps the good man differs from others most by seeing the truth in each class of things, being as it were the norm and measure of them. . . . We . . . choose the pleasant as a good, and avoid pain as an evil (*NE* III.4 1113a31–b1).

Without appropriate training and habituation, then, a person will be unable to grasp what is good. What a person *naturally* takes pleasure in, and thus perceives as good, will rarely converge with what really is good, and verbal instruction alone will be powerless to substantially alter those perceptions.

There is a second form of habituation presupposed or involved in the concept of practice, a form that corresponds to Plato's insistence that people must be surrounded with images of the good in order to know and develop a kinship with it. Aristotle holds that "the many" lack "even a conception of what is admirable and truly pleasant, since they have never tasted it" (X.9 1179b14–15). In light of his empiricist principle that all thought derives from sense experience,[25] we can infer from this—literally "[the many] being without a taste of them [the admirable and truly pleasant] *(ageustoi ontes)*"—that we are to understand the claim that those who are poor and uneducated lack a conception of what is good, fine, beautiful, or admirable *(kalon)* quite literally. A taste of things *kalon* and truly pleasant is, of course, easier to come by than an opportunity and the means necessary to practice good habits in the way one must in order to become virtuous. So if it is common for people to lack even *this,* it is all the more clear that the development of good character requires a great deal that many people have no assured access to. Good birth and nurture, good models, good moral coaching and guidance, access to the means necessary to performing specific good actions, and even the very concept of what one should be aiming at, may lie ineluctably beyond a person's reach.

Thus, Aristotle's view is that neither an acquaintance with the good, nor true moral beliefs, nor a capacity to guide oneself in accordance with reason are acquired spontaneously. They must all be cultivated. Since fidelity to reason requires putting instruction and persuasion suitable to promoting the autonomous virtue of all citizens before force, Aristotle is evidently committed to the proposition that a just system of law must be grounded in these forms of education. Even if we acknowledge that he regards punishment as itself educative or corrective in some instances, we have every reason to think that he regards it as it is portrayed in the *Protagoras,*, as a "catastrophe" (*Prot.* 325c; §2.2), both futile when relied on exclusively and unjust if the educative methods more suitable to nurturing the capacities of reason have not run their course.

If the *complicity version* of *FCJ* is thus implied by Aristotle's views, the *direct* textual evidence for his accepting, assuming, or intending it when he makes his arguments for public education is very slim indeed. In addition to his remark about punishment in *Pol.* VII.13, there is one passage which deserves comment. In his discussion of responsibility and the grounds of punishment and censure in *NE* III.5, Aristotle appears to formulate the Platonic argument that wrongdoing arises from ignorance and a lack of capacity to do the right thing, and to concede that this would preclude punishment if the ignorance and lack of capacity are attributable to inadequate education. The passage is a notoriously difficult one, however, and must be examined in the context of Aristotle's larger account of responsibility and the setting established by Plato's *Protagoras* and *Laws*. By undertaking this examination we will be able to see that although Aristotle's primary objective in *NE* III.5 is to repudiate the Socratic *asymmetry thesis*, or defend his own claim that virtuous and vicious acts are equally voluntary, his substantive view of the appropriate conditions for punishment is no different from Plato's, and to that extent entails the stronger Platonic educational program associated with the rejection of Socratic intellectualism as a foundation for just punishment.

Before turning to this, we will do well to close this chapter by asking why Aristotle did not state either version of *FCJ* more explicitly, if it is the most compelling argument he might have given on behalf of a public system of education. An answer suggested by the character of his audience, and the broad strategies of argument we have seen him deploy,[26] is that he may have seen no point in doing so. I have argued that he took his audience to include some who would have wished to pursue the common good, and some who would have pursued only their own perceived good and the perpetuation of their own rule, and I have tried to show that he has arguments tailored to the motives of each. What gives *FCJ* its special force is the proposition that the state will not be in a position to *justly* punish offenders unless it establishes the conditions for informed and rational consent to the laws and properly initiates citizens into compliance with them through education. From the point of view of one who was already committed to the legislative pursuit of the common good, this would be superfluous, however, and from the point of view of a corrupt ruler it would be beside the point. It could have no place in the kind of appeal to the desire for stable rule which Aristotle pursues (§ 4.2). It is a proposition which we might expect Aristotle to acknowledge at some point, as he seems to in *NE* III.5, but not to attach a great deal of importance to.

If *FCJ* may be counted the most compelling argument which it is possible to extract from *Pol.* VIII.1 and allied texts, this is because the nature of a modern audience's commitment to justice would place it largely, if not entirely, between the two audiences Aristotle intended to address. Whatever we in liberal democracies think about distributive justice or the state's role in facilitating the pursuit of happiness, we are apt to concede that the most minimal of states must have law, and must enforce that law at times. This argument, *FCJ*, suggests that to create legitimate law, and to justly enforce it, a state must have some *public system* for ensuring the provision to all of whatever education is required for informed and rational consent to law, and whatever education is essential to creating a reasonable likelihood of voluntary compliance with it. In its *form*, then, *FCJ* is an argument which is more universally compelling than any other we have seen, for it comes to rest in the most minimal conception of a state we can conceive.

With this preliminary conception of the character and implications of the *argument from the foundations of corrective justice* in mind, we must close this chapter and leave to the next the task of elaborating and examining the argument in connection with Aristotle's views on corrective justice and responsibility

6

Education and the Foundations of Justice

A number of objections may still be raised to my suggestion that we have grounds for regarding the *argument from the foundations of corrective justice (FCJ)* as Aristotelian. The task of this chapter will be to respond to these, provide what additional evidence there is for attributing the *complicity version* of this argument to Aristotle, and offer such elaboration and examination of both versions of it as may be appropriate.

First, Aristotle does have an account of corrective justice which we have so far ignored, but it is widely assumed that it applies only in the sphere of private law, that is to say in twentieth-century terms, in civil actions in tort, which the recent literature has focused on, and contracts, and not in the sphere of criminal law. It is also assumed that there is no connection in Aristotle's thought between corrective justice and justice in distributions of any kind, including distributions of education. If these assumptions are correct, then the idea of corrective justice in Aristotle cannot be linked to punishment and the necessary conditions for it, nor in any other way to the equitable distribution of education that is the same for all. I will show that these consumptions are not correct, that there is no reason to doubt that Aristotle's concept of corrective justice has application in the domain of criminal justice, and that there is no reason to infer from his distinction between corrective justice and distributive justice that there are no relationships between the two.

Second, I have promised to show that in *NE* III.5 Aristotle acknowledges that a lack of capacity to comply with law arising from educational failure precludes punishment. The traditional line of interpretation of *NE* III.5 has it that Aristotle holds we are all responsible for our own states of character, since we produce them through our own actions, and that for this reason we are morally responsible for the actions flowing from our character. If this interpretation were correct, it would mean that Aristotle breaks sharply with the Platonic view of responsibility and liability to punishment and what it preserves of the Socratic view.

I have held, on the contrary, that there is a strong continuity between Aristotle's view and Plato's, and I will need to show in some detail that the evidence for this continuity—the evidence that Aristotle follows Plato in denying the existence of any autonomous capacity to choose one's character that would justify a state in administering punishment without regard to its own complicity in the existence of vice and wrongdoing—provides us with the best understanding of the nature of the objection which Aristotle entertains at 1114a3, and the nature of his response.

The interpretation of *NE* III.5 which I will develop here has the merit of resolving the apparent inconsistency in Aristotle's position on the origins of character which arises under the traditional readings. In doing this I will show that what is often taken to be a flaw in Aristotle's theory of moral development is not.[1] His remarks about the origins of character in Books I and X of the *Nicomachean Ethics* are quite evidently consistent with the account of the *Politics*, while those occurring in III.5 do not seem to be. The difficulty revolves around the question of whether there are necessary conditions for good character that are beyond a person's control and must be externally supplied. The view of the *Politics* is that there are, and the view entailed by traditional interpretations of III.5 is that there are not. This inconsistency must be resolved, and it is resolved on the interpretation I will offer.

Having answered these objections pertaining to Aristotle's accounts of corrective justice and responsibility, and having wrung as much evidence of Aristotle's endorsement of the *complicity version* of *FCJ* from *NE* III.5 as it can yield, I will then consider more closely the principles of consent and complicity underlying the two versions of FCJ, and will attempt to sort through what we should find compelling in them, and what FCJ really entails.

6.1 THE SCOPE AND ALLEGED INDEPENDENCE OF CORRECTIVE JUSTICE

There is a view of Aristotle's conception of corrective justice which has enjoyed some following among tort theorists in recent years, according to which corrective justice is *distinct* from distributive justice and entirely *independent* of it.[2] The distinctness of the two is, of course, asserted by Aristotle in a well-known passage in the *Nicomachean Ethics*, and no one could seriously doubt that he does take the *forms* of these two kinds of justice to be distinct:

> What is just in distributions of common assets will always fit the [geometrical] proportion mentioned above. . . . On the other hand, what is just in transactions is certainly equal in a way, and what is unjust is unequal; but still it fits numerical proportion, not the [geometrical] proportion of the other species (1131b28–32a2; Irwin 1985a).

He goes on to say that justice in transactions, or corrective justice, "treats the people involved as equals, when one does injustice and the other suffers it," looking "only at differences in the harm," and ignoring the differences in merit between the two parties that would be determinative in distributive justice (1132a3–6).

It seems to be widely assumed that this formal distinction between distributive and corrective justice precludes any substantial relationship between the two, and various conclusions are then drawn from this. Most interestingly, perhaps, the authority of this Aristotelian notion of corrective justice is invoked in one way or another in support of a private law conception of tort liability, in opposition to any vision of it as an instrument of public policy through which larger distributive aims might be promoted. "Aristotle's account stands opposed to . . . the utopianism of the social reformer, the economic calculations of the maximizer of efficiency, and the romantic nihilism of those who proclaim that law is dead," says Weinrib (1987, 152), referring in turn to Unger 1983, Posner 1977, and Kairys 1982. Not so far removed from this is Richard Epstein's well-known attempt to invoke the notion of corrective justice on behalf of a private law conception of torts, with the apparent aim of sharply limiting corporate liability (Epstein 1980). Posner, in turn, has argued that Aristotle's view is in fact essentially compatible with his own economic theory of law (Posner 1981), but his scholarship has not been compelling enough to alter the impression that Aristotle's notion of corrective justice implies a private law conception of torts and stands opposed to a progressive politics of law.

What is rather remarkable about all of this, apart from the generally cavalier and, in the case of Weinrib, obscure treatment of the Aristotelian texts, is how little it has been recognized that Aristotle's formal distinction between distributive and corrective justice does not preclude his holding that there are varieties of corrective justice which presuppose forms of distributive justice. It is generally *assumed* that formal distinctness entails normative independence, but clearly it does not. For all Aristotle says about the nature of corrective justice, he might nevertheless hold that imposing at least some kinds of sanctions is inappropriate unless certain forms of distributive justice have been attained.

Weinrib's argument is that "the irreducible unity of a transaction disqualifies the possibility of an instrumental understanding of private law" (1987, 148), but this assumes incorrectly that what may be interpreted as a transaction can never also be interpreted as a distribution. The argument is, in any case, neither Aristotle's nor Aristotelian in spirit, and it ignores the larger context of Aristotle's legal thought, and the purposes he thinks law should serve. It ignores the fact that for Aristotle *all* law is an instrument of political rule, and none of it *private* in the modern sense that Weinrib intends. Indeed, it is clear that Aristotle had no such distinction in mind as the modern one between criminal law and torts, and that everything he says about corrective justice might just as reasonably be applied to our criminal law.[3] He uses his term for corrective justice, *diorthôtikon*

(*NE* V.4 1131b25), much as Plato has Protagoras speak of punishment as corrective *(euthunousês)* legal action or correction *(euthunai)* (*Prot.* 326d–e), to speak of setting right or rectifying all manner of wrongs, including adultery, wounding, and killing (1132a4–8), by negating the assailant's gain *(kerdos)* with a penalty (9–14). It is a bit odd, then, that recent attention to Aristotle's remarks about corrective justice has occupied itself so single-mindedly with applications in the law of torts.

Although Aristotle would not have called corrective justice an "instrument of public policy," he did, as we have seen, regard law in general as one of the two fundamental tools of the legislator's craft, and he thought that legislators should exploit its full potential in pursuing the state's natural aim. That aim, as we have seen, is the promotion of a partnership in pursuit of the best life, which requires promoting the virtue and well-being of all citizens, and the resolution and elimination of conflict,[4] including most particularly the ever present conflict between rich and poor. Aristotle assumed that these aims could be accomplished in part through laws which were implemented or enforced, as the Athenian homicide code was,[5] through privately initiated actions. Thus, if my purpose here were to develop a theory of torts consistent with Aristotle's view of the larger purposes of the law concerned with interpersonal harms, I would connect the idea of restoring "equality" between the two parties to a harm, not with the troubled notion of making the aggrieved party "whole again" through compensation, but rather with the goal of resolving conflict, and through the ancient notion that anger may be appeased and "vengeance bought off."[6] I would also press the claim that the notion of "restoring equality" was itself a quite progressive one not long before Aristotle's time, inasmuch as it introduced a range of protected rights held by rich and poor alike, and thereby rejected forms of aristocratic privilege which had been common before the democratic reforms of Solon. This is a project for another occasion, however.

My concern here is with criminal law, and if I am right about Aristotle's endorsement of either or both versions of the *argument from the foundations of corrective justice*, then he cannot regard corrective justice and distributive justice as entirely independent. Rather, he must regard corrective justice as resting in the achievement of an equitable distribution of education. Let us proceed, then, to Aristotle's account of responsibility and consider what evidence it may provide that he does indeed endorse the *complicity version* of *FCJ*.

6.2 RESPONSIBILITY FOR ACTIONS AND FOR CHARACTER

Aristotle says at the close of *NE* III.5 that states of character "are in our power and voluntary," because they are produced by voluntary actions which it is in our power to do or not do (1114b29–15a3). Many commentators have inferred from this that he believes an agent would not be responsible for what he does if he were not also responsible for having the state of character that explains his doing what he does, and that he argues that we are all of us in fact responsible for having the characters we do.[7] Understood this way, he seems to hold that an agent, *A*, is not responsible for any *x*, unless *A* is *radically responsible* for *x*. That is, he seems to hold that for *A* to be responsible for *x*, *A* must be the uncaused cause of *x*, and *A*'s producing *x* must be unconditionally avoidable.

This reading is surely anachronistic in imputing to Aristotle a modern concept of *freedom of the will* and the belief that moral responsibility *requires* freedom of the will. It is also profoundly at odds with Aristotle's account of the formation of moral character and rational capacities: his view that people are naturally constituted in such a way as to act in pursuit of what they perceive to be good, that their perceptions of the good are determined by their moral training and habituation, and that their capacity to act in pursuit of higher goods in the face of conflicting present goods and prospects of pain must be produced by training and practice. Strangely enough, commentators have adopted this traditional reading of *NE* III.5 and criticized Aristotle for supposedly failing to realize that early training would be a threat to responsibility for character.[8] Clearly, Aristotle did grasp the role of early training and education in character formation, and it is the commentators who err in failing to search for other interpretations of III.5. Since his own well-developed account of character formation could not have been far from his mind when he wrote III.5, it would be most appropriate to conduct that search on the defeasible presumption that his accounts of responsibility, character formation, and the polis's natural and proper role in that formation are compatible.

In contemplating the anachronism of the standard reading, it is useful to recognize that the doctrine that moral responsibility requires freedom of the will entered the tradition through Saint Augustine's positing of free will in response to the theological problem of evil, which is to say the problem of how a god who was the radical creator of the universe and human nature would not be implicated in the wrongdoing of those who possess that nature, and how, if he is implicated in that wrongdoing, he could be in a position to blame human beings for what they do (Augustine 388–91, 3). The idea of a free will, wrote Hobbes, is the idea "of a will of man not subject to the will of God" (Hobbes 1651, xlvi.31), and if this is correct, then it is unclear why a secular conception of morality and moral responsibility would require any such idea. The theological need to theoretically preclude divine complicity in human wrongdoing, however, is *similar* to the requirement that the polis in its legislative and educative capacities, i.e., the state, not be complicit in a citizen's wrongdoing if it is to justly censure and punish. The important difference is that the assumption of a god who invents human nature out of whole cloth and with unlimited foresight has been understood to require the assumption of a capacity of choice which severs all connection between a person's nature and the quality of his or her actions—thereby breaking any connection between the quality of those actions and God[9]—whereas

Aristotle's rather plausible account of moral development and the difference a polis can make to it requires only good faith educative efforts toward those whose possession of ordinary human rational potential both demands those efforts—as an obligation of fidelity to reason (§4.1)—and makes them beings for whom virtue and vice are possible (*NE* VII.6 1149b31–50a1).

It would take us too far afield to pursue the lengthy analysis of the evidence which these claims call for, but if they are correct, then the modern doctrine that moral responsibility requires free will provides no reason at all to favor the standard interpretation of III.5, and a proper understanding of it is interestingly consistent with the view that we can interpret Aristotle as adopting the Socratic view of complicity, without hesitating to regard his account of responsibility as an account of *moral* responsibility. The traditional interpretation assumes that freedom of the will is required for moral responsibility, interprets Aristotle as having an account of moral responsibility, and infers that his remarks about the voluntariness of character traits is an attempt to assert a form of freedom of the will. Other accounts share this modern assumption about moral responsibility and infer from Aristotle's moral psychology, and sometimes facts about the context of Greek thought, that his account of responsibility is *not* an account of moral responsibility.[10]

I am advocating a third approach that asserts a deeper continuity between ancient and modern accounts of responsibility, resting in a principle of noncomplicity. Aristotle does not speak of "moral responsibility" *per se*, but simply of responsibility *(aitia)*. While *aitia* is a kind of causal *(aitos)* relationship between an agent or the agent's state of moral character and an item of conduct or product of conduct, Aristotle seems to regard a judgment of responsibility as both a retrospective moral assessment which may be formulated in praise and blame, as when we say, e.g., that some damage, *d*, is *A*'s fault, and a warrant—*in a well-ordered society*—for imposing sanctions such as censure and punishment. Thus, I do not see any good reason to deny that Aristotle's account of responsibility is an account of moral responsibility, but neither do I regard the attribution of moral responsibility as having the unconditional justificatory force, in fact or for Aristotle, that has been assumed so often in the modern era. Judgments of moral responsibility are *diagnostic* first, and *justificatory* only second and often problematically.

With this preface, I will now sketch out the broad contours of Aristotle's account of responsibility, and then proceed to *NE* III.5 itself.

6.21 The Human Being as an Origin of Action

It is obvious that responsibility and voluntariness are closely linked in the *Nicomachean Ethics*, but what the relationship is exactly is less clear, and perhaps less clear still is what the nature of either of these is, positively speaking. Considerable confusion has been created, no doubt, by the fact that the *NE* devotes a great deal of attention to involuntariness, so that the definition of voluntariness seems to derive from it; but this confusion can be rectified through a closer reading of the *NE* itself, as well as through a comparison with the *Magna Moralia* and the *Eudemian Ethics*, both of which proceed by defining voluntary action before involuntary action, and not in terms of it.[11]

The causal character of *aitia,* or responsibility, is evident in Aristotle's remark in *NE* III.5 that "man is a moving principle or begetter of his actions as of children" (1113b18–19). This same idea recurs at greater length in both of the earlier works, including *EE* II.6 as follows:

> Every substance is by nature a sort of principle; therefore each can produce many similar to itself, as man man, animals in general animals, and plants plants. But in addition to this man alone of animals is also the source of certain actions; . . . as elsewhere, the source or principle is the cause of all that exists through it (1222b16–30).

Following this he says that praise and blame are given "only for what we ourselves are causes of, . . . that virtue and badness have to do with matters where the man himself is the cause and source of his acts" (1223a11–15). Here we see first the claim that only human beings are capable of action, virtue, and vice, and further the implied claim that this is the case because no other kind of creature is so constituted as to be the right kind of source of motion. Besides this general requirement for being properly subject to attributions of responsibility, namely that the subject of those attributions possess the rational capacities or "power of choice or calculation" normal to human beings (*NE* VII.6 1149b31–50a3), we see the further requirement that one can only be properly held responsible for those particular things that one is the "cause and source" of. We will need to consider each of these requirements in turn after noting what Aristotle says about biological begetting in the *MM*.

What is interesting in the *MM* treatment of the topic is that we are told that action springs from principles in much the way that a tree springs from a seed, the seed being "a kind of principle *(archê)*" (1187a33–34). A seed, of course, is the origin of a tree without being its *radical* origin, or one whose disposition to produce that tree is not shaped and made what it is by prior causes. This is consistent with the statement in the *NE* that we beget our actions as we do our children, and it suggests that whatever Aristotle concedes to the objection posed at 1114a3 in *NE* III.5, it is not, as William Hardie suggests, that "the agent's activity, although a moving principle, is not an original or spontaneous principle of movement," since it is determined by character (Hardie 1980, 175). Springing from character is precisely what makes activity spontaneous, in Aristotle's view.

To continue, however, we must ask what it is about human beings that makes Aristotle regard them alone as capable of action, and thereby subject in general to judgments of responsibility. A good place to start is with Aristotle's remarks regarding children and other animals, for there we find an account of the attributes of civilized adults which make them, but not other animals and children, full-fledged agents who are properly regarded as generally responsible for what they do. These attributes come under the heading of choice or decision *(prohairesis)*, which animals are incapable of because they lack "deliberative imagination" *(DA* 343a5–10). Both children and animals act from appetite, or desire that is not mediated by deliberation, he implies *(NE* III.1 1111a24–27; *Phys.* 197b4–8), whereas "when we have decided as a result of deliberation, we desire in accordance with our deliberation" *(NE* III.3 1113a12–13). Deliberation, as Aristotle describes it, is probably best understood as an activity that includes identification of the constituents of an end (Wiggins 1980, 225), as well as selection of means that are appropriate to an end *(NE* III.3 1112b13), and involving the ability to recognize and respond to the relevance of various relevant considerations *(NE* VI.5 1140b5–6 and 16–21). Aristotle seems to assume that children lack these forms of reasoning required for deliberation, and they are thus not sources and causes of *action*, properly speaking, and not full-fledged moral agents *(EE* 1224a27–30).

Besides reasoning or thought, choice also requires a state of character or conception of the good, which children lack at least by and large, since states *(hexeis)* of this kind are formed over time through "activities exercised on particular objects" *(NE* 1105b10–12), and endure in a way that children's preferences typically do not. "The origin *(archê)* of action," Aristotle says:

> . . . is choice *(prohairesis),* and that of choice is desire *(orexis)* and reasoning *(logos)* with a view to an end. This is why choice cannot exist either without intellect and thought *(nou kai dianoia)* or without a state of character *(êthikês . . . hexiôs);* for good action and its opposite cannot exist without a combination of intellect and character. Intellect itself, however, moves nothing, but only intellect which aims at an end and is practical. . . . Hence choice is either desiderative thought or intellectual desire, and such an origin of action is a man *(kai toiautê archê anthrôpos)* *(NE* VI.2 1139a32–b5).

So it is having the capacity for choice or decision that makes fully developed human beings sources of action, and not merely sources of motion, and this capacity for choice requires the capacities of reasoning involved in deliberation and a state of character or stable structure of ends or conception of the good.

6.22 Voluntariness and Responsibility

Turning now from this general condition for responsibility to the idea that we are responsible for just those things that have their source and cause in us, Aristotle says in *NE* VI.5 that "the origin of what is done is that for the sake of which it is done" (1140b15–16). This suggests that it is, at least roughly, the dependency of differences in conduct on the agent's state of character, with its conception of the good or proper ends of action, that makes that conduct the agent's and subject to praise or blame. This is essentially what we find at work in Aristotle's account of voluntariness, which begins with the observation that "on voluntary passions and actions praise and blame are bestowed, on those that are involuntary forgiveness, and sometimes also pity" (*NE* III.1 1109b30–32).

Aristotle's account of voluntariness *(to hekousion)* and involuntariness *(to akousion)* begin from the premise that

> Those things . . . are thought involuntary, which take place under compulsion or owing to ignorance; and that is compulsory of which the moving principle is outside, being a principle in which nothing is contributed by the person who acts or is acted upon (1109b35–10a3).

He goes on to consider the puzzling case of "mixed" actions, which a person would not ordinarily choose to do, but does under threat of something worse, such as in throwing cargo overboard in order to save a ship in a storm. Since the moving principle is in the agent and the act is "worthy of choice at the time" when it is done (1110a12), an act of this kind is "voluntary, but in the abstract perhaps involuntary; for no one would choose any such act in itself" (1110a17–19). What Aristotle seems to have in mind here is that even in many difficult and threatening circumstances people can be expected to choose what is best in the circumstances, and to the extent that they do or do not they have acted in a way that reflects the state of their character or conception of the good, and are thus open to praise or blame. In modern terms, one who does the best that circumstances permit can offer an adequate justification for his or her action, and it is this justification that shields the agent from any blame for doing something that should not ordinarily be done.

By contrast, Aristotle recognizes that there are also circumstances in which a person may be forgiven for doing "what he ought not under pressure which overstrains human nature and which no one could withstand" (1110a24–25). Although we might expect him to say that in these cases a person's capacity to make a rational decision has simply been overwhelmed by fear, and the connection between the person's particular preferences or state of character and the act broken,[12] he does not. He admits as an *excusing* condition only those forms of compulsion in which "the cause is in the external circumstances and the agent contributes nothing" (1110b1–3), such as in being "carried somewhere by a wind" (1110a3).

Having said this, Aristotle then entertains and denies the Socratic asymmetry thesis, in what is evidently its Platonic formulation, since it is concerned with the inability to do what is right in the presence of pleasures and pains:

> it is absurd to make external circumstances responsible, and not oneself, as being caught by such attractions [pleasures], and to make oneself responsible for noble acts but the pleasant objects responsible for base acts (1110b13–15).

The argument he offers in denying the existence of any asymmetry is that since it is in pursuit of the "pleasant and noble" that "all men do everything they do," if one regarded pleasant and noble objects as having "compelling power" over people, then "all acts would be . . . compulsory" (1110b9–10; cf. 1111a25–11b3). In saying this, Aristotle is of course not denying that good people alone are able to judge "each class of things rightly" and see "the truth in them" (III.4 1113a30–33), so neither can he be denying that in some sense people of good character are able to act well and people of bad character are not. His concern here is evidently to defend the everyday and juridical use of the category of the voluntary to mark off acts that are attributable to a person's being the kind of person he or she is. This is a sensible thing to do, because the finding of fact it involves—the determination that a harm is the fault of one person and not another, or of neither but instead a peculiarity of the circumstances—is an essential preliminary to any resolution of the bad feelings and potential for continuing conflict that arise from interpersonal harms. The concept of responsibility is, as I have said, an essentially diagnostic one.

This pattern of analysis followed by a response to the Socratic view is then repeated in Aristotle's account of ignorance as a sufficient condition for involuntariness. Just as the agent must contribute nothing if the force of circumstances is to qualify as exculpating compulsion, an agent must not be the source of his or her own ignorance if the ignorance is to entail involuntariness and a lack of responsibility. This consideration gives rise to a third category of actions, which are neither voluntary nor involuntary. The kind of ignorance that makes an act involuntary must be ignorance that originates outside of the agent, for otherwise the act *does* have its origin and cause in the agent. Yet voluntariness requires knowledge of the circumstances (*NE* III.1 1111a22–24), so when an act is done in ignorance of the circumstances of action, and that ignorance is the agent's own fault, then responsibility arises because the act and any resulting harm have their source and cause in the agent, even though the act is not voluntary. So clearly Aristotle does not want to restrict responsibility to voluntary action, as is sometimes thought.[13] He thinks we are responsible for some action that is not voluntary as well.

So we find Aristotle distinguishing involuntary acts done *by reason of* ignorance, or caused by ignorance which is explained by the circumstances and not by a defect of the agent's character, from acts done *in* ignorance, though he never gives us a name in the language of voluntariness *(hekousion)* for this category of action that is neither voluntary nor involuntary. The distinction is introduced in *NE* III.1:

Acting by reason of ignorance seems also to be different from acting *in* ignorance; for the man who is drunk or in a rage is thought to act as a result not of ignorance but of one of the causes mentioned, yet not knowingly but in ignorance (1110b25–27).

The causes that are mentioned are evidently internal to the agent (the propensity for rage) or within the agent's control (being drunk). Being within the agent's control, the operation of that cause is thus a reflection of, or explained by, the agent's state of character. By contrast, the unknown peculiarities of the circumstances of action may make an actor faultlessly ignorant of things material to the character of the act, and in that case the action is involuntary under certain descriptions (1110b33–11a21).

As Susan Sauvé Meyer has shown in great detail, the idea here is that the agent's state of character must be the intrinsic efficient cause of the act under the relevant description for the agent to be responsible for the act under that description (Meyer 1993, 100 ff.).[14] Put somewhat differently, a characteristic of an act must be traceable to the actor's desires, conception of the good, or state of character—in contemporary terms, his or her preferences—for the actor to be responsible for the act described as having that characteristic. If serving tea was only lethal because there was no reason to suspect that the tea had been laced with cyanide, then it is no reflection on the host, and he cannot be properly said to have voluntarily killed his guests or to be responsible for their deaths. The pattern of causal explanatory reasoning at work here may be regarded as *contrastive*: a person is the source and cause—essential efficient cause—of a harm if and only if one could have relied upon a person of acceptably good character to have acted in such a different way in the same circumstances that the harm would not have occurred.

Following these remarks on ignorance, involuntariness, and what is neither voluntary nor involuntary, Aristotle returns to the doctrines of Socrates, by first confirming the Socratic view that all wrongdoing involves ignorance, and then insisting that this should not matter to deciding what is voluntary or involuntary:

> Now every wicked man is ignorant of what he ought to do and what he ought to abstain from, and error of this kind makes men unjust and in general bad; but the term "involuntary' tends to be used not if a man is ignorant of what is to his advantage—for it is not ignorance in choice that makes action involuntary (it makes men wicked), nor ignorance of the universal (for *that* they are *blamed*), but ignorance of the particular circumstances of the action and the objects with which it is concerned (1110b28–11a1).

This passage again confirms that Aristotle is making a distinction between acting involuntarily and being unjust in one's state of character owing to ignorance of the nature of what one chooses over a long span of time. His point here is that ignorance of the good does not make one's pursuit of the bad involuntary, or make one not responsible for the harm one does, but this is consistent with holding that it would be futile and unjust to censure and punish people who had never enjoyed the benefits of moral training and education.

6.23 *Nicomachean Ethics* III.5

Aristotle returns again at the start of *NE* III.5 to the Socratic dictum that "no one is voluntarily wicked or involuntarily blessed," and denies the asymmetry again on the grounds that a man is "a moving principle or begetter of his actions as of children" and "the acts whose moving principles are in us must themselves also be in our power and voluntary" (1113b17–22). This is the same pattern of argument as in the *MM*, and again this suggests that in general one need not be the source of the source in oneself of one's actions, in order to be the source of one's actions, anymore than one must be one's own parent in order to be the parent of one's child. This prompts a repetition of evidence regarding the conventional use of the terms "voluntary" *(hekousion)* and "involuntary" *(akousion),* including a reference to the punishment that legislators mandate for "those who do wicked acts (unless they have acted under compulsion or as a result of ignorance for which they are not themselves responsible)" (1113b24–25), and for those

> thought responsible for the ignorance, as when penalties are doubled in the case of drunkenness; . . . and so too in the case of anything else that they are thought to be ignorant of through carelessness; we assume that it is in their power not to be ignorant, since they have the power of taking care (1113b30–14a3).

One thing to be noted in this passage is that it says not that everyone has the power of taking care, but that the attribution of responsibility for ignorance *depends upon the assumption* of a power of taking care.

What follows immediately is the objection, "But perhaps a man is the kind of man not to take care" (1114a3–4). This would seem to be again the Platonic form of the Socratic objection, since it is concerned not simply with ignorance, but with the capacity to not be ignorant, even in the presence of pleasures such as those of alcohol, which Plato and Aristotle agree one needs training to resist (§2.42, §5.3). It is Aristotle's answer to this objection which was long regarded as the key to his theory of responsibility, which is to say his alleged assertion that we are all responsible for having the states of character we do, and only for this reason responsible for our actions:

> they [who lack the capacity to take care] are themselves by their slack lives responsible for becoming men of that kind, and men are themselves responsible for being unjust or self-indulgent, in that they cheat or spend their time in drinking bouts and the like; for it is activities exercised on particular objects that make the corresponding character. . . . Now not to know that it is from the exercise of activities on particular objects that states of character are produced is the mark of a thoroughly senseless person. Again, it is irrational to suppose that a man who acts unjustly does not wish to be unjust. . . . But if without being ignorant a man does the things which will make him unjust, he will be unjust voluntarily (*NE* 1114a4–13).

Aristotle insists here that people *ought* to recognize that their actions contribute to their becoming people of a certain kind, but he cannot say—in light of his own account of the formation of desire, moral perception, and understanding—that those who have been brought up badly are capable of becoming anything but bad. The sentences that follow seem to acknowledge this by invoking a medical analogy suggestive of the legislator's educational responsibilities:

> Yet it does not follow that if he wishes he will cease to be unjust and will be just. For neither does the man who is ill become well on those terms. Although he may perhaps, be ill voluntarily, through living incontinently and disobeying his doctors. In that case it was *then* open to him not to be ill, but not now, when he has thrown away his chance. . . . So too, to the unjust and to the self-indulgent man it was open at the beginning not to become men of this kind, and so they are unjust voluntarily; but now that they have become so it is not possible for them not to be so (*NE* 1114a13–23).

Through the image of disobeying the doctors from whom one has presumably received appropriate instruction, Aristotle invokes the provision of such instruction—by analogy, the instruction and training which a good legislator would provide—as a background assumption essential to sustaining his defense of the conventional use of the categories of voluntariness and involuntariness in imposing censure and punishment. In doing this, he accepts the force of the Platonic objection which has prompted this response, and observes that *if* we assume a background of proper education, then an unjust person's lack of capacity to know and do the right thing will be self-inflicted and not the state's fault, inasmuch as he ought to know that his actions are instrumental in forming his state of character. He acknowledges that the voluntariness of wrongdoing, as it is conventionally understood, can only be a sufficient condition for punishing someone if instruction, persuasion, and training have been put before force, as the *principle of fidelity to reason* demands, and the state thereby freed of any complicity in the wrongdoing.[15]

When Aristotle says, then, that "at the beginning" the unjust and self-indulgent had a chance "not to become men of this kind," what he must mean by the beginning is at the conclusion of their proper upbringing and education or sometime thereafter. Meyer argues that he has in mind a fixed point of admission to adulthood, coinciding with an Athenian youth's enrollment as a citizen or *dokimasia*, and there is a good deal of sense in this (Meyer 1993, 124–126, 141). It is only at that point that an Athenian youth would have stood directly before the law, for instance. But the text gives us no reason to think that Aristotle precludes the possibility of a person reaching midlife, say, in a state of habitual virtue, but not complete or fully secure virtue, and succumbing to the seductions of newly found power or untried pleasures, or being consumed by jealousy, hardship, or vengeance brought on by unforeseen circumstances. Aristotle countenances the corruption of good character in such ways in his remarks in *Pol.* II.7 on the dangers of allowing people to accumulate too much wealth, and in *Rh.* II.13, as I noted in §2.2 in connection with related themes in *Laws* II 653c–d and the suggestion in the *Protagoras* that incapacitating misfortune would overthrow only someone who is capable, not the chronically incapable. . . .

. . . a good man may eventually become bad with the passage of time, or through hardship, disease, or some other circumstance that involves the only real kind of faring ill, which is the loss of knowledge (344d–45b).

Given these indications of Aristotle's belief that it is possible for a person to fall at any point in life from a better state of character to a worse one, if he or she begins and continues to do the wrong things, it seems most reasonable to suppose that he is here in III.5 allowing that a person can be responsible for falling into a vicious and incapacitated state of character whenever that might occur after the completion of a suitable education.[16] What Aristotle has in mind by a suitable education in virtue, we have already seen.[17]

The context of Aristotle's reference to bringing ruin upon oneself through incontinent living in defiance of one's doctor's orders (at 1114a15–16) suggests that he intends medical art as a model for legislative art—not as it is actually practiced, but as it should be—in this instance as in others.[18] Appearing as it does in the context of a discussion of blame and punishment, the reference is strongly suggestive of similar clauses in *Laws* V 727c (in the prelude to the laws as a whole: "when he delights in pleasures contrary to the advice and praise given by the lawgiver") and IX 853b (the prelude to the law of capital offenses, with its reference to the education the accused is presumed to have enjoyed). A rather striking combination of thematic elements is also shared by *NE* III.5 and *Laws* I 644b–46d, with its "divine puppet" passage (644e) and insistence that education is essential if people are to become rational, autonomous, and law abiding. The whole discussion of education in this passage in *Laws* I is set in the context of a discussion of drunkenness, the loss of control involved in drunkenness, and how the legislator might use regulated drinking parties in fashioning education which could prevent such loss of control or promote self-rule in accordance with reason. In the *NE* passage, drunkenness and the loss of control involved in drunkenness appear at 1113b31 and 1114a6 and 27, and at 1113a15–18 and 22–31 are related to voluntary bodily defect, a topic appearing in much the same form in the *Laws* passage at 646b–c. This cluster of thematic elements shared by *Laws* 644b–46d and *NE* III.5, and the prominence of education in the former, suggest Aristotle had the former in mind when he wrote the latter. This also reinforces the conclusion that he is acknowledging here that the legitimacy of censure and punishment rest on prior appropriate educational efforts on the legislator's part, and that these efforts must provide the same education for all citizens and include not just instruction but training which enables people to act more in conformity with reason than they otherwise could.

Another related passage worth noting is Aristotle's own remarks on drunkenness and liability in *Pol.* II.12. His comment there on the law of Pittacus, which provides that "if a drunken man do something wrong, he shall be more heavily punished than if he were sober," is that this ignores the excuse that may be offered and looks "only to expediency," rather than justice (1274b18–23). The inconsistency between this and his endorsement of the same convention in *NE* III.5 is curious, but the position in *Pol.* II.12 may be considered closer to that of the *Laws*, insofar as the incapacity involved in drunkenness and in being "drunk with pleasure" are treated as closely analogous in *Laws* I,[19] and the conventional juridical uses of voluntariness and involuntariness are rejected because wrongdoing arises from just such incapacity and the ignorance it involves (*Laws* IX 860c–64b). What is most likely is that the passage in the *Politics* predates the one in the *Nicomachean Ethics*, and that what is different in the latter arises from a desire, which Aristotle did not yet have when he composed *Pol.* II.12, to reconcile the conventional uses of voluntariness and involuntariness with Plato's claim that "those who are able to rule themselves are good, those who cannot are bad" (*Laws* I 644b).

With these basic points of interpretation and textual etiology in hand, we need to continue by considering two remaining points of contention, and finish with a brief look at a second objection and response which appears in *NE* III.5.

One point we must be clear on is that Aristotle's view cannot be that properly raised and educated people acquire an unqualified capacity to freely choose bad actions and a bad state of character, and become bad by *choosing* these. If they have been well brought up and educated they will *not* choose them, because they would not desire to and would take no pleasure in doing so. Roberts makes essentially this point in objecting to Meyer's suggestion that what Aristotle envisions is youths choosing between the activities "that will complete or preclude the formation of a virtuous character" (Roberts 1995, 578; Meyer 1993, 126), and Meyer, for her part, does not make it clear how it could be consistent with Aristotle's psychology for a person who had enjoyed the advantages of a good upbringing and education to "throw it all away," as we say. Whether Aristotle is contemplating youths at the threshold of virtue or people of any age who have acquired virtue that is habitual but not complete, some account is required of how a descent into vice, ignorance, and incapacity can result from a person's own voluntary actions, without bad actions or character being objects of choice.

The assumption I believe we must make is that although an adequate upbringing and education will make every reasonable effort to develop the capacity and disposition to resist pleasures and pains to the extent that they should be resisted, a person of limited experience of the world will remain vulnerable to at least some fears, desires, and strong disturbing emotions elicited by difficult and unfamiliar circumstances. Any of these might cause a person to lose sight of things important to the quality of his actions and the difference those actions will have to the kind of person he is becoming. As Aristotle says in his account of *akrasia*, or weakness of will, it is possible to have knowledge in a sense, yet not have it

> as in the instance of a man asleep, mad, or drunk. But now this is just the condition of men under the influence of passions; for outbursts of anger and sexual appetites

and some other such passions, it is evident, actually alter our bodily condition. . .
(*NE* VII.3 1147a13–16).

Aristotle is suggesting here that the intoxication of desire and alcoholic intoxication are alike in causing a physically mediated corruption of perception
(1147b15–17), which leads people to voluntarily act in a way that is contrary to
what their deliberations lead them to choose, oblivious all the while to the risk
to their ends and to their character if they grow accustomed to acting in that way.
Aristotle says nothing to rule out the operation of this mechanism of ignorance
in those who are generally virtuous but *akratic*—or simply inexperienced—with
respect to particular objects of choice, including "victory, honor, wealth" and the
like (VII.4 1147b30). The relevance of this to his position in III.5 is suggested
by the reference to "living incontinently" at 1114a16.

A person who is well prepared for virtue but inexperienced might also mis-
judge friends and associates, and be seduced by them into misjudging situations
and the risks inherent in them. In *Republic* VIII, Plato describes a course of descent from a just state of character to an unjust one, emphasizing the seductively
corrupting influence of associates who have mistaken conceptions of happiness,
and there is perhaps an echo of this in Aristotle's reference in *NE* III.5 to people
"spend[ing] their time in drinking bouts and the like" (1114a5–6), since that is
something one would do with undesirable associates. The desire that displaces
the actor's grasp of the correct end might in this case be the desire for compan-
ionship, misdirected through inexperienced judgment; the perceptual error material to doing what is directly destructive of good character would arise from
the seductive influence of the companions' errors.

Perceptual errors arising in either of these ways could lead a person of considerable virtue to act in ways he does not see are self-indulgent and unjust, and
as Aristotle says in *NE* II.1, "it is from the same causes and by the same events
[viz., what we practice] that every virtue is both produced *and destroyed
(eptharatai)*" (1103b6–7; emphasis added). What must be assumed is that he
should have known better than to pursue such pleasures immoderately or accept
such people's vision of happiness, and that most people who had received the
same adequate training and instruction *would have* known better. For on this assumption the statesman can with justice conclude that it is something in the person himself, and not the inadequacy of the education provided, that explains his
weakness and failure.

A second point we must be clear on is that the passage in *NE* III.5 which we
have been examining does not qualify or alter the relationship between voluntariness and responsibility identified in the preceding section (§6.22). An actor remains responsible for an act (under a description) or event just in case the
actor's state of character is the source and cause, or intrinsic efficient cause, of
the act (under that description) or event. What this passage does is lay down a
condition for using responsibility or the absence of involuntariness to justify
punishment and harsh censure; to justify any response which is not, as Plato says,

"of the most gentle character, full of understanding" (*Laws* IX 863c). As I suggested above, Aristotle seems to regard a judgment of responsibility as a diagnostic determination that a given act or event arose from and is explained by a person's state of moral character. He does not seem to regard a determination of responsibility as a sufficient license in itself for imposing sanctions. This is not to say that judgments of responsibility may not be formulated in praise and blame suitable for use in the moral instruction of both children and adults. Aristotle clearly does approve of using them in this way, as Roberts rightly emphasizes (Roberts 1989b, 25–26), but there are grounds not only in the *Laws*, but also in *Prot.* 325b–c and *Pol.* VII.13 1332a12–16, for regarding this educational use as distinct from the use of judgments of responsibility in licensing harsh and forceful penalties, whether curative in intent or suitable to one beyond cure. The considerations arising under the *principle of fidelity to reason*, demanding that persuasion and instruction be put before force and violence, constrain this latter use but not the former, and I have argued that Aristotle acknowledges this in *NE* III.5.

A second objection in the dialectic of *NE* III.5 repeats in a somewhat different form the Platonic version of the Socratic asymmetry thesis, and Aristotle's answer is cautious and limited to defending the equal voluntariness of good and bad actions (1114a31–b2). For this purpose he need not assert that appropriately educated bad people will have had some control over what ends appear good to them. It is sufficient to construct the following dilemma:

> Whether, then, it is not by nature that the end appears to each man such as it does appear, but something also depends on him, or the end is natural but because the good man does the rest virtue is voluntary, vice also will be none the less voluntary; for in the case of the bad man there is equally present that which depends on himself *in his actions* even if not in his end. If, then, as is asserted, the virtues are voluntary (for we are ourselves somehow part-causes of our states of character, and it is by being persons of a certain kind that we assume the end to be so and so), the vices also will be voluntary; for the same is true of them (1114b17–25; emphasis added).

This does not challenge in any way the Socratic dictum that ignorance is a barrier to harsh censure and punishment, provided there is still any hope that instruction and persuasion may remedy that ignorance. What this passage does, in effect, is assert that even if actors have no control over the ends they pursue, their actions in pursuit of those ends depend upon the actors themselves, in the sense of originating in them, and are thus voluntary, whether they are good or bad. This follows from Aristotle's account of voluntariness, which holds that if the ends we pursue are *our* ends, then our actions in pursuit of those ends have originated in *us*, are attributable to our being the way we are, and are subject to praise and blame.

This, and what Aristotle has said in response to the first objection, is all the argument that he gives us in *NE* III.5, and so when he says in summing up that the virtues are states of character which "are in our power and voluntary" (1114b26–30), this clearly does not report a considered judgment that it is entirely up to us what ends we pursue. He must mean that there is a conditional sense in which virtuous and vicious actions are both in our power (namely, that the kinds of actions we perform depend upon our states of character), and that through our voluntary actions we can either confirm ourselves in a state of virtue, or fall, through growing accustomed to doing the wrong thing, into a less desirable state of character. We must conclude that Aristotle's views do not imply that agents can freely choose their ends, nor that such freedom is a necessary condition for responsibility. Yet he assigns responsibility for the promotion of good character development to the statesman, and Aristotle's handling of the medical analogy in III.5 confirms that he would count the statesman's conscientious sponsorship of a public system of education as a necessary condition for people being punished and censured for the harm they do. It confirms that the *complicity version* of the *argument from the foundations of corrective justice* is at least implicit in Aristotle's accounts of education, moral development, and corrective justice.

6.3 THE PRESUPPOSITIONS OF CORRECTIVE JUSTICE

Michael Philips observed some years ago that "the theory of punishment is importantly connected with the theory of state authority," because "the moral justification of punishment by the state is obviously importantly connected to the moral justification of the state's authority" (Philips 1986, 393). He noted, quite aptly, that the full significance of this had received little notice in recent work on the justification of punishment. By contrast, its significance does seem to have been appreciated by Socrates, Plato, and Aristotle in what I have called here the *argument from the foundations of corrective justice (FCJ)*.[20]

The threat of punishment may be required to create and preserve the rule of law, but punishment also *presupposes* a rule of law, and thus a background of good faith effort to establish a rule of law through such noncoercive and largely educational measures as may be reasonably thought sufficient to establish civil order. In the absence of those measures the legitimacy of speaking of the enforcement *of law* would be in doubt, and so there arise issues of fundamental importance regarding the content and scope of distribution of the education that is necessary to establishing the norms of public life, and inducing individuals to comply (or initiating them into compliance) with those norms. Since compliance with law is ineluctably a *de jure* condition for uninterrupted enjoyment of a range of important goods and rights, and since compliance is likely to be substantially causally influenced by preparation for compliance, the distribution of such preparation or education must be viewed as an important issue of distributive justice. Thus, corrective justice may presuppose a form of distributive justice, i.e., a just distribution of goods of a sort that is essential to becoming and remaining a full member of the society bound by the law to be enforced. Putting it bluntly, there may be failures to include individuals in full membership in society—to initiate them into the compliance with law that is a condition for full membership—that are so serious as to make *punishment* morally improper even in the face of serious violations of law.

What rationally compelling implications this view of legitimate punishment may have for contemporary law and education is not altogether clear, of course. This unclarity rests, in part, in the uncertain status of the principles on which the two versions of *FCJ* rest. We need to begin by asking whether there are versions of the *consent* and *complicity* principles relied on above which may warrant acceptance, and then determine what is entailed by these principles in a modern setting.

Aristotle nowhere duplicates the list of conditions for meaningful consent suggested at *Crito* 51d–53a, but this list, and Plato's account of the "double method" employed by good doctors and the preludes to the laws, provide a general indication of what Aristotle would have understood by proper conditions for consent. They derive from, and attempt to do justice to, the same principle of fidelity to reason which we have found cause to attribute to Aristotle. What we have in the first instance, then, is a rather rich notion of consent, and the idea that consent of this sort is a requirement for legitimate law and enforcement of law. Second, we have found reason to infer that Aristotle's view is that moral responsibility or blameworthiness for a legally proscribed wrong is not a sufficient basis in itself for a state to impose censure and punishment, if the laws lack authority or the state is itself implicated in the wrong. Although this deserves further comment, there is nothing remarkable about it, since the right to punish, as it is normally claimed by governments, is patently relational to begin with. It applies only to actors and conduct within the jurisdictional authority of the laws to be enforced.

A reasonable course for us to take, then, is to begin by considering how much of this notion of consent might be salvaged, supposing that we might be able to agree that consent is necessary for the law to have authority. A sympathetic line to take would be to try to identify the conditions that would be necessary for consent to be genuine, or free, or properly informed; and taking this line one might well agree that meaningful popular authorization of law would require some of the very things we have reason to think Aristotle would insist on. It might include not only publication of the reasons for the laws being as they are, but also education that would by and large enable people to appreciate and assess the force of those reasons. Without the first condition, consent would not be properly informed, one might insist, and without the latter condition, consent would not be fully competent and free, in one important sense of the word "free." It would not be free in precisely the sense that one would lack the capacity to be rationally self-determining in the relevant domain of choice.

This line of thinking may be summed up by distinguishing three forms of consent. The first is "simple consent," or consent that is merely voluntary, in the sense of noncoerced. Consent theories in the classical liberal mold, when they rely on a notion of real consent, whether "express" or "tacit," might *seem* to have simple consent in mind, though it is not so clear that they really do. The second form of consent is "informed consent," by which I mean consent given to something which one knows not only the essential features of, but also the reasons held to favor it, and with knowledge of the alternatives which there are known good reasons to consider. The typical supposition about adults negotiating an original contract is that these conditions are actually met. The third form of consent, with its assumptions of adequate information and rational ability, I will call "rational consent." Rational consent would reflect people's interests with as much reliability as can be guaranteed by reasonable educative efforts, aimed not only to inform but to cultivate abilities to reason and judge.[21]

There is a good deal to be said for this notion of rational consent, since it is a fair approximation of the kind of consent we should rationally prefer to be giving, when we give our consent. In some sense we would all like to be perfectly rational, and to give our consent only when it is perfectly rational for us to do so, but only if coming to be this rational were without cost. Surely it would not be without cost, however, so the kind of consent we should rationally wish to give is consent which is as rational as it could be made to be by an education which enhances rationality up to, but not beyond, the point at which the marginal cost to us of that education ceases to pay for itself through the marginal gains in rationality it is likely to yield.

Moreover, on classical liberal assumptions about the natural course of development of a person's powers of reason, the conditions for this kind of consent would seem to be met by adult original contractors. The Aristotelian view may then be rather more like a classical liberal view than it might first seem to be, the principal differences arising from the former's less optimistic view of the likelihood of a person's coming to possess a rational will without substantial educational efforts, and from its notion that legitimacy requires the creation of conditions favorable to real, ongoing consent. A related difference is that the liberal "state of nature" theories hold that government authority is *derived from* popular authorization, whereas Aristotle regards rule as legitimate only if it is *exercised through* consent, a requirement pertaining to its *manner*.

Turning from *consent* to *complicity*, we have seen that the notion that reason, virtue, and self-control are *attainments* which individuals do not have the wherewithal to secure through their own unaided powers is an aspect of the Aristotelian account which may be understood to have significance beyond any connection it may have with the notion of consent. The view that these attributes are attainments of this sort seems to me correct, and it suggests a principle to the effect that if it is a community's or state's fault that a person turns out badly, then the authority of that community or state cannot be invoked in censuring and punishing that person for the harms that come about owing to his or her badness. This "noncomplicity" principle has the advantage of being morally sound. Given the power of a state, or political community in its legislative and educative capacities, to influence behavior, there is a burden of care it must bear in seeking to establish a rule of law. Its authority to censure and punish must be *established* through its own good faith efforts, on this principle, and the scope of that authority may be considered to be limited to those it has taken reasonable care to incorporate into the life of the community, in accordance with its requirements, but also in the enjoyment of those conditions "favorable to the practice of virtue."

We normally assume that moral responsibility is a sufficient condition for imposing moral censure, i.e., harsh moral criticism, but this seems to me rather implausible in general, and the present claim in particular is that there is a speaker-relative constraint on the appropriateness of censure, and not just actor-relative constraints (the "actor" being in a legal context the defendant). Moral censure is undeniably an important aspect of actual criminal proceedings and punishment (Duff 1986, 39ff.), and so criminal punishment as we know and practice it would seem to be precluded when censure is precluded. This is not to say that if the conditions for rational consent were met, but the conditions for noncomplicity were not met, that our hands would be completely morally tied and all effective avenues to security closed. If we were in no position to censure or punish, we might nevertheless claim a right of self-defense and find alternative means through which to exercise that right. We might also claim a right to exact compensation for damage done, to the extent that a defendant is capable of rendering it. Even conceding this, however, might saddle us with a need for very extensive reform, and it is unthinkable that such reform could be preferable to making adequate educational investments in children to begin with.

But why must these investments be public ones, administered through a public system of education, and not provided at home? Why not regard the burden of *FCJ* as falling on parents? The answer to this I would offer is that doing so would seem to leave us with two options, neither acceptable: we might expect parents who provide inadequate upbringing and education to compensate their children who suffer criminal convictions, or we might establish inadequacy of education as an excuse sufficient to preclude conviction. Two obvious problems with the first option are that parents may be in no position to make any form of compensation, and that even if they are there is no appropriate form of compensation for the loss of moral and social standing entailed by public censure and the loss of liberties and rights of citizenship, including voting rights in most of the United States (Mauer 1998), imposed by a criminal conviction. It would also be intolerable to allow parental failure as an excuse when charges are brought against their children, for deviant norms could then be self-perpetuating, and a system of common law would not have been effectively created. In some societies it is *possible* that spontaneously occurring forms of education would be quite adequate, but there is nevertheless truth in Aristotle's apparent view that initiation into compliance with law must not be left to chance, if the state is to have *assurance* that it is in the right in bringing criminal penalties to bear on its citizens and residents.

This is a powerful argument for a public system of education, but not I think for a system in which attendance at a public school is mandatory. It seems to justify a system in which public measures are taken to ensure that everyone receives an adequate education, and evidence of a private education's fulfillment of state requirements is accepted as grounds for exemption from public schooling.

The principle of noncomplicity has enjoyed no small acceptance among philosophers of the Western tradition, though most notably in connection with the theological problem of evil which I have already referred to.[22] The question that is crucial in understanding the principle's implications for secular moral judgments and the sanctions of both morality and law is what would properly count as a good faith effort, or by contrast, an effort that is so deficient that the individual's badness may be properly judged the state's fault. The view of Plato and Aristotle—if Crito's instruction through the laws and the manner of the "free" doctor of the *Laws* is any indication—would seem to be that those who are to undertake this initiation must proceed by attempting to "commune with" and create relationships of trust with the young, so as to create those conditions in which there is a reasonable chance that they will learn that compliance with law will serve *their* ends and not only those of others, and will accept the principles embodied in law as their own. The young must be drawn into, and made part of, the community bound together by common law, by a kind of attraction, as Plato says, on the assumption that many of them would be unlikely to become a part of it otherwise. To the extent that something like this is correct, and it does not seem to me very far off the mark, it does give us a measure, if only rough, of what is adequate.[23]

Even in the absence of a well-defined threshold of adequate state investment in the foundations of consent and voluntary compliance, one can identify a problem of fairness in instances where such investments are made inequitably. In the face of seriously unequal efforts to enable those who are growing up to come to a rational acceptance of and compliance with law, what is most reasonable may be the view that it is unfair to let the burden of legal sanctions fall as heavily on those who were not properly prepared to accept law as on those who were. This might be developed through a general notion of "equal protection" of the law, understanding by this a principle of natural justice which might or might not be implied by the equal protection clause of the Fourteenth Amendment to the U.S. Constitution. To the extent that a government must engage in certain activities in order to institute a rule of law in the first place, one might consider it under a general duty to engage in those activities in ways that do not place some individuals more at risk of suffering criminal convictions than others. If it is wrong to police or prosecute one segment of the population more aggressively than another, because it unfairly puts the members of that segment at greater risk of conviction, then there is reason to hold that differential investments in moral socialization which influence the likelihood of later criminal activity are also suspect.

6.4 A RADICAL PROPOSAL

What this amounts to, then, is first of all the suggestion that the conditions for one's giving rational consent to the law must be met in order for the law to have legitimate jurisdiction over one, and second that the state must not be at fault for one's inclination to engage in crime if one is to be properly punished. If these conditions have not been met, then there is a sense in which appropriate efforts have not been made to make one part of the society whose full privileges are formally and often substantially contingent upon compliance with law. This goes to the substance of public education in the broadest sense, and demands some form of public system of education. Moreover, it is surely true that a great deal of the burden rests with early upbringing and socialization,[24] so the provisions of family and welfare law, and forms of intervention to assure that every child receives adequate care and socialization, are as much to the point as provisions for adequate schooling are. Nor should the importance of other spheres of socialization beyond home and school be ignored. In any case, where efforts to provide the foundations for rational acceptance of the legitimacy of law are widely or entirely absent there would be no law with any legitimate claim on anyone, and where they are lacking only with respect to particular individuals, one would have to regard those individuals as beyond its scope. Further, where people are allowed to turn out substantially less inclined to accept and comply with law than they might have been through reasonable state efforts, those of whom this is true cannot in good faith be censured or punished by the state. As my remarks about the conditions under which children accept social norms and law suggest, these two lines of thought converge in the idea that a proper foundation for acceptance of law supplies both the grounds for consent and the capacity to comply.

These principles are not far removed from those of classical liberalism, and the critique of punishment which they give rise to would rest on some of the same claims of fact which a Marxist critique of punishment would. Accepting Jeffrie Murphy's "Marxism and Retribution" (1973) as a suitable guide to the Marxist view, it is readily apparent that there are points of convergence pertaining to both consent and complicity. The latter is evident in Murphy's conclusion that it is unjust "to punish people who act out of those very motives that society encourages and reinforces," and in his suggestion that a good deal of crime may in fact arise from motives encouraged by society, such as "greed, selfishness, and indifference to one's fellows" (236). More broadly, he suggests that "criminals typically are not members of a shared community of values with their jailers," and that this is owing to social and economic inequalities which undermine the social sentiments of sympathetic identification and reciprocity (237).

While I would not disagree with either of these claims, the latter seems to me particularly important. There is support for it in the substantial case that can be made through comparative criminological studies for the idea that crime rates are influenced both by workforce participation rates and, independently of that, by the extent of inequality in a society (Currie 1985). Moreover, these are claims about the foundations of social learning of the sorts which are essential to establishing a broad acceptance of law, and I am sympathetic to the idea that at least some industrial nations are doing less toward securing those foundations than they could be reasonably expected to. I would note, however, that this rests on claims about the prospects for reciprocal feelings of goodwill or sympathy extending across class lines, which is perhaps not directly relevant to the dominant pattern of violent crime in the United States, where aggressors and their victims tend to share low socioeconomic status (Reiss et al. 1993, 5). So it may be more directly to the point to focus not on the foundations for broad social reciprocity, but on the question of whether children have decent people in their lives who care about them enough to enable them to care about themselves and others, and thus to form a significantly motivating attachment to the social morality prescribed by the law. There are arguably many children in the United States who now lack this, and are brought up not in accordance with the standards of "decent" society, but in accordance with a brutal "code of the streets."[25] Many others who do come from "decent" homes are subject to simultaneous countersocialization on the street, which in recent years has not stopped even at killing a five-year-old for refusing to steal.[26]

Quite apart from what might be done for such children through providing their parents with better opportunities and assistance, there is evidence of gross failure in the direct socialization undertaken by the state through the medium of public schooling. For one thing, the lower academic "tracks" into which students of low socioeconomic status tend to be placed are unlike others in being characterized by classrooms distinguished by their lack of trust, cooperation, and good will. As Jeannie Oakes concludes in a major study of tracking,

> [observed] differences [in classroom relationships] have a strong potential for leading students differentially either toward affiliation with and active involvement in social institutions or toward alienation from and a more negative involvement in the institutions they encounter (Oakes 1985, 134).

Indeed, there is reason to conclude that the higher incidence of misconduct and criminality among students assigned to lower tracks is in part a consequence of the more hostile climate of the classrooms they are assigned to. More generally, there are factors common to most public schools which have made the typical contact between teachers and students insubstantial and unlikely to generate sympathetic identification, and there is evidence linking these factors to the incidence of crime and violence. Specifically, there is evidence suggesting that the anonymity of large schools, the alienation produced by "hostile and authoritarian attitudes on the part of teachers toward students," and the impossibility of meaningful contact created by high student-to-teacher ratios and a schedule of many short periods of study in a day, each with a different teacher, are all associated with high levels of violence in schools.[27]

Turning now from complicity to consent, there are similarities between Murphy's Marxism and the Aristotelian view on this theme as well, but also significant differences arising from their somewhat different conceptions of consent. "Central to the Social Contract idea," says Murphy, "is the claim that we owe allegiance to the law because the benefits we have derived have been voluntarily accepted." They have been voluntarily accepted, the story goes, because "as rational [people, we] can see that the rules benefit everyone ([ourselves] included) and that [we] would have selected them in the original position of choice," and seeing this we stay and accept those benefits (Murphy 1973, 237). The basis for critique consists then of two claims of fact: that the social classes which produce the larger numbers of criminals do not derive much benefit from the existence of law, and even if they did would lack any means by which to emigrate and thereby forego those benefits. Thus, on two counts, they could not be properly said to consent to the authority of law by voluntarily accepting its benefits.

What is different in the Aristotelian critique is that it could, but need not, make use of the claim that the body of law in question does not benefit members of disadvantaged classes, and that it need not take emigration to be a necessary condition for withholding consent. Law must aim at the good of all citizens to be just, by Aristotle's standards, but on his account the substantive justice of law is not directly related to whether anyone has given his or her consent to it. On his view it is not enough that *a rational person* would consent to a body of law, because *instituting* a rule of law requires far more than this. One does not earn consent simply by conceiving of laws that are substantively attractive. It is necessary, in addition, that people *be* rational, which they turn out to be only under favorable circumstances, and that they be appropriately informed. It is necessary, in other words, that they be in a position to give rational consent to the rule of law they are bound by, so even if the laws *are* beneficial to everyone, they lack authority on the Aristotelian view if people have not been prepared to see that. Thus, even without concerning ourselves with the benefits of law to the poor, or what one might accept as a refusal of consent, one can find a basis for critique in the existence of avoidable ignorance and incomprehension of the rational basis for the law. I would cite in this connection some of the same facts noted above, including those that point to a failure to cultivate trust in the credibility of authority figures, and add that deficiencies of intellectual development, low academic attainment, and the use of corporal punishment by parents are important predictors of who will commit criminal offenses (Reiss et al. 1993, 7, 383, 388–91). The use of corporal punishment with children is significant not only in providing them with a model for aggressive behavior, but also insofar as it is a style of behavioral management which *fails to cultivate a responsiveness to reason.*

Beyond this, and closely connected, is the Aristotelian thought, more radical than anything in Marx, that the acquisition of a rational will, of self-control, and the capacity to comply with law, is an attainment which requires timely and very substantial social investments which are far from universally forthcoming. Several childhood traits predictive of later violent criminality may be described as deficits of rational self-control, namely hyperactivity, impulsivity, and deficits of attention, concentration, and ability to defer gratification (Reiss et al. 1993, 7). Whatever role genetic factors may play in these traits, they are surely in part learned, and not only remediable through instruction, but also preventable to some degree through parental training. Studies of experimental interventions have indeed shown success in improving the self-control and social skills of aggressive children, and in teaching them alternatives to the aggressive behavioral strategies they have typically learned quite early in their lives (Reiss et al. 1993, 385ff.). To the extent that we know or could learn how to effectively promote the development of rational self-control in children whose families are not up to the task, the burden of the Aristotelian argument is not only that there is a weighty moral imperative to do so, but that the legitimacy of our systems of criminal punishment rests on doing so.

It is possible, of course, to regard education that inculcates virtue, self-control, and a willingness to obey the law as an oppressive form of social control, but the fact remains that the privileges of full membership in a society governed by law are contingent upon conformity with that law, and conformity is itself an attainment of sorts that becomes more likely when social investments of the right kind are made, and less likely when those investments are not made. When those investments are deficient or made in a discriminatory manner, and we are faced, as we are in the United States, with crime rates which far exceed those of other industrialized nations (Reiss et al. 1993, 3–5; Currie 1985, chap. 1) and vary widely between the groups in whom we have invested quite differently, we must regard ourselves as faced with gross injustice which no appeal to individual choice can undo.

7

Justice and the Substance of Common Care

The aim of this final chapter will be to elaborate the consequences of Aristotle's arguments for educational equality, content, and choice. This will require that we examine more precisely the substance and the "sameness for all" of the education which the Aristotelian arguments for public education mandate. It may appear that the *argument from a common end (CE)* and the *argument from the foundations of corrective justice (FCJ)* will not get us very far toward what we typically think of as obvious curricular necessities. Yet I will argue here that they demand as rich a fundamentally compulsory curriculum as we should want: one which includes moral and civic education, preparation for work, and an initiation into the life of the mind focused on the structures of reason and evidence. I will also address the matter of how far Aristotle's arguments take us toward an adequate defense of schooling that is common, or brings together students of all kinds in a society, and schools that are public in the sense of being operated by agencies of government.

Beginning with educational equality, I will adduce some general considerations concerning the difficulties involved in establishing a concept of educational equality and illustrate them in connection with a recently influential model of equality which fails the Aristotelian requirement of aiming at genuinely common goods. This will set the stage for defining the forms of educational equality mandated by *FCJ* and the *appeal to respect for reason* outlined in §4.1. These will include equality with respect to moral and civic education, with respect to admission to the life of the mind (which is to say the forms of inquiry and knowledge), and— perhaps surprisingly—with respect to preparation for work. I will argue that Aristotle's conception of justice demands, in economies such as ours, that comprehensive reasonable efforts, including educational efforts, be made with the aim of achieving full employment. The conclusion follows by extension from *FCJ*: to the extent that education makes a difference to employability, and thereby criminal risk, its impact must as a matter of fundamental justice be equitable, but employability can only be a genuinely common good, and so a coherent object of educational equality, in a full-employment economy.

This first section of the chapter yields a mandatory four-part curriculum which involves the cultivation of both moral and intellectual virtues, and I will turn in the second section to the significance of this for moral education. In doing this, I will examine Aristotle's endorsement of the doctrine of the unity of virtue and consider some opposing concerns about moral education and instruction in critical thinking which generate a puzzle about how one can succeed in combining both in a single coherent program of instruction.

In the chapter's third section, I will address the insufficiency of the grounds on which Aristotle's defense of public education has been dismissed, and consider the extent to which his arguments demand common schooling and leave room for educational choice or reliance on a free market in schools. I will conclude that the arguments for common schooling and for the preservation of public systems of education are strong. I will also conclude that the arguments for privatizing education are weak, because market forces cannot be expected to improve schools in all the ways that should be important to us, because appeals to parental authority are insufficient in principle and because the evidence has not borne out the expectation that privatization would improve schools.

7.1 JUSTICE AND EDUCATIONAL EQUALITY

There is no one idea of educational equality. Nor, among the many that have been formulated, is there any one idea of educational equality that is obviously superior to its rivals. There are several reasons for this. One is that the idea of educational equality is often only vaguely formulated. This breeds confusion. It makes the merits and deficiencies of the idea hard to assess without a good deal of analysis, and that analysis is not always forthcoming. Another reason is that it is hard to find decisive grounds favoring any one conception of equal education over and against all the others. This is true, in turn, not only because decisive grounds for interesting conclusions are hard to come by in general, even when one is not particularly confused, but for three special reasons as well.

7.11 Equality and Its Forms

The first of these special sources of difficulty is that although equality has the appearance of something simple, straightforward, and appealing, it is not attainable in its simple, ideal form by human communities. The forms of equality that are attainable stand opposed to each other along a whole host of dimensions of form.[1] One example of this arises from the fact that human beings are not completely alike in what they value or derive benefit from. Since they are not, the simple and appealing idea of everyone having the *same valuable things* divides into the somewhat opposed ideas of everyone having the *same things* (which Rae calls "lot-regarding" equality) and everyone being alike in how much they *value* or benefit from what they have (which Rae calls "person-regarding" equality) (Rae et al. 1989, 82–101). In this and like ways the *one* gives rise to the *many*, and in this process of division the appeal of simple equality is spread awkwardly among incompatible alternatives. Thus impoverished by its wealth of progeny, the ideal of equality cannot impose order in its own house.

A second source of special difficulty in securing the foundations of a concept of educational equality or equal educational opportunity is that questions about the substance of the education or educational opportunities to be equalized are only resolvable on some specification of what the *aims* of the education are to be. Indeed, the choice between "equal education" and "equal educational opportunity" is itself largely determined by the choice of aims, since the fundamental reason for lowering one's sights from equality *per se* to mere equality of opportunity is that the kind of thing we aim to distribute fairly cannot be *directly* distributed.[2] For instance, if literacy is a goal of education, then we may wish to speak partly or entirely in terms of "educational equality" and regard literacy as an outcome which all children with the capacity to become literate should be enabled to reach. More cautiously, we may recognize that literacy cannot be directly distributed, and speak of equalizing either the *means* or the *prospects* of becoming literate (Rae et al. 1989, 64–76), and possibly of the former as "equal educational opportunity" with respect to the educational outcome of literacy,[3] and of the latter as "equal education" in literacy (since equalizing prospects involves much more than equalizing opportunities or the external means to success). By contrast, if we take the central goal of education to lie beyond the immediate results of instruction, in something like the broadening of life options or the enhancement of socioeconomic status, then we will almost certainly speak of "equal educational opportunity" and take its substance to be something like the equalization of prospects in life or prospects of middle-class status, or more modestly the equalization of opportunity to get an education that will improve those prospects.

Given this role of aims or goals in determining the substance of equality in education, no conception of equality will be adequately grounded unless the identification of the aims involved is also well grounded. Yet the identification of aims almost never is well grounded, either in theory or in practice, and little attention is ever directed toward rectifying this. Many aims are suggested by both theorists and reformers, but almost never on the strength of any serious normative justification.

A third and final special difficulty in securing the foundations of a concept of equality is that to succeed one must not only justify some conception of the aims of education, but also justify state control over some relevant *domain of allocation* or pool of resources which can be distributed. The extent to which the resources justifiably controlled by the state coincide with those required to fully attain the goals which are justified is quite important to the character of the equality one will be able to defend. To insist that a state is accountable for the equal distribution of a domain of goods (a "domain of account") of which it controls only a portion of (its "domain of allocation") is going to create tensions, especially if there are good reasons why the state should not control much more of that domain of account than it already does (Rae et al. 1989, 48–63). These tensions will tend to push one away from a strategy of "global equalization" (i.e., equalization with respect to the entire domain of account) and toward a variety of less ambitious alternatives. The proper scope of state powers and resources is quite a difficult matter in its own right, of course, and this suggests that the difficulties in establishing the legitimacy or necessity of any conception of equality in education are fairly staggering, all told.

These are some of the difficulties which have caused education theorists to become "bogged down in conceptualizing what educational equality really mean[s]" (Oakes 1985, xiii), but the enumeration of these difficulties also provides a framework for judging the adequacy of conceptions of educational equality, and for constructing one which is adequate. Our purposes here will be well served now by illustrating this through an examination of the merits and deficiencies of Amy Gutmann's well-known "democratic threshold" of equal educational opportunity (Gutmann 1987, 136–9), beginning with the prima facie advantages of defending a threshold of equality, as opposed to absolute relational equality.

A threshold of equality seems on the face of it to be a threshold, or level of investment or attainment, below which no relevant individual will be allowed to fall. Equality under a threshold may thus be no more than a kind of *relative* equality, since a threshold is a kind of "floor" but not a "ceiling." To the extent that it mandates efforts to raise those falling below the specified "floor" to a level that is no longer below it, it may reduce inequality, but it does not aim to eliminate it. A threshold imposes no upper bound on permissible variations in investment or attainment above the floor it imposes. An ideal of equality cast in the form of a threshold is thus a weaker or less pure form of equality than a strictly relational one, which would impose pair-wise equality between all the individuals or blocks of individuals in a population or segment of a population. It would also appear to be a more easily attainable form of equality than its purely relational counterpart, unless the threshold is set so high as to eliminate any variation above it. (That is, unless it is set so high that it would impose pure relational equality on the population in question. I will call a threshold of this kind a *maximal* threshold, and one that is so low that no intervention is required to bring every member of a population above it a *minimal* threshold.) Ease of attainment is an advantage of considerable importance because equality of educational outcomes in particular is often regarded as generally unattainable (Coleman 1990, 63–5), but also more significant morally than equality of inputs. The relative equality mandated by an outcome threshold that is moderately difficult to attain seems an attractive compromise by this measure. A related advantage is that equalization up to such a threshold would also appear to be less vulnerable to the charge that any prospect of attainment would depend upon unacceptable infringement of individual and family autonomy. Thus, there are apparent general advantages to thinking in terms of thresholds of equality somewhere on the scale between the minimal and maximal endpoints I have described.

7.12 A "Democratic Threshold" of Educational Equality

The best-known attempt to develop a view of this kind is Amy Gutmann's notion of a "democratic threshold" of equality. I will argue that her vaguely delineated "threshold" does not have the virtues which thresholds might generally be expected to have. In fact, the "threshold" she describes is vulnerable to exactly the objections which she makes against one of the alternatives she rejects, the so-called "equalization" view of equality. Thus, I will clarify and object to the *form* which her concept of equality takes. In doing that I will also pave the way for some doubts about the substantive foundations of her threshold.

The most plausible alternative to Gutmann's threshold which she considers is what she calls the *equalization* view of equal educational opportunity. According to this view the state must "use education to raise the life chances of the least advantaged (as far as possible) up to those of the most advantaged" (Gutmann 1987, 131). The state must pursue prospect-regarding equality with respect to life outcomes, in other words. Since those prospects are presumably influenced by factors other than the amount and quality of educational resources bestowed by the state, equalization entails a strategy of compensatory inequality in the distribution of those resources. This gives rise to Gutmann's most fundamental objection, which is that this compensatory strategy may entail that children with better than average prospects will receive no state education, if the resources available do not raise the worse off to either parity or some plateau short of it. This she takes to be unacceptable, as she does the interference in family life and homogenization of children which a full equalization of prospects would arguably require. These are problems which arise from insisting on global equality in the face of morally significant barriers to expanding a relatively limited domain of allocation.

Gutmann's alternative to equalization has two parts. The first is her *democratic authorization principle*, which grants authority "to democratic institutions to determine the priority of education relative to other social goods" (136). The second is her *democratic threshold principle*, according to which "inequalities in the distribution of educational goods can be justified if, but only if, they do not deprive any child of the ability to participate effectively in the democratic process" (136).

Having stated these principles, she then reveals an important feature of her "threshold" principle when she observes that it limits the state's discretion under the "authorization" principle, by "imposing a moral requirement that democratic institutions allocate sufficient resources to education to provide all children with an ability adequate to participate in the democratic process" (136). This makes it clear that when the threshold principle refers to "the distribution of educational goods" this does not mean merely "the distribution of those educational goods which the state chooses or is presently able to distribute" (i.e., the presently available domain of allocation). For in that case, given the way the principle is formulated, it would have distributional implications which are quite restrictive at low levels of investment in education (it would demand equality in the enjoyment of whatever educational goods the state made available, if those goods were insufficient to enable everyone to participate "effectively" in democratic processes), but no implications whatsoever for how much should be invested. Since Gutmann does take it to have such implications, we must understand the threshold principle to cover every form of educational good present in a society, whether or not the state itself has had anything to do with its distribution.

If this is true, however, then there is first, and most trivially, an inaccuracy in Gutmann's description of the baseline of resource allocation which this creates. Given the terms of her threshold, what must be allocated is enough educational resources to ensure that everyone is enabled to participate *effectively* in democratic processes, not simply to participate, as she says. This, then, is the baseline part of her democratic threshold, represented by the horizontal line *b* indicated in figure 7.1. It is an absolute or noncomparative threshold, which represents some minimum level of ability to participate "effectively" in democratic processes.

To this baseline Gutmann later adds the complicating observation that "the threshold of an ability to participate effectively in democratic politics is likely to demand more and better education for all citizens as the average level and quality of education in our society increases" (139). Educational adequacy is thus *relative* and "dependent on the particular social context," she says, and she suggests that since this is true "the best way of determining what adequacy practically entails may be a democratic decision-making process that follows upon public debate and deliberation" (137). Ignoring for the moment this last suggestion, the idea seems to be that *some* gap between the most and least democratically capable members of society is compatible with universal "effective" participation, but that this gap cannot become too big or the effectiveness of the less capable will be compromised.

The effect of this observation is to define a composite threshold consisting of an absolute or nonrelational baseline segment (*b* in figure 7.2), whose length corresponds to the acceptable gap or distance between the most and least capable citizens, and a relational segment (*r* in figure 7.2) which rises from the baseline and runs parallel to the line of strict equality (*e* in figure 7.2) at the fixed distance from it corresponding to that acceptable difference in democratic capabilities.

The relational component of this democratic threshold is, in fact, just what one would expect, given Gutmann's original statement of the threshold, and the

Figure 7.1

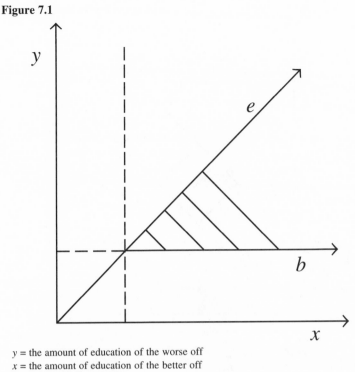

y = the amount of education of the worse off
x = the amount of education of the better off
e = strict (relational) equality
b = democratic baseline threshold

premise that participation in democratic politics is a competitive activity. But this means that her threshold is defined in a way that is parasitic on the concept of equalization, and differs from it only in establishing a baseline of mandatory education and tolerating some deviation from strict equality. The form of equalization which she rejects is one with a different goal from her own, of course, but even the combination of these differences leaves her threshold vulnerable to the criticisms she brings against equalization. Simply put, one cannot escape the difficulties inherent in global equalization simply by opening up a modest zone of acceptable deviation from pure equality and lopping off the lower end of the curve.

Putting this more concretely, the political assets of privileged and highly influential people might render the political capabilities of others comparatively ineffectual, perhaps by shaping the terms of public debate in unseen ways, thereby placing their society to the right of r in figure 7.2. Even though the problem is somewhat less acute than it would be for strict equalization, the solution it calls for is the same, if this influential minority has secured its influence even without

Figure 7.2

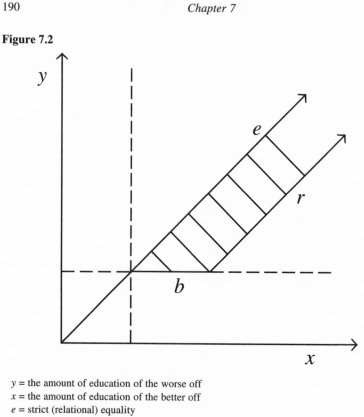

y = the amount of education of the worse off
x = the amount of education of the better off
e = strict (relational) equality
b = democratic baseline
$r+b$ = democratic threshold

the advantage of any public schooling: either pour public resources into the least capable, while excluding the more capable, or interfere with families and children in ways that Gutmann rejects. Unless one can confidently say that even very large differences of political efficacy are tolerated by her threshold, one must concede that the relative equalization which it demands will entail essentially the same problems as equalization, except that the aim which her threshold rests on is decidedly more compelling than the one associated with the form of equalization she criticizes.

Gutmann has drifted almost imperceptibly into regarding politics as an arena of competition, and education as aiming to give citizens a competitive advantage, or a minimum of competitive disadvantage, in their efforts to dominate one another in this arena. As I noted in my opening description of Athenian education, and in discussing Aristotle's concern that education direct citizens toward goods that are not essentially contested, it is hard to see how competitive advantage of any kind can be a coherent goal for a system of public education, or a good with respect to which education can be equalized.[4] This is not to say that it would be wrong for schools to make efforts to reduce the political disadvantage of the poor and others who are likely to reach adulthood ill-equipped to promote their own interests through political activity. Rather, first, it is to say that because political advantage is an intrinsically competitive good, any promise to enable people of ordinary means to become effective political participants through better education is likely to be an empty promise, since there is every reason to expect those of greater means to use those means to preserve their advantage. Education *in itself* cannot be expected to be "the great equalizer" politically, any more than it can be economically. Second, it is to say that as good as it would be to shrink the gap in political influence between those who wield it and those who lack it, the political good to be brought about by education must be conceived of as a common good, and not as the advancement of the private competitive advantage of one group over another, in order to make sense as an object of collective choice or the goal of a public system.

Of course, this raises the question of how well defined this threshold is in the first place, and especially what is meant by "effective" participation in democratic processes. To do something effectively normally means to do it in such a way as to produce the effect one desires, but it is hard to see how this could be a standard for participation in competitive democratic processes, unless one is contemplating a citizenry with very low expectations. Even if all one hopes for is that the votes one casts be effective in the sense of being the ones most consistent with one's interests, there would seem to be no end to the education that would be necessary.

Gutmann hopes to sidestep demands to produce a clearer standard by suggesting, as I noted above, that the job of producing such clarity is best left to the democratic decision-making process itself. This will seem to many an appropriate concession, but I think it is not. This threshold of democratic equality is meant to establish a democracy-preserving limitation on the discretion of democratic majorities. Majoritarian deliberations about the setting of this threshold would be suspect in the same way that such deliberations regarding encumbrance of minority voting rights would be. If Gutmann is on the right track in the first place, then voting rights and politically significant education must both meet some *fair* standard of equality as a precondition for democratic processes being fair.

This brings us, finally, to Gutmann's foundational argument that education which promotes political competence is essential to the effective use of constitutionally recognized rights to engage in political speech and to vote, and thus should count as a constitutionally recognized fundamental interest. Without discussing the U.S. Supreme Court's rejection of this argument in *San Antonio Independent School District v. Rodriguez*,[5] Gutmann does try to find evidence that some such argument has gained a foothold in the law (Gutmann 1987, 137), but the case is not a strong one. In *Rodriguez* the Court acknowledged that education is relevant to the effective use of constitutionally guaranteed rights to speak and vote, but it did not concede that any "identifiable quantum of education is a constitutionally protected prerequisite to the exercise of either right" (36).

Again, one might argue not from the U.S. Constitution, but on some other grounds, that a proper democracy requires the threshold of educational equal opportunity which Gutmann recommends. She produces no such argument, however, so although the idea of a democratic threshold of equality is intuitively attractive, its foundations are less clear, and it is less substantively determinate, and less attractive in its form, than one might hope.

In a more recent work, Amy Gutmann and Dennis Thompson argue in a more Rawlsian manner (Rawls 1993), from an ideal of civic equality and an associated concept of reciprocity. They hold that reciprocity requires citizens and public officials to appeal in political argument and in defense of the laws to "reasons that are shared or could come to be shared by" all "who are motivated to find fair terms of social cooperation," and to rely on empirical claims which are "consistent with reliable methods of inquiry" (Gutmann and Thompson 1996, 14, 65, 15). On this account, any defensible conception of democracy would be grounded in such a notion of civic equality, and would regard universal education which develops the skills and virtues of deliberation as an essential means to enabling and disposing adults to treat each other as civic equals. What schools should do, they say, is

> aim to develop their students' capacities to understand different perspectives, communicate their understandings to other people, and engage in the give-and-take of moral argument with a view to making mutually acceptable decisions (359).

Presumably, they will also have to instruct students in the "reliable methods of inquiry" in which the empirical claims made in public life are to rest, and contribute to the creation of fair opportunities to secure nonbasic economic and social goods.[6]

One virtue of this approach is that it is grounded not in a specific, controversial account of democracy, but in a moral requirement that people respect the reason in each other, not just in their private transactions, but in public life. Another of its virtues is that it conceives of civic education as aiming to produce genuinely common goods: the abilities and virtues conducive to mutual respect, social cooperation, good judgment, and wise choices. It is in these respects a more Aristotelian approach than the one Gutmann seems committed to in *Democratic Education*. Having said this, however, let us return to the Aristotelian arguments themselves and examine their significance for educational equality in light of the foregoing.

7.13 Equality and Common Goods

Aristotle's arguments for public education are rooted, in much the way that Gutmann and Thompson's account of education for deliberative democracy is, in a concept of respecting the reason in ourselves and others. In certain respects, then, we can expect that the significance of his arguments for public education that is the same for all would be much the same as theirs. This is most obviously true within the sphere of civic and moral education, but also in somewhat different ways with respect to education in the methods of inquiry and in preparation for work.

Both versions of the *argument from the foundations of corrective justice (FCJ)* rest on the principle of respect for the reason in ourselves and others, which I have called the *principle of fidelity to reason*, and establish educational prerequisites for just law and its enforcement—law that rests in truthful instruction and rational persuasion, rather than force. I have emphasized the educative burden on the state involved in creating the conditions for rational and informed consent and compliance, including the importance of establishing relationships of trust and sympathy between teachers and students, and building communities of learning which establish the psychosocial conditions for a child's accepting the civilizing norms of social life. This is a burden which includes both instruction to develop the capacities of reason and communicate the reasons for existing laws being as they are, and the social aspects of schooling and supervised practice that are material to a child's being *moved by* those reasons.

The kind of educational equality this seems to mandate is a baseline threshold of equality in the enjoyment of educational goods which suffice to create the conditions for rational acceptance of the law's demands, insofar as there *is* reason to accept those demands, and a reasonable prospect of voluntary compliance with them. One way to define this baseline of minimally adequate education would be to set it at a level sufficient to sustain a high level of acceptance and voluntary compliance within the adult population generally. This would be a natural way to understand talk of "the same education for all," in connection with the idea of putting persuasion and instruction before force as a general approach to establishing a rule of law. On the other hand, this would not do justice to three features of Aristotle's account: (1) his belief that the state's role in promoting the common good includes regulating childbirth and early child care to make them as conducive as possible to the development of virtue; (2) his acceptance of principles of respect for reason which seem to call for putting reason and persuasion before force *as much as possible;* and (3) his concern to unite every faction and potential faction within a polis under one common law and ethic of cooperation. Each of these points deserves comment.

Aristotle rightly regards early care and training as an important foundation for the development of both moral and intellectual virtues, and defends a legislative policy of comprehensive or global equalization that contributes materially to the development of virtue. In a society which makes little legislative effort to promote desirable development during the preschool years, or even to protect children from abuse and trauma that is profoundly damaging to their development (Cicchetti and Toth 1995; Rogosch et al. 1995; Toth and Cicchetti 1996; Cicchetti and Toth 1997; Shields and Cicchetti 1998), a policy of global equalization would demand *compensatory* efforts during the school years. This policy would demand conscientious efforts to give each child what he or she needs to develop well, rather than giving all children the same things in the same amount at school. The principle of putting persuasion, instruction, and the nurturing of reason before force *as much as possible*, demands no less than this. If children have come to school in disparate states of moral and intellectual development and will be judged equally before the law when they leave it (an overgenerous assumption, given the recent trend in American law toward judging young criminals as adults, not on the strengths of their upbringing and instruction, but because of the inhumanity of their acts), then the burden of educational equality entailed by *FCJ* must be interpreted as a burden, compensatory in many cases, to meet the individual developmental needs of all children by the time they have completed their required years of schooling. Finally, we arrive at a similar result by considering Aristotle's concern to unite all groups within cities under one common law. A threshold of educational equality sufficient to bring about a high level of acceptance and compliance with law within the general citizenry of a city or state might not produce high levels of acceptance and compliance within some subpopulations of citizens. That would be a quite unsatisfactory result from Aristotle's point of view, and would suggest that a more appropriate threshold would require educational efforts which would at least generate high levels of acceptance and compliance in each social subgroup within the population of citizens.

On three grounds, then, the form of educational equality that would be most consistent with Aristotle's educational thought would not be a form of *marginal* equality up to a baseline of educational "inputs" sufficient to allow most children to grasp what is good in the laws and accept their burdens. It would be, on two grounds, a form of *global* equality up to such a baseline. Since the second of these grounds is morally compelling, being nothing more than an application of a duty to respect the reason in others, we should regard this form of equality as not only commended by Aristotelian principles, but obligatory in any society which establishes a system of law. What this requires, in part, is that the state ensure that the psychosocial conditions essential to the progress of moral development be available to every child, however deficient a child's prior experience might be as a basis for becoming moral, developing good moral judgment, and grasping the reasons for laws being as they are. This seems a rather modest and reasonable benchmark of adequate care, but schools in the United States, especially those which serve the residents of cities, typically do not measure up to this standard. I noted in the preceding chapter that there is evidence linking the deficiencies in these schools to the incidence of crime and violence in them, and a fitting thing to add is that if we are going to continue to allow many children to endure catastrophic deprivation in the years before they begin school, it is hardly enough to merely create a wholesome and nurturing moral climate in these schools.

So far I have cast this argument *FCJ* in a way that rests in the *principle of fidelity to reason*'s requirement that citizens and state alike respect the reason in others:

The Argument from the Foundations of Corrective Justice

P1: It is neither practical nor just (i.e., consistent with respect for the reason in others) to impose law through force and violence. A rule of law must instead be established through education preparatory to rational consent to the law and autonomous compliance.

P2: The state must itself establish a system which ensures the universal provision of such education (i.e., a public system of education) in order to establish a universal right to censure and punish those who violate the law.

P3: No state exists without law and its enforcement.

C: Thus, justice requires that all states have public systems of education.

What justice requires, more precisely, is that any level of government which makes and enforces laws has a system for ensuring the adequacy of education for all who are subject to those laws. This does not preclude systems in which individual schools and local districts retain a great deal of control over their own affairs, and there are some reasons to prefer such systems, but it does mean that higher levels of government cannot absolve themselves of regulatory or financial responsibility through a preference for localism. Responsibility rests at every level of political organization that aims to bind a people together under a common rule of law.

I have also noted that punishment under any system of law involves a loss or suspension of fundamental rights, making compliance with law a condition for the secure enjoyment of those rights. And I have noted that one might invoke a notion of equal protection of the laws, according to which a fundamental requirement of justice is that the state not put some citizens more at risk than others of suffering a loss or suspension of fundamental rights, through unequal distribution of goods whose distribution the state has a duty to oversee (§6.3). With these additional premises, one may bring the educational equality mandated by *FCJ* within the scope of constitutionally protected fundamental rights in much the way that Gutmann (1987) attempts to, for it becomes a fundamental requirement of justice that those educational goods foundational to securing compliance with law be equally distributed. A salient difference, however, is that this argument pertains not to the "effectiveness" with which the rights are exercised, but the more sharply delineated matter of losing the rights altogether, at least for a time.

Thus, there are three advantages of the conception of educational equality generated by *FCJ* over and against Gutmann's "democratic threshold." First, it can be construed as relying on the idea of state action putting one at risk of losing a right altogether, rather than the more elusive notion of the "effectiveness" of one's use of a right. Second, this conception of educational equality has the advantage of identifying a simple baseline threshold, which has the attractions noted in §7.11, that Gutmann's threshold turned out not to have. It can do this because what is at stake is providing children with genuinely common goods: the foundations for favorable moral development and a rational understanding of the merits of the laws. Third, this conception relies on a notion of respect for persons which generates claims about what justice in even the most minimal state requires, and in doing this it sidesteps the controversies surrounding substantive conceptions of democracy and their justification.

The objection might be pressed at this point that even if all of this is true, the education which *FCJ* compels us to equalize is too narrow in its substance to be of much interest. This might seem to be the case if one conceives of a preparation for obedience to the law as a simple matter of establishing habits of respect and obedience, but we have seen that this is very far from Aristotle's mind. Among other things, we have seen that the *consent version* of *FCJ* demands education which prepares citizens for rational and informed consent to laws, both existing and proposed (§3.12), and that this demands a very significant measure of intellectual training to develop the capacities of critical reason, as well as truthful instruction in the reasons for the laws. Although I have not said this explicitly, an education preparatory to giving consent to proposed laws would also have to involve instruction in the nature of governmental processes, which is to say the ways in which public deliberations take place and in which one may participate, unless this is too obvious to require explanation. The character and quality of this instruction should enable children of ordinary abilities to understand the processes of government well enough to know how to participate in those processes and register their consent or dissent in the ways they are entitled to.

There are three related points, all bearing on moral and political education, that deserve some elaboration, and two more bearing on instruction in the methods of inquiry and preparation for productive labor. The first is that Aristotle's conception of respect for the reason in others demands preparation for obeying the laws "in the manner of a citizen," which is to say voluntarily when the reasons for obeying them are adequate, but *only* when the reasons are adequate. Proper obedience is thus understood to involve exercises of critical reason and autonomous judgment, quite apart from what is involved in giving rational consent, and there are good reasons for this. A state has no legitimate interest in its citizens obeying laws that it would be wrong to obey. On the contrary, the very interest which justifies systems of criminal law is an interest in citizens refraining from wrong conduct and doing what's right, since this is most protective of other's interests and conducive to the common good. Moreover, a state must recognize the possibility that in some circumstances some of its laws might require conduct which would be wrong. In such circumstances, it has an interest in citizens being able to rationally evaluate the laws and act from autonomous good judgment in disobeying them, just as it does in the case of military orders which are illegal by the standards of sound international law. This interest calls for education suitable to developing the capacities of reasoning, perception, and good judgment essential to judging and applying laws, and developing knowledge of the laws and the reasons for them.

A second point is that Aristotle derives from his general principle of respect for the reason in others a presumptive right of self-rule resting in a person's possession of normal human rational potential, and assumes on that basis that an acceptable education for citizens preparatory to being ruled by law must also be preparatory to *sharing in* rule.[7] Sharing in rule includes for Aristotle, and for any state whose system of corrective justice involves trial by jury, not only exercises of collective judgment in public debate and deliberations bearing on possible new laws and matters of public policy, but also exercises in the administration of justice in enforcing existing laws. This requires preparation for exercises of collective deliberation, judgment, and action, just as I have said the *consent version* of *FCJ* itself does. This will require on Aristotle's account, as much as on Gutmann and Thompson's, instruction in the methods of inquiry that are germane to answering empirical questions bearing on the issues of public life. It will also be greatly facilitated by common schooling that enables children of different kinds to practice such deliberation and collective action together.

A third point is that Aristotle is an advocate of free moral inquiry and incremental political and legal reform, enacted through popular consent (§3.12, §4.32). Unlike the Plato of the *Laws*, who seems to regard critical moral reflection and what little impetus to progress there may be as the exclusive privilege of the elders of the Nocturnal Council, Aristotle shows no sign of restricting the distribution of this function any further than to hold that political science can only be productively pursued by those who are morally serious and have had some experience of the world. Wherever the impetus to reform might lie, it requires a public which is not trained in habitual obedience to one fixed set of laws for all time, but is receptive to the reasons that might be given on behalf of new laws and the moral aspirations and insight they express. Moreover, we have seen that Aristotle holds that the additive and perceptual character of practical wisdom makes it possible for citizens engaged in collective debate and deliberation to grasp things more completely than any of them could alone, and improve each other's moral understanding and judgment in doing so. With this, and his remark that "the guest will judge better of a feast than the cook" (*Pol.* III.11 1282a22–23), he opens the possibility that ordinary citizens gathered in their assemblies and courts may themselves make and instigate progress. Moreover, quite apart from the importance of preserving the possibility of intergenerational progress, we have seen that it is essential to Aristotle's conception of a city capable of promoting happy lives that it make room for continuous moral development, conversation, and contemplation. Education that is compatible with the possibility of free moral inquiry, collective deliberation, and progress must begin in the inculcation of habitual virtue, but also cultivate the intellectual virtues in a way that aims toward autonomous virtue, good judgment, and continued moral growth and inquiry. As I noted in chapter 4 (§4.34), such education should also provide children with a foundation of previous experience in mutual trust, common action, and common success, in collaboration with others unlike themselves whom they will face as fellow citizens later. This requires common schooling, a point I will return to in the final section of this chapter.

Let us consider now the instruction in the methods of inquiry called for by the *consent version* of *FCJ*, and by the consideration that mutual respect demands that citizens be prepared to be ruled and share in rule alike. This would be accomplished presumably through instruction in logic or general techniques of argument analysis, and instruction in a variety of disciplines or branches of knowledge, focused on their manner and canons of investigation. Aristotle's *De Partibus Animalium* opens with a description of a complete education as one which enables a person to master those canons and form reasonable judgments of the quality of reasoning in all branches of knowledge (639a1–15). Although this is an impossibly high standard, an education which would enable citizens to contribute to public debate in the right kinds of ways would have to approximate this at least to the extent of providing a general sense of the nature of reasoning and evidence in the natural and human sciences. This does not demand *more* study of history, economics, mathematics, and a sampling of the natural and behavioral sciences than children in industrialized countries typically receive, but it probably does require more effective instruction in the patterns of discovery, confirmation, and explanation in these fields of inquiry. The arguments which commend this result as a requirement of justice suggest that what would be adequate is an initiation into these methods and modes of reasoning which would enable children of normal abilities to arrive at the threshold of full citizenship, able to offer reasons of an appropriate kind in public transactions and rely on empirical claims that are "consistent with reliable methods of inquiry," as Gutmann and Thompson say.

Apart from the significance of intellectual training for participation in collective self-rule, it is important to recall again that Aristotle has other grounds for regarding the development of intellectual virtue to be the highest end of education (§3.5). Even if we reject the conception of *eudaimonia* on which this rests, there is some reason to hold, as I did in chapter 4 (§4.1), that a natural duty of respect for the reason in ourselves and others generates "imperfect" duties of mutual aid in the development of our rational capacities. I held that a public system of education could provide one efficient means to collectively satisfying these duties, and it is appropriate to reiterate this here.

Finally, there are several reasons to regard an adequate preparation for work or respected forms of productive labor as a further requirement of justice, both by Aristotle's lights and in fact. First, this seems to follow from a modification of the argument *FCJ*. As Aristotle notes, unemployment or being poor and without means to support oneself is an important risk factor for criminality (§4.33; Currie 1985, 104–41, 263–74). Since government policy, including education policy, has a substantial impact on patterns of employment, and in this and other ways on patterns of criminality, one must regard equality of impact on the prospects for respected employment as a requirement of justice in education and public policy generally. I have noted previously that as long as respected employment remains a contested good there can be no meaningful measure of equality in the education preparatory to such employment, and it follows that educational efforts must be coordinated with appropriate economic policies. The aim of economic policy must be to maintain a full-employment economy, so that, even if the more desirable jobs are strongly contested, ongoing access to work that confers social respect and a basis for self-respect is not, for it is respect and a sense of full membership in society that is most salient to criminality. Only against the background of such a policy can one define any meaningful threshold of adequacy in the education preparatory to employment, a threshold which requires that every child be adequately prepared for a least one respected form of work which can be obtained even if everyone else obtains respected work.

The difference that employment makes to criminality has less to do with being in a state of need than with the social rewards and forms of supervision entailed by employment. We have seen that Aristotle argues in *NE* X.9 that laws should be enacted to safeguard the habits essential to preserving adult virtue, and it is not much of an extrapolation from this to argue that legislation should aim to maintain a full-employment economy, since the supervision provided by law enforcement agencies is both less effective in inducing obedience to law and more burdensome than the supervision entailed by employment. The latter consists not only of intentional monitoring by supervisors, and incidental monitoring by co-workers, but also a more pervasive system of norms, expectations, and social contacts that is easily overlooked: people who have steady and respected work tend to have as their associates outside of work other people who are similarly employed and respected, and the knowledge that breaking the law would entail a serious loss of standing within that circle of associates is a potent incentive to obey the law (Currie 1985, 116–17). Conversely, those who do not work regularly are not subject to comparable supervision through many hours of the day, and are more likely on the whole to have nonworking associates and to have less to lose in any number of ways, including with regard to their reputation, if they break the law. As irksome as supervision on the job may sometimes be, it is advantageous to working people to the extent that it provides a social world helpful to preserving much that is important to them, including their *de facto* status as full citizens (Shklar 1991, 64, 67, 92).

Second, we have seen Aristotle argue that sharing in rule, or ruling and being ruled as justice demands, is undermined by economic inequality (§4.34). His view is that as disparities in economic power grow, trust and goodwill are eroded, the ability to collaborate in pursuit of the common good dissolves in contempt, envy, and hostility, and impartial justice and the rule of law itself are severely strained, if not obliterated, by the arrogance of the privileged and the incapacity of the very poor. "Thus arises a city, not of freemen, but of masters and slaves," he writes (*Pol.* IV.11 1295b22). To the extent that education preparatory to work matters to maintaining moderation in wealth and the possibility of mutual respect and trust, and thereby to cooperation in collective self-governance, the arguments which demand education preparatory to participation in collective self-governance also demand adequate preparation for work and conscientious efforts to ensure the universal availability of work. In any country, such as the United States, in which being employed is a *de facto* condition for full citizenship and the possibility of engaging in respected political speech, this is all the more true (Shklar 1991, 98–101).[8]

Third, in his account of the content of public education Aristotle includes what is necessary in the way of practical arts. He assumed as a background to this an agrarian economy based in land capital which could be passed from father to son, not a modern economy based largely in human capital, which can only be transmitted and acquired through education. In a world such as ours, what is necessary in the practical arts can be nothing less than what suffices to create the human capital or abilities on which productive and respected employment depends. Thus, a suitable adjustment of Aristotle's account to accommodate the differences between an ancient economy and a modern one would yield preparation for work as a necessary component.

An objection which might be lodged against this conclusion is that Aristotle conceived of liberal education, or the education suitable to a freeman, as an education which aims almost entirely at the proper use of leisure in the activities that fulfill a person's highest human potential, and that he regarded productive labor as a degrading obstacle to the fulfillment of that potential. These attributions are beyond dispute, but the nature of the interpretive exercise we are engaged in at this juncture demands that we ask what kinds of reforms Aristotle might have regarded as suitable for a constitution of the kind we have. In an economic order in which it is—contrary to Aristotle's assumption—*possible* for people to secure some leisure of the relevant kind through accumulating and investing their own human capital, and impossible for most of them to secure such leisure in any other way, it is not absurd to regard the "necessary measure" of training in the practical arts as entailing an adequate preparation for productive employment, provided we also note that Aristotle would have counseled us to favor policies and regulations that would shorten the work week and distribute work more evenly.[9]

Fourth, Aristotle holds that a state cannot be just without being dedicated to mutual advantage, or the happiness of all citizens, and I noted in §5.15 that this demands equitable educational investments in the forms of education material to mutual advantage and happiness. Creating the conditions, including the educational conditions, for universal respected employment is crucial to creating a society of mutual advantage, and consequently one in which a sense of justice can stand as a bulwark against factionalism, political instability, and crime.[10]

Finally, stable and respected employment is important to the capacity of parents to care well for their children, through both the resources and the ongoing character development it provides (Currie 1985, 191). Aristotle calls for legislative measures to ensure favorable patterns of child care (*Pol.* VII.17), and in a world such as ours it is hard to see how those measures could be adequate without being favorable, both educationally and in other ways, to full and adequate employment.

All told, then, Aristotle's arguments for public education suffice to establish that a public system of education is required as a matter of fundamental justice, and is the responsibility of any government at any level which makes and enforces laws. His arguments also suffice to establish some important forms of educational equality as a basic requirement of justice, and mandate a required curriculum of moral and political education, a broad introduction to the forms of human knowledge and their methods of inquiry, and preparation for work.

7.2 CULTIVATING THE MORAL AND INTELLECTUAL VIRTUES

Having shown on several grounds that the content of the education mandated as a matter of justice by Aristotle's arguments includes both moral and intellectual virtues, it will be instructive now to examine the curricular agenda this entails, and especially what it entails for how we think about moral education and what is acceptable and desirable in the way of moral education in public schools. In order to do this, we must first return to Aristotle's account of the moral and intellectual virtues and get a clearer understanding of his view of their relationships to each other. That is, we must examine his account of the unity of virtue.

7.21 The Unity of Virtue

One of the most familiar aspects of Aristotle's account of virtue is the distinction he draws between the intellectual and moral virtues at the end of Book I of the *Nicomachean Ethics*:

> . . . some kinds of virtue are said to be intellectual and others moral, contemplative wisdom *(sophia)* and understanding *(sunesis)* and practical wisdom *(phronêsis)* being intellectual, generosity *(eleutherio tês)* and temperance *(sôphrosunê)* moral (I.13 1103a5–7).

This division of the virtues follows the pattern of his division of the soul or psyche. "By human virtue *(anthropine aretê)* we mean not that of the body, but that of the soul," he says (I.13 1102a16). Understanding the soul to be the source and cause of growth and movement, he divides it into rational and irrational elements, and divides the irrational part itself into the desiring part responsible for initiating movement and the nutritive part responsible for growth. Setting aside the nutritive part of the soul, and having implicitly identified the rational and desiring elements as the parts of the soul that contribute to action, Aristotle then says that "virtue is distinguished into kinds in accordance with" the difference between the rational and desiring parts of the soul (I.13 1103a4). That is to say, he identifies the moral virtues as states of the desiring part of the soul, and intellectual virtues as states of the rational part of the soul. Moral virtues thus come to be defined as dispositions to feel and be moved by our various desires or emotions neither too weakly nor too strongly, but in a way that moves us to choose and act as reason would dictate and allows us to take pleasure in doing so (II.5– 6). Intellectual virtues are later defined as capacities or powers of understanding, judgment, and reasoning which enable the rational parts of the soul to attain truth (VI.2 1139b11–13), the attainment of truth being the function of the calculative or practical part no less than the scientific or contemplative one.

Having drawn this distinction between the intellectual and moral virtues at the end of Book I, Aristotle opens Book II with a remark about the origins and development of virtue that contrasts these forms of virtue in a way that would seem quite significant for the enterprise of moral education:

> Virtue, then, being of two kinds, intellectual and moral, intellectual virtue in the main owes both its birth and its growth to teaching . . . while moral virtue comes about as a result of habit, . . . none of the moral virtues arises in us by nature . . . (I.1 1103a14–20).

The obvious implication of this for the moral upbringing and education of children is that moral virtue is not something that can be taught or engendered through verbal instruction alone, but is rather something that can only be brought about by ensuring that children consistently act in the right ways. The development of habit presumably requires consistency of conduct, or conduct that is consistently shaped in all its details toward what is desirable, and Aristotle's claim here is that habit is the proximate origin of moral virtue. The development of good habits is thus the target at which moral instruction should aim:

> by doing the acts that we do in our transactions with other men we become just or unjust, and by doing the acts that we do in the presence of danger, and being habituated to feel fear or confidence, we become brave or cowardly. The same is true of appetites and feelings of anger. . . . Thus, in one word, states arise out of like activities. . . . It makes no small difference, then, whether we form habits of one kind or of another from our very youth; it makes a very great difference, or rather *all* the difference (II.1 1103b17–25).

As interest in Aristotle has spread beyond the universities to the larger educational community, what has received the most attention is this idea that moral learning is properly concerned with developing virtues of character and requires supervised practice of the right kinds.[11] Yet Aristotle's account of the development of moral virtue is not as simple as it may appear to be from these opening passages. Although he distinguishes the moral and intellectual virtues, he also holds that no one is fully virtuous or has true moral virtue without having the intellectual virtue of practical wisdom (VI.13 1144b7–17, 1144b30–32), and that no one can become practically wise without first possessing natural or habitual moral virtue (VI.12 1144a29–37, VII.13 1144b20). These interdependencies are grounded in the premise that humans are a union of intellect and desire (VI.2

1139a32–b5). They are explained more specifically by a conception of goodness or virtue as not merely a form of moral innocence, but rather what enables its possessor to achieve outward success in pursuing the proper ends of action (I.12 1101b2–3,[12] II.9 1109a24–29), and by the view that although it is the function of thought to identify the proper ends of action, its capacity to do so is limited by the fact that people tend to regard what they are accustomed to taking pleasure in as good (III.4, VI.5 1140b7–19). Since virtue is what enables one to perform actions that *successfully* pursue good ends, it will require success in the intellectual tasks of discerning what is salient in the circumstances of action and thinking through what it is best to do. Good habits formed under the guidance of *others'* good judgment will not fully equip one to face life's complexities. On the other hand, to the extent that one's conception of the proper ends of action and perception of the circumstances of action are formed and limited by one's emotional dispositions, one can only have the intellectual virtue of practical wisdom or *phronêsis* if one is morally virtuous.

These interdependencies between the intellectual and moral virtues are exceedingly important to Aristotle's theory of virtue and the human good, and my purpose in this section will be to explore their significance for moral education. I shall begin by saying a few words about their role in Aristotle's ethical theory, and then shift my attention to their bearing on current curricular developments. Aristotle's account of the relationships between the moral and intellectual virtues suggests the importance of integrating what is now promoted under the rubrics of character education and instruction in critical thinking, and it provides a useful starting point for thinking about how to succeed in integrating these pedagogical enterprises. If his account is correct, then neither can be complete without the other, although they are popularly perceived to be in conflict and little theoretical consideration has been devoted toward a synthesis.[13] I shall devote much of my attention here to examining some philosophical obstacles which seem to stand in the way of a synthesis, and I shall do so in a way that sets the issues on a larger historical stage, in order to see better what is at stake and to appreciate better what is distinctive in the Aristotelian view.

Aristotle distinguishes the moral and intellectual virtues but he also asserts the double-edged thesis that practical wisdom both presupposes and completes moral virtue. In taking this position he follows Plato in rejecting the moral intellectualism of Socrates, while also preserving the doctrine of the unity of virtue. Virtue "in the strict sense" involves practical wisdom, and this explains, he says, why

> some say that all the virtues are forms of practical wisdom, and why Socrates in one respect was on the right track while in another he went astray; in thinking that all the virtues were forms of practical wisdom he was wrong, but in saying they implied practical wisdom he was right. . . . [I]t is . . . the state that implies the *presence* of right reason, that is virtue; and practical wisdom is right reason about such matters. Socrates, then, thought the virtues were forms of reason (for he thought they were, all of them, forms of knowledge), while we think they *involve* reason.

It is clear, then, . . . that it is not possible to be good in the strict sense without practical wisdom, nor practically wise without moral virtue. But in this way we may also refute the dialectical argument whereby it might be contended that the virtues exist in separation from each other; the same man, it might be said, is not best equipped by nature for all the virtues, so that he will have already acquired one when he has not yet acquired another. This is possible in respect of the natural virtues, but not in respect of those in respect of which a man is called without qualification good; for with the presence of the one quality, practical wisdom, will be given all the virtues (VI.13 1144b16–45a2).

Practical wisdom entails the presence of all the virtues because although one may have some natural or habituated virtues in some degree without having them all, if one lacks the perceptions associated with even one form of virtue, then one's perception of moral particulars, conception of the proper ends of action, and deliberations about what to do will all be corrupted in at least that one respect. There will be situations in which the emotions associated with the missing form of virtue will be felt too strongly or weakly and will lead one astray. It is in this way that practical wisdom entails the presence of all the virtues, and since true virtue requires practical wisdom this implies that one cannot have any one virtue fully without having all the others.

This unity of virtue thesis is a centerpiece of Aristotle's ethical theory inasmuch as it grounds his central thesis about the essential place of virtue in a happy life. As we saw in chapter 3 (§3.11), he holds that happy lives involve activity of the rational soul "in accordance with the highest virtue," namely *sophia* or contemplative wisdom, and it follows from his views on the unity of virtue that such activity is impossible without moral virtue (Kraut 1989; Korsgaard 1986; cf. *Laws* I 631c; §2.4).

For our purposes, however, what has most immediate importance is Aristotle's distinction between habituated virtue and full or true virtue, and his conception of the consummation of virtue in *phronêsis* (practical wisdom, good judgment, or practical intelligence). There are several reasons to accept the idea that true virtue is the proper object of moral instruction.

7.22 Why "True" Virtue?

First, only a true virtue is good without qualification, and it is surely better for people to acquire traits that are good without qualification than ones that are not. On the one hand, supposing that it is possible to have moral knowledge without having a settled disposition to do what one knows is right, it is not unreasonable for us to prefer that our fellow human beings acquire not only the knowledge but the disposition to act on it. On the other hand, a moral disposition that is not guided by understanding and good judgment can have bad consequences for both its possessor and others. Loyalty *in due measure* is a good and fine thing, for instance, but conceived as a disposition that is not accompanied by good judgment it exposes its possessors to risks of manipulation and betrayal, and may induce them to inflict wrongful harm in the service of their affiliations.[14] The disadvantages of blind loyalty are significant enough that one may reasonably doubt whether it is a good thing to inculcate it, but the same cannot be said of loyalty that is judicious.

A second reason for regarding true virtue as the appropriate object of moral instruction is that, as we saw in §7.13, justice (the *complicity version* of *FCJ*) requires that we morally educate children, and respect for human beings as rational creatures requires that we do this in a way that is conducive to the emergence of autonomous moral judgment and understanding, which is to say genuine, and not just habitual, virtue.

A third related reason is that justice (the *consent version* of *FCJ*) requires that the conditions be created for rational consent to the laws, existing and proposed, in the manner appropriate to a citizen, which is to say in a manner arising from a desire to do the right thing, and guided by autonomous good judgment. Rational consent is only possible to the extent that justice is *transparent*. That is, it is only possible to the extent that laws and institutions are open to inspection, and citizens have been educated in both the powers of inspection and judgment and the cooperative virtues on which the very enterprise of collective deliberation and consent depends. True, and not just habitual, virtue is demanded both in the giving of rational consent and in a citizen's manner of compliance with law.

Finally, quite apart from any consideration of law and governments, a moral community is by all rights an enterprise whose functions, such as guidance and correction, are more or less universally distributed among its members. There are no reasons why this should not include exercises of moral judgment which may create pressure toward modifications and progress, and if it does include these, then a moral order is an enterprise which demands widely distributed moral intelligence and autonomous judgment, not just obedience. It demands true virtue.

7.23 The Paradox of Progressive Morality

Let us suppose, then, that it is clear that true virtue in Aristotle's sense is the appropriate aim of moral instruction, and that this entails cultivation of both the moral and intellectual virtues. The popular perception of an opposition between inculcation of "community values" and encouragement of critical thinking suggests there are at least prima facie tensions in this project of instructional synthesis, arising from the objections that may be lodged against each side of this instructional divide by the other. It will be useful to enumerate these objections, identify the tensions which this enumeration yields, and take stock of the moral tradition's attempts to grapple with them.

The objections or problems which I shall survey here I shall call: (1) the problem of indoctrination; (2) the problem of foreclosed options; (3) the problem of force; (4) the problem of skepticism; (5) the problem of local variation, and (6) the problem of free-riding. The problems of indoctrination and free-riding together give rise to a bind, or paradox, which I shall call the *paradox of progressive morality*.

1. *Indoctrination*. A common fear about moral education is that it will inevitably be indoctrinating, in the sense that it will establish beliefs which are not all evidently true, and will do so in such a way that those beliefs are not easily dislodged at any later time. The dimly perceived specter of Plato's *Republic* looms in the background of this fear, and we have seen that Aristotle's moral psychology inherits some of the *Republic*'s fundamental assumptions. It is commonly assumed now, as then, that the powers of reason take time to develop in children, and that until those powers have developed, their beliefs remain vulnerable to manipulation. Another Aristotelian and Platonic assumption with broad contemporary currency is that what we have been habituated to in our youth tends to exercise an *enduring* influence on what we desire and perceive to be good. A third assumption, also evident in Aristotle's thought and derived from Plato's, is that children become neither good nor responsive to reason without an upbringing that surrounds them with good models and guides them toward good habits. On these assumptions, moral habituation may be supposed both a prerequisite for critical thought, as Aristotle held, *and* an obstacle to its unfettered employment. Is it not generally true that one is not in a good position to judge the conception of the good one has been raised in, since one will tend to see what one has grown accustomed to as good?

2. *Foreclosed options*. A second and related objection is that in suppressing alternative conceptions of the good, moral habituation restricts life options. The child's so-called "right to an open future" is breached.

3. *Force*. A third objection is that moral habituation necessarily involves *force*, and is thus morally suspect, particularly in government schools. If moral habits must be cultivated without the benefit of children being antecedently reasonable, then a substantial reliance on force may seem inevitable. Peter Simpson's work on Aristotelian educational theory exemplifies exactly this line of thinking, in insisting that in the Aristotelian account of becoming good, habits of good conduct can only be established by force, since they cannot be established by rational persuasion (Simpson 1990, n. 13).

4. *Skepticism*. Coming at this from the other side, one might worry that children are all too easily initiated into the deadly game of logic, that once immersed in its culture of criticism, they can all too effectively wash themselves and each other in a "cynical acid"[15] which eats away even the sturdiest moral fibers, denuding them of the sheltering fabric of culture, community, and tradition. One need only imagine that the attitude of the critical thinker is to believe just what there is adequate reason to believe, and that there are no rational foundations for morality, or none that can be easily discovered.

5. *Local variation*. A fifth problem is that even if there are rational foundations for morality *generally*, there will almost certainly be legitimate local variations, since some problems of social coordination will have no single best solu-

tion. Different interests may be balanced somewhat differently, leaving the members of each of the various moral communities pained in one way here, in another way there. What is local in this way appears, and is in some sense, arbitrary. This renders it vulnerable to critical scrutiny, however valuable and irreplaceable it may be.

6. *Free-riding*. Even if there were easily discernible foundational arguments for morality generally, and for any merely local rules, one might fear that instruction in critical thinking will embolden children in their embrace of self-interested arguments to free-ride on public morality, to take advantage of the self-restraint of those who accept the demands of morality. The idea of morality as a system of conduct-guiding norms is that it provides reasons for action that take precedence over all others. Its norms are solutions to problems of social coordination which yield mutual advantage when complied with, and this mutual advantage provides us all with reasons of prudence to prefer life in a community constrained by such norms. Some people may understand how this provides a rational foundation for morality, but not fully accept what it demands, namely that we all accept the reasons of morality as compelling reasons, even when the reasons of prudence counsel a different course. The price of morality's benefits is accepting *limits on our liberty to govern ourselves by our own reason*, but how rational will this seem to one who is encouraged by instruction in critical thinking to think for herself?

The situation in which "everyone is governed by his own reason" is inevitably "a condition of war," says Hobbes (1651, xvi.4), but the "fool," without denying the existence of a social covenant, "questioneth whether injustice . . . may not sometimes stand with that reason which dictateth to every man his own good. [He questions whether] it be not against reason [to violate the covenant]" (xv.4). "The force of words being . . . too weak to hold men to the performance of their covenants," and virtue being too rare, we must authorize a sovereign to establish moral law by force of arms and the suppression of academic freedom, says Hobbes (xiv.31, xviii.9, xlvi.23 OL). If we are to find some principled grounds on which to resist the repugnantly illiberal aspects of this Hobbesian solution, we need to show either that habits of virtue, and the sentiments, perceptions, and inclinations of which they are composed, are robust and resistant to any corrupting influence that critical reason might have, or that critical reason can be counted on to counsel fair play and adherence to moral norms.

Surveying this list, we find three forms of the concern that moral training compromises individual freedom and three forms of the concern that the liberating capacity of critical reason undermines fidelity to common morality. At least four of these concerns were on the philosophical agenda at its outset, and have been perennially at the heart of philosophical concern with education, the problems of *local variation* and *foreclosed options* being the exceptions. I will set these exceptions aside in what follows, and begin my discussion of the others with some brief remarks on their place in the philosophical tradition.

We saw in chapter 2 (§ 2.1) that Thrasymachus argues in Book I of Plato's *Republic* that laws aim at the advantage of the rulers alone, while those who have made the laws "declare what they have made—what is to their own advantage— to be just for their subjects" (338e). His argument confronts Socrates with a problem of indoctrination which the Socratic elenchus cannot answer, but which Plato hopes to. The elenchus offers no hope of arriving at a consistent set of *true* beliefs unless one has begun with beliefs which are weighted toward the truth to begin with. In the face of systematic error, which could arise from systematic deception, it is powerless, and this points up the desirability of having some basis for judging a society which is independent of what is taught in it.

Thrasymachus's consistent disdain for conventional morality may also be considered an expression of moral skepticism, to be answered by Plato's theory of moral knowledge, while the challenge from Glaucon that follows in Book II shows how the free-rider problem arises even among those who accept the rationality of entering into a social covenant to create and enforce a common morality. It is in hopes of answering this free-rider problem that Plato spends the better part of Books II–IX trying to show that virtue is not simply an instrumental good, related to happiness only unreliably through external sanctions, but an internal good of the psyche without which no one can have any prospect of happiness. It is, at least in part, in hopes of answering this problem that Rousseau later undertakes to convince us that Emile can *without benefit of instruction* discover the natural laws of morality and physics, and from the latter the existence of God and the afterlife (thus, the essential elements of "natural religion").[16]

Thrasymachus represents the problem of force, no less than the problem of indoctrination, and we saw that Plato affirms in response that in the best kind of city children are educated by "persuasion" embodied in music and poetry, and not by "force," as they are in deficient cities (III 401b–402a, VIII 548c). In the *Republic* (III 401b–402a, VIII 548c, IX 590c–d) as in the works of Locke (1693, §31–85), the resistance to using force in education rests in the idea that reliance on force tends to undermine the development of responsiveness to reason, and the idea that force need be used only sparingly, since children are quite ready to imitate those who are praised and admired, and quite inclined to adopt the standards and way of life of those who take care of them.

What this brief historical introduction begins to reveal is that the problems of indoctrination and free-riding are the most challenging. The problem of force depends upon failing to recognize the ways in which children are drawn to the good without force or rationally compelling argument. Plato, Aristotle, and Locke all had a reasonably good understanding of how this occurs. On Aristotle's account, what is lacking in most children without moral training is specifically an attachment to what is admirable *(kalon)* or appropriate *(prepon)* (*NE* X.9 1179b4– 26), and argument alone will not engender such an attachment; but this does not mean that children are without other motives that can be relied upon to persuade them, often without force, to engage in conduct that will allow them to develop a taste for what is admirable or appropriate, and a devotion to it for its own sake.[17]

They thereby become responsive to reasons of a distinctively moral kind, which Aristotle regards as practical reasons of the highest order.

By contrast, what may seem the obvious adequate response to the problem of indoctrination is not adequate. That response would note the reference, in my statement of the problem of indoctrination, to establishing "beliefs which are not all evidently true" and hold that there is no problem if we take care to inculcate only beliefs which are evidently true. I think there is a lot of good sense in this response, and that public school districts in the United States typically do attempt to exercise such care when they pursue initiatives in character education. Non-violence and mutual respect are on the list, but beliefs about sexual orientation, gender roles, and what constitutes a family are not. When the various constituencies in a district are brought to the table, their initial apprehensions about "whose values" are to be taught give way to a consensus that is remarkably stable across districts.

As gratifying as such success may be, however, we have to make some allowance for our collective fallibility. Recognizing our fallibility, and making allowance for the possibility of moral progress, should lead us to embrace the ideal of a moral community that is held together by norms that are open to public evaluation and revision, a community that chooses fundamental law for itself and makes moral progress by revising it over time. Even if we take care to find common ground in what we teach, if we teach it in a way that precludes any possibility of thinking beyond it, then the ideal of a progressive common morality is compromised, and a form of the problem of indoctrination remains.

The problem of skepticism is also an easier one than the free-rider problem. Although it is periodically fashionable to profess moral skepticism, the contractarian view that it is mutually advantageous and therefore rational to impose on ourselves duties of mutual respect, or at least self-restraint, is not only an attractive fall-back position in theory, but is easily grasped as self-evident in practice. Although there may be specific provisions of particular moral codes that may not be mutually advantageous, the general proposition that moral order is mutually advantageous seems true. On the other hand, the free-rider problem would remain unsolved even if the problem of skepticism *were* solved.

Taken together, the problems of indoctrination and free-riding create something of a bind or dilemma, a *paradox of progressive morality*, if you will:

1. Either one's capacity to critically evaluate the morality one is habituated into is limited by the perceptions and sentiments one acquires in that habituation, or it is not.

2. If it is limited in this way, then no consistent system of morality is open to internal public scrutiny, and no one brought up in that system has any rational assurance that it is not deficient.

3. If one's critical capacity is not limited in this way, then the perceptions and sentiments which incline one to give the reasons of morality priority can be undermined by critical thinking, resulting in moral free-riding.

The problem, in short, is how morality can both command our fidelity and be open to effective public scrutiny and appropriate revision. It would seem that it can only have one of these properties at the expense of the other.

The classical and modern traditions share a common aspiration to solve the free-rider problem by means of a theoretical demonstration that it is rational to be moral, but divide on the questions of whether the requisite moral knowledge can be *easily* acquired and whether it can be acquired *independently* of one's prior moral beliefs. To the extent that it can be acquired *easily* and *independently* of one's prior moral beliefs and perceptions, a solution to our paradox may be found in the possibility of us all having moral knowledge.

As we have seen, the Platonic and Aristotelian view is that moral habituation and the true moral beliefs it engenders provide an essential foundation for becoming reasonable and acquiring moral insight, and that such insight is difficult to achieve. When a person who has been properly cared for and trained acquires the ability to reason, reason will confirm the sound perceptions established by that training and care (*Rep.* 402a). Belief must precede knowledge, as it were. But in the circumstances that prevail in most cities, most people will never acquire that knowledge, and the preservation of their incomplete virtue will require some modest enforcement of laws which embody divine reason or natural moral law (*NE* X.9 1180a1–4). Though the texts are less clear on this point, the view of Aristotle and the later Plato may be that even the moral insight of people of considerable practical wisdom may not obviate the need for some form of external assistance.[18]

By contrast, the view that emerges in the early modern period is that faith and reason converge, but may do so independently of one another. According to the doctrines of *natural reason* and *natural religion*, human beings possess as a gift of nature a faculty of reason by which they can easily discover within themselves a knowledge of God, moral law, and the afterlife. Such knowledge of the moral law and its divine enforcement would provide us all with assurance that virtue pays and provide an independent measure of human laws and customs. It is this doctrine that provides Rousseau with a solution to the tension he sees between domestic and public education, between education in the interests of the child and education in the interests of society. On a proper understanding of natural law, which the child will allegedly discover for himself, these interests coincide.

I am not sanguine about the prospects for making good on the idea that there is easily, and thus widely, attainable moral knowledge which not only provides an independent measure of the soundness of whatever moral code one has grown up with, but also a compelling motive to be moral. The Aristotelian account of virtue and reason seems more plausible in this respect. If such knowledge is not widely attainable, however, what possibilities for escaping the *paradox of progressive morality* remain? I can think of four which may warrant some consideration.

First, one might hypothesize that reason can outstrip the sentiments, that what one rationally judges to be best will not always be possible for one emotionally.

If this is true, then critical reason may be able to provide evaluations of one's moral mother tongue sufficient for moral progress, even as it remains the language of one's heart. Progress would be intergenerational, not intragenerational, and the sentiments of each generation would bind its actions, if not its tongue. A difficulty with this suggestion is that if the advances in moral judgment are not put into practice in any way, it is not clear how intergenerational progress can proceed. Inconsistencies between speech and conduct are as likely to engender cynicism as progress, especially on Aristotelian assumptions about how moral virtues are cultivated.

Second, one might argue that allowance for fallibility in our identification of fundamental moral principles is misplaced, that what we think of as moral progress is progress in the consistency and sensitivity of application of the same fundamental principles which have been transmitted already through many generations. On this line of argument, there is no harm in people being forever bound in their sentiments, conduct, and perception of the good by the correct fundamental morality they are brought up in. That will prevent them from exploiting opportunities to free-ride, while a training in critical thinking and moral case analysis will develop their capacity for advancing moral progress through sensitive and creative application of the fundamental principles they have learned. This is a solution quite consistent with the moral finality of Plato's *Republic* and *Laws*, but not obviously compatible with Aristotle's conception of *phronêsis*. The idea that moral insight is tied up with the discernment of particulars and is aggregative (Sherman 1989, 13–55) does not lend itself to this suggested partitioning of principle and application.

Third, a suggestion which is more authentically Aristotelian than either of the preceding is that, as a body of citizens reaches better collective judgments about matters of moral concern, it can and should bind itself under new laws, thereby creating for itself the motivation to act in a more enlightened way. This is possible, by Aristotle's lights, even if people who have been brought up well, and have acquired a conception of what is admirable *(kalon)* or appropriate *(prepon)* and a seriousness about doing what is admirable or appropriate, remain in some danger of backsliding. Given the advancement of moral insight and judgment which such people can attain when they bring their somewhat different perspectives together in conversation, they will at least be in a position to advance enlightened legal reform, and will wish to, and they will thereby bind themselves under morally progressive laws, while both instructing and binding those who have not achieved the same progress of understanding. As we have seen, Aristotle stakes a great deal of his political theory on the idea that legal reform can be an effective instrument of moral progress, provided the instructional and motivating force of law is not undermined by changing it too much or too frequently (*Pol.* I.2 1253a30–39, II.8 1269a14–23).

A final possibility is that if children are initiated into habitual practices of giving and taking reasons, including moral reasons, they will become both morally serious and committed critical thinkers, motivated by conceptions of themselves as both moral and devoted to the truth. Being motivated in this way will preclude free-riding, since selfishness and making an exception of oneself will be incompatible with a desire to be moral; but if thoughtfulness about what counts as a reason has been cultivated, it is hard to see how the perceptions and sentiments formed by such an upbringing would preclude an examination of fundamental morality and a potential for moral progress. On this alternative, one pictures the intellectual virtues as themselves originating in training or habituation in accordance with norms of reason, as much as in teaching, and one pictures training in the habits of virtue as also including a training in the practice of giving adequate reasons for what one does and respecting the adequate reasons that others give. This is not a straightforwardly Aristotelian view to the extent that it rejects the idea that reason emerges late, identifies a stage of habituation in norms of reason, and sees habits of giving and taking reasons as part of the habituation of ethical virtue. In these ways it is a more obviously Lockean view than Aristotelian, but the differences may be more apparent than real. Locke regards children as able to grasp reasons, though not the deepest reasons, and he thinks it a good thing to initiate children from the earliest possible age in the practices of reason giving. I am not sure that Aristotle's conception of moral habituation precludes any of this, since it must surely promote the development of rational and self-critical capacities if it is to promote true virtue (Sherman 1989, 157–99). What *is* precluded on Aristotle's account is the view that children are responsive to reason in the sense of grasping and being moved by appeals to what is good, admirable, or appropriate; but this is not to say that they are incapable of reasoning or unresponsive to other kinds of reasons.

This final solution is in some ways the most attractive, but a great deal remains to be examined. This must suffice, however, as an indication of the agenda for the theory and practice of moral education entailed by Aristotle's view of the relation between the moral and intellectual virtues.

7.3 THE CASE FOR PUBLIC EDUCATION

The foregoing investigations have led us to a number of conclusions bearing on the necessity of a public education. One of these is that justice requires a public (i.e., state operated) system of education which provides an adequate moral, political, and disciplinary education, and an education preparatory to respected work, for all children. A second is that this is the responsibility of all levels of government that make and enforce laws. A third is that there are good reasons to favor common schooling which brings children of all kinds together in schools and classrooms which accord them equal respect and status and which adopt cooperative methods of instruction to encourage children to deliberate and work together. Since the arguments for the first two of these conclusions are collected together in §7.13 above, there is no need to recapitulate them here. On the other hand, it will be useful to address the inadequacy of the grounds on which Aristotle's arguments for public education have been dismissed. It will also be useful to review the arguments for common schooling, since they have not yet been collected together, and to summarize the significance of all of these arguments for proposals to privatize education in one way or another.

As I said at the outset of this investigation, Aristotle's educational thought has received little scholarly comment, and when the arguments for public education *have* received comment they have been hastily dismissed. One recent work whose treatment of this topic warrants a response is Fred Miller's landmark treatise, *Nature, Justice, and Rights in Aristotle's Politics* (1995). Miller recognizes that Aristotle regards the care and education of citizens as preeminently important to the polis's natural political agenda, but he dismisses this as untenable. His main objection rests in the idea that Aristotle's conception of the polis illicitly conflates the notions of state and society:

> The end of the polis *qua* society is the virtuous and happy life, but it does not follow that the function of the polis *qua* state is to use coercive force against its citizens so as to make them virtuous and happy. Aristotle, in making such an inference, is confusing the two senses of 'polis' and is assigning to the polis *qua* state a function which properly belongs only to the polis *qua* society (360).

One very surprising feature of these remarks is the reference to "coercive force." Aristotle's concern, as Miller recognizes, is with promoting virtue, but he does not believe that anyone is made virtuous by force, except in the very marginal sense that a child's virtue may be promoted by compulsory school attendance laws and school rules that are subject to enforcement when they are not voluntarily complied with, or that an adult's virtue is safeguarded from ruin by laws that discourage ruinous acts. It would be truer to Aristotle to say that he thinks that the polis *qua* state should take responsibility for nurturing virtue and rationality in a way that provides a foundation for adult freedom (in accordance not with the law *per se*, but with the individual's own grasp of the demands of reason), than to suggest he is unleashing all the coercive power of the state in forcing citizens "to conform to an official code of morality" (361).

One of the most important lessons about schools that we can derive from Aristotle is that we subvert their mission and proper role in laying the foundation for voluntary and rational acceptance of the proper demands of law to the extent that we rely not on education itself, but on surveillance and force, in attempting to create good order within their walls. By Aristotelian standards, to capitulate to a primary reliance on force within schools themselves is tantamount to abandoning any serious pretence of a just rule of law in the society at large. The alternative demanded by justice and respect for reason is that schools devote themselves to building relationships of trust and mutual goodwill, predicated on respect, mutual advantage, and responsibility rooted in the cultivation of a disposition to think things through and act accordingly. A common response to school initiatives devoted to these ends is to complain that they take time away from the proper academic business of schools, but all the evidence we have suggests that attention to "social and emotional" learning of this kind promotes academic achievement by enabling teachers to create a culture of learning which children want to be part of (Lewis 1995; Elias et al. 1997).

Having said this, I would readily concede that Aristotle cannot just assume that it is the business of the polis *qua* state to take on the burden of moral education. Where Miller sees a confusion, however, I have found all the elements of an *argument from the foundations of corrective justice*, which shows that it cannot be just for a society *in its lawmaking capacity*—i.e., *as a state*—to leave to chance whether citizens turn out to be good and rational and able to comprehend the reasons for the laws being as they are. Without an adequate public system of education, the polis *qua* state would often be, in its relationship with the criminal offender, in the position of putting force and violence before instruction and persuasion, and we have found good reasons to conclude that Aristotle would regard this as unjust.

This argument depends, as we have seen, on an important difference between Aristotle and liberals like John Locke, which Miller nowhere acknowledges, namely their very different views on the development of reason and human goodness. Locke's view, that the untutored reason of individuals in a state of nature would allow most of them to easily grasp the elements of natural moral law and adhere to that law, would be regarded by Aristotle as not only false but an invitation to injustice in more than one way, since it is only through law and the education that must precede it that we become rational and human. If Aristotle is right about this, as I think he is, then this represents a significant threat to classical liberal thought and its presumption that the state bears no responsibility for laying the foundations for rational consent to the laws and voluntary compliance with them.

In defense of his claim that moral education is "properly" the business of the private associations constituting the polis *qua* society, Miller cites the natural diversity of values, the repression involved in trying to eliminate that diversity (365), and the potential pitfalls of placing the power to control moral education in the hands of public officials (373). With regard to diversity, I would respond that it is essential to determine the intended scope of moral education: are we talking about inculcating a common morality of justice and self-restraint or trying to make everyone a philosopher? The former is no threat to any forms of diversity we should value, though the latter is, and I have suggested an appropriate concession to pluralism which accommodates this, yet leaves the more compelling aspects of Aristotle's educational views intact (§5.15). Miller's concerns about who should have the authority to morally educate are too empirically complicated to try to sort through here, but there is a distinctly un-Aristotelian and antistatist bias to them. He worries about "special-interest groups ... defin[ing] the agenda for coercive moral education" (373), but does not ask whether the vested interests of the local communities with political control over public schools in the United States might be more favorable to the public interest than the motives that "private" organizations such as corporations would bring to education. He asks whether public providers may "underestimate the costs that are borne by the public," but does not ask whether the relative accessibility of information about the operations of public institutions in democratic societies vis-a-vis information about private organizations would allow the public to better judge those costs and how well the public interest is being served. The experience of seeing local school districts build public consensus around the frameworks for character education programs inclines me to be more sanguine about public control than Miller appears to be. The more important feature of this debate, however, is that apart from dismissing the idea of a common morality of justice out of hand, Miller's argument for the state having no proper role in moral education is not an argument from principle so much as from empirical speculation.

7.31 Common Schooling

Unlike the arguments for a public system of education rooted in principles of mutual respect, the arguments for common schooling do not establish requirements of justice. Rather, they identify important public goods which there is some reason to think we can effectively promote through educating children of disparate backgrounds together. They do not show that no other means to achieving these goods are possible, nor that there are no competing goods worthy of consideration. The goods the arguments for common schooling identify are very weighty ones, however, and in the absence of credible alternative means to achieving these goods, they warrant the adoption of the most promising means to effectively integrating schools.

The first of these arguments, which runs through many books of the *Politics*, rests in the idea that schools and other public institutions should promote mutual goodwill, trust, and friendship between children of all kinds in order to create a more socially unified and politically stable society (§5.14, §5.15). An aspect of this argument identified in §5.14 is the thesis that the development of the virtues which citizens should exercise in relation to each other requires a foundation of practice in relation to each other, which is to say in relation to a representative sample of others, and not simply in relation to those whom citizens of diverse backgrounds are predisposed to associate with. A related but distinct argument, noted first in §4.34 and outlined in the first section of this chapter, is that the capacity of citizens of diverse backgrounds to participate productively in collective deliberation and self-rule requires the right kind of practice, and that common schools can provide a suitable venue for such practice. As Eamonn Callan, has said,

> the exercise of reasonableness presupposes deliberative settings in which citizens with conflicting beliefs and ends can join together to ask how they might live

together on terms that all might endorse on due reflection. Such settings must straddle the cleavages that divide them from each other. That being so, the Aristotelian thesis [that virtues are acquired through their exercise] would suggest that the growth of reasonableness requires at some stage that reciprocity be practised in dialogical contexts that straddle our social cleavages (Callan 1997, 177).

A third argument, resting on the requirement of adequate instruction in the academic disciplines, is suggested by evidence that separate schooling is almost inevitably unequal and deficient in what it provides those who are cut off from the mainstream of a society's intellectual life. The United States Commission on Civil Rights concluded in its 1967 report, *Racial Isolation in the Public Schools*, that

> The central truth which emerges from this report and from all the Commission's investigations is simply this: Negro children suffer serious harm when their education takes place in public schools which are racially segregated, whatever the source of such segregation may be (193).

The evidence of the intervening decades is that this remains true, largely because of the difficulties which separate schools face in replicating the cultures of learning more typical of schools dominated by children who already belong to the cultural and intellectual mainstream of society.[19]

Aristotle's concerns about social division, distrust, inequality, and the barriers these pose to a stable and just political system are significant enough to warrant establishing and maintaining a public system of schools which at least provides substantial incentives for children from all parts of our cities to spend part of their time learning and growing up together in settings which accord and communicate equality of status.

7.32 Privatization and Parental Choice

With regard to the question of how far Aristotle's arguments take us toward any position on the relative merits of achieving our educational goals through publicly operated schools versus privately operated ones, we must distinguish two kinds of arguments for privatization: one concerned with the choice of means to whatever educational goals we have, another with parental authority and choice. We must also distinguish these questions about what is effective and just in the abstract, from questions about whether it is sensible to support privatization and voucher initiatives in the political climate which now prevails in the United States.

The arguments for school choice or voucher systems resting in appeals to parental authority have come most often from religious fundamentalists, and have taken the form of asserting that the free exercise of their religion entails a right not only to transmit it to their children, but to do so in ways that shield their children from any opposing points of view. These arguments have coexisted with remarkably successful efforts to censor the texts used in public schools (Delfattore 1992) and a similarly remarkable growth in home schooling, and have the goal of creating state subsidies or full tuition grants for separate religious schooling. Though far fewer in number, there are parents who object to the value content of the public schools available to them on other grounds—because they mirror the vapid consumerism and anti-intellectualism of American culture, for instance—so these arguments from parents' authority over their children's moral development might be advanced on nonreligious grounds as well (Arons 1986).

One response to these arguments is that, at least in their dominant form, they would yield a form of school choice entailing state funding for religious schooling, and that this would obliterate a cornerstone of the American understanding of separation of church and state. I am not much moved by this objection, and there is no precedent for it in Aristotle, of course. Eamonn Callan has argued with much cogency that there are patterns of support for religious schooling which might be favorable to securing the kind of educational goods I have been concerned with here, inasmuch as they create incentives for parents to accept appropriate regulation of their children's schooling in exchange for fully funded denominational schooling (Callan 2000). What is not clear, however, is whether parents who do not want their children to learn to think things through for themselves would accept such arrangements. It may well be that it is only by resisting any state funding for denominational schooling that we can preserve adequate incentives for families to enroll their children in schools which satisfy the requirements established by the arguments we have considered here.[20]

The first important point which I would insist on, then, is that any arrangements that promote school choice must be consistent with securing the forms of educational content and equality described above. Given this requirement, it is not immediately obvious which arrangements might be acceptable, especially in light of what is known of the curricular choices made by fundamentalists who choose separate schooling at their own expense. It could not be consistent with legitimate state interests to fund schools in which children are not exposed to any sources of information, including books, magazines, or newspapers, that are not produced by fundamentalist presses (Delfattore 1992).

The second important question at stake is how much weight should be given to the collective goods promised by common schooling vis-a-vis the interest that parents have in using separate schooling to consolidate their influence over the formation of their children's religious and moral identities. I am sympathetic to arguments for according considerable weight to parents' interests in their children's identities (Callan 2000), but a characteristic of such arguments is that they rest more in parental anxieties than in demonstrable fact. It is not unreasonable to suppose that common schooling will tend to have a homogenizing effect on children, but if children tend to gravitate toward like-minded friends, and in most public schools there are others who share their faith, then perhaps the threat to parents' legitimate interests in their children's identities is not as great as it seems. So although these parental interests must be accorded some weight in the design of public systems of education, I am inclined to think that the interests which may be promoted by common schooling are weighty enough to make it unwise to publicly subsidize separate religious schools.

In sum, the arguments for educational privatization resting in appeals to parental authority or religious freedom seem insufficient to outweigh the interests which favor common schooling, and the arguments from justice require that any concessions to choice must be qualified by reasonable measures to insure that all children receive adequate instruction of the kinds outlined in §7.13.

Arguments from the efficacy of markets often suggest that market mechanisms would be a panacea for all the various problems which plague the American school system. This is not the place to survey and evaluate these arguments, but it is fair to say that they are highly speculative. What information costs must parents bear to make good choices, and how many parents will be able to bear those costs? Will choice lead parents to be more productively involved in their children's education and schools because they are happy to have a choice, or less involved because they will assume the schools are better and do not need their participation, and because the exercise of choice is likely to increase the average distance from home to school and discourage unnecessary trips? How strong would the inflationary pressures on grades be, and how much would that undermine actual educational achievement? Will the choices available to parents really improve in the ways we need them to improve? The difficulties involved in projecting the answers to these and many other questions make it impossible to regard the argument from market efficiency as a theoretically compelling one, let alone an empirically established one.

What is clear is that in order to meet the requirements established by Aristotle's arguments, any scheme of privatization would have to: (1) provide parents with the full price of admission; (2) ensure that all schools meet the minimal standards I have identified; and (3) establish ground rules for admission and incentives favorable to creating diverse student populations in every school.[21] Partial grants or vouchers cannot meet the requirements of equity or the goal of integration identified above, and there are good reasons to doubt that the choices parents would make would be favorable to every aspect of the educational content and equality I have described.

It has been my experience that many parents care a great deal about their children "getting ahead," which is to say outdoing and prevailing over their peers—so much so that it is not uncommon now for suburban families to hold their children back from entering school when they are first old enough to be admitted, so they will be more physically and intellectually developed than their classmates—and much less about whether their children are civil, respectful, and reasonable in their dealings with others. We live in a culture still dominated more than we publicly admit by an ethic of outward success, in which one is "nobody" without such success, and is worthy of respect as a peer only to the extent that one prevails over others. In these circumstances it is quite absurd to suppose that privatization and parental choice are mechanisms of reform that will enable schools to more effectively promote the common goods identified by Aristotle and the early American advocates of public schooling. In economic terms, these goods are externalities which would fall beyond the scope of the incentives created by privatization. So while we can engage in empirical speculation about the possible benefits of privatization and choice, we cannot plausibly contend that the educational aims and forms of equality required by justice can be secured without government action to provide and mandate them. If any system of privatized schools could be adequate to the demands of justice, it would be in large measure through mechanisms of regulation or public oversight and not through market mechanisms. This is not to say that mechanisms of choice could not be useful in improving the quality of education in some ways, for they might be, but this remains to be seen.

The last question to be addressed is whether it is sensible, in light of the arguments we have considered, to favor the kinds of voucher proposals which have been proposed and submitted for public approval. Here the question is clearer than in the abstract, I believe, but also farther removed from the high ground of theory on which most of this investigation has been conducted. What seems evident is that, in the present distinctly inegalitarian political climate, no remotely adequate proposal is likely to come forward or could prevail if it did. What seems most probable is simply that systems of public schools would be weakened by the diversion of funds into subsidies which are large enough to make the private schooling some parents already acquire more affordable, but too small to create the mobility essential to creating any significant incentives to innovation and improvement. There are other grounds as well for doubting that we would succeed in creating the kind of free market in schooling assumed by arguments from market efficiency. In an era in which the federal government of the United States has all but abandoned the use of antitrust laws to block further concentration of the control of news and information in the hands of a small number of corporations, I find the suggestion that we could create a robustly competitive market in schooling improbable. The extent of corporate control over information and the terms of public debate in American classrooms is troubling enough as it is (Manning 1999). Speaking less probabilistically, the experiments with privatization to date have not been encouraging (Ascher, Fruchter, and Berne 1996; Richards, Shore, and Sawicky 1996; Flam and Keane 1997). [22]

What is undeniable is that we Americans entered a difficult period in our national educational history in the 1980s, with the encouragement given to the fundamentalist right and a decade of highly publicized reports alleging educational failure. Where we will succeed in going from here is not entirely clear, but we must not lose sight of the fact that the American system of public education is almost without parallel in the world in its ambition to provide all children with a general education. The international comparisons on which our schools are condemned have seldom taken this into account or inferred from the close correlation of urban social disintegration with declining test scores that the work of preserving what we value in our civilization cannot be borne by schools alone (Cremin 1989). The problems in our schools are not likely to be remedied by choice or any other structural reforms in the administration of schools, because these problems are largely a by-product of the disintegration of our neighborhoods and cities, and the eclipse of our aspirations to public service. What matters in the end is whether we can find enough teachers committed to the nearly all-consuming form of public service that teaching is, and create the social, economic, and other conditions that will allow teachers to create communities of care, justice, and inquiry in their classrooms.[23] Without a renewed commitment to both public education and the health of our communities, it is hard to see how this will be possible.

7.33 Conclusion

The contrast between the modern and ancient versions of the problem of the relationship of morality and law is rooted in different experiences of conflict, but also in rather different accounts of how human beings become rational and good. The early modern period was preoccupied with the Reformation wars, and thus with the question of religious freedom. Between Hobbes, Locke, and Rousseau we see three different accounts of the proper relationship between church and state, resting in three different accounts of how conflict inspired by doctrinal differences and the claims of conscience might be resolved. The assertion of rights of conscience prevailed, most famously in Locke's *Letter concerning Toleration*, and is still with us in calls for school choice as a means of giving parents more complete authority over the formation of their children's hearts and minds (Arons 1986). The suggestion that with public education we risk evils comparable to those over which the Reformation wars were fought is misplaced, however. The dangers lie not in us becoming too much like each other in our moral convictions, but too different and inclined to demonize each other, and in failing to treat our children not just as means to the fulfillment of our desire to replicate ourselves, but as ends in themselves, worthy of respect as rational beings.

The problems of the Greeks were different, and no less relevant to our own. Despite the occurrence of some well-known impiety trials, religious persecution was "in principle impossible within the Greek system," for Greek cities "knew neither Church nor dogma," and were generally tolerant of unbelief (Zaidman and Pantel 1992, 11–12). The question of fundamental concern in the world of fourth-century Greece, as the great alliances crumbled in the aftermath of the Peloponnesian War and conflict over land and debts brought down governments with regularity (Finley 1953, 1983), was how to create order that is both stable and good. Public schooling and an associated moderation of economic and social inequality were the means to political stability and social unity offered first by

Plato, and then in a more attractive form by Aristotle, as an alternative to economic expansion built on military expansionism—the course pursued by Athens and advocated by Aristotle's pedagogical competitor, Isocrates. The postwar economic boom in the United States encouraged the notion, not unlike that of the Athenians, that an "expanding economic pie" could buy domestic tranquility without common schooling, and in the face of deep racial and socioeconomic inequality. But if we are now, in the face of growing disparity between the rich and the poor, descending into a "new civil war" (Hacker 1992b), then we could do worse than to take Aristotle seriously.

Notes

INTRODUCTION

1. For an admirable attempt to reconstruct the balance of *Pol.* VIII see Lord 1982.

2. Most notable and convincing in this regard is Miller 1995.

3. See esp. Jaeger 1948. See Wians 1996, including esp. Pellegrin 1996, for some reappraisals of what may be inferred about the course of Aristotle's philosophical development.

4. Leon Kojen defended essentially this view in his talk on a draft of this book, presented at the World Congress of Philosophy in Boston, 14 August 1998.

I will sometimes leave the word *polis* (pl. *poleis*) untranslated, or use the anglicized plural "polises." There is no single English word that adequately captures it, and there is something to be said for the idea that Aristotle was after all writing with a particular form of political institution in mind. Nevertheless, I will also use the terms "city" and "state" in some contexts. A polis was an autonomous political association of perhaps two thousand to one hundred thousand citizens, together with many noncitizens, occupying an urban settlement *(asty)* and its surrounding territory *(chôra)*. In some respects it is best thought of as a city, an urban area which serves as a center of commerce, manufacturing, the arts, and other aspects of social life. On the other hand, as an autonomous political entity that makes laws for itself, a polis must also be thought of as in some ways like a modern state. I will use the word "state" particularly when what is at issue are the powers and burdens that are inseparable from the enterprise of making and enforcing law, and the word "city" particularly in discussing matters to which the scale of a polis is important, such as civic unity and the naturalness of living in a polis.

5. This is certainly true of Burnyeat 1980 and Sherman 1989, which are the most influential works in this genera. Though not a work on Aristotle's educational thought per se, an important exception is Bodéüs 1993.

6. For interpretations of the *NE* as directed strictly to the private pursuit of moral development, see Betbeder 1970 and Gauthier and Jolif 1970. Bodéüs seems to me entirely correct in concluding that

Aristotelian ethics, far from describing an individual ethics alien to politics, presents, on the contrary, the essential body of learning with which the legislator must fortify himself when legislating. Conversely, one might say that the main body of political issues discussed by the philosopher also presents learning which is to provide direction for heads of household, who are often responsible for the education of children and thus need to act, in a restricted context, as if they were lawgivers (Bodéüs 1993, 123).

7. See Swanson 1992 for a portrayal of Aristotle as a champion of the private sphere, and Mulgan 1994 for corrective observations focused on her associated portrayal of Aristotle as a "crypto-feminist."

8. It also requires attention to other works, such as the *Rhetoric, Eudemian Ethics,* and the disputed *Magna Moralia.* I shall not ignore these works, but I shall follow tradition and the dominant view of them in treating the *Nicomachean Ethics* as the mature expression of Aristotle's ethical theory.

9. *Phronêsis* "must also recognize the particulars," Aristotle writes, "for it is practical, and practice is concerned with particulars" (*NE* VI.7 1141b14–16). He holds that grasping the particulars (of situations in which one must deliberate and act) is a matter of perception and develops through training, experience, and conversation.

A secondary practical aim of political science is to guide individual heads of households in the management of their domestic affairs. See *NE* X.9 1179b29–34 and *NE* I.2 1094b7–11, where Aristotle explains why the science of the highest good for man is political science, even though it may be used by an individual (in the "private" sphere, outside the powers of any office) or for the benefit of a single individual.

10. Aristotle uses *euêmeria* in a way that seems interchangeable with *eudaimonia* at *EE* I.4 1215a27, *Pol.* III.4 1278b29, and *Pol.* VIII.5 1339b4–5, though in other passages, such as *NE* I.8 1099b7 and X.8 1178b33, *euêmeria* takes on a different sense. In some contexts "well-being" seems the right choice, because although Aristotle identifies *eudaimonia* (happiness, flourishing) as the highest good for human beings, and believes that the best kind of polis would be one that enables all of its citizens to be happy, he also seems to hold (as I shall argue in chapter 3) that polises should aim at the well-being of all their inhabitants, even those who are precluded by their natures from being happy. Happiness determines a scale of well-being along which they can progress, and should be enabled to progress, even though they can never reach its terminus.

11. Aristotle says at *NE* V.2 1130b22–27 that

practically the majority of the acts commanded by the law are those which are prescribed from the point of view of virtue taken as a whole; for the law bids us practice every virtue and forbids us to practice any vice. And the things that tend to produce virtue taken as a whole are those of the acts prescribed by the law which have been prescribed with a view to education for the common good.

12. See Godwin (1798, 235–39) and Mill (1859, 301–4).

13. See Elias et al. 1997 and the notes to §7.2.

14. Jefferson's theoretical subordination of political education to the larger purpose of securing the happiness of all is Aristotelian in spirit if not in name. The preamble to Jefferson's 1778 *A Bill for the More General Diffusion of Knowledge* reads in part:

[The] most effectual means of preventing [a government from degenerating into tyranny] would be to illuminate, as far as practicable, the minds of the people at large. . . . And whereas it is generally true that that people will be happiest whose laws are best, and best administered, in proportion as those who form and administer them are wise and honest; whence it becomes expedient for promoting the publick happiness that those persons, whom nature hath endowed with genius and virtue, should be rendered by liberal education worthy to receive, and able to guard the secret deposit of the rights and liberties of their fellow citizens, and that they should be called to that charge without regard to wealth, birth or other accidental condition or circumstance; but the indigence of the greater number disabling them from so educating, at their own expense, those of their children whom nature hath fitly formed and disposed to become useful instruments for the public, it is better that such should be sought for and educated at the common expense of all, than that the happiness of all should be confided to the weak or wicked (Jefferson 1778, 526–27).

15. It is worth noting that the "revisionist" historians whom Kaestle is concerned to rebut do not disagree with the view that the American public school movement was concerned above all with character traits. See Katz 1968 and Bowles and Gintis 1976. Where they differ is in insisting, on what is now widely regarded as too little evidence, that the function or intent of public schooling was to preserve inequality and oppress the working class, on whom it was imposed. Bowles and Gintis argue that it is by promoting different virtues in children of different social classes that schools fulfil this function (131–41). For a study of public school coalitions which lends support to Kaestle, see Peterson 1985. See also Cremin (1988, 17–49) and Tyack (1974, 72–77).

16. As one commentator wrote in 1968:

It is foolish to proclaim the day and hour that the Public School Movement died, equally foolish to assign its precise moment of birth. No one can doubt, however, that there was such a movement . . . (McClellan 1968, 1).
. . . we are beginning to question most of the basic assumptions which underlie [it] (3).

17. See, e.g., Cookson 1994 and Henig 1994.

CHAPTER 1: GREEK *PAIDEIA* AND SOCRATIC PRINCIPLES

1. This is the number recorded in the catalogue of Aristotle's works prepared by Diogenes Laertius. Tradition has it that Aristotle had made a study of as many as three-hundred constitutions.

2. Here and elsewhere Aristotle refers to Sparta *(spartê)* and the Spartans using the terms Lacedaimon, Lacedaimonians, and Laconians. There is no ideal way to translate *koinê*, an adverbial form of *koinos*, which means "common" or "shared in common." Reeve's "do so as a community" and Kraut's "make this a common project" are both more literal than Rackham's "conduct it on a public system," but it is pretty evident that doing

something as complicated as educating children as a community or a common project requires a system of some sort.

3. Aristotle consistently understands the educational significance of common meals
to be their value in promoting friendship or unifying a city, and the testimony of Plutarch,
in his life of Lycurgus, the great Spartan law-giver, suggests that one way in which
Lycurgus intended them to promote unity was by contributing to the elimination of luxury
(*Lyc.* X). He writes of the common tables that

> . . . the Cretans call them "andreia," but the Lacedaemonians, "phiditia,"
> either because they are conducive to *friendship* and friendliness, "phiditia"
> being equivalent to "philitia"; or because they accustom men to simplicity
> and *thrift*, for which their word is "pheido." But it is quite possible, as some
> say, that the first letter of the word "phiditia" has been added to it, making
> "phiditia" out of "editia," which refers merely to meals and *eating*. They
> met in companies of fifteen, a few more or less, and each one of the din-
> ing companions contributed monthly a bushel of barleymeal, eight gallons
> of wine, five pounds of cheese, two and a half pounds of figs, and in addi-
> tion to this, a very small sum of money for such delicacies as meat and fish.
> Besides this, whenever anyone made a sacrifice of first fruits, or brought
> home game from the hunt, he contributed a portion to the meals. For when-
> ever anyone was preoccupied with a sacrifice or the chase, he was allowed
> to eat at home, but the rest had to be at the meal. For a long time this cus-
> tom of eating at common meals was rigidly observed. . . .
>
> Boys also used to come to these public meals, as if they were attending
> schools of sobriety; there they would listen to political discussions and see
> instructive models of liberal breeding (*Lyc.* XII.1–4).

See also Xenophon, *Lac. Pol.* V generally, and especially 5–6, where it is suggested that
an aim of the Spartan common meals was to provide a means by which "the experience
of the elders might contribute largely to the education of the juniors." For a related account of the Cretan common meals, see Strabo, *Geography* X.4.20. And see Powell (1988,
122–23, 126) on the role of the Spartan common meals in promoting a sense of equality
(encouraged by the Spartan term *homoioi*, "peers," for its citizens), attenuating the
citizen's contact with his family, and eliminating the *symposion*, or private drinking party
of the wealthy.

4. Aristotle, who was writing roughly forty years after the Spartans' defeat in 371,
implies himself at *Pol.* II.9 that the Spartans were defeated owing to a shortage of men,
but he may have been misled in some respects by Spartan propaganda, which aimed "to
discourage the idea that there was anything clever about her military actions, which an
intelligent opponent might learn to counter at little cost. Instead, emphasis was laid on
the hardness of Spartan hoplites and of their training, which enemies from more comfortable cities might despair of matching" (Powell 1988, 228). See also 97 and 229ff.,
and Marrou (1956, 19). Note that all dates pertaining to the ancient world refer to the
pre-Christian era—hence "371" rather than "371 B.C."

5. The date of origin of the ephebic system is uncertain. It is generally agreed that
"there are no texts about ephebes certainly datable before 334/3" (Lewis 1973, 254]), but
circumstantial evidence suggests that the system was established in the early fourth century. See Schnapp (1997, 22–23).

6. I rely here and throughout this section on Beck (1964, 72–146), Golden (1990, 51–79), Lynch (1972, 32–67), Marrou (1956, 3–45), and Powell (1988, 227–31). For commentary on Marrou, see Downey 1957.

7. The archaeological record provides many images of girls in dancing and music lessons, and one of a girl who is carrying writing tablets by a strap and is apparently being led to school by her *paidagôgos*. Although these are evidence of "a specialized education for young girls," as Schnapp says (Schnapp 1997, 48), it is not clear which girls received this education. Beck offers a fairly optimistic reading of the evidence (Beck 1964, 85–88), and Golden the more disheartening appraisal that these may represent courtesans, rather than respectable citizen girls (Golden 1990, 72–74). See also Powell (1988, 341ff.) on female literacy and the education of girls generally.

8. Lynch (1972, 34) suggests "at least two different buildings, one for *gymnastikê* and one for *mousikê*."

9. The norms of Athenian life would have discouraged parents from performing this task themselves. Leisure was embraced as an ideal and a mark of high social class for both sexes, and women were separated and largely confined to their homes. It is worth noting, however, that the latter norm appears to have weakened toward the close of the fifth century as a consequence of losses suffered in the Peloponnesian War and the flight of over twenty thousand slaves. In the period that followed, which had evidently run its course by the mid-fourth century, there was more pressure on women to work both within and outside their homes, and it is conceivable that some may have performed the functions of the *paidagôgos* themselves. Similarly, there is evidence that poor Athenian women were never prevented from going out of their homes, but it is doubtful that their households could have paid for schooling. See Powell (1988, 337–64) and *Pol.* IV.15 1300a4–7 and VI.8 1323a3–6, on the need of poor women to work and the impossibility of preventing them from leaving their houses.

10. Thus, when Socrates concedes in the *Crito* that the Athenian laws "instruct[ed] [his] father to educate [him] in the arts and in physical culture" (50d–e), one cannot assume that this is what the law instructed all fathers to do. See §1.32.

11. "Education is not only a traditional aristocratic concern," writes Lord, citing *Pol.* IV.15 1299b24–25, IV.8 1293b34–38, IV.8 1294a19–22, and VI.2 1317b38–39, "but a distinguishing feature of the aristocratic class, not to say perhaps the most important element constituting its collective identity" (Lord 1990, 213). See also Marrou (1956, 39–40), on the "scorn and suspicion" with which the aristocrats regarded the development of schools, and their view that suitable birth or ancestry is a necessary condition for virtue, without which education is useless.

12. Without a *common* advantage it is hard to see how any system of education could be an object of collectively rational public choice. Even if it were true that what all people strongly prefer is to outdo or prevail over one another, any system that gives one part of a population a greater chance of satisfying this preference than it would otherwise have would thereby give the rest of that population a worse chance of satisfying it than it would have had. The choice of such a system could not be *collectively* rational, and in a system that *is* justified by its capacity to secure common advantages it could not be collectively rational to commit public or common resources to the pursuit of "positional" goods, which are "valuable to some people only on condition that others do not have" them (Hollis 1982, 236), unless promoting them is necessary to, or an efficient means to, securing other nonpositional goods.

13. Cf. Plutarch, *Lyc.* XVI.4. Xenophon's attribution of the classical form of Spartan education to Lycurgus was probably contrived to lend it the respectability of ancient origins. See Marrou (1956, 19). See also Powell (1988, 217–18) on the Spartans' fabrication of "ancestral constitutions" and manipulation of their own history to suit political ends.

14. Aristotle says as much at *NE* V.9 1128b10–11, where he notes that *aidôs* "is defined as a kind of fear of disrepute" and makes people blush.

15. This did include morally edifying instruction in music and poetry, which Plutarch describes some pages later in XXI.

16. Noting the idealization of Spartan education by "fanatical partisans," especially "amongst her old enemies in Athens," and by modern German scholars, Marrou remarks that, "It is difficult for a French historian, writing in 1945, to speak of it with complete detachment. From K. O. Müller 1824 to W. Jäger 1932, German scholarship lauded it to the skies as a product of the Nordic spirit possessed by the Dorians—the conscious embodiment of a racial, militarist, totalitarian policy—a model, miraculously before its time, of the ideal which from the time of Frederick II, Scharnhorst, and Bismarck to the Nazi Third Reich, never ceased to inspire the German soul" (1956, 23).

17. See chapter 3, §3.12.

18. Since Greek men generally married women quite a bit younger than themselves, and would thus have been generally much more experienced and knowledgeable than their wives, one need not regard this as resting on an invidiously sexist assumption.

19. "When he claims the assent of nearly everyone, he is primarily thinking of the members of the Academy. He is not especially concerned with people in general," writes Burnet (1900, 1).

20. Compare *Pol.* VII.1 1323a39–b1 with *Ap.* 30b.

21. Compare *NE* VII.2 1145b23ff. with *Prot.* 352b–c.

22. Compare *Pol.* IV.2 1289b5–6 with *St.* 291e, and Aristotle's theory of the "mean" in *NE* II.6 with *St.* 309c and 283c–85c.

23. On the dating of Plato's dialogues into the early Socratic dialogues, in which Socrates is portrayed essentially as he was; the middle and late dialogues, in which Plato expounds two phases of his own philosophy; and those which are transitional from the early to the middle, see the introduction to Kraut 1992 and Brandwood 1992.

24. Aesop's fable of "The North Wind and the Sun," which dates to the fifth or sixth century, purports to show that "persuasion is often more effective than violence" (Gagarin and Woodruff 1995, 147). Democritus (c. 460–380) writes that "It is clearly better to promote *aretê* by means of exhortation and persuasion than by law and compulsion" (160). Most famously, Gorgias (c. 480–375) contrasts persuasion and force in his "Encomium of Helen" (6–8), but he has in mind a kind of persuasion that makes an induced act involuntary, which is very far from what Plato has in mind (190–95, and esp. 193). See Bobonich 1991, which suggests that there is "something of a deliberate paradox" in this and similar usages (366, n. 6). On the frequent contrasts between *peithô* and *bia* in Greek tragedy, see Buxton 1982.

25. See chapter 2, §2.1.

26. This probably refers to the same Solonian law discussed by Schmitter (1975) and above in §1.1. Kraut suggests that this passage refers to a different law, but in doing so seems to rely on the idea that Solon's called upon fathers to teach their sons a *craft (technê* in the expression *technên didaschesthai)* (Kraut 1984, 91 n. 1). On Schmitter's wider

interpretation of the expression *technên didaschesthai*, there is no reason to think it was not this Solonian law that called upon the parents of Socrates to educate him in music and "gymnastics" (Schmitter 1975, 288).

27. On Xenophon's depiction of Socrates generally, see Vander Waerdt (1994, articles 5–8), and Vlastos (1991, 99–106).

28. When Socrates refers to "the god" *(ton theon)* he clearly has in mind, at least some of the time, Apollo, who fits the description "the god, the one in Delphi" *(Ap.* 20e) who has called him to service, he says. It is possible that in some instances he means Zeus, whom he invokes by name at 17c, 25c, 26d, 26e, and 35d, such as when he refers to "the god" as passing judgment on him (35d) and knowing his future (42a), for it was Zeus who was said to punish all human injustice, and whose thought was believed to be "identical with future happenings" (Lloyd-Jones 1983, 5).

29. In judging their failure to perceive this gulf as *blameworthy*, Socrates no doubt assumes that their cities will have instructed them in the differences between gods and men.

30. David Reeve concludes that Socrates believes piety "is simply knowledge," since he believes all virtue is knowledge and tells Euthyphro (at *Euth.* 14b) that his definition of piety, which includes a knowledge condition and more, could be briefer (Reeve 1989, 65). This cannot be the whole of what Socrates believes about the nature of piety, however, and the course of Reeve's own argument suggests that Socrates believed that piety is "service to the gods" *(Euth.* 13d) in the cause of knowledge or wisdom (Reeve 1989, 65). This is quite compatible with the attributions I am making here, which refer both to striving ("service") and to the attitude of respect or reverence for the divine, which provides the motive or reason without which acts having the outward form of service would not exhibit the virtue of piety. Gregory Vlastos, for his part, argues that piety is doing god's work (Vlastos 1991, 176), but also ignores the question of motive and attitude.

31. Socrates says in the first of these passages that he believes "it is not allowed by the laws of god *(ou . . . themiton)* that a better man be injured by a worse one." In the latter he has the idealized laws of Athens speak to him of their "brothers, the laws of Hades" *(adelphoi oi en Haidou nomoi).*

32. Kraut develops this and related points in great and convincing detail (Kraut 1984, 54–114), and my debt to his work will be evident in what follows. One salient point is his conception of what is entailed by the city's insistence that it is like a parent to citizens: not that unconditional obedience is owed, since the Greeks did not think that adults owe their parents obedience any more than we think they do, but that it is appropriate to explain oneself to a parent or city whose wishes one cannot comply with.

33. Having heard Crito's arguments Socrates says at 46b, that "I am the kind of man who listens only to the argument that on reflection seems best to me. I cannot, now that this fate has come upon me, discard the arguments I used; they seem to me much the same." After some discussion he concludes at 48a that, "We should not then think so much of what the majority will say about us, but what he will say who understands justice and injustice, the one, that is, and the truth itself." In short, he insists on an objective standard of judgment and resists the idea that his circumstances and interests should lead him to judge the arguments any differently from how he did before.

34. See *Ap.* 30a–b and 38a, which are referred to in §1.3. One must wonder whether Socrates would qualify this account of what fidelity to reason demands, by adding that one may receive divine guidance that corrects or supplements the determinations of one's

own reason. He refers to his "divine sign" as sometimes intervening to turn him "away from something [he is] about to do" (*Ap.* 31d), and he infers from its failure to turn him away from his response to the proposal of a death sentence that it is better for him to be dead than alive (*Ap.* 41d). He thus seems ready to accept divine warnings that his own deliberations have fallen short of the mark, and to accept on divine evidence conclusions which go beyond anything he could know through rational inquiry (in the example at hand, the relative advantages of life and death). As David Reeve has convincingly argued (Reeve 1989, 66–70), Socrates' acceptance of divine guidance rests in his rationally examined beliefs about the wisdom and virtue of the gods, but no more than that "He does not need to justify each particular command and prohibition independently of the fact that he believes it to have a divine source" (70). The evidence suggests, then, that Socrates believes that some people, including perhaps some authors of constitutions, receive true beliefs or knowledge by divine inspiration, and that makes the burden of complying with reason more complicated. People might sometimes have to weigh their own reasoned determinations against the possibility that a given law embodies the word of god. Yet there is little indication in the dialogues before us that Socrates has thought through the complications this entails. In evaluating the laws of Athens in the *Crito* he simply examines them on their merits (50d–e), and he tells us nothing here of how one might seek to distinguish genuine divine inspiration from things that might be mistaken for it. (On Socrates' beliefs about revelation and its dependence on not taking the nature of things [e.g., beauty] for granted, his beliefs about the philosopher's "possession by god," etc., see *Sym.* 209d–12c and *Phdr.* 249c–50d.)

35. Hugh Lloyd-Jones writes that from the time of Homer onward, "Offenders against oaths or strangers were considered as offenders also against the *time* [honor] of Zeus, and since a god punished offenders against his *time*, were punishable by him" (Lloyd-Jones 1983, 7). He argues more generally that in the theology of both the *Iliad* and *Odyssey*, as in that of Hesiod and later Greek sources, Zeus is supreme among gods, knowing and determining all things, imposing one *Dikê* (order, justice) on the universe and human beings, and punishing all the injustices which human beings commit against each other. Zeus is portrayed as equipping kings with their scepters and the customs and principles of justice (*themistes*) by which they will rule (6), and granting the authority to the members of local aristocracies (*basileis*) to guard those customs and principles through just verdicts and the like (32).

36. These references are discussed by David Levy (1998).

37. Kraut says that an aim of Plato's in putting Socratic political philosophy "in the mouth of the city's imaginary spokesmen" is to suggest that it is a philosophy which "can serve as a public charter that a city and its citizens can appeal to in dealing with each other" (Kraut 1984, 40). I would add that Plato is also displaying the mode of persuasion which Socrates believed should prevail in public life.

38. See e.g., *Phdr.* 246e–48e and 253d–54e. An important passage which I shall take note of in chapter 2, §2.4, is *Laws* 766a.

39. "We give two alternatives, either to persuade us or to do what we say" (52a).

40. Cf. Aristotle's remark that "while people hate *men* who oppose their impulses, even if they oppose them rightly, the law in its ordaining of what is good is not burdensome" (*NE* X.9 1180a22–24).

41. See notes 28, §1.3, and 35, §1.31.

CHAPTER 2: THE ARGUMENTS OF PLATO

1. The form of dialectical questioning which Socrates subjects his interlocutors to in the early dialogues, and which was practiced also by the Sophists, was known as the *elenchos* or *elenchus*, meaning scrutiny, interrogation, or refutation. The objective and condition for success in elenctic questioning was to drive the respondent into a contradiction, thereby revealing a lack of expertise on the topic under discussion. See Vlastos 1983 and *Rep.* VII 534b–c.

2. Because it has almost nothing to say about education, I will pass over the *Statesman*, but it is worth noting that John Cooper (1999) has made a strong case for interpreting Plato as holding in that work that although the *authority* to rule is not dependent upon securing consent, the *manner* in which a true king or statesman would rule is through consent (*St.* 276e) obtained by speeches and the deliberations of an assembly (implied by remarks about the persuasion of "large numbers of people in a crowd" at 304c–d). True statesmen *lead* their cities by instruction and persuasion in much the way that the leaders of democratic Athens led it, in this account. Cooper's defense of this interpretation could be supplemented by noting the importance of putting persuasion before force to achieve the statesman's proper goals: the greatest happiness of the citizens (301d, 311c), civic harmony (309c, 310e), and autonomous virtue arising from an education that instills secure true moral beliefs (309ac–e). Thus, despite this dialogue's notorious difficulties (see e.g., Klosko 1986b, 188 ff.), there is a good case to be made for the claim that it exhibits the same fundamental commitment to putting instruction and persuasion before force that we have seen in the Socratic dialogues.

3. The preface to the law of impiety in Book X consists in large part of an extended constructive argument for the existence of the gods, the purpose of which is to persuade atheists to change their minds.

4. On the relationship between the *Republic* and *Laws* see Morrow (1954, 8), Stalley (1983, 8–10, 13–22), and Laks 1990. Laks suggests that the former is a city inhabited by gods and the latter a city inhabited by men. Stalley suggests that "a ruler who could direct every detail of common life in accordance with knowledge would have to be more than human. In the world as it actually is the best we can do is imitate knowledge by means of law" (18). But neither Laks nor Stalley draws the conclusion which I do here that a second-best city would be one whose laws are able to avoid moral error entirely (i.e., encode divine law without error) through divine inspiration. Both suggest that the Kallipolis is ideal in the sense of being more unified and harmonious, which presupposes inhabitants who are god-like in being unperturbed by lower desires. I would agree that this is an important measure of what is ideal for Plato, since he says as much at *Laws* V 739d, but hold with Reeve (1988) that Plato's presumption in the *Republic* is that a city designed on the basis of genuine moral knowledge could create such harmony by shaping people's desires more favorably than any actual city can. If this is correct, then the determinative idealization pertains to knowledge and not to desire per se, even if social unity is the most definitive measure of what is politically ideal.

I should note by way of clarification that in describing the *Republic* as a city of moral knowledge I do not mean to preclude a role for divine inspiration in the framing of the laws of the Kallipolis. Plato has Socrates suggest at IV 427b–c that the most important laws, pertaining to piety, are to be established by the Delphic Apollo. For the most part, however, he argues that the education of the guardians will enable them to frame the best laws themselves (IV 425d–e).

5. If Plato assumes this understanding of the nature of virtue will be acquired through the systematic methods of his "later dialectic," announced in the *Phaedrus* (265d ff.) and exhibited most clearly in the *Statesman* and the *Sophist*, then it would be an understanding which places its object within a comprehensive system of explanatory and justificatory relationships and qualifies as knowledge (*epistêmê*). See *Tht.* 202c–d, *Philebus* 55d–59c, Nehamas (1999a, 19–22) and (1999b, esp. 235–41), and related references. However, there is no suggestion in the *Laws* that Magnesia's laws *rest in* such knowledge, or that it would equip a person with the godlike wisdom of a philosopher-king.

6. My account of these owes a great deal to Reeve (1988, chap. 1). In general, I accept Reeve's view that much of the point of *Republic* I is to expose the deficiencies of the elenchus and the craft analogy.

7. Cephalus says, among other things, that "When the appetites relax and cease to importune us, . . . we escape from many mad masters" (329c–d), much as Plato speaks of the appetites at VIII 561a, IX 577d and 588e–89a, etc.

8. E.g., courage in the *Apology* and *Phaedo*, though he cannot define it in the *Laches*; piety in any number of dialogues, though he cannot define it in the *Euthyphro*; moderation in the *Charmides*, though he cannot define it there.

9. The fact that the Socratic elenchus is displayed in this way in Book I and later attacked in Book VII is one of the reasons for concluding that a central purpose of Book I is to display the deficiencies of Socratic method and doctrine to be corrected in Books II–X. See Reeve (1988, 22–24).

10. Unless, contrary to Plato's assumption, one were confronted with people whose beliefs are known to the questioner to be so corrupt that the danger of true beliefs being abandoned is outweighed by the potential benefit of false ones being abandoned.

11. See note 3 to this chapter. The form of argument is a constructive one which provides the person who has fallen into error with reasons for adopting a true belief, and thus for abandoning its negation.

12. Meno states the paradox at 80d: "How will you look for it [the nature of virtue], Socrates, when you do not know at all what it is? How will you aim to search for something you do not know at all? If you should meet with it, how will you know that this is the thing that you did not know?"

13. Socrates' statement of the theory of recollection is followed by the disclaimer, "I do not insist that my argument is right in all . . . respects" (86b).

14. This evidently establishes the precedent for Aristotle's later restrictions on his own audience in *NE* I.2 (1094b28–95a11).

15. At *Crito* 47b–e Socrates suggests that just as the body is ruined by improper diet and exercise, so too the soul is corrupted by unjust actions. He would presumably add that just actions make the soul healthier and stronger, which is consistent with a commitment to *cultivating* reason by encouraging its use and strengthening it through use. Although this suggests an incipient concept of practice, it is not linked, as it is in Plato's thought, to the idea that the dominance of the reasoning part of the soul must be established through training, i.e., practice and other forms of education that not only inform and strengthen rational judgment, but strengthen it as a moving force in relation to other moving forces in a person. The effect of denying the natural (i.e., unaided) supremacy of reason in the soul (which is not to say its *proper*, and so in another sense natural, supremacy) is to give the responsibility to cultivate reason this two-fold character.

16. This is obscured somewhat by the common practice of imputing a deterrence theory of punishment to Protagoras, reading "deterrence" into *apotropês*, when "prevention" would be more literal (324b). See Stalley (1995, 10). In the context of modern penal theory, the language of deterrence suggests that punishments function as costs that are artificially attached to crimes (with uncertain probability) and taken into account more or less rationally by actors contemplating the commission of crimes. There is no indication that Protagoras has anything like this in mind, and not, e.g., that punishments give people pause to reflect on the wrongness of what the law prohibits (i.e., instruct them), or change their character by causing certain desires to atrophy (i.e., train their passions). He says at 325a–b that we "instruct and punish those who do not share in it [virtue], man, women, and child, until their punishment *makes them better*" (emphasis added).

17. See §2.5.

18. Christopher Taylor notes quite accurately that "The main problem [in interpreting this passage] is how to take the statement that the victim of misfortune cannot help being bad" (Taylor 1991, 145), but he seems to overlook the tensions between this statement and Socratic intellectualism. He cites as related texts *Nicomachean Ethics* III.1 and V.8, which pair "necessity" (the action originating wholly outside of the actor) with ignorance (146), but a comparison which sheds more light on the references to becoming bad "with the passage of time, or through hardship" and losing one's knowledge would be to *Laws* II 653c–d and *Rhetoric* II.13, where Plato and Aristotle speak of the corruption of feelings, perceptions, and good character by the hardships of life. Plato refers specifically to the erosion over time of the benefits of an education that trains the emotions. For discussion of related motifs in Greek theater see Nussbaum 1986.

19. Allowing once again for the possibility that some laws will be revealed by the Delphic oracle.

20. *Paideia* may have referred originally to child rearing, and by Plato's time most properly to schooling outside the home, but it could be used to denote the whole range of cultural and civic influences on the formation of character, including such things as festivals, public art, and performances. Later, in the Hellenistic Age, when Greek formal education became more dominantly literary in content, *paideia* came to signify the whole of the Greek cultural tradition embodied in literature. See Jaeger 1939–44 and Marrou 1956.

21. Plato identifies education in *mousikê* with education by persuasion at VIII 548b–c.

22. No less an authority than Aristotle interprets the *Republic* as making no provision for educating the producers (*Pol.* II 1264a30–40), and Reeve (1988, 186–88) reviews the various reasons for concurring and concludes that

> there is compelling reason to think that Plato intends primary education to be for future rulers and guardians only. . . . And—on the positive side—there is reason to think that Plato intends future producers to receive a traditional apprenticeship training in the single polis craft for which they have as high a natural aptitude as for any other. Hence it is training in a craft that releases an appetitive psyche from the rule of unnecessary appetites . . . (190).

While I agree with this judgment that in the Kallipolis "training in a craft is to a producer what primary education is to a guardian" (190), I think it underestimates the breadth of the city's educational provisions, and overestimates the burden which Plato expects training in crafts to bear. We have just seen that Plato regards law as educating every class of citizen, and as resting in the supervision of *mousikê, gymnastikê*, and games, in order, as Gregory Vlastos says, to equip the children of "all three classes" with "the right beliefs and, what is more, with the right emotive charges, so that what one comes to call 'just' one will feel irresistibly attractive and its contrary disgustingly ugly" (Vlastos 1973, 137). Reeve suggests, in effect, that as long as a future producer grows up imitating the right craft, the city will be unconcerned with his or her other pastimes; but it is hard to imagine Plato agreeing that practicing a craft would provide adequate security against the effects of habitual gambling or other pastimes which invite irrationality and undermine the association between production and consumption which he wants to foster. Reeve recognizes the need in the Kallipolis for training that frees the producers from the domination of *pleonectic* desires, but insists this is nothing other than training in crafts and denies that it is educative, on the grounds that it does not reshape the soul (Reeve 1988, 189). He says later, however, that the producers will receive "training and education . . . to moderate their unnecessary appetites so that these will not threaten the stability of the Kallipolis" (190–91), which seems to take back the claim that the producers are to receive no education, and to concede that their training *is* educative since it inculcates a measure of moderation. He argues, contra Vlastos, that this is not "*musical* moderation" (310 no. 8), but the distinction is suspect and hardly justifies the conclusion that the producers do not need to be moderate and do not become moderate in any degree through aspects of their upbringing and training that are supervised by the city. He cites IV 431d–32a, as Vlastos does, but ignores the agreement reached there that consensus or harmony in the Kallipolis requires that both the rulers and the ruled be moderate, and insists implausibly that moderation is a virtue possessed by them jointly but not severably.

23. It is conceivable, of course, that Plato may think some human beings are so conspicuously deficient in spirit (and thus the potential love of honor) or the normal capacities of reason (and thus the potential love of wisdom) that efforts to educate them can soon come to an end. This is suggested by the lines immediately preceding those which I quoted at the start of this section, in which Plato says that "the condition of a manual worker is despised" because his "best part is naturally weak" and so unable to "rule the beasts within him" that it is better for him "to be the slave of that best person who has a divine ruler in himself" (IX 590c). See Vlastos (1995, 90 ff.). This would seem to be the precedent for Aristotle's position on "natural slavery" in *Politics* I, and it is a disturbing passage, but one which should not be interpreted as indicative of Plato's attitude toward the entire producing class. Not all producers are manual laborers, and we have in Cephalus a portrait of one who possesses the virtues of moderation and piety to a significant degree, and has not only benefited from education but has bestowed it to moral advantage on his son Polemarchus (note their references to Sophocles, Pindar, and Simonides), even though neither has the potential to be a lover of wisdom. See §2.1.

Similarly, although Plato's moral commitments require that truthful and cogently reasoned instruction be used to the greatest extent possible, he may think that fabrications such as the notorious "myth of the metals" (III 414b–15d) bring people of deficient reason closer to grasping the good than is possible through appeals to evidence and argument. See Reeve (1988, 208–12) for a well-developed defense of the view that Plato advocates only "verbal," not real, lies, and that "the world views available to the producers and guardians in the Kallipolis are intended to be as close to the truth as their natural abilities and ruling desires allow" (212).

24. Although the passage at 467a seems fully accepting of the adequacy of unregulated and privately procured instruction in crafts, it is worth noting that in Book VIII Plato identifies the existence in oligarchies of poor people without means of supporting themselves as "the greatest of all evils" (552a) and attributable to "lack of education, bad rearing, and a bad constitutional arrangement" (552e). Given these remarks, he might well say that in some cities the remedies for this "greatest evil" would include efforts on the city's part to take responsibility for both the general (i.e., moral) education and craft training of the poor.

25. It is easy to overlook how high a standard the *Laws* sets for a rule of law which operates through consent and lets no one stand above the law, free from accountability for violations of the public trust. In a paper presented at the Western Division meetings of the American Philosophical Association in the spring of 1940 (Morrow 1941), Glenn Morrow outlined in persuasive detail the mechanisms through which Plato would ensure that public officials abide by the law, citing among other passages VIII 846b, where Plato says that

> If any magistrate is thought to have rendered an assessment of penalty with unjust purpose, he shall be liable for double damages to the injured. Whoever wishes may bring suit in the common courts against the magistrates for unjust decisions rendered in cases brought before them.

Morrow then observed, quite accurately, that "these and other texts show quite clearly that any person who considers he has been wronged by an official may bring suit for damages against the offending official," but he seriously overstated the availability of such remedies in the United States of 1940 when he then held that this suggestion of Plato's "has close analogies with the civil suit against an officer which is allowed by our law" (Morrow 1941, 155). It was in fact not until 1946, while the Nuremberg trials were being conducted in the name of restoring the rule of law in Europe, that Congress passed the Federal Tort Claims Act, waiving the *sovereign immunity* which the federal government had previously enjoyed. It has only been by degrees through the intervening years that the states have followed suit, and important limitations on liability remain (Keeton 1984, 1032–51).

26. How close is not clear, but would depend very much on the extent to which citizens are stimulated to further inquiry. See Bobonich (1996, 255).

27. Christopher Bobonich, in his important article on the *Laws*, concludes on persuasive grounds that the preludes are intended to provide "a rational grasp of basic ethical principles" so that a "free person will be able to see for himself how he is to decide and to act and will be able to regulate his behavior accordingly" (Bobonich 1991, 384). I think this is correct, but also that Bobonich is somewhat off target in surmising that the possession of such "rational understanding" is to be promoted because it is "part of what it is for a free person to be virtuous" (387). Rational understanding is to be promoted because it is essential to full virtue, but more fundamentally because it is essential to the flourishing of the divine aspect of human nature itself. Plato's grounds for excluding slaves are probably that they do not possess intact capacities of reason, and he might exclude resident aliens of normal rational capacity on the grounds that the city does not owe them the same duties of care that it owes its citizens, who are bound by reciprocal duties. See §1.33. This is admittedly speculative, but it would account for the distinction between

free citizens and others which Bobonich's suggestion responds to, while making clearer moral sense.

28. The argument for control of the poets is replicated at II 659c–60a; the necessity of ensuring that the message of education is that virtue pays is defended at II 660d–61c; the savagery of human beings without law is noted at VI 766a–b; the importance of regulation of birth and nurture is argued at VII 790b; the importance of "the bonds" of the regime (custom, habit, unwritten law) is urged at VII 793b–d and linked to the regulation of children's games at VII 797a–d, song and dance at VII 798a–e, and poetry at VII 801d.

29. That this is the concept of nature or *phusis* at work here is suggested not only by the internal logic of the argument, but also by Plato's repeated uses of medical metaphors for statesmanship, since in medicine what is natural is for living things to repair and preserve themselves, and for doctors to assist that self-repair and self-preservation. See von Fritz and Kapp (1977, 116).

30. In suggesting through these historical arguments that what is constitutionally legitimate is conducive to the perpetuation of rule, Plato also provides a form of argument for legitimate rule which engages the motives of actual rulers. This may be a manifestation of a broader concern in this dialogue to illustrate the manner in which philosophy may succeed in making a difference to politics. See Pangle (1980, 375 ff.). The tradeoff between duration and scope of power that is involved here is even more explicit in Plutarch's rendering of the first version of the argument, which includes elements which may have been familiar to Plato's audience. Plutarch writes of the Spartan king, Theopompus:

> This king, they say, on being reviled by his wife because the royal power, when he handed it over to his sons, would be less than when he received it, said: "Nay, but greater, in that it will last longer." And in fact, by renouncing excessive claims and freeing itself from jealous hate, royalty at Sparta escaped its perils, so that the Spartan kings did not experience the fate which the Messenians and Argives inflicted upon their kings, who were unwilling to yield at all or remit their power in favor of the people. . . . it was in very truth a divine blessing which the Spartans had enjoyed in the man who framed and tempered their civil polity for them (*Lyc.* VII 2–3).

This account may derive from the elegiac poetry of Tyrtaeus, a near-contemporary of Theopompus, who is mentioned at *Laws* I 629a, II 667a, and IX 858d.

31. Cf. the theory of justice and law proposed by Thrasymachus in *Republic* I (338d–39a) and discussed in §2.1.

32. See Roberts (1987, 32–34) and note my discussion of *Prot.* 325b–c in §2.2.

33. In his account of the causes of wrongdoing in Book IX, the Athenian Stranger enumerates "three kinds of basic faults": "anger and fear" (i.e., excess or deficiency of spiritedness), "pleasures and desires," which operate through "persuasive deceit that is irresistibly compelling" (presumably in those who do not receive effective moral training), and ignorance (864b; 863b). Note that while ignorance is named here as one of several causes of wrongdoing, pleasure is said to deceive, which clearly implies that one who does wrong under the influence of pleasure does it in a state of ignorance, even though ignorance is not the cause of the wrongdoing. The same would apply to anger and fear, presumably, since we learn at I 645e that "sensations, memory, opinions, and

thought . . . desert a man if he fills himself with drink," and at I 649c–d that anger, love, pride, fear, wealth, strength, "and everything else that turns us into fools and makes us drunk with pleasure" makes us unusually bold. If we are ignorant like a drunkard in all of these states, it implies that there are ethically salient forms of ignorance that cannot be eliminated through instruction (i.e., telling and persuading), but only through training the passions.

34. Cf. *Rep.* III 411c–e.

35. For an analysis of the frequency of various forms of argument and exhortation to virtue in these preludes, see Laks 1991.

36. Note also that by Book XII even Megillus, the Spartan, has come to insist that to hold a belief while being "unable to give a demonstration of it through argument" is slavish or contrary to what befits a free citizen (966b).

37. Note, however, Bobonich's correction of Morrow's somewhat one-sided emphasis on the role of nonrational "enchantment" (Bobonich 1991, 367–69). There are commentators who reject the idea that the aim of these preludes and the education which prepares the ground for them is to provide the citizens with moral understanding and cogent justifications for their moral beliefs and the laws. Stalley, e.g., quite rightly rejects the extreme view of Popper, who holds that these preludes are nothing but "lying propaganda" (Popper 1966, 270), but Stalley holds nevertheless that the preludes are "exhortations rather than arguments" and that it is their "literary qualities" that Plato admires, citing as a basis for the latter claim 811c–e (Stalley 1983, 43). Many of the preludes displayed in the *Laws* do employ arguments giving reasons why the law should be obeyed, however, and Stalley's reading of VII 811c–e seems far off the mark. Robert Hall offers evidence in support of the view I have adopted here (Hall 1981, 95), but characterizes the preludes as simply providing "some awareness of how [compliance with the law serves] toward the attaining of his morality" (95). This ignores the evidence that they outline and defend central tenets of Socratic and Platonic moral theory and provide reasons for why compliance is in the citizen's interest.

38. It is the *evidentiary* relevance of a background of effort to create conditions favorable to virtue that is most clearly implied in this passage, but that evidentiary import is a direct consequence of its causal relevance. Thus, if the immediate import of the passage is that a failure to educate might have evidential relevance to choosing a lesser and "corrective" punishment (one that is itself educative) over death, it also suggests indirectly that lack of care by the state is causally relevant, and that a just system of law would not punish without first educating.

39. Although Socrates' intellectualism dictates a concern with ignorance as the sole obstacle to virtue, it follows from his view that people unfailingly act in pursuit of the apparent good, that if they are ignorant of the true good, they will be unable to pursue it. As we have seen, Plato has a more complex account of what makes a person without a proper upbringing and education unable to comply with law and the dictates of reason.

CHAPTER 3: GROUNDWORK FOR AN INTERPRETATION OF *POLITICS* VIII.1

1. The announced task of the *Statesman* is to define statesmanship (258c), but after the question is put whether "the statesman and king and slave-master, and the manager

of a household" all share the same form of expertise (258e), it is quickly agreed that the difference in size between households and cities is all that separates these from each other (259b), and that statesmanship and kingship are the same thing (259d).

2. See note 2 to chapter 2.

3. The suggestion that the wife's deliberative faculty is *akuron* has baffled commentators. It might be a *qualitative* judgment, and if it is it might be explained by the fact that Greek men typically married women who were roughly twenty years younger than themselves and without experience of the world. See Mulgan 1994. On the other hand, it might not be a judgment of the quality of a wife's deliberations, but an acknowledgment of the fact that the deliberations of a Greek wife were *circumstantially* without effect, inasmuch as she lacked a position of authority. To describe the husband's rule over his wife as constitutional would in any case seem to entail the concession that she is *entitled* to share in rule to the extent that she acquires experience and thus maturity of judgment in matters of importance to the household.

4. The basic principles endorsed by Aristotle would make it ideal for all the inhabitants of a city who have a share in virtue to be citizens and (what is the same, on his account) be entitled to participate in rule, but he seems to regard this as an unattainable ideal on the grounds that cities require forms of work that are incompatible with the exercise of practical wisdom (see e.g., *Pol.* VII.4 1326a17–25, VII. 8 1328a23–36, VII.9 1328b34–29a2). He also seems to regard the qualifications for citizenship as changeable in light of various problems that may arise, rather than fully determined by fundamental rights (see e.g., VI.4 1319b6–14 and VI.6 1320b25–37). See also Kraut (1996, 762 ff.), responding to Miller 1995.

5. See note 9 to the Introduction.

6. The final chapter of the *Nichomachean Ethics* (X.9) is clearly intended as a transition to the *Politics*, which suggests Aristotle may have regarded it as preparatory to the latter, and at *Pol.* VII.1 he says he will only repeat what has been said in his "exoteric" lectures "concerning the best life" (1323a22–23), which suggests similarly that he assumed familiarity with the *Nichomachean Ethics*.

7. Aristotle says in *NE* X.7 that complete happiness is activity of "the most divine element in us," and "that this activity is contemplative we have already said" (1177a16–18), presumably in I.5 (where he eliminates the life of enjoyment as too slavish and the life of politics as too superficial, leaving the contemplative life as the best [1096a4–5]) and I.7 (where he says that the "human good turns out to be activity of soul in conformity with excellence . . . the best and most complete" [1098a16–18], which can only mean in conformity with *sophia*). Despite these linkages, there is an interpretive tradition which holds that the evidence of *NE* I stands in some tension with the evidence of Book X, with most of the confusion arising from a failure to see that the most important and psychologically fundamental reason why the contemplative life involves the possession and exercise of the moral virtues is that the development and dominance of reason, and thus *sophia*, depends upon it (much as we saw at the start of §2.4). I will take up this matter of the unity of the virtues in §7.21. See Kraut 1989 for a convincing reconciliation of the texts which supports the interpretation I outline here.

8. Contrary to what has often been inferred from Aristotle's suggestion that human beings are "political" by nature, which (as I have said) only means that they are city (polis) dwellers by nature (Cooper 1990), in the three senses outlined at the start of this section.

9. John Cooper suggests an alternative and more holistic account of the sense in which

noncitizens share in the advantages of a city (Cooper 1990), which is rejected on reasonable grounds by Fred Miller (1995, 211, n. 52).

10. Peter Simpson takes a very different view of this chapter, when he holds that according to Aristotle natural slaves "differ as much from free persons as the body from the soul, or as wild animals from human beings" (Simpson 1990, 153). Aristotle does indeed say at 1254b5 that "the soul rules the body with a despotical rule," and five lines later (1254b10) that "The same holds good of animals in relation to men," and finally at 1254b16–20 that, "Where there is such a difference as that between soul and body, or between men and animals . . . the lower sort are by nature slaves. . . . " But the "difference" that "holds good" in all these cases is simply, as the larger context of the chapter makes clear, that in each case there is a "distinction between the ruling and the subject element" (1254a30–31) that is "natural and expedient" (1254b8–9), which is to say natural and good for the subject element. Nothing in the passage implies that in each case the ruling and subject elements are different from each other *in the same way*. Moreover, it is important to note that Aristotle speaks of *tame* animals, and not *wild* ones, as Simpson says, when he speaks of the natural rule of men over animals. It is likely that Aristotle conceives of wild animals as ones that are ungoverned (not ruled), in fact, and if slaves and tame animals are governed in similar ways it might be as much through praise as through any other means.

11. "Virtually everything you say to a slave should be an order, and you should never become at all familiar with them. . . ."

12. See the introduction for a full list of supporting passages.

13. Since my interest here is primarily in what Aristotle's remarks on slavery reveal about his account of governance in general, I have not mentioned that the conditions of fact that have to be met for him to regard slavery as just cannot possibly be met. It goes without saying that the merit of Aristotle's test of the legitimacy of slavery is limited to precluding slavery on any terms less mutually beneficial.

14. See the introduction for a complete list of the relevant passages.

15. A briefer, parallel passage concerning justice in the distribution of offices or shares in rule is at *NE* V.3 1131a24–28.

16. As will soon become clear, they could be justified also on this second ground to the extent that Aristotle would generalize them to range over not only "the many," or in other words members of the *dêmos* who lack the prerequisites for studying political science—namely good character, worldly experience, and leisure—but also those who *can* master political science.

17. See note 9 to the introduction, and the related text. The differences between Aristotle's position and Plato's in the *Republic* are large, clear, and emphasized in at least some respects by Aristotle himself in *NE* I.6, but how different Aristotle's position is from Plato's in the *Laws* is less clear.

18. Nancy Sherman develops this idea that perceptual adequacy is for Aristotle a matter of achieving a well-rounded grasp of the particulars or seeing something "in the round," in Sherman (1989, 13 ff.).

19. Note the related passage at *NE* V.6 1134a35–34b2: "we do not allow a *man* to rule, but reason (*logon*)." Urmson and Ross take the unnecessary liberty of substituting *nomon* (law) for *logon* (Barnes 1984, 1790). See also *Pol.* III.11 1282b1–2, where Aristotle says that "laws, when good, should be supreme."

20. Cf. *Rep.* IV 445d, where Plato says

the constitution we've been describing . . . has two names. If one outstanding man emerges among the rulers, it's called kingship; if more than one, it's called an aristocracy.

21. It is for this reason that Fred Miller says that this second best constitution satisfies the "principle of unanimity," roughly the requirement that all citizens regard the constitution as an acceptable one, from which it follows that "the constitution must have the consent of the governed" (Miller 1995, 273)—their *tacit* consent, in any event.

22. See *NE* I.1 and 2, and particularly 1094a26–28 and 1094b11–12, where politics or political science (*hê politikê*) is called the master art or craft (*architektonikês*) and is identified as the form of inquiry Aristotle is engaged in.

23. See Jaeger 1957 and Lloyd 1968.

24. See *Politics* IV.1 1288b21–89a7. On the aims and intended audience of the *Politics* see Bodéüs 1991 and 1993, Lord (1984, 9–11), and P. A. Vander Waerdt's criticisms of Bodéüs, in Vander Waerdt 1985.

25. Though it should be noted that Plato does acknowledge at *Laws* 746a–c that when social and material circumstances do not permit the full realization of a model regime "the most just thing to do in each case" is to "contrive to bring about whatever is the closest" to it of those arrangements that are possible.

26. See e.g. Thomas Pangle's interpretive essay on the *Laws*, in Pangle 1980, and Klosko 1986a.

27. The identity of these "starting points" has been a subject of controversy. (See, e.g., Irwin [1988b, 347 ff.], which errs in its estimation of Plato's and Aristotle's confidence in being able to answer skeptics [348], but is probably right in its argument that Aristotle's method is not merely dialectical, but relies on an account of the soul.) These starting points would evidently have to be the kinds of moral beliefs or facts both (1) shared by well-bred Greeks, and (2) relied upon in arguments in the *Nichomachean Ethics,* such as the one in I.5 (establishing the identity of the best kind of life by appeals to the slavishness of the life of enjoyment and the superficiality of the life of honor), which follows the "digression" (I.5 1095b13–14) in I.4 in which Aristotle says a student of political science "must have been brought up in good habits. For the facts are the starting point . . . and the man who has been well brought up has or can easily get starting points" (1095b5–8). A student who came to Aristotle's lectures in possession of these moral "facts" or beliefs could expect to have them worked into a coherent and interconnected whole yielding a systematic understanding or knowledge of the good and its promotion. Or so Aristotle presumes.

28. Having in mind a wild animal, and not a tame one, no doubt.

29. Aristotle says in *Pol.* VI.3 that "although it may be difficult in theory to know what is just and equal, the practical difficulty of inducing those to forbear who can, if they like, encroach, is far greater, for . . . the stronger care for none of these things" (1318b2–6). Lynch (1972) provides evidence that Aristotle's school was in fact open to students who were not well-born (78–79), and that he made a practice of giving public ("exoteric") lectures to large audiences (91–92), but Lynch also provides evidence that Aristotle believed he had "put philosophy in an orderly form which causes no difficulty whatever for the wise, but is of no use to liars and imposters" (92, n. 37).

30. In the sphere of action, an *archê,* or first principle, is "that for the sake of which" an action is done (*NE* VI.5 1140b15–16), an aim, concept of the good, or universal premise from which deliberation begins (VII.8 1151a14–18).

31. See Stockton (1990, 103–15). Most of these offices amounted to what one might call "junior" archontal offices (30).

32. See Connor 1992, Powell (1988, 274–98), and Stockton (1990, 123ff.) on the nature of political leadership in democratic Athens.

33. It should be noted that the drafting and ratifying of *nomoi* (laws), as opposed to decrees (*psêphismata*), was by some time in the first half of the fourth century no longer a function of the Assembly, but of a distinct legislative body of *nomothetai*, who were randomly selected from the pool of six thousand citizens who were registered each year for jury duty. This should not be seen as an abridgment of the fundamental sovereignty of the *ecclêsia*, for the work of the *nomothetai* still had to be initiated by the *ecclêsia*, and the distinction between *nomoi* and *psêphismata* was, in any case, not very clear (see Stockton [1990, 67–84]), but Aristotle seems to have doubted the Assembly's capacity to exercise independent judgment. The demagogues "hold in their hands the votes of the people, who obey them," he says at 1292a27–28.

34. William Frankena's assertion (Frankena 1965, 61) that Aristotle offers in VIII.1 a series of arguments for the *twin theses* that the state should both regulate and "take complete charge of" education is clearly off the mark, then, in failing to note that Aristotle says that he will consider three questions *in turn*.

35. The Rackham 1944 translation of the *Politics* provides another instance of this.

36. In *Pol.* IV.1 1289a15–20, Aristotle speaks of a constitution as a *taxis* concerning the distribution of offices, where authority rests, and what the end of each community shall be, but there is no reason to think that he is arguing for anything so comprehensive as this in arguing that education is important enough to justify making some arrangement regarding it, *unless it is already assumed that a public system is being created*. Establishing a constitution and establishing a public system of education would be alike, presumably, in involving principles for assigning people to its various roles, specification of where authority rests, and a specification of aims.

37. I will consider this in more detail at the opening of chapter 4.

38. See §2.43.

39. On the breadth and accuracy of Aristotle's knowledge of the *Laws,* see Morrow 1960a and Ernest Barker's note on "The Debt of Aristotle to the *Laws*" (Barker 1947, 380–82). Barker's view that "the scheme of education in Book VII of the *Politics* is propounded with constant reference to the Laws" (381), is now widely accepted.

40. On Plato's provisions for common meals in the *Laws,* see David 1978.

41. Aristotle is often understood to hold that states of character are *permanent,* and if this is right there would be no need for measures aimed at *preserving* the ones that are desirable. A great deal of evidence (not the least of which is *NE* 1179b35–80a4 itself) suggests that he did not regard virtue (except possibly complete virtue) as permanent, however, but rather as a state of development of the active capacities of the soul which can neither be generated nor preserved without proper exercise. He says at *NE* II.1 1103b7–8 that "it is from the same causes and by the same means that every virtue is both produced *and destroyed*" (emphasis added). See note 18 to chapter 2.

42. Carnes Lord and Christopher Rowe are among those who identify a reference to the *Laws* here. See Lord (1990, 209) and Rowe (1991, 70–71).

43. He thus stands in a tradition of Greek thought running back to Simonides, for the law "always had, in the eyes of the Greeks, the function not only of prohibition and surveillance, but of education," writes Jacqueline de Romilly, adding that though they re-

garded punishment as educative, their view was that "the educative role of the laws could not be limited to that" (de Romilly 1971, 229–39).

44. As Lord (1982, 92–104) argues.

45. See note 3 to chapter 1, on the role of boys in Spartan common meals.

46. I have been concerned here with both law and culture as educative, and have thus ignored Aristotle's provisions in VIII.16 concerning childbirth and the early development of the child's body. He obviously regards these too as an important part of the city's care of its children, but I will consider them to be preparatory to education, rather than a part of education.

47. I examine the relationships between the moral and intellectual virtues at much greater length in §7.21.

48. Aristotle provides some confirmation of this with his remark that "letters" are useful for "money-making, household management, learning, and many political activities" (VIII.3 1338a15–17).

49. For more discussion of the educational and ethical significance of music in Aristotle, and Greek thought generally, see Anderson 1966.

50. This may reflect some notion of reciprocal obligations of care and obedience proper to a citizen, of the kind I suggested in discussing the *Crito* and the *Laws*. See §1.33 and note 27 to chapter 2.

CHAPTER 4: WHY EDUCATION IS IMPORTANT

1. These being, in his words, that "(1) attention to the education of youth is demanded in the interest of the constitution (12–18), . . . and (2) it is demanded because some training is required before men can act virtuously (18–21)" (Newman 1902, vol. 3, 499).

2. See §3.11.

3. One might find a philosophical basis for asserting this duty in the argument that it would be rational to agree to some appropriately qualified version of it as a fundamental regulative principle of any human society. Given the advantages of rationality over irrationality, including its mutual advantages when the substance of rationality is understood to encompass mutually advantageous coordinative principles of social action, I have no doubt that such an argument could be made. On this conception of rationality and the foundations of morality, see Baier 1995 and Gauthier 1986.

4. For a review of the evidence and refutation of the Rousseauian "growth" model, see Purdy (1992, 87–123), Damon 1988, and Rogoff 1990.

5. I will defer detailed discussion of Aristotle's version of the unity of virtue thesis until chapter 7 (§7.21). It has some relevance here, insofar as Aristotle holds that education is not only directly necessary for the development of rationality (wisdom), but also indirectly necessary for it, since one cannot be fully rational (wise) without being fully virtuous and cannot be fully virtuous without education. His view is that without a training in virtue a person does not become capable of acting in accordance with the demands of reason or responsive to reasoning which appeals to moral premises, is not able to perceive accurately what is good, bad, and relevant, does not learn from the perceptions of good and wise people in the way a potential friend of them could, and does not develop discriminating judgment in the things that matter in the way that a person who practices reasoning with the right ends in view does.

6. See e.g., *Pol.* VII.1 1323a24–b12, and esp. 1323a39–b1, where Aristotle says (following *Ap.* 30b) that "mankind does not acquire or preserve the virtues by the help of external goods, but external goods by the help of the excellences."

7. The polity or constitutional form of government was identified in §3.12 as a legitimate form of constitution, second in quality to an aristocracy, but the best that most actual cities could hope to achieve.

8. Miller 1995 develops at 45–56 a trenchant analysis of the provocative but misleading claim in *Pol.* I.2 that "the polis is by nature clearly prior to the family and to the individual, since the whole is of necessity prior to the part" (1253a 19–20). This passage has suggested to some commentators that a polis is an end in itself, akin to an organism, which should take priority over the happiness or good of individual citizens, just as the good of an individual should take priority over the good of any of his or her bodily parts. On Miller's account, Aristotle is only claiming that the polis is prior in completeness and self-sufficiency, i.e., that "human beings cannot realize their natural ends without the polis" (53), but can as part of one.

9. To appeal to his (perceived) self-interest is not to appeal to what is good for him, one should note. The two will often fail to coincide, in Aristotle's view, since people with political ambitions are usually drawn to politics by their love of honor and misunderstanding of what the happiest life for human beings is.

10. Aristotle asks in a related passage in *Pol.* II.8, of a city ruled by only one of its three classes, "if the two other classes have no share in the government, how can they be loyal citizens?" (1268a24–26).

11. See Rowe (1991, 57–69). The textual anomalies which had been considered grounds for shifting IV–VI are reviewed at 57–59.

12. As Miller points out, the concept of a "majority" which Aristotle deploys in this context takes into account both the number of citizens and their "quality" (Miller 1995, 285–93).

13. Reeve's translation and the Barnes revision of Jowett's are in this instance clearly superior to those of either Rackham or Lord, for they alone follow the wording of the Greek, on which *both* the prospects for persuasion and the ability to participate fall within the scope of the consideration that there are practical constraints imposed by "existing circumstances." Rackham and Lord both shift the clause, *ek tôn huparchontôn* (out of existing circumstances), so that it applies only to the ability to participate, whereas it would appear, from the word order in the Greek, that Aristotle intends this clause to apply also to the prospects for persuasion. "Existing circumstances," as they pertain to the prospects for easy persuasion, would surely include the *aims* which existing regimes actually pursue and are receptive to pursuing. Simpson's wording is closer to Reeve's and Jowett and Barnes's, but does not clearly identify the need to obtain cooperation and the need for arrangements to be feasible more generally as distinct requirements: "what should be done is to introduce the sort of arrangement that, given what people already have, they will easily consent to or could easily participate in. . . ."

14. Polansky's remarks at (*op. cit.*) 341 and 342 are quite compatible with this line of thought, in fact, except that he never draws the conclusion that Aristotle sought or intended to direct his concerns to the attention of actual leaders, whether as his immediate audience or through the students of political science who made up his audience.

15. For further discussion of constitutional stability and the preservation of regimes compatible with the position I have taken here see Miller (1995, 183–90, 269–71, 293–309).

16. We could regard equality with respect to virtue as a distinguishable aspect of the quality of a constitution, but this would yield some redundancy. We have already seen in §4.1 how the city's natural aim, respect for reason, and the promotion of happiness demand efforts to promote the common possession of virtue, and in §5.1 we will see the importance of the common possession of virtue to constitutional unity. To regard the common possession of virtue as a constitutional good in its own right would not generate any interestingly distinct line of argument.

17. To bring about a full realization of the constitution's underlying principles does not mean that if the regime is, say, democratic, then it should aim to realize the greatest amount of democracy possible. As we have already seen, this would be contrary to Aristotle's advice at *Pol.* VI.5 1320a1–4, and in Books V and VI generally. The sense of "full realization" intended here pertains not to how fully the principles of the regime exhibit a particular form such as democracy, monarchy, or oligarchy, but rather to how fully developed and implemented the law deriving from its guiding principles is, whatever those principles may be. Aristotle, in judging actual regimes, does give considerable attention to the importance of their laws conforming to the principles of their own constitutions (a prerequisite for a well-ordered constitution), a fact emphasized somewhat excessively by Richard Bodéüs in (Bodéüs 1991). Fred Miller takes a more balanced view in Miller (1995, 183–90).

18. As noted previously, this thesis will be taken up a greater length in chapter 7,§7.21.

19. See note 29 to chapter 2, and related text.

20. There was indeed in Athens a force of Scythian slaves whose assistance could be called upon in maintaining order during meetings of the *ecclêsia*, and individual magistrates could also call upon the assistance of small numbers of slaves in such matters as the enforcement of verdicts, but there was no force empowered with the general policing functions of a modern police force.

21. See in chapter 3, §3.11 and note 21 and related text. In this chapter see esp. note 10 and related text.

22. Aristotle refers to such goods as "contested" *(perimacheta)* at *Pol.* 1271b8, *NE* 1168b19, and elsewhere. See Irwin (1985b, 160ff.).

23. For further discussion of luxury *(truphê)* in the political thought of Plato and Aristotle, see Berry (1994, 45–62).

24. See chapter 3, §3.5.

25. As I suggested in §4.1. The same indirect contributions to desirable habituation could be cited in connection with education that establishes compliance with law (§4.31 and §4.32), practices of moderate property acquisition and the sharing of property in common (§4.33), and patterns of cooperation, trust, and friendliness which unite a polity.

26. For the sake of brevity, I omit here several lines of text and several connecting arguments which are not of immediate interest to us.

CHAPTER 5: WHY EDUCATION SHOULD BE PUBLIC
AND THE SAME FOR ALL

1. In addition to the passages referred to already, such as *Pol.* II.5 1263b37–38, one could cite *EE* VII.1 1234b23–24, where Aristotle says that "it is thought to be the special business of the political art to produce friendship."

2. Aristotle's view that the virtues are intrinsically socially beneficial is revealed most clearly, perhaps, by his remarks on justice in the *Nicomachean Ethics*. "We call those acts just that tend to produce and preserve happiness and its components for the political society," he says at *NE* V.1 1129b17–19, a just act being a virtuous act considered in relation to the city and its other inhabitants. Similarly, at *NE* VIII.9 1160a13–14, he describes the just as "that which is to the common advantage. "See also *Pol.* III.6 1279a17–19, III.12 1282b16–18, III.13 1283b35–42; and Roberts (1989, n. 8 and related text).

3. On the place of this concept of naturalness in *Pol.* I, see Roberts (1989, 192–95), and on the three aspects of the naturalness of the polis and its parts generally, see §3.11 and Miller (1995, 30–45).

4. See, e.g., Price (1989, chap. 7).

5. Aristotle says in *NE* IX.10 that "one cannot have with many people the friendship based on virtue and on the character of our friends themselves" (1171a19–20), but perhaps he means, not that one cannot have friendships based in virtue with many people, but that one cannot have many such friendships arising from knowledge of the *particular* states of character of one's friends. By emphasizing the conjunction in this way (i.e., that denying the conjunction does not entail denying the first conjunct), one might reconcile this passage with the idea that the citizens of a good polis may have a regard and liking for each other's character arising from a *general* knowledge of their fellow citizens and a more intimate knowledge of only a few.

6. Those being in her words that "a friend wishes and does good to the friend for the friend's own sake; wishes his friend to exist for his own sake; spends time with the friend; makes the same choices; shares the friend's joys and sorrows" (243).

7. An apparent difficulty with this claim is that Aristotle never takes a clear and consistent stand on whether the imperfect varieties of friendship involve mutual goodwill. He often uses *philia* in a rather wide sense that includes these lesser varieties, but in other instances adds the more restrictive qualification that perfect friendship is *real* friendship (*EE* VII.2 1238a19–20) or friendship *in the highest degree* (*NE* VIII.3 1156b10, VIII.4 1157a13, IX.6 1167b10, IX.8 1168b2). His account is thus suspended uncomfortably between the view that the attributes of friendship, including goodwill, are present in the lesser friendships only with qualification or to a lesser degree, and the view that these varieties of friendship lack such attributes as goodwill, and so count as friendship only under a qualified definition, or with qualification, or to a lesser degree. All such uncertainty is precluded in the present instance, however, since it is clear that mutually recognized goodwill is essential to the kind of partnership in the city that Aristotle wants friendship to secure.

8. The problem, intuitively, is that it is impossible to have an attitude toward an individual whom one does not know in any way, through either acquaintance or description. Formally, the problem is that one cannot validly infer the *de re* instantiations of a *de dicto* universal: from "c_1 desires that $(x)(Tx)$," where "c" is a citizen, "T" is the predicate "thrive," and the domain of x is c's fellow citizens, one cannot infer the instantiations "c_1 desires *for* c_2 that Tc_2," "c_1 desires *for* c_3 that Tc_3," . . . "c_1 desires for c_n that Tc_n," where n is the number of citizens in c_1's city.

9. For a useful discussion of Aristotle's conception of learning through "critical practice," and the place in this practice of interaction between learner and environment, see Sherman (1989, 176–91).

10. See chapter 3, §3.4 and §3.5.

11. See note 4 to chapter 4, and related text.

12. On the importance of stability to individual well-being, see chapter 4, §4.31 and §4.32.

13. The first clause of the first premise of that argument, that legislators should promote the happiness of all citizens as much as possible, is strong enough to sustain a conclusion to the effect that legislators should take measures to ensure that all citizens are properly educated.

14. Given the importance of race, and the role of race in determining socioeconomic status in contemporary America, an obvious place to begin would be with studies of racial divisions and their effects, such as Andrew Hacker's *Two Nations* (Hacker 1992a). A related locus of research would be the role of racial injustice and hostility in undermining an equitable administration of criminal justice, and thereby belief in the very idea of common justice. One symptom of the erosion of this belief is racially based "jury nullification" (Butler 1995), though its occurrence has probably been exaggerated (Leipold 1997).

15. See note 12 to chapter 1, and related text.

16. Tom Green affirms the antecedent clause of this statement and formulates its consequent clauses as the *law of zero correlation* and the *law of last entry*. The first holds that "there is a point in the growth of the [school] system at which there is no longer any correlation between educational attainment and . . . the distribution of non-educational social goods ordinarily associated with educational attainment" (Green 1980, 91). Put more concretely, as the market becomes saturated with people with a credential such as a high school diploma, the value of that credential in obtaining social goods drops to zero. A corollary of this is that as the value of that credential drops, the "social liabilities" associated with lacking it increase (97). The second law holds that "no society has been able to expand its total educational enterprise to include lower status groups *in proportion to their numbers in the population* until the system is 'saturated' by the upper and middle status groups" (108). This means that if members of this lower status "group of last entry" do obtain a credential which has conferred competitive advantage on others, they will do so *on the whole* in conditions of market saturation, which will make the credential economically and socially worthless, and if they fail to obtain this credential they will suffer liabilities which they would not have in the absence of a system capable of achieving market saturation. It can scarcely be rational for this group of last entry (i.e., lower status groups) to support a public system of education on these terms. Such a system can be collectively rational, as I have said, only if it promises to confer goods of a kind whose structure permits common possession or enjoyment.

17. *Brown v. Board of Education,* 347 US 483 (1954).

18. See also Banks 1993, and Allport 1954, which first established that interracial contact reduces racial prejudice when the following factors are present: (1) the group setting is cooperative rather than competitive; (2) common goals are pursued; (3) all parties are accorded equal status; (4) the participants get to know each other as individuals; (5) the contact is institutionally authorized.

19. See, e.g., Braddock (1980, esp. 179 and 185), Allport 1954, and Slavin 1983. Robert Slavin reports that

> The results of the studies relating cooperative learning to intergroup relations clearly indicate that when students work in ethnically mixed coop-

erative learning groups, they gain in cross-ethnic friendships. The research indicates that the effects of cooperative learning on intergroup relations are strong and long lasting" (87).

He also notes that the research generally supports Gordon Allport's "contact theory," but suggests that the critical variable is not contact as such, but a setting which creates equality of situational status. In a more recent work, he adds that the research "showed positive effects of cooperative learning on close, reciprocated friendship choices—the kind of friendships that should be most difficult to influence" (Slavin 1995, 54).

20. It will come as no surprise to most Americans that the flight of whites from urban school districts in the United States has resulted in increasing concentrations of children in schools that are not racially and economically mixed, and in widening disparities of quality between the education provided to the urban poor and to the suburban middle class (Berne 1994, 1–23; Kozol 1991).

21. Miller (1995) defends at length the claim that Aristotle uses the language of rights, and has a theory of natural rights. This is most plausible with regard to entitlements to share in rule (which I have regarded in this work as *prima facie* entitlements; see §3.1) and entitlements that are properly protected through compensatory forms of corrective justice. See Cooper (1996), Curren (1997), and Kraut (1996).

22. Miller makes the illuminating observation that Aristotle assumes that nothing composite has order, constitutes a unified whole, or is goal-directed, except through a ruling principle, in the case of a body its soul, and in the case of a polis its constitution (*Pol.* I.5 1254a28–36):

> In Aristotle's metaphysics the source of unity *(to henopoioun)* of a thing is by nature its authoritative *(kata phusin kurion)* and ruling principle *(archon)*, and this is the formal cause. . . . The constitution performs a similar function in Aristotle's politics (Miller 1995, 151).

23. There are models of "democracy," in the modern sense, that involve mass participation that is quite minimal and remote from the consequential decisions to be made (Held 1987). Systems of these kinds seem to call for little if anything in the way of a public system of education to underwrite the quality of governance, so there are grounds to refrain from holding that it is in the *nature* of democracy as such to place special demands of this kind on education. What does seem true, however, is that there are serious threats to the well-being of present and future generations which are not being solved (such as looming environmental catastrophes), that the potential solutions are at least in some measure political, and that the prospects of finding and adopting those solutions would be improved by universal education in the moral and intellectual virtues which Aristotle commends, the intellectual virtues necessary to finding the solutions no less than the virtues of self-restraint necessary to adhering to them (Purdy 1992, 167).

24. See notes 27 and 30 to chapter 3, and related text.

25. See, e.g., *DA* 432a7, *Sens.* 445b16, and *A. Post.* 81a38, which are cited by Jonathan Barnes (1979, 39).

26. See the end of §4.1 and the start of §4.2 in chapter 4.

CHAPTER 6: EDUCATION AND THE FOUNDATIONS OF JUSTICE

1. See, e.g., Williams (1985, 38).

2. This corrective justice "school" of thought has included Jules Coleman (1983 and other works), George Fletcher (1972), John Borgo (1979), Frederick Sharp (1976), Richard Epstein (1980), and most recently Alan Strudler (1992). It is Ernest Weinrib, however, who has most studiously defended the idea that Aristotle regards corrective and distributive justice as independent. See particularly Weinrib 1987 and §IV of Weinrib 1988.

3. In discussing Aristotle's notion of corrective justice, Weinrib writes that "Aristotle observed that what we would now call private law has a special structure of its own" (1987, 977–78). Since Aristotle recognized no category of law corresponding to our private law (rather only the sorts of harms which fall under our criminal code, but which could only be privately prosecuted under Athenian law) it is quite unclear how he could have made any such observation.

4. There is evidence for this in his concern, evident throughout the *Politics*, that law unite, and not divide, cities, and also in his insistence in *NE* III.1 that an expression of regret for an unintended harm is a necessary condition for escaping legal responsibility. The best explanation for his linking responsibility and regret in this way is that without the expression of goodwill conveyed by regret, even an unintended harm may incite antagonistic feelings and generate conflict.

5. It is worth noting that many features of what remains of this code suggest that its fundamental purpose was not to punish or compensate, but to resolve conflict. See Gagarin (1981, ch. 8).

6. See Smith 1987.

7. A fairly recent example of this traditional line of interpretation is Terry Irwin's. He argues that the central claim in *NE* III.5 1114a6–13 is that "most adults . . . are still capable of effective deliberation about the sort of people they should be," and so can be praised or blamed for the states of character they come to have, and consequently the actions flowing from those states of character (Irwin 1980, 140–41).

8. See, e.g., Furley (1977, 53).

9. This provides a more plausible account of when and why "moral agents became ghosts" than Alasdair MacIntyre's suggestion that it was owing to certain aspects of his Lutheranism that Kant broke radically with what preceded him (MacIntyre 1982, 306–09) or Bernard Williams's and Thomas Nagel's suggestions that Kant was concerned to preclude "moral luck" (Williams 1981; Nagel 1979). On Kant's denial that there is any such thing as luck, and his assertion that everything "happens in accordance with the foresight of God" and "is grounded in His good providence," see Kant (1775–80, 94–95). It is seldom recognized that the first outspoken critic of Leibniz's view that human freedom consists of a person's acts being a function of his or her nature, those acts being avoidable in the conditional sense that a person would act differently if endowed with a different nature by God (Leibniz 1679, 266), was not Kant but Christian August Crusius, who pointed out the theological inadequacies of the Leibnizian account and partitioned Leibniz's *principle of sufficient reason* in a way that prefigured Kant's partitioning of the world into that which is causally necessitated by the laws of nature (phenomenal) and that which is intelligible through its adherence to laws of reason (noumenal). Lewis White Beck (1969) provides a brief introduction to the role of Crusius as a predecessor of Kant,

but the only work I am aware of which addresses the bearing of the former's work on freedom and the principle of sufficient reason on the latter's development is a doctoral dissertation by Reinhard Finster (1984).

10. This seems to be true of Arthur Adkins's account of responsibility in Greek thought generally (Adkins (1960) and is asserted by Susan Sauvé Meyer ((1993, 128, n. 7) to be true of Jean Roberts's (1989) and possibly my own previous interpretation of Aristotle on this topic (Curren 1989). My view in that paper was actually no different from what I have just outlined here, except that while I interpreted Aristotelian responsibility as having both moral and legal aspects, I argued that the legal background to *NE* III.5 is particularly useful to understanding Aristotle's concerns there with ignorance and incapacity. In the meantime I have arrived at a substantially different view, developed below, which accepts Roberts's argument that Aristotle's dominant concern in III.5 is the Socratic asymmetry thesis, that he denies the asymmetry thesis, but that he does so in a way that does not depart substantially from "the Platonic conception of vice as ignorance and disease" (Roberts 1989b, 33). Some aspects of my earlier view remain, including those adopted by Meyer (see Meyer 1993, 129, n. 8; 141, n. 24).

11. My argument does not depend on the authenticity or dating of the *Magna Moralia*, but I will call attention to passages from it which have confirmatory value if it is authentic. I do regard the *MM* as authentic, moreover, on the strength of arguments that appeal to the apparent philosophical development running from the *MM*, through the *EE*, to the *NE*. On the authenticity of the *MM*, see Cooper 1973. I agree with Cooper's observation that "on some issues the simpler treatment found in the *Magna Moralia* presents more adequately a basic insight which the other, more elaborate treatments tend to obscure" (328).

12. Harry Frankfurt (1988) offers such an account of compulsion as an excusing condition. As my remarks above suggest, I agree with him that compulsion may sometimes function as an *excuse* in this way, but disagree with his claim, contra Nozick 1969, that it can never function as a *justification* in the manner that Aristotle suggests.

13. See, e.g., Irwin 1980, where Terry Irwin offers as his final formulation of Aristotle's analysis of moral responsibility: "*A* is responsible for doing *x* if and only if (a) *A* is capable of deciding effectively about *x*, and (b) *A* does *x* voluntarily" (132).

14. "The intrinsic effect of an efficient cause," she says

> is a result of the type that the causal power is productive of *(poiêtikê)* or that it naturally produces *(pephuke poiein)*. This is what the causal power produces reliably or "always or for the most part" (Meyer 1993, 104).

15. Meyer says that

> in arguing that people are responsible for their states of character, Aristotle has in mind agents who have already had pointed out to them the sorts of activities that they must perform and avoid in order to develop a virtuous disposition. And he is claiming that such knowledge is insufficient to make them virtuous. Both virtue and vice are still open to those who possess such knowledge, and it is up to them whether they become virtuous by following the prescribed activities . . . (Meyer 1993, 140).

On this reading, the target of this argument in III.5 is Socratic intellectualism, which Aristotle has rejected in II.4, saying "They [who think that knowledge or reasoned instruction is sufficient for virtue] act like the sick who listen carefully to the doctors, but carry out none of the doctors' prescriptions" (1105b12–16). The similarity of reference to doctor's orders in the two passages is tantalizing, but this reading rests in the mistaken premise that Socratic intellectualism "motivates" the asymmetry thesis (141) in a way that would allow Aristotle to undercut the latter by undercutting the former. As we have seen, Plato and Aristotle both reject Socratic intellectualism and preserve a form of asymmetry between virtue and vice, in holding that virtuous people see the moral truth and the vicious do not, that virtue is a healthy state of soul, and that vice is a diseased and incapacitated one. Meyer suggests, in effect, that in this passage in III.5 Aristotle assumes that what is required in addition to reasoned instruction to develop virtue is just performing the right activities as an adult; but clearly he does not assume this, and it is hard to see how the *point* of the passage could be to deny intellectualism. Clearly what Aristotle has been at pains to do is defend a conventional use of the terms, *akousion* and *hekousion*, without giving up the substance of the Platonic account of the nature and origins of vice which he shares (Roberts 1989b, 23, 32–33), and the point of 1114a3–22 is to identify the assumption on which they can be reconciled. Roberts also misses this point, and ignores several striking features of this passage—such as the role of incapacitation and its three images of falling from a capable state into an incapacitated one—in holding that "the whole point of the passage is to show that . . . firmness of character is not to be confused with nature," since Aristotle exempts from blame what exists by nature, as opposed to what is learned or acquired (*NE* III.5 1114a22–31; Cf. *Prot.* 323d–24a; §2.2). See also Broadie (1991, 166–74). If this were the "whole point of the passage," one would expect to see Aristotle speak here of states of character generally and not just bad and defective ones, and it would be enough for him to say again that states of character are acquired through education and practice, instead of arguing that when education has been provided the actor, not (by implication) the statesman, is the cause of the actor's own defective state of character.

16. For our purposes here, it is not essential to resolve the matter of whether Aristotle has in mind people who have received an adequate education and become actually virtuous, though not completely and securely so, or people who have received that education and are not yet virtuous. Meyer builds a case for the latter interpretation resting on the claim that in *NE* X.9 Aristotle is distinguishing two "stages" of habituation, "the second of which is *up to the developing agents themselves*" (Meyer 1993, 124; italics added), when he says that we shall need laws "to cover the whole of life; for most people obey necessity rather than argument, and punishments rather than what is noble" (*NE* X.9 1180a4–5). She argues that "when Aristotle claims . . . that we become virtuous by performing virtuous actions . . . the sorts of activities he has in mind belong to" this alleged second "stage" of habituation and not the first, since the kinds of things mentioned ("exchanges with people," "dangerous situations," and "drinking") are clearly the domain of adult activities rather than those of a child (125). There are at least two serious errors in this line of argument. First, it does great violence to the passage in X.9. How can Aristotle be making a distinction there, made nowhere else in his account of moral development, between an early compulsory stage of habituation and a subsequent stage "up to the developing agents themselves," when the point of the passage is that laws are needed to ensure the continuation of good habits, since most people only "obey necessity"? Since

Aristotle regards the laws as having greater compulsive power than parents (*NE X.9* 1180a19–21), he cannot be. Second, while it is true that children will not have engaged in some of the activities that adults do, the truth in this falls far short of sustaining the thesis that a youth at the conclusion of an adequate education will not be virtuous, but will stand instead at "the crucial moment when she chooses between the alternative courses of action" (Meyer 1993, 126). It ignores the fact that Aristotle lived in a world in which Spartan boys were expected to secure meals by stealing and "setting upon people when asleep or off their guard" (*Lyc.* xvii.3–4), which is an obvious example of children engaging in exchanges with people and facing danger, and that like Plato he held that children's play and activities should resemble as much as possible the activities they will engage in as adults (*Pol.* VII.17 1336a31–35). The very passage which Meyer relies on (*NE* II.1 1103b17–25) implies as much with its insistence on the importance of forming the right habits "from our very youth," since this can only mean that the very habits that are crucial to adult virtue must be established in youth. As we saw in chapter 2, Plato proposes to make supervised experience in drinking a part of education precisely in order to ensure that citizens will not encounter alcohol only as adults and without an established capacity and disposition to consume it in moderation (*Laws* 635c–d; §2.42). Thus, it seems truer to Aristotle's conception of virtue and its development to regard the well-educated youth as having attained a kind of virtue, but not complete virtue, since the latter would require practical wisdom and wider experience than he or she will have had. Though, as I said, it is not essential to the main points I am trying to establish here that this be so.

17. Citing *Prot.* 325e–26a and 327e–28a, Meyer suggests that Aristotle "has in mind a social context very much like the one in the Athens of his time" (Meyer 1993, 140, n. 23), and so presumably nothing more than the education which an Athenian youth would have received as a matter of course, in the absence of the legislation which Aristotle calls for. If this were correct, it would mean that we do not have the materials here for an argument for public education, but it is hard to see how this could be correct, given the considerable evidence that Aristotle was dissatisfied with the quality of moral education in Athens.

18. See note 23 to chapter 3, and related text.

19. See note 33 to chapter 2, and related text.

20. It was also recognized by Jeffrie Murphy (1973), and in the next section of this chapter I will note the points of contact between the Marxist critique, as Murphy presents it, and the radical consequences of an Aristotelian view.

21. "Rational consent," as I am using the term here, thus does not mean *ideally* rational consent. The notion of "*reasonable* educative efforts" introduces some indeterminacy into the idea of "rational consent" which I will not be able to resolve here, given the complexity of what might constitute reasonable education.

22. As I have said, it is this theological problem which gave rise to the myth, which descended from Augustine into the Christian Enlightenment, of a radically and innately "free will." The point I am concerned to establish here is that if we abandon this myth in favor of Plato and Aristotle's more plausible pre-Christian view of the efforts required to produce a good and rational will, then we are faced with a problem not only for theology, but for secular human communities as well.

23. John Rawls's description (Rawls 1971, 490–91) of the way in which the development of a sense of justice depends upon personal attachments is probably correct. See

Power (1989) and Ryan and Stiller (1991). Rawls's view suggests that social virtue is unlikely to emerge or prevail in the absence of a sense of justice, and a sense of justice is not likely to emerge in a child to whom authority figures (i.e., individuals who represent or manifestly adhere to acceptable principles of social life) do not communicate a clear intention to act for the child's good. On belief in the fairness of law and its administration as a factor in obeying the law, see also Tyler (1990).

24. Summarizing the findings of a large body of research, Albert Reiss and his coauthors note that "violent offenders tend to have experienced poor parental child rearing methods, poor supervision, and separations from their parents when they were children. . . . In addition, they tend disproportionately to come from low-income, large-sized families in poor housing in deprived, inner-city, high-crime areas" (Reiss et al. 1993, 367).

25. Elijah Anderson, a prominent sociologist, argues that

> For [a significant minority of hard-core street youths] the standards of the street code are the only game in town. The extent to which some children— particularly those who through upbringing have become most alienated and those lacking in strong and conventional social support—experience, feel, and internalize racist rejection and contempt from mainstream society may strongly encourage them to express contempt for the more conventional society in turn. In dealing with this contempt and rejection, some youngsters will consciously invest themselves and their considerable mental resources in what amounts to an oppositional culture to preserve themselves and their self-respect. Once they do, any respect they might be able to garner in the wider system pales in comparison with the respect available in the local system; thus they often lose interest in even attempting to negotiate the mainstream system (Anderson 1994, 94).

26. In October 1994 a five-year-old boy, Eric Morse, was thrown to his death from a window in a Chicago housing project by two boys, ages ten and eleven, because he had refused to steal candy for them. The story was reported on the front page of the *Chicago Tribune* (Kuczka and McRoberts 1994).

27. The relevance of school size, teacher attitudes, and factors related to the extent of teacher contact with individual students is borne out by studies of school crime summarized in Scrimger and Elder (1981, 12). Taken together, these studies suggest that the quality of student-teacher relationships has significance for the moral socialization of at least some children.

CHAPTER 7: JUSTICE AND THE SUBSTANCE OF COMMON CARE

1. Douglas Rae and his coauthors develop a highly illuminating analysis of the dimensions along which equality divides (Rae et al. 1989, 20–44).

2. Another reason for speaking of "equal educational opportunity" is a conception some may have of teaching as merely offering opportunities to learn, which children are free to take advantage of or not as they please. This is not only a very un-Aristotelian

understanding of the nature of teaching, but one which ignores the role in actual teaching of persuading and motivating students, as well as simply telling them what to do.

3. Opportunity having to do with means and the absence of external constraints, as distinct from ability.

4. See note 12 to chapter 1 and related text (§1.1) and note 16 to chapter 5 and related text (§5.15).

5. 411 US 1 (1973).

6. Gutmann and Thompson hold that, "Basic opportunity in education is . . . necessary for fair opportunity in employment" (320), but refer the reader to Gutmann 1987 for details.

7. See §3.1, §4.34, and note 23 to chapter 5, and related text in §5.21.

8. "Only earning offers citizens their standing," writes Judith Shklar. "Not to work is not to earn, and without one's earnings one is 'nobody'" (Shklar 1991, 92). She argues that this tenet of traditional American ideology "creates a presumption of a right to work as an element of American citizenship" (99).

9. As I noted in §5.15, the adaptation of Aristotle's *argument from constitutional unity* and *argument from a common end* to circumstances in which moderate value pluralism must be assumed also diminishes the role of Aristotle's distinction between the practical arts and what is fitting for leisure in defining a suitable curriculum.

10. As Elliott Currie writes, without stable work roles which provide positions of respect for all citizens, a society "cannot make good on its side of the social contract: it cannot credibly promise that being good will result in doing well" (Currie 1985, 263). He argues that economic policies unfavorable to full employment in the United States have contributed substantially to a level of criminal violence far exceeding those of other industrialized nations, and concludes that "we have encouraged . . . the social and economic forces that undermine social cohesion . . . then invoke a grossly outsized penal system to contain the predictable consequences, without notable success" (226). On the role of "inequalities that are perceived as unjust" in engendering crime, see also 162 and 144–79 generally.

11. Two examples of the use being made of the Aristotelian dictum that we learn justice and lyre-playing alike "by doing" (1103a31–b2) are the arguments currently being given for public service requirements for high school graduation in the United States ("service learning") and a recent variant of "control theory." Harris Woffard, former director of the Peace Corp and current director of the Corporation for National Service, has recently cited Aristotle in defense of service learning requirements in a speech given at the White House/Congressional Conference on "Character Building" (Washington, D.C., 7 June 1996). He argues that if children are to become generous or benevolent they must devote some of their energies to helping others. Gregory Bodenhamer, a former juvenile probation officer who now trains parents, teachers, and school administrators in techniques for managing difficult adolescents, has developed a self-consciously Aristotelian account of parenting (Bodenhamer 1995). One illustration of his Aristotelianism is his insistence that children should not be told that it is their choice to do the right thing or something else, with a reminder of the consequences of bad choices. Many children will care more about doing what they want to do at the moment than about future consequences, and will soon grow accustomed to choosing the worse over the better. The better and more Aristotelian approach is to insist on acceptable conduct and provide supervision sufficient to induce it.

12. Rackham (1934) translates *NE* I.12 1101b2–3, "praise belongs to goodness, since it is this which makes men capable of accomplishing noble deeds," which captures better than the alternatives the background notion, pervasive in Aristotelian ethics, that virtue is what enables a person or thing to do well what is appropriate to it.

13. The idea that there is a direct opposition between inculcation of morality and instruction in critical thinking is evident, among other places, in the criticisms leveled at the U.S. courts for endorsing the view that state and local authorities have a legitimate interest in inculcating "community values" through the public schools. See, e.g., van Geel 1983 and Roe 1991. It is also evident in Julia Annas's observation, in her commentary on Plato's *Republic*, that some educationalists "think that a child's intellectual autonomy is destroyed by too thorough a training in accepting group values at an early age," a problem faced by Plato "in an especially acute form" (Annas 1981, 87). A rare effort toward synthesis is Pritchard 1996.

14. It was for such reasons, offered by a community representative who had served in the Vietnam War, that loyalty and patriotism were recently struck from a tentative list of "core values" to be taught in a public school district in New York State. Courage and honesty remained on the list, although similar objections could be made to them. This inconsistency could be attributed to a failure to consistently consider the traits under discussion as entailing the good judgment needed to "hit the mean" between different kinds of error. My observations from the trenches of the character education movement suggest that unrecognized vacillations between true and merely habitual virtue are common.

15. The phrase is Oliver Wendell Holmes's.

16. See Rousseau (1762), 98–99 (on the child's discovery of property rights), 168–77 (on astronomical, kinematic, and other scientific discoveries), and 313–14 (on the discovery of God through the design argument).

17. Note Aristotle's references to children being moved by affection (*NE* X.9 1180b4–7) and by love and respect for elders (*Pol.* I.12 1259b11–12), and to social instincts which create some natural tendency to cooperation (*Pol.* I.2 1253a30). Simpson's suggestion that there is no middle ground between being moved by reason and being moved by force (Simpson 1990, n. 13) rests on a misunderstanding of the context of Aristotle's remark about the form of the rule of the soul over the body at *Pol.* I.5 1254b2–31 in Aristotle's discussion of natural slavery. See Simpson (1990, 153) and note 10 to chapter 3 above.

18. See, e.g., *Rh.* II.3; *Laws* 653c–d, where Plato describes the religious festivals of a city as restoring the virtue which people tend to lose over the course of their lives; and Lord 1982, which argues that Aristotle develops a similar view through the idea that public performances of tragedies induce a cathartic purging of emotions that tend to accumulate and corrupt practical wisdom. (Cf. note 18 to chapter 2 and related text.) Commentators commonly attribute to Aristotle the assumption that "wisdom must be so solid and steady an understanding of the truth that its knowledge can never be dislodged" (Cooper 1998, 266), but it is hard to find grounds for attributing to him the view that a person who is once wise is thereby permanently wise. In general he seems to hold the view that life is a struggle against death and that the preservation of the virtues that depend upon life is also a struggle that we are bound to lose eventually (Gill 1989, 230–34).

19. For a vivid portrayal of the cultural norms which characterize racially isolated inner-city schools, see the opening chapter of Suskind 1998. A complicating factor is that some forms of more specialized separate schooling, such as for black males only, or for girls only, have been more successful than ordinary mixed schools. This suggests that

although we should be aiming at common schooling that is adequate in the ways I have indicated, in the short run we may come closer to achieving these goals through a system that tolerates some separate schooling.

20. I say this recognizing that there may be no adequate grounds for denying parents a qualified right to choose home or private schooling, and no acceptable way to oversee some aspects of home schooling that the state has a legitimate interest in.

21. Cf. Brighouse (1996, 468 ff.) and Brighouse 2000.

22. For a more hopeful assessment of the lessons of these experiments and the potential for good that may be achieved through choice mechanisms, see Brighouse 2000.

23. On those other conditions, see Damon and Colby 1996

Bibliography

Adams, J. 1778. *A Defence of the Constitutions of Government of the United States of America*. In *The Works of John Adams, Second President of the United States, 1850–56*. ed. C. F. Adams. Vol. 6, 3–220. Boston: Little, Brown.

Adkins, A. 1960. *Merit and Responsibility*. Oxford: Clarendon Press.

———. 1967. "*Polupragmosune* and 'Minding One's Own Business': A Study in Greek Social and Political Values." *Classical Philology* 71 (4): 301–27.

———. 1971. "Homeric Values and Homeric Society." *Journal of Hellenic Studies* 91: 1–14.

———. 1973. "Aretê, Technê, Democracy and Sophists: *Protagoras* 316b–328d." *Journal of Hellenic Studies* 93: 3–12.

Allan, D. 1965. "Individual and State in the *Ethics* and *Politics*." In *La "Politique" d'Aristote*, ed. R. Stark et al., 53–85. Geneva: Foundation Hardt.

Allport, G. 1954. *The Nature of Prejudice*. Reading, Mass.: Addison-Wesley Publishing Co.

Anderson, E. 1994. "The Code of the Streets." *Atlantic Monthly* 273 (5): 80–94.

Anderson, W. D. 1966. *Ethos and Education in Greek Music*. Cambridge, Mass.: Harvard University Press.

Annas, J. 1977. "Plato and Aristotle on Friendship and Altruism." *Mind* 86 (344): 532–54.

———. 1981. *An Introduction to Plato's Republic*. Oxford: Clarendon Press.

———. 1990. "Comments on J. Cooper." In Patzig 1990, 242–48.

———. 1993. *The Morality of Happiness*. Oxford: Oxford University Press.

———. 1996. "Aristotle on Human Nature and Political Virtue." *Review of Metaphysics* 49 (4): 731–53.

Annas, J. and R. Waterfield. 1995. *Plato, Statesman*. Cambridge: Cambridge University Press.

Arons, S. 1986. *Compelling Belief: The Culture of American Schooling*. Amherst, Mass.: University of Massachusetts Press.

Ascher, C., N. Fruchter, and R. Berne. 1996. *Hard Lessons: Public Schools and Privatization*. New York: Twentieth Century Fund Press.

Augustine. 388–91. *On Free Choice of the Will*. Trans. T. Williams. 1993. Indianapolis: Hackett Publishing Co.

Baier, K. 1995. *The Rational and the Moral Order: The Social Roots of Reason and Morality*. Chicago: Open Court Press.

Ballantine, J. 1983. *The Sociology of Education*. Englewood Cliffs, N.J.: Prentice-Hall.

Banks, J. A. 1993. "Multicultural Education for Young Children: Racial and Ethnic Attitudes and Their Modification." In *Handbook of Research on the Education of Young Children*, ed. B. Spodeck, 236–50. New York: Macmillan Publishing Co.

Barker, E. 1947. *Greek Political Theory*. London: Methuen.

Barnes, J. 1979. "Aristotle's Concept of Mind." In *Articles on Aristotle. 4. Psychology & Aesthetics*, ed. J. Barnes, M. Schofield, and R. Sorabji, 32–41. London: Duckworth.

———, ed. 1984. *The Complete Works of Aristotle, The Revised Oxford Translation*. Princeton: Princeton University Press.

———. 1990. "Aristotle and Political Liberty." In Patzig 1990, 249–63.

———, M. Schofield, and R. Sorabji, eds. 1977. *Articles on Aristotle. 2. Ethics and Politics*. London: Duckworth.

Beck, F. A. G. 1964. *Greek Education*. London: Methuen.

Beck, L. W. 1969. *Early German Philosophy: Kant and His Predecessors*. Cambridge, Mass.: Harvard University Press.

Berne, R. and L. O. Pincus, eds. 1994. *Outcome Equity in Education*. Thousand Oaks, Calif.: Corwin Press.

Berry, C. 1994. *The Idea of Luxury*. Cambridge: Cambridge University Press.

Betbeder, P. 1970. "Ethique et Politique selon Aristote." *Revue des Sciences Philosophiques et Théologiques* 54 (3): 453–88.

Bobonich, C. 1991. "Persuasion, Compulsion and Freedom in Plato's *Laws*." *Classical Quarterly* 41 (2): 365–88.

———. 1996. "Reading the *Laws*." In *Form and Argument in Late Plato*, ed. C. Gill and M. M. McCabe, 249–82. Oxford: Clarendon Press.

Bodenhamer, G. 1995. *Parent in Control*. New York: Simon & Schuster.

Bodéüs, R. 1991. "Law and the Regime in Aristotle." In Lord and O'Connor 1990, 234–48.

———. 1993. *The Political Dimensions of Aristotle's Ethics*. Albany, N.Y.: State University of New York Press.

Borgo, J. 1979. "Causal Paradigms in Tort Law." *Journal of Legal Studies* 8 (3): 419–55.

Bowles, S. and H. Gintis. 1976. *Schooling in Capitalist America*. New York: Basic Books.

Braddock, J. H. 1980. "The Perpetuation of Segregation Across Levels of Education: A Behavioral Assessment of the Contact-Hypothesis." *Sociology of Education* 53 (3): 178–86.

———, R. Crain, and J. McPartland. 1984. "A Long-Term View of School Desegregation: Some Recent Studies of Graduates as Adults." *Phi Delta Kappan* 66 (4): 259–64.

Brandwood, L. 1992. "Stylometry and Chronology." In Kraut 1992, 90–120.

Brighouse, H. 1996. "Egalitarian Liberals and School Choice." *Politics & Society* 24 (4): 457–86.

———. 2000. *School Choice and Social Justice*. Oxford: Oxford University Press.

Broadie, S. 1991. *Ethics with Aristotle*. New York: Oxford University Press

Burnet, J. 1900. *The Ethics of Aristotle*. London: Methuen.

Burnyeat, M. 1980. "Aristotle on Learning to be Good." In Rorty 1980, 69–92.

Bury, R. G. 1926. *Plato, The Laws*. Cambridge, Mass.: Harvard University Press.

Butler, P. 1995. "Racially Based Jury Nullification: Black Power in the Criminal Justice System." *Yale Law Journal* 105 (3): 677–725.

Buxton, R. 1982. *Persuasion in Greek Tragedy*. Cambridge: Cambridge University Press.

Callan, E. 1997. *Creating Citizens: Political Education and Liberal Democracy*. Oxford: Clarendon Press.

———. 2000. "Discrimination and Religious Schooling." In *Citizenship and Diversity*, ed. W. Kymlicka and W. Norman, 45–67. Oxford: Oxford University Press.

Carter, S. L. 1998. *Civility*. New York: Harper Collins.

Cicchetti, D. and S. L. Toth. 1995. "A Developmental Psychopathology Perspective on Child Abuse and Neglect." *Journal of the American Academy of Child & Adolescent Psychiatry* 34 (5): 541–65.

———, eds. 1997. *Developmental Perspectives on Trauma: Theory, Research, and Intervention*. Rochester, N. Y.: University of Rochester Press.

Cohen, D. 1995. *Law, Violence, and Community in Classical Athens*. Cambridge: Cambridge University Press.

Coleman, Ja. 1990. *Equality and Achievement in Education*. Boulder, Col.: Westview Press.

Coleman, Ju. 1983. "Moral Theories of Torts: Their Scope and Limits. Part II." *Law and Philosophy* 2 (1): 5–36.

Connor, W. R. 1992. *The New Politicians of Fifth-Century Athens*. Indianapolis: Hackett Publishing Co.

Cookson, P. 1994. *School Choice*. New Haven: Yale University Press.

Cooper, J. 1973. "The *Magna Moralia* and Aristotle's Moral Philosophy." *American Journal of Philology* 94 (4): 327–49.

———. 1977. "Aristotle on the Forms of Friendship." *Review of Metaphysics* 30 (4): 619–48.

———. 1985. "Aristotle on the Goods of Fortune." *The Philosophical Review* 94 (2): 173–96.

———. 1987. "Contemplation and Happiness: A Reconsideration." *Synthese* 72 (2): 187–216.

———. 1990. "Political Animals and Civic Friendship." In Patzig 1990, 220–41.

———. 1994. "Ethical-Political Theory in Aristotle's *Rhetoric*." In Furley and Nehamas 1994, 193–210.

———. 1996. "Justice and Rights in Aristotle's *Politics*." *Review of Metaphysics* 49 (4): 859–72.

———, ed. 1997. *Plato, Complete Works*. Indianapolis: Hackett Publishing Co.

———. 1998. "The Unity of Virtue." *Social Philosophy & Policy* 15 (1): 233–74.

———. 1999. "Plato's *Statesman* and Politics." In *Reason and Emotion*, ed. John Cooper, 165–91. Princeton: Princeton University Press.

Cremin, L. 1988. *American Education: The Metropolitan Experience 1876–1980*. New York: Harper & Row.

———. 1989. *Popular Education and Its Discontents*. New York: Harper & Row.

Curren, R. 1989. "The Contribution of *Nicomachean Ethics* iii 5 to Aristotle's Theory of Responsibility." *History of Philosophy Quarterly* 6 (3): 261–77.

———. 1993–94. "Justice, Instruction, and the Good: The Case for Public Education in

Aristotle and Plato's *Laws*." *Studies in Philosophy and Education* 11 (2–4): 293–311; 12 (4): 103–26; 13 (1): 1–31.

———. 1995a. "Justice and the Threshold of Educational Equality." In *Philosophy of Education 1994*, ed. M. Katz, 239–48. Urbana, Ill: Philosophy of Education Society.

———. 1995b. "Punishment and Inclusion: The Presuppositions of Corrective Justice in Aristotle and What They Imply." *The Canadian Journal of Law and Jurisprudence* 8 (2): 259–74.

———. 1997. Review of Miller 1995. *Reason Papers* 22 (Fall): 144–53.

———. 1999a. "Critical Thinking and the Unity of Virtue." In *Philosophy of Education 1998*, ed. S. Tozer, 158–65. Urbana, Ill.: Philosophy of Education Society.

———. 1999b. "Cultivating the Intellectual and Moral Virtues." In *Virtue Ethics and Moral Education*, ed. D. Carr and J. Steutel, 67–81. London: Routledge.

Currie, E. 1985. *Confronting Crime*. New York: Pantheon.

Damon, W. 1988. *The Moral Child*. New York: The Free Press.

——— and A. Colby. 1996: "Education and Moral Commitment." *Journal of Moral Education* 25 (1): 31–37.

David, E. 1978. "The Spartan *Syssitia* and Plato's *Laws*." *American Journal of Philology* 99 (4): 486–95.

Defourney, M. 1932. *Aristote: Etudes sur la Politique*. Paris: Éditions Beauchesne..

Delfattore, J. 1992. *What Johnny Shouldn't Read: Textbook Censorship in America*. New Haven: Yale University Press.

de Romilly, J. 1971. *La loi dans la penseé Grecque*. Paris: Société d'Édition "Les Belles Lettres."

Dover, K. J. 1974. *Greek Popular Morality in the Time of Plato and Aristotle*. Berkeley: University of California Press.

Downey, G. 1957. "Ancient Education." *Classical Journal* 52 (8): 337–45.

Duff, R. 1986. *Trials and Punishments*. Cambridge: Cambridge University Press.

Düring, I. 1961. *Aristotle's Protrepticus: An Attempt at Reconstruction*. Göteborg, Sweden: Elanders Boktryckeri Aktiebolag.

Düring, I. and G. E. L. Owen, eds. 1960. *Aristotle and Plato in the Mid-Fourth Century*. Göteborg, Sweden: Elanders Boktryckeri Aktiebolag.

Elias, M. et. al. 1997. *Promoting Emotional and Social Learning: Guidelines For Educators*. Alexandria, Va.: Association for Supervision and Curriculum Development.

Engberg-Pederson, T. 1983. *Aristotle's Theory of Moral Insight*. Oxford: Clarendon Press.

England, E. B., ed. 1921. *The Laws of Plato*. 2 vols. Manchester: Manchester University Press.

Epstein, R. 1980. *A Theory of Strict Liability*. San Francisco: Cato Institute.

Fine, G. 1992. "Inquiry in the *Meno*." In Kraut 1992, 200–226.

Finley, M. I. 1953. *Land and Credit in Ancient Athens, 500–200 B.C.* New Brunswick, N.J.: Rutgers University Press.

———. 1980. *Ancient Slavery and Modern Ideology*. New York: Viking Press.

———. 1983. *Politics in the Ancient World*. Cambridge: Cambridge University Press.

Finster, P. R. F. 1984. "Spontaneität und Freiheit: Eine Untersuchung zu Kants theoretischer Philosophie unter Berücksichtigung von Leibniz, Wolff und Crusius." Ph.D. diss., Universität Trier, Germany.

Flam, S. and W. Keane. 1997. *Public Schools/Private Enterprise*. Lancaster, Penn.: Technomic Publishing Co.

Fletcher, G. 1972. "Fairness and Utility in Tort Theory." *Harvard Law Review* 85 (3): 537–73.

Fowler, H. 1914. *Plato*, vol. 1. Cambridge, Mass.: Harvard University Press.

Frankena, W. 1965. *Three Historical Philosophies of Education*. Chicago: Scott, Foresman and Co.

Frankfurt, H. 1988. "Coercion and Moral Responsibility." In *The Importance of What We Care About*, ed. H. Frankfurt, 26–46. Cambridge: Cambridge University Press.

Frede, M. 1987. "Philosophy and Medicine in Antiquity." In *Essays in Ancient Philosophy*, ed. M. Frede, 225–42. Minneapolis: University of Minnesota Press.

Freese, J. 1926. *Aristotle, The "Art" of Rhetoric*. Cambridge, Mass.: Harvard University Press.

Furley, D. J. 1977. "Aristotle on the Voluntary." In Barnes, et. al. 1977, 47–60.

———— and A. Nehamas, eds. 1994. *Aristotle's Rhetoric: Philosophical Essays*. Princeton: Princeton University Press.

Gagarin, M. 1981. *Drakon and Early Athenian Homicide Law*. New Haven: Yale University Press.

———— and P. Woodruff, trans., eds. 1995. *Early Greek Political Thought from Homer to the Sophists*. Cambridge: Cambridge University Press.

Gauthier, D. 1986. *Morals by Agreement*. Oxford: Clarendon Press.

Gauthier, R. A. and Y. A. Jolif. 1970. *L'Ethique à Nicomaque*. 2d ed. 4 vols. Louvain-Paris: Publications Universitaires.

Gill, M. L. 1989. *Aristotle on Substance*. Princeton: Princeton University Press.

Godwin, W. 1798. *Enquiry concerning Political Justice*. Ed. K. C. Carter. 1971. Oxford: Clarendon Press.

Golden, M. 1990. *Children and Childhood in Classical Athens*. Baltimore, Md.: Johns Hopkins University Press..

Green, T. F. 1980. *Predicting the Behavior of the Educational System*. Syracuse, N.Y.: Syracuse University Press.

Gutmann, A. 1987. *Democratic Education*. Princeton: Princeton University Press.

———— and D. Thompson. 1996. *Democracy and Disagreement*. Cambridge, Mass.: Harvard University Press.

Hacker, A. 1992a. *Two Nations: Black and White, Separate, Hostile, Unequal*. New York: Ballantine Books.

————. 1992b. "The New Civil War." *The New York Review of Books*. 23 (April): 30–33.

Hall, R. W. 1981. *Plato*. London: George Allen & Unwin.

Hammond, N. G. L. 1986. *A History of Greece to 322 B.C.* 3d ed. Oxford: Clarendon Press.

Hardie, W. F. R. 1980. *Aristotle's Ethical Theory*. 2d ed. Oxford: Clarendon Press.

Hart, H. L. A. 1961. *The Concept of Law*. Oxford: Clarendon Press.

Hedrick, C. and J. Ober, eds. 1996. *Dêmokratia: A Conversation on Democracy, Ancient and Modern*. Princeton: Princeton University Press.

Held, D. 1987. *Models of Democracy*. Stanford, Calif.: Stanford University Press.

Henig, J. 1994. *Rethinking School Choice*. Princeton: Princeton University Press.

Hobbes, T. 1651. *Leviathan, Or the Matter, Form, and Power of a Commonwealth Ecclesiastical and Civil*. Ed. E. Curley. 1994. Indianapolis: Hackett Publishing Co.

Hollis, M. 1982. "Education as a Positional Good." *Journal of Philosophy of Education* 16 (2): 235–44.

Hornblower, S. and A. Spawforth. 1996. *The Oxford Classical Dictionary*. 3d. ed. Oxford: Oxford University Press.

Hubbard, B. and E. Karnofsky. 1982. *Plato's Protagoras*. London: Duckworth.

Irwin, T. 1977. *Plato's Moral Theory*. Oxford: Clarendon Press.

———. 1980. "Reason and Responsibility in Aristotle." In Rorty 1980, 117–55.

———. 1985a. *Aristotle, Nicomachean Ethics*. Indianapolis: Hackett Publishing Co.

———. 1985b. "Moral Science and Political Theory in Aristotle." *History of Political Thought* 6 (1–2): 150–68.

———. 1986. "Socratic Inquiry and Politics." *Ethics* 96 (January): 400–415.

———. 1988a. "Disunity in the Aristotelian Virtues." *Oxford Studies in Ancient Philosophy*. Supplementary Vol., 61–78. Oxford: Clarendon Press.

———. 1988b. *Aristotle's First Principles*. Oxford: Clarendon Press.

Jaeger, W. 1939–44. *Paideia: The Ideals of Greek Culture*. 3 vols. Oxford: Basil Blackwell.

———. 1948. *Aristotle: Fundamentals of the History of His Development*. Trans. R. Robinson. 2d ed. Oxford: Clarendon Press.

———. 1957. "Aristotle's Use of Medicine as Model of Method in His Ethics." *The Journal of Hellenic Studies* 77: 54–61.

Jefferson, T. 1778. *A Bill for the More General Diffusion of Knowledge*. In *The Papers of Thomas Jefferson*. J. P. Boyd, ed. Vol. 2, 526–35. Princeton: Princeton University Press.

Jones, H. L. 1969. *The Geography of Strabo*. Cambridge, Mass.: Harvard University Press.

Kaestle, C. 1983. *Pillars of the Republic: Common Schools and American Society 1780–1860*. New York: Hill and Wang.

Kairys, D., ed. 1982. *The Politics of Law*. New York: Pantheon.

Kant, I. 1775–80. *Lectures on Ethics*. Trans. L. Infield. 1979. Indianapolis: Hackett Publishing Co.

Katz, M. 1968. *The Irony of Early School Reform*. Boston: Beacon Press.

Keeton, W. P. 1984. *Prosser and Keeton on Torts*. 5th ed. St. Paul, Minn.: West Publishing Co.

Keyt, D. 1993. "Aristotle and Anarchism." *Reason Papers* 18 (Fall): 133–52.

———. 1996. "Aristotle and the Ancient Roots of Anarchism." *Topoi* 15 (1): 129–42.

——— and F. Miller, eds. 1991. *A Companion to Aristotle's Politics*. Oxford: Basil Blackwell.

Klosko, G. 1986a. "Rational Persuasion in Plato's Political Theory." In *The Politics of Fallen Man*, ed. M. Goldsmith and T. Horne, 15–31. Sidmouth, England: Sovereign Printing Group.

———. 1986b. *The Development of Plato's Political Theory*. New York: Methuen.

Korsgaard, C. 1986. "Aristotle on Function and Virtue." *History of Philosophy Quarterly* 3 (3): 259–79.

Kozol, J. 1991. *Savage Inequalities: Children in America's Schools*. New York: Harper Collins.

Kraut, R. 1984. *Socrates and the State*. Princeton: Princeton University Press.

———. 1989. *Aristotle on the Human Good*. Princeton: Princeton University Press.

———, ed. 1992. *The Cambridge Companion to Plato*. Cambridge: Cambridge University Press.

———. 1996. "Are There Natural Rights in Aristotle?" *The Review of Metaphysics* 49 (4): 755–74.

———. 1997. *Aristotle, Politics Books VII and VIII.* Oxford: Clarendon Press.

Kuczka, S. and F. McRoberts. 1994. "Five-Year-Old Was Killed Over Candy: Boy Refuses to Shoplift and Is Dropped Fourteen Floors to His Death, Police Say." *Chicago Tribune,* Saturday, 15 October, 1A.

Laks, A. 1990. "Legislation and Demiurgy: On the Relationship Between Plato's *Republic* and *Laws.*" *Classical Antiquity* 9 (2): 209–29.

———. 1991. "l'utopie legislative de Platon." *Revue Philosophique de la France et de l'etranger* 116 (4): 417–28.

Lamb, W. R. M. 1924. *Plato,* vol. 2. Cambridge, Mass.: Harvard University Press.

Leibniz, G. 1679. "On Freedom." In *Gottfried Wilhelm Leibniz: Philosophical Papers and Letters,* Trans, ed, L. Loemaker. 1969. 2d ed. Dordrecht, Netherlands: D. Reidel Publishing Co.

Leipold, A. 1997. "Race-Based Jury Nullification: Rebuttal." *John Marshall Law Review* 30 (Summer): 923–27.

Levy, D. 1998. The Digression in Plato's *Theaetetus.* Paper presented at the University of Rochester, 4 May 1998.

Lewis, C. 1995. *Educating Hearts and Minds: Reflections on Japanese Preschool and Elementary Education.* Cambridge: Cambridge University Press.

Lewis, D. 1973. "Attic Ephebic Inscriptions." *Classical Review* 23 (2): 254–56.

Liddell, H. G., R. Scott, and H. S. Jones. 1976. *A Greek English Lexicon.* Oxford: Clarendon Press.

Lloyd, G. E. R. 1968. "The Role of Medical and Biological Analogies in Aristotle's Ethics." *Phronesis* 13 (1): 68–83.

Lloyd-Jones, H. 1983. *The Justice of Zeus.* Berkeley: University of California Press.

Locke, J. 1689. *A Letter concerning Toleration.* J. Tully, ed. 1983. Indianapolis: Hackett Publishing Co.

———. 1693. *Some Thoughts concerning Education.* In *Some Thoughts concerning Education and Of the Conduct of the Understanding.* R. W. Grant and N. Tarcov, eds. 1996. Indianapolis: Hackett Publishing Co.

Long, R. 1996. "Aristotle's Conception of Freedom." *Review of Metaphysics* 49 (4): 775–802.

Lord, C. 1982. *Education and Culture in the Political Thought of Aristotle.* Ithaca, N.Y.: Cornell University Press.

———. 1984. *Aristotle, The Politics.* Chicago: University of Chicago Press.

———. 1990. "Politics and Education in Aristotle's 'Politics'." In Patzig 1990, 202–15.

———. 1996. "Aristotle and the Idea of Liberal Education." In C. Hedrick and J. Ober 1996, 271–88.

——— and D. O'Connor, eds. 1991. *Essays on the Foundations of Aristotelian Political Science.* Berkeley: University of California Press.

Lynch, J. 1972. *Aristotle's School.* Berkeley: University of California Press.

MacDowell, D. 1978. *The Law in Classical Athens.* Ithaca, N.Y.: Cornell University Press.

MacIntyre, A. 1982. "How Moral Agents Became Ghosts." *Synthese* 53 (2): 295–312.

Manning, S. 1999. "Students for Sale: How Corporations Are Buying Their Way into America's Classrooms." *The Nation,* 27 September, 11–18.

Mansnerus, L. 1993. "Kids of the 90's: A Bolder Breed." *The New York Times,* Sunday, April, sec. 4A, 14–17.

Marchant, E. C. 1923. *Xenophon, Memorabilia and Oeconomicus.* Cambridge, Mass.: Harvard University Press.

———. 1925. *Xenophon, Scripta Minora*. Cambridge, Mass.: Harvard University Press.

Marrou, H. 1956. *A History of Education in Antiquity*. London: Sheed and Ward.

Mauer, Marc. 1998. *Losing the Vote: The Impact of Felony Disenfranchisement Laws in the United States*. Washington, D. C.: Sentencing Project and Human Rights Watch.

Mayhew, R. 1997. *Aristotle's Criticism of Plato's Republic*. Lanham, Md.: Rowman & Littlefield Publishers.

McClellan, J. 1968. *Toward an Effective Critique of American Education*. Philadelphia: J. B. Lippincott Co.

McGlew, J. 1993. *Tyranny and Political Culture in Ancient Greece*. Ithaca, N.Y.: Cornell University Press.

Meyer, S. 1993. *Aristotle on Moral Responsibility*. Oxford: Basil Blackwell.

Mill, J. S. 1859. *On Liberty*. In *Collected Works of John Stuart Mill*. J. Robson, ed. 1977. Vol. 18, 213–310. Toronto: University of Toronto Press.

Miller, F. 1995. *Nature, Justice, and Rights in Aristotle's Politics*. Oxford: Clarendon Press.

———. 1996. "Aristotle and the Origins of Natural Rights." *Review of Metaphysics* 49 (4): 873–907.

Morrow, G. 1941. "Plato and the Rule of Law." *Philosophical Review* 50 (2): 105–26. Reprinted in Vlastos 1978, 144–65.

———. 1953. "Plato's Conception of Persuasion." *Philosophical Review* 62 (2): 234–50.

———. 1954. "The Demiurge in Politics: The *Timaeus* and the *Laws*." *Proceedings and Addresses of the American Philosophical Association* 27: 5–23.

———. 1960a. "Aristotle's Comments on Plato's *Laws*." In Düring and Owen, eds. 1960, 145–62.

———. 1960b. *Plato's Cretan City*. Princeton: Princeton University Press.

Muir, J. V. 1982. "Protagoras and Education at Thourioi." *Greece & Rome* 29 (1): 17–24.

Mulgan, R. G. 1977. *Aristotle's Political Theory*. Oxford: Clarendon Press.

———. 1994. "Aristotle on the Political Role of Women." *History of Political Thought* 15 (2): 179–202.

Müller, K. 1824. *Die Dorier*. Breslau: Max.

Murphy, J. 1973. "Marxism and Retribution." *Philosophy and Public Affairs* 2 (3): 218–43.

Nagel, T. 1979. "Moral Luck." In *Mortal Questions,* ed. T. Nagel, 24–38. Cambridge: Cambridge University Press.

Nehamas, A. 1999a. "Meno's Paradox and Socrates as a Teacher." In *Virtues of Authenticity,* ed. A. Nehamas, 3–26. Princeton: Princeton University Press.

———. 1999b. "*Epistêmê* and *Logos* in Plato's Later Thought." In *Virtues of Authenticity*, 224–48. Princeton: Princeton University Press.

Nettleship, R. L. 1906. *The Theory of Education in the Republic of Plato*. Chicago: University of Chicago Press.

Newman, W. L. 1902. *The Politics of Aristotle*. 4 vols. Oxford: Clarendon Press.

Nozick, R. 1969. "Coercion." In *Philosophy, Science, and Method: Essays in Honor of Ernest Nagel,* ed. S. Morgenbesser, P. Suppes, and M. White, 440–72. New York: St. Martin's Press.

Nussbaum, M. 1986. *The Fragility of Goodness*. Cambridge: Cambridge University Press.

Oakes, J. 1985. *Keeping Track*. New Haven: Yale University Press.

Ober, J. 1989. *Mass and Elite in Democratic Athens*. Princeton: Princeton University Press.

Panagiotou, S., ed. 1987. *Justice, Law and Method in Plato and Aristotle*. Edmonton: Academic Print and Pub.

Pangle, L. S. and T. Pangle. 1993. *The Learning of Liberty: The Educational Ideas of the American Founders*. Lawrence: University Press of Kansas.

Pangle, T. 1980. *The Laws of Plato*. Chicago: University of Chicago Press.

Patzig, G., ed. 1990. *Aristotles' "Politik."* Göttingen, Germany: Vandenhoeck & Ruprecht in Göttingen.

Pellegrin, P. 1996. "On the 'Platonic' Part of Aristotle's *Politics*." In Wians 1996, 347–57.

Perrin, B. 1914. *Plutarch's Lives*. Vol. 1. Cambridge, Mass.: Harvard University Press.

Peterson, P. 1985. *The Politics of School Reform 1870–1940*. Chicago: University of Chicago Press.

Philips, M. 1986. "The Justification of Punishment and the Justification of Political Authority." *Law and Philosophy* 5 (4): 393–416.

Polansky, R. 1991. "Aristotle on Political Change." In Keyt and Miller 1991, 323–45.

Popper, C. 1966. *The Open Society and Its Enemies*. Vol. 1. Plato, 5th ed. Princeton: Princeton University Press.

Posner, R. 1977. *Economic Analysis of Law*. 2d ed. Chicago: University of Chicago Press.

———. 1981. "The Concept of Corrective Justice in Recent Theories of Tort Law." *Journal of Legal Studies* 10 (1): 187–206.

Powell, A. 1988. *Athens and Sparta: Constructing Greek Political and Social History from 478 B.C.* London: Routledge.

Power, F. C., A. Higgins, and L. Kohlberg. 1989. *Lawrence Kohlberg's Approach to Moral Education*. New York: Columbia University Press.

Price, A. W. 1989. *Love and Friendship in Plato and Aristotle*. Oxford: Clarendon Press.

Pritchard, M. 1996. *Reasonable Children*. Lawrence: University Press of Kansas.

Purdy, L. 1992. *In Their Best Interest? The Case against Equal Rights For Children*. Ithaca, N.Y.: Cornell University Press.

Rackham, H. 1934. *Aristotle, The Nicomachean Ethics*. Cambridge, Mass.: Harvard University Press.

———. 1944. *Aristotle, Politics*. Cambridge, Mass.: Harvard University Press.

———. 1971. *Aristotle, Eudemian Ethics*. Cambridge, Mass.: Harvard University Press.

Rae, D. et al. 1989. *Equalities*. Cambridge, Mass.: Harvard University Press.

Rawls, J. 1971. *A Theory of Justice*. Cambridge, Mass.: Harvard University Press.

———. 1993. *Political Liberalism*. New York: Columbia University Press.

Reeve, C. D. C. 1988. *Philosopher-Kings: The Argument of Plato's Republic*. Princeton: Princeton University Press.

———. 1989. *Socrates in the Apology*. Indianapolis: Hackett Publishing Co.

———. 1998. *Aristotle, Politics*. Indianapolis: Hackett Publishing Co.

Reiss, A. et al. 1993. *Understanding and Preventing Violence*. Washington, D.C.: National Academic Press.

Richards, C. E., R. Shore, and M. B. Sawicky. 1996. *Risky Business: Private Management of Public Schools*. Washington, D. C.: Economic Policy Institute.

Roberts, J. 1987. "Plato on the Causes of Wrongdoing in the *Laws*." *Ancient Philosophy* 7: 23–37.

————. 1989a. "Political Animals in the *Nicomachean Ethics.*" *Phronesis* 34 (2): 185–204.

————. 1989b. Aristotle on Responsibility for Action and Character." *Ancient Philosophy* 9 (1): 23–26.

————. 1995. Review of Meyer 1993. *The Philosophical Review* 104 (4): 577–79.

Robinson, R. 1995. *Aristotle, Politics Books III and IV.* Oxford: Clarendon Press.

Roe, R. 1991. "Valuing Student Speech: The Work of Schools as Cognition and Conceptual Development." *California Law Review* 79 (4): 1269–1345.

Rogers, K. 1993. "Aristotle's Conception of *To Kalon.*" *Ancient Philosophy* 13 (2): 355–71.

Rogoff, B. 1990. *Apprenticeship in Thinking: Cognitive Development in Social Context.* Oxford: Oxford University Press.

Rogosch, F. A., D. Cicchetti, A. Shields, and S. L. Toth. 1995. "Parenting Dysfunction in Child Maltreatment." In *Handbook of Parenting, Vol. 4: Applied and Practical Parenting,* ed. M. H. Bornstein, 127–59. Mahwah, N. J.: Lawrence Erlbaum Associates.

Rorty, A. 1980. *Essays on Aristotle's Ethics.* Berkeley: University of California Press.

Rossell, C. H. 1990. *The Carrot or the Stick for School Desegregation Policy.* Philadelphia: Temple University Press.

Rousseau, J.-J. 1762. *Emile.* Trans. A. Bloom. 1979. New York: Basic Books.

Rowe, C. 1991. "Aims and Methods in Aristotle's *Politics.*" In D. Keyt and F. Miller 1991, 57–74.

Ryan, R. and J. Stiller. 1991. "The Social Contexts of Internalization." In *Advances in Motivation and Achievement.* Vol. 7, ed. M. L. Maehr and P. R. Pintrich, 115–49. Greenwich. Conn.: JAI Press.

Sabine, G. H. 1973. *A History of Political Theory.* 4th ed. Hinsdale, Ill.: Holt, Rinehart and Winston.

Saunders, T. 1991. *Plato's Penal Code.* Oxford: Clarendon Press.

————. 1995. *Aristotle, Politics Books I and II.* Oxford: Clarendon Press.

Schmitter, P. 1975. "Compulsory Schooling at Athens and Rome?" *American Journal of Philology* 96 (3): 276–89.

Schnapp, A. 1997. "Images of Young People in the Greek City-State." In *A History of Young People In The West,* ed. G. Levi and J.-C. Schmitt, Vol. I, 12–50. Cambridge, Mass.: Harvard University Press.

Schofield, M. 1996. "Sharing in the Constitution." *Review of Metaphysics* 49 (4): 831–58.

Schollmeier, P. 1994. *Other Selves: Aristotle on Personal and Political Friendship.* Albany, N.Y.: State University of New York Press.

Scrimger, G. and R. Elder. 1981. *School Security Handbook.* Sacramento: California State Office of the Attorney General.

Sharp, F. 1976. "Aristotle, Justice and Enterprise Liability in the Law of Torts." *University of Toronto Faculty of Law Review* 34 (1): 84–92.

Sherman, N. 1989. *The Fabric of Character: Aristotle's Theory of Virtue.* Oxford: Clarendon Press.

Shields, A. and D. Cicchetti. 1998. "Reactive Aggression among Maltreated Children: The Contributions of Attention and Emotion Dysregulation." *Journal of Clinical Child Psychology* 27 (4): 381–95.

Shklar, J. 1991. *American Citizenship: The Quest for Inclusion*. Cambridge, Mass.: Harvard University Press.

Simpson, P. 1990. "Making the City Good: Aristotle's City and Its Contemporary Relevance." *The Philosophical Forum* 22 (2): 149–66.

———. 1995. "Political Authority and Moral Education." *Public Affairs Quarterly* 9 (1): 47–62.

———. 1997. *The Politics of Aristotle*. Chapel Hill: University of North Carolina Press.

Sisson, E. 1940. "Human Nature and the Present Crisis." *Philosophical Review* 49 (2): 142–62.

Slavin, R. 1979. "Effects of Biracial Learning Teams on Cross-racial Friendships." *Journal of Educational Psychology* 71 (3): 381–87.

———. 1983. *Cooperative Learning*. New York: Longman.

———. 1995. *Cooperative Learning: Theory, Research, and Practice*. 2d ed. Boston: Allyn and Bacon.

Smith, S. 1987. "The Critics and the 'Crisis': A Reassessment of Current Conceptions of Tort Law." *Cornell Law Review* 72 (4): 765–98.

Sorabji, R. 1980. *Necessity, Cause, and Blame: Perspectives on Aristotle's Theory*. Ithaca, N.Y.: Cornell University Press.

———. 1990. "Comments on J. Barnes." In Patzig 1990, 264–76.

Stalley, R. F. 1983. *An Introduction to Plato's Laws*. Indianapolis: Hackett Publishing Co.

———. 1995. "Punishment in Plato's *Protagoras*." *Phronesis* 40 (1): 1–19.

Stockton, D. 1990. *The Classical Athenian Democracy*. Oxford: Oxford University Press.

Strudler, A. 1992. "Mass Torts and Moral Principles." *Law and Philosophy* 11 (4): 297–330.

Suskind, R. 1998. *A Hope in the Unseen*. New York: Broadway Books.

Swanson, J. 1992. *The Public and the Private in Aristotle's Political Philosophy*. Ithaca, N.Y.: Cornell University Press.

Taylor, C. C. W. 1991. *Plato, Protagoras*. Rev. ed. Oxford: Clarendon Press.

Toth, S. L. and D. Cicchetti. 1996. "The Impact of Relatedness with Mother on School Functioning in Maltreated Children." *Journal of School Psychology* 34 (3): 247–66.

Tyack, D, 1974. *The One Best System: A History of American Urban Education*. Cambridge, Mass.: Harvard University Press.

Tyler, T. R. 1990. *Why People Obey the Law*. New Haven: Yale University Press.

Unger, R. 1983. "The Critical Legal Studies Movement." *Harvard Law Review* 96 (3): 561–675.

U. S. Commission on Civil Rights. 1967. *Racial Isolation in the Public Schools*. Washington, D.C.: U.S. Government Printing Office.

Vander Waerdt, P. A. 1985. "The Political Intention of Aristotle's Moral Philosophy." *Ancient Philosophy* 5 (1): 77–89.

———, ed. 1994. *The Socratic Movement*. Ithaca, N.Y.: Cornell University Press.

van Geel, T. 1983. "The Search for Constitutional Limits on Governmental Authority to Inculcate Youth." *Texas Law Review* 62 (2): 197–297.

Vlastos, G. 1941. "Slavery in Plato's Thought." *Philosophical Review* 50 (3): 289–304.

———. 1972. "The Unity of Virtues in the *Protagoras*." *The Review of Metaphysics* 25 (3): 415–58.

———. 1973. "Justice and Happiness in the *Republic*." In *Platonic Studies*, ed. G. Vlastos, 111–39. Princeton: Princeton University Press.

———, ed. 1978. *Plato: A Collection of Critical Essays*. Notre Dame, Ind.: University of Notre Dame Press.

———. 1983. "The Socratic Elenchus." In *Oxford Studies in Ancient Philosophy*. Vol. 1, ed. J. Annas, 27–58. Oxford: Clarendon Press.

———. 1991. *Socrates: Ironist and Moral Philosopher*. Ithaca, N.Y.: Cornell University Press.

———. 1995. "The Theory of Social Justice in the *Polis* in Plato's *Republic*." In *Studies in Greek Philosophy*. Vol. 2, ed. D. W. Graham, 69–103. Princeton: Princeton University Press.

von Fritz, K. 1954. *The Theory of the Mixed Constitution in Antiquity*. New York: Columbia University Press.

———. and E. Kapp. 1977. "The Development of Aristotle's Political Philosophy and the Concept of Nature." In Barnes, Schofield, and Sorabji 1977, 113–34.

Weinrib, E. 1987. "Aristotle's Forms of Justice." In Panagiotou 1987, 133–57.

———. 1988. "Legal Formalism: On the Immanent Rationality of Law." *Yale Law Journal* 97 (6): 949–1016.

Wians, W., ed. 1996. *Aristotle's Philosophical Development*. Lanham, Md.: Rowman & Littlefield Publishers.

Wiggins, D. 1980. "Deliberation and Practical Reason." In Rorty 1980, 221–40.

Williams, B. 1981. "Moral Luck." In *Moral Luck,* ed. B. Williams, 20–39. Cambridge: Cambridge University Press.

———. 1985. *Ethics and the Limits of Philosophy*. Cambridge, Mass.: Harvard University Press.

Yack, B. 1993. *The Problems of a Political Animal: Community, Justice, and Conflict in Aristotelian Political Thought*. Berkeley: University of California Press.

Zaidman, L. and P. Pantel. 1992. *Religion in the Ancient Greek City*. Cambridge: Cambridge University Press.

Index

About the Author

Randall Curren is associate professor at the University of Rochester, where he has held appointments in both the Department of Philosophy and the Margaret Warner Graduate School of Education and Human Development since 1988.